CANADIAN CONTENT
THIRD EDITION

NELL WALDMAN
SARAH NORTON

HARCOURT
BRACE
CANADA

Harcourt Brace & Company, Canada

Toronto Montreal Fort Worth New York Orlando
Philadelphia San Diego London Sydney Tokyo

Canadian Cataloguing in Publication Data

Main entry under title:

Canadian content

3rd ed.
ISBN 0–7747–3518–X

1. College readers. 2. English language — Rhetoric.
I. Norton, Sarah, 1941–   . II. Waldman, Nell Kozak, 1949–
PE1417.C35 1996   808' .0427   C95–930076–7

Publisher: Heather McWhinney
Editor and Marketing Manager: Kelly Cochrane
Projects Manager: Liz Radojkovic
Editorial Assistant: Martina van de Velde
Director of Publishing Services: Jean Davies
Editorial Manager: Marcel Chiera
Supervising Editor: Semareh Al-Hillal
Production Editor: Sheila Barry
Production Manager: Sue-Ann Becker
Production Co-ordinator: Carol Tong
Copy Editor: Paula Pike, WordsWorth Communications
Cover Design: Opus House
Interior Design: Pronk & Associates
Typesetting and Assembly: Sharon Moroney
Printing and Binding: Best Book Manufacturers, Inc.

Cover Art: "The Raven and the First Men" by Bill Reid. Courtesy of the University of British Columbia Museum of Anthropology. Photograph taken by W. McLennan.

∞ This book was printed in Canada on acid-free paper.

3 4 5   00 99 98

PREFACE

To the Instructor

Canadian Content, Third Edition, is a reader designed for Canadian college and university students taking a first-level composition course. Most of the forty selections new to this edition—many of them never previously anthologized—are by or about Canadians. At this time in our country's history, it is appropriate, even urgent, to concentrate on the questions of who we are, where we have come from, and how we are similar to or different from our neighbours, so that we may choose intelligently where we want our common destiny to lead. To provide students with new perspectives on and insights into our diverse community, many of the selections new to this edition focus on the experience and uniqueness of being "Canadian."

Like its predecessors, this edition includes readings and instructional text for the four traditional rhetorical modes: narration, description, exposition, and argumentation. Narrative and descriptive prose provide a useful starting point for students not only because students are familiar with these forms from high school, but also because they will find powerful and affecting prose in the selections that constitute Unit One. However, since most of the writing that students are required to do in school and on the job is expository, most of this book is devoted to explaining and illustrating the six basic expository strategies. The first eight units are arranged in ascending order of difficulty: from narration and description to exemplification, process analysis, classification and division, comparison and contrast, cause and effect, definition, and finally argumentation, which requires the application of several expository techniques in addition to persuasive ones. The ninth unit, Further Reading, includes eight fairly sophisticated essays that employ a combination of rhetorical strategies. New to this edition are a brief introduction to writing documented essays together with a list of topics designed to give students practice in writing documented essays based on selections in the text.

We acknowledge at the outset that the rhetorical patterns treated here individually are, in "real life" writing, most often found in combination. In our experience, however, students find it helpful to analyze and practise these patterns of development one at a time. When all have been mastered, students can then combine them in various ways to suit their purpose. ·

The essays within each unit are arranged from simplest to most complex; thus, an instructor can assign readings suited to the level of the class, or can lead students through a progressively challenging series of assignments in a single rhetorical mode. In choosing the selections for this text, we kept in mind three criteria: first, each essay had to be well written—an example of good standard English prose, neither very formal nor highly colloquial, the kind of prose we want our students to learn to write. Second, each selection had to exemplify one of the rhetorical modes: the structure and development had to illustrate clearly, if not exclusively, the pattern under discussion. Finally, we looked for pieces that were both informative and interesting, selections that would stimulate thought, provoke class discussion, and promote our students' understanding of themselves, of others, and of the world around us.

Throughout the text, we emphasize that there is no one "best" way of approaching a topic. There are always many approaches to choose from when organizing and developing an idea, and the "best" choice depends on a careful analysis of one's audience, subject, and purpose. In other words, we present the traditional rhetorical modes not as compositional straitjackets but as methods of invention, options to explore when considering how to approach a particular subject.

Many instructors prefer to organize their courses around themes rather than structural patterns, so we have included a second Table of Contents organized by theme. The Further Suggestions for Writing (page 401), which encourage students to consider similarities and differences between essays throughout the text, should be particularly useful to instructors who prefer the thematic approach.

Each unit begins with an introduction written in an informal, accessible style. Where possible, examples and allusions have been drawn from the students' culture, not just to make the point clear, but also to make the writing process less intimidating. One of the goals of this text is to demystify the writing process. The introductions encourage the student to ask specific questions about his or her subject and then to formulate a thesis statement that, tentatively at first, more definitively after several drafts, summarizes the essay in a single sentence. Whether or not this sentence appears in the final draft, the exercise of formulating and refining a thesis statement serves to clarify both the student's thinking and the paper's organization.

Many students resist composing a traditional essay outline. The thesis statement—which is an outline in miniature—ensures that the student has done the preliminary thinking and organizing that a well-structured paper requires. Students sometimes object to this "blueprint" approach to composition, protesting that "real writers don't write this way." True: novelists, poets, playwrights, and many other professional writers do not approach writing this way. Nevertheless, as the selections in this text clearly illustrate, "real" writers do pay careful attention to the organization and development of their prose. A few, such as Bertrand Russell and Martin Luther King, Jr., even employ a formal thesis statement.

Most of our students, of course, do not aspire to become professional writers. Their goal is to write competently within the context of their company, business, or profession. Unfortunately, many students arrive at college without much training or practice in writing clear prose; hence, we have emphasized structure throughout this text. Most college students, in our experience, respond positively to a practical, no-nonsense approach to writing such as the one we present here.

Immediately following the introduction in each unit, there is a short model essay that illustrates the prose structure being presented. To show students how a single subject may be approached from different points of view and supported in different ways, all the model essays focus on the subject of education and have been designed to illustrate the introductory and concluding strategies that are explained in the List of Useful Terms at the back of the book.

Within the units, each selection is followed by a short biographical note and by definitions of the most difficult words and allusions. Please note that our "meanings" are not intended to be exhaustive definitions; we have explained each word or phrase specifically as it appears in its context. Not all potentially problematic terms have been glossed, only those that the majority of students are likely to have difficulty with: terms that lack contextual clues as to their meaning or that are essential to the reader's understanding of the text. We expect students to use their dictionaries to clarify the meaning of other words they may not know.

Two sets of questions follow each essay. The Structure and Strategy questions are designed to lead the students to an understanding of *form*: how the piece is put together and why the writing strategies employed are effective. The Content and Purpose questions are designed to encourage the students' analysis of the *content* of the piece, to deepen their understanding of meaning.

Words or phrases that are included in the List of Useful Terms appear in capital letters in the questions. For example, if a question explores an author's use of DICTION, the typeface serves as a cue to consult the List of Useful Terms for an explanation of the word "diction."

We have included a few Suggestions for Writing after each essay. These suggestions lead either to a paper with a form similar to that of the essay under discussion or to one that responds in some way to the content of the piece. At the end of each unit, Additional Suggestions for Writing give students practice in the specific rhetorical form that is its focus. And finally, at the end of the book, we have provided Further Suggestions for Writing, a list of topics to encourage students to identify and explore thematic and formal links between two or more selections in the text.

Acknowledgements

This text, like its predecessors, has been very much a co-operative effort. We wish to acknowledge the contributions of Pierre Coupey, Barbara North, and Annette Pope, who reviewed the text and commented most helpfully on its strengths and weaknesses. We are also indebted to the many readers whose suggestions helped shape the form and content of this edition. In particular, we thank Ritva Seppanen, Andrew McLelland, Robin Conover, Cliff Werier, Sabrina Reed, Sandra Bit, Nicholas J. Collins, Tim Chamberlain, Hugh Cook, Ramona Montagnes, Anthea Kyle, and Barbara Brown. Special thanks are due to John Dixon, of Capilano College; Joan Rike, of Vancouver Community College; and Phil Zacharatos, of the Ministry of Forests, B.C., who took the time to provide biographical and factual information we would otherwise have been unable to confirm. And finally, we would like to thank the thousands of students and teachers across Canada whose use and enjoyment of the first two editions have made this third edition possible.

About the Cover Art

On our cover, Bill Reid's sculpture interprets an ancient Haida creation myth. Raven, bored with the pretty but lifeless world in which he found himself, sought company and entertainment. Flying over a beach one day, he spotted a gigantic clamshell that was closed tight, trapping dozens of little creatures inside. Raven prodded and pried at the shell and eventually coaxed the creatures, the first humans, out into the light of day. Like the clamshell, the selections in this book contain ideas, imagination, vision, and life. Readers who patiently and persistently dig beneath the surface will be rewarded with knowledge and entertainment to inspire and brighten their world.

A Note from the Publisher

Thank you for selecting *Canadian Content,* Third Edition, by Nell Waldman and Sarah Norton. The authors and publisher have devoted considerable time to the careful development of this book. We appreciate your recognition of this effort and accomplishment.

We want to hear what you think of *Canadian Content.* Please take a few minutes to fill in the stamped reader reply card at the back of the book. Your comments and suggestions will be valuable to us as we prepare new editions and other books.

CONTENTS

By Unit

Unit Three: Process Analysis: Explaining "How"   127

Unit Four: Classification and Division: Explaining Kinds and Parts   167

Unit Five: Comparison and Contrast: Explaining Similarities and Differences   199

Unit Six: Cause and Effect: Explaining "Why"   227

Unit Seven: Definition: Explaining "What" 271

Unit Eight: Argument and Persuasion: Appealing to Reason and Emotion 307

Unit Nine: Further Reading 349

Further Suggestions for Writing 401

List of Useful Terms 405

Author Index 417

CONTENTS

By Theme

On Canada

On the Contemporary Scene

On the Cultural Mosaic

On History

On the Arts, Media, and Sports

On Morals and Ethics

On Politics

On Relationships

On Science, Technology, and Nature

On Language and Writing

1. How to Read with Understanding

Every college student knows how to read—sort of. The trouble is that most of us don't read very efficiently. We don't know how to adapt our reading style to our purpose. Most people aren't even aware that there are different kinds of reading suited to different purposes.

Basically, there are two kinds of reading: **surface reading**, which is casual reading for pleasure or for easy-to-find facts. This is the kind of reading we engage in when we enjoy a novel, magazine, or newspaper. The second kind of reading is **deep reading**. This is the type required in college courses and on the job: reading to acquire the knowledge, facts, and ideas we need in order to understand a topic. This kind of reading has practical rather than recreational purposes. Both kinds of reading can bring us personal satisfaction, but one is undeniably more difficult than the other.

Deep reading, or analytical reading, is the kind that most of us don't do as well as we would like. As with any other skill, there is a technique involved that can, with practice, be mastered. In general, there are three basic guidelines to follow: figure out as much about the piece as you can *before* reading it; identify what you don't understand *while* reading it; and review the whole thing *after* reading it.

Specifically, there are seven steps to reading with understanding:

1. Remove Distractions

Every year, teachers hear hundreds of students protest that they are able to read perfectly well while listening to music, watching television, talking on the phone, or filing their nails. These students are right. They can read under those circumstances, but they can't read for understanding. To read analytically, you have to focus your attention completely on the text. Reading for understanding is an *active* process, requiring your full concentration and participation. For example, you should learn to read with a pencil in your hand, if you don't already do so. Only half the task of making the meaning clear belongs to the writer; the other half belongs to you. Understanding is something you have to work at.

Find a quiet spot, with a good reading light, where you can be alone with your book, your pencil, and your dictionary. We'll get to the dictionary later.

2. Preview Before You Read

Human beings cannot learn facts, ideas, or even words in isolation. We need a context, a sense of the whole into which the new piece of information fits. The more familiar you are with the context and content of a piece before you begin to read, the better able you will be to read with understanding—whether you're reading three sentences or three volumes.

Figure out as much as you can before beginning to read. How long is the piece? You'll want to estimate how much time you'll need to complete it. What's the title? The title usually points to something significant about the writer's topic or purpose. Like the label on a candy bar, the title of an article tells you something about what's inside. Who wrote it? Knowing something about the author helps you predict what the essay might be about. Is the author dead or alive? What is his or her nationality: Canadian, American, or Tasmanian? Is she a humorist or a social critic? Or is he a journalist or an academic? Is the author a specialist in a particular field?

What about the body of the work? Does it include any diagrams or illustrations? Are there subheadings that indicate the division of the material into main ideas? Finally, for the readings in this text, don't forget the context we've provided for you: the unit in which each essay is found gives you a clue to the kind of organization and development you can expect.

3. Read the Selection All the Way Through

This is a very important step, and it isn't always easy. Most inexperienced readers have a fairly short attention span—about eight to ten minutes (about the length of program time between commercials)—and they need to train themselves to increase it. You need to read a piece all the way through in order to get a sense of the whole; otherwise, you cannot fully understand either the essay or its parts.

As you read the essays in this text, note the words marked with a °: it signals that the meaning of the word or phrase is given in the Words and Meanings section following the essay. If you're unfamiliar with the term, check the definition we offer and continue reading. Underline any other words whose meaning you cannot figure out from the context. You'll look them up later.

This first time through, withhold judgment. Don't allow your prejudices—in the root sense of the word, "prejudgments"—to affect your response at this stage. If you decided in advance that the topic is boring ("Who cares about beef stew?") or the style is too demanding ("I couldn't possibly understand anything entitled 'Patriotism Redux'"), you cheat yourself out of a potentially rewarding experience. Give the writer a chance; part of his or her responsibility is to make the writing interesting and accessible to the reader. Another point to keep in mind is that reading is like any other exercise: it gets easier, or at least less painful, with practice. You'll get better at it and soon be able to tackle increasingly difficult challenges.

You haven't forgotten your pencil, have you? Here's where it comes into the act. Try to identify the main parts of the essay as you read: the INTRODUCTION, the parts into which the BODY is divided, and the CONCLUSION. If they are obvious, underline the THESIS—often expressed in a thesis statement in the introduction—and each main point, usually expressed in the TOPIC SENTENCE of a PARAGRAPH. When you come across a sentence or passage you don't understand, put a question mark in the margin. Key terms that appear in CAPITALS in the introductions and in the questions following the selections are explained in the List of Useful Terms at the end of the book.

Good writers "set up" their material for you: they identify their subject early, and indicate the scope of their essay. They use various TRANSITIONS to signal to the reader that they have concluded one idea and are moving on to another. Note, however, that this first read-through is not the time to stop and analyze the structure and writing strategies in detail. You need to read the piece a second (or even a third) time to accomplish such analysis successfully.

If you've been practising what we've been suggesting so far, you will *not* have stopped to look up INTRODUCTION, BODY, CONCLUSION, THESIS, TOPIC SENTENCE, PARAGRAPH, or TRANSITION in the List of Useful Terms. The time to look up the meaning of these and any other unfamiliar terms is when you have finished reading through this whole section.

4. Look Up the Meaning of Any Words You Didn't Understand

Here's where your dictionary comes in. Look up the words you underlined as you read through the essay—but don't just seize on the first definition given and assume this is the meaning the author intended. Read *all* the meanings given. Note that some words can be used both as nouns and as verbs; only one set of meanings will be appropriate in the context you are reading. When you're satisfied you've located the appropriate definition, jot it down in the margin beside the mystery word.

Now go back and reread any passages you marked with a question mark the first time through. Once you have figured out any vocabulary problems that initially bothered you, and now that you have an overview of the whole piece, you should find that the meaning of those confusing passages is much clearer.

5. Read the Questions Following the Selection

After you've answered all your own questions about the piece, go through the questions on Structure and Strategy and Content and Purpose that we have provided. You won't be able to answer them all at this point. The purpose of reading the questions now is to prepare yourself for a second, closer reading of the essay. These questions will guide you eventually to a thorough understanding of the piece. At this point, however, all you need to know are the sorts of questions you'll be considering after your second reading.

6. Read the Selection a Second Time—Slowly, Carefully

Got your pencil ready? Identify the INTRODUCTION, the part of the essay that establishes the subject, the limits of the subject, and the writer's TONE. If you haven't already done so your first time through, underline the THESIS and main points. Make notes in the margins. Use the margins to jot down in point form an outline of the piece, to add supplementary—or contradictory—evidence, or to call attention to particularly significant or eloquently expressed ideas. Circle key TRANSITIONS. The physical act of writing as you read helps keep your attention focussed on the essay and serves to deepen your understanding of its content and structure.

Think about the AUDIENCE the writer is addressing. Are you included in the group for whom the writer intended the essay? If not, you should remember that your reactions to and interpretations of the piece may differ from those of the intended readers. For example, if you are black, your response to Staples's essay, "Just Walk

On By," will probably be somewhat different from that of the white, middle-class readers who are Staples's primary target.

During your second reading, identify the writer's main PURPOSE. Is it to inform, to persuade, or to entertain? Notice, too, how the writer develops the main points. Be sure you distinguish between the main ideas and the supporting details—the EXAMPLES, ILLUSTRATIONS, DEFINITIONS, ANALOGIES—that the writer has used to make the ideas clear to the reader. As you read, be conscious of the writer's TONE: is it humorous or serious, impassioned or objective, formal or informal? Good writers choose their tone very carefully, since it directly affects the reader's response, probably more than any other technical aspect of writing.

Finally, consider the CONCLUSION of the essay. Does it simply restate the thesis or expand on it in some way? Are you left with a sense of the essay's completeness, a feeling that all questions raised in the piece have been satisfactorily answered? Or do you feel that you've been left dangling, that some of the loose ends have yet to be tied up?

At this point, you have a decision to make. Are you satisfied that you understand the essay? Are the writer's purpose, thesis, main ideas, and method of development all clear to you? If so, go on to step 7. If not—as often happens when you are learning to read analytically, or when you encounter a particularly challenging piece—go back and read it through a third time.

7. Answer the Questions Following the Selection

Consider the questions carefully, one by one, and prepare your answers. Refer to the selection often to keep yourself on the right track. Most of the questions don't have simple, or single, answers! Jot down your answers in point form or in short phrases in the margins of the text.

The purpose of the questions is to engage you as deeply as possible in the structure and meaning of each piece. As you analyze *what* the writer has said (the content and purpose) and *how* he or she has said it (the structure and strategies), you will come as close as you can to full understanding. At this point, you are ready to test your understanding in classroom discussion or through writing a paper of your own.

2. How to Write to Be Understood

Learning to read with understanding will help you write so that what you say is clearly understood. As you become conscious of the process readers use to make sense of a piece of writing, you will become increasingly skilful at predicting and satisfying the needs of *your* readers. For years, you've probably been told, "Keep your audience in mind as you write." By itself, this is not a particularly helpful piece of advice. You need to know not only *who your audience is*, including how much they know and how they feel about your subject, but also *how readers read*. These two pieces of knowledge are the keys to writing understandable prose. (We are assuming here that you have a firm grasp of your subject matter. You cannot write clearly and convincingly about something that you don't really understand.)

As long as you know what you are writing about and whom you are writing for, there are five steps you can take to ensure that your readers will understand what you have to say. The approach we present here applies to all kinds of expository and persuasive writing; that is, to any piece of writing in which your purpose is to *explain* something—a process, a relationship, a complex idea—or to *persuade* your readers to think or act in a particular way.

Writing a paper is like going on a journey: it makes sense—and it's certainly more efficient—to fix on your destination and plan your route before you begin. Your **subject** is your destination. Your **main points** determine the route you select to get to your destination. In other words, the main points determine the kind of paper you are going to write.

In this text, we explain eight basic ways to organize a paper: eight different approaches to explaining a subject, eight different routes to a destination. Something we want to emphasize is that there is no *one* way to explain a subject. A subject, like a destination on a map, can be approached from many different directions.

Take education, for example. It is a very broad, general subject. Now, if you flip through the introductions to the first eight units of this book, you will see that each introduction contains a model essay illustrating the organizational pattern explained in that unit. All of these model essays are on the subject of education, but they are all different. We've limited the subject eight different ways, chosen eight different sets of main points, eight different organizational patterns—eight different paths to the goal. Read these model essays carefully, and you'll discover how the pattern discussed in each unit can lend shape, coherence, and unity to the subject you're writing about.

As you will have discovered by now, people who are reading for information, for understanding, don't like surprises: no bumps or potholes, no sudden shifts in direction, no dead ends. They appreciate a well-marked, smooth path through the writer's prose. So your task is to identify the path for them, set them on it, and guide them through to the end. If you can keep them interested, even entertained, on their journey, so much the better. As you read through the selections in this book, you will encounter a variety of stylistic devices that you can use to add interest and impact to your own writing.

Here are the five steps to clear, well-organized writing:

1. clarify your subject
2. identify the main points of your subject
3. write a thesis statement
4. develop the paragraphs
5. revise your paper.

If you follow these five steps carefully, in order, we guarantee that you will write papers that an attentive reader will be able to understand—and perhaps even enjoy.

Steps 1, 2, and 3 are the *preparation* stage of the writing process. Be warned: these three steps will take you as long as—if not longer than—steps 4 and 5, which involve the actual *writing*. There is a general rule that governs all expository and persuasive writing: the longer you spend on preparation, the less time the writing will take, and the better your paper will be.

Step 1: Clarify Your Subject

The subject of your paper or report may be one assigned by a teacher or by your supervisor. At worst, you may have to come up with one on your own. Choosing a satisfactory subject can be the most difficult part of writing an easy-to-understand piece of prose. Inexperienced writers often choose a subject that is far bigger than either their knowledge or the space allotted them can justify.

A suitable subject is one that is both *specific* and *supportable*. A thorough, detailed discussion of a single, specific topic is much more satisfying to read than a general, superficial treatment of a very broad topic. This is why Wade Davis chose to discuss three highly specific examples rather than to generalize broadly about ecological disasters in his essay "The End of the Wild" (see Unit Two). You can narrow a broad subject by applying one or more limiting factors to it. Think of your subject in terms of a specific *kind*, or *time*, or *place*, or *number*, or *person* associated with it. Davis, for example, limited his subject in terms of kind (bird, animal, and forest), time (twentieth century), and place (North America).

A subject is supportable if you can develop it with examples, facts, quotations, descriptions, anecdotes, comparisons, definitions, and other supporting details. These supporting details are called EVIDENCE; we will discuss its use more fully under step 4, below. Evidence, combined with good organization, makes your discussion of a subject both clear and convincing.

Step 2: Identify the Main Points of Your Subject

Once you have clarified your subject, think about the approach you're going to use to explain it. There are many possible ways of thinking and writing about any subject. In a short paper, you can deal effectively with only a few aspects of a subject, even a very specific one. But how do you decide what is the best approach to take? How do you decide which aspects of your subject to discuss and what main points to make and explain?

One way to sort through these choices is to do some preliminary research. Another technique some writers use is to jot down everything they can think of about their subject until they "freewrite" or "brainstorm" their way to an organizational pattern. Perhaps the surest way to approach a subject—especially if you're stuck for ideas—is to ask yourself some specific questions about it. Apply the following list of questions, one at a time, to your subject and see which question "fits" it best—which question calls up in your mind answers that approximate what it is you want to say. (The symbol "S" stands for your subject.)

If this is the question that fits	Then this is the kind of paper you will be writing
1. What does S look like? 2. How did S happen?	DESCRIPTION/NARRATION
3. What are some significant examples of S?	EXAMPLE
4. How is S made or done? 5. How does S work?	PROCESS ANALYSIS

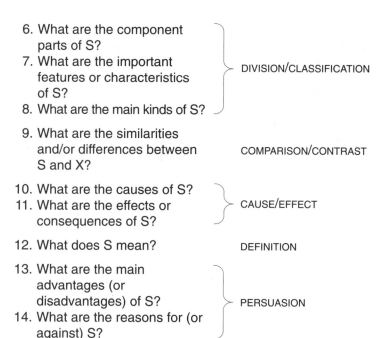

6. What are the component parts of S?
7. What are the important features or characteristics of S?
8. What are the main kinds of S?

DIVISION/CLASSIFICATION

9. What are the similarities and/or differences between S and X?

COMPARISON/CONTRAST

10. What are the causes of S?
11. What are the effects or consequences of S?

CAUSE/EFFECT

12. What does S mean?

DEFINITION

13. What are the main advantages (or disadvantages) of S?
14. What are the reasons for (or against) S?

PERSUASION

These questions suggest most of the different ways you can look at or think about a subject. When you discover the question that elicits the answers that are closest to what you know and want to write about, then you will have discovered what kind of paper you need to write. The answers to the best question are the aspects of the subject you will discuss; they become the main points of your paper. The eight different types of papers listed in the right-hand column above correspond to the rhetorical patterns presented in this text. To find out how to arrange and develop your main points to produce an effective paper, turn to the introduction of the appropriate unit.

Step 3: Write a Thesis Statement

A **thesis statement** in your INTRODUCTION is the clearest way to organize a short paper of 350 to 800 words. It plans your paper for you, and it tells your reader what he or she is going to read about. Remember: "no surprises" is the watchword when you write, unless you're writing mystery stories. To continue the analogy between reading an essay and taking a trip, the thesis statement is a kind of map: it identifies both your destination and the route. Like a map, it keeps your reader (and you) on the right track.

To be specific, a thesis statement clearly tells your reader the subject of your paper, the main points you will discuss, and the order in which you will discuss them. Not all essays contain thesis statements. In some of the essays in this book, for example, you will notice that the THESIS is implied rather than explicitly stated. We recommend, however, that you include a thesis statement in every paper you write. There is probably no writing strategy you can use that is more helpful to your readers' understanding of what you've written.

To write a thesis statement, you join your *subject* to the *main points* (arranged in an appropriate ORDER) by means of a linking word such as *are, because, since, include,* or a colon. Here is a simple formula, or blueprint, for a thesis statement (S stands for your *subject*; a, b, c, d stand for your *main points*):

> S consists of a, b, c, d....

The introduction to each unit of this text contains a formula to follow when constructing a thesis statement for the particular type of paper presented in that unit.

Here are some examples of thesis statements taken from essays included in our collection:

"There are three dimensions of a complete life: length, breadth, and height." (*The Dimensions of a Complete Life*)

"Three passions, simple but overwhelmingly strong, have governed my life: the longing for love, the search for knowledge, and unbearable pity for the suffering of mankind." (*What I Have Lived For*)

"General education is an essential part of the curriculum because it enhances one's ability to build a career and to live a full life." (*Why Are We Reading This Stuff, Anyway?*)

"Most educators agree that the principal causes of failure in school are lack of basic skills, lack of study skills, and lack of motivation." (*Why Do They Fail?*)

Note that the main points in a thesis statement should be expressed in PARALLEL STRUCTURE. See the List of Useful Terms for an explanation of parallel structure.

Step 4: Develop the Paragraphs

Each of your main points will be developed in a paragraph, sometimes in two or three paragraphs. Each paragraph should contain a TOPIC SENTENCE that clearly states the main idea or topic of that paragraph. Often, the topic sentence comes at the beginning of the paragraph so that the reader knows what to expect from the very beginning. The next five, six, or more sentences develop the topic. The key to making the paragraph unified (see UNITY) is to make sure that every one of the supporting sentences relates directly to the topic. An adequately developed paragraph includes enough supporting information to make the topic clear to the reader.

How do you decide what is the best way to develop a particular paragraph? How much support should you include? What kind of support should it be? To make these decisions, try putting yourself in your reader's place. What does he or she need to know in order to understand your point clearly? If you ask yourself the seven questions listed below, you'll be able to decide how to develop your topic sentence.

1. Is a **definition** needed? If you're using a term that may be unfamiliar to your readers, you should define it—phrasing it in your own words, please, rather than citing a quotation from a dictionary. The Introduction to Unit Seven will show you how to define terms.

2. Would two or three **examples** help clarify the point? Providing examples is probably the most common method of developing a topic. Readers may be confused or even suspicious when they read unsupported generalizations or statements of opinion. Providing specific, relevant examples will help them to understand your point. The Introduction to Unit Two will show you how to use examples effectively.

3. Is a series of steps or stages involved? Are you explaining a **process** to your reader? Sometimes the most logical way to make your point clear is to explain how something is done—that is, to relate, in order, the steps involved. The Introduction to Unit Three will give you detailed directions for this kind of development.

4. Would a **comparison** or **contrast** help make your explanation clearer? Your reader will find it easier to understand something new if you explain it in terms of something he or she is already familiar with. A *comparison* points out similarities between objects, people, or ideas; a *contrast* shows how the objects, people, or ideas are different. The Introduction to Unit Five provides a detailed description of this technique.

5. Would **specific details** be useful? Providing your reader with concrete, specific, descriptive details can be a very effective way of developing your topic. Such details create an image in the mind of the reader—of general appearance, size, shape, texture, or direction, for example. Descriptive details are also

useful in creating or intensifying the mood you are trying to convey. In some paragraphs, numerical facts or statistics are useful in supporting your point—just be sure your facts are correct and your statistics up to date! See the Introduction to Unit One for instructions on writing effective description.

6. Would **narrating a story** be an effective way of getting your idea across? Everyone loves to read a story if it's well told and relevant to what's being discussed. Use of a personal anecdote to illustrate a point can be a very effective way of helping your readers not only understand your point but also remember it. A good story contains the basic narrative elements of event, place, and sequence; it also helps contribute to the tone and purpose of your essay. The Introduction to Unit One will give you guidelines to follow when using a narration to develop a point.

7. Would a **quotation** or **paraphrase** be appropriate? Would your reader be convinced by reading the words of someone else who shares your opinion? Occasionally, you will find that another individual—an expert in a particular field, a well-known author, or a respected public figure—has said what you want to say so well that your own paper can only benefit from including it. Quotations, so long as they are kept short and not used too frequently, can also add EMPHASIS to an idea. Sometimes, you don't want to quote directly from another writer, but to rephrase the writer's idea in your own words. It's up to you to decide what the essential points are and then word them in a way suited to the needs of your paper. This technique is called PARAPHRASING.

Whenever you use a quotation or a paraphrase, of course, you *must* acknowledge your source. See Writing the Documented Essay (page 15) for instructions on how to find and use source material.

If you glance at the unit titles in the Contents, you will see that some of these methods of paragraph development are also structural principles on which whole essays can be based. Because of their multipurpose character, it is essential that you become familiar and comfortable with all seven strategies.

The methods you choose to develop a point should be determined by your readers' needs and expectations. If you have a clear picture of your audience, you'll be able to choose the appropriate kinds and amount of development they require if they are to follow you with ease. You can, of course, use more than one method to develop a paragraph; sometimes a comparison can be effectively coupled with a quotation, for example. There is no fixed rule that governs the kind or number of development strategies required in any particular paragraph or essay. The decision is yours. Your responsibility as a writer is to keep in mind what your readers know and what they need to know in order to understand the points you're making.

Once you have developed your main points, you will add two important paragraphs: the INTRODUCTION and CONCLUSION. All too often, these parts of a paper are dull, clumsy, or repetitive. But they shouldn't be and they needn't be. If carefully constructed, these paragraphs can effectively catch your reader's attention and clinch your argument. The List of Useful Terms contains specific strategies you can choose from when crafting a beginning and ending for your paper.

As you write your paragraphs, keep in mind that you want to make it as easy as possible for your reader to follow you through your paper. TRANSITIONS and TONE can make the difference between a confusing, annoying paper and an informative, pleasing one. *Transitions* are words or phrases that show the relationship between one point and the next, causing a paragraph (or a paper) to hang together and read smoothly. Transitions are like the turn signals on a car: they tell the person following you where you're going. The List of Useful Terms will give you suggestions for appropriate transitional phrases, depending on what kind of relationship between the ideas you want to signal.

Tone is the word used to describe a writer's attitude toward the subject and the reader. A writer may feel angry about a subject, or amused, or nostalgic, and this attitude is reflected in the words, examples, quotations, and other supporting details he or she chooses to explain the main points. Good writing is usually modulated in tone; the writer addresses the reader with respect, in a calm, reasonable way. Writing that is highly emotional in tone is not often very convincing to the readers: what gets communicated is the strength of the writer's feelings rather than the writer's depth of knowledge or validity of opinion about the subject.

Two suggestions may help you find and maintain the right tone. First, never insult your reader unintentionally with phrases such as "Any idiot can see that...," or "No sane person could believe...," or even "It is obvious that...." Remember that what seems obvious to you is not necessarily obvious to someone who has a limited knowledge of your subject or who disagrees with your opinion. Second, don't condescend—talk down—to your reader, and don't use heavy-handed sarcasm. On the other hand, you need not apologize for your opinion. You've thought about your subject and taken considerable time to develop it. Present your information in a positive rather than a hesitant way: avoid phrases such as "I tend to believe that..." or "I may be wrong, but...." Have confidence in yourself and in your ideas.

Step 5: Revise Your Paper

At last you've reached the final step in the writing process. Even though you are by now probably sick of the whole project and eager to be rid of it, *do not* omit this important final step. Revising (which means "taking a look back") is essential before your paper is ready to be sent out into the world. Ideally, you should revise your paper several days after writing it. After a "cooling-off" period, you'll be able to see your work more objectively. If you reread it immediately after you've finished writing it, you're likely to "read" what you *think* you've written—what's in your head rather than what's actually on the page.

Thorough revision requires at least two reviews of your paper. The first time you go over it, read it aloud, slowly, from beginning to end, keeping your audience in mind as you read. Is your thesis clear? Are all the points adequately explained? Has anything been left out? Are the paragraphs unified and coherent? Are there any awkward sentences that should be rephrased?

The second time you read your paper through, read it with the Editing Checklist (on the inside of the back cover) in front of you for easy reference. Pay special attention to the points that tend to give you trouble; for example, sentence fragments, verb errors, apostrophes, or dangling modifiers. Most writers know their weaknesses. Unfortunately, it's human nature to focus on our strengths and try to gloss over our weaknesses. This is the reason why editing your work can be a painful process. Nevertheless, it is an absolutely essential task. You owe it both to yourself and to your reader to find and correct any errors in your writing.

If you are a poor speller, you will need to read your paper a third time. This time, read it through from the end to the beginning to check your spelling. When reading from back to front, you're forced to look at each word individually, not in context, and thus you are more likely to spot your spelling mistakes. If you are truly a hopeless speller, ask someone to identify the errors for you. Better yet, learn to use a spell-checking program on a word processor.

A final word of advice: whether you are in school or on the job, always make a copy of your paper before you hand it in. You wouldn't want to have to go through this whole process again because your paper got misplaced!

If you follow these five steps carefully, you and your reader will arrive at your destination without any accident, mishap, or wrong turns. The journey should be relatively painless for you, and informative—perhaps even enjoyable—for your reader.

3. Writing the Documented Essay

For some essays or research assignments, you will be required to locate and integrate other people's ideas, knowledge, or expert opinion into your paper. You will use the written (or, occasionally, spoken) words of external sources to help make your ideas clear and prove your point to your reader. As any good lawyer knows, proving a point depends on two things: finding enough good evidence and presenting it effectively. The kind and quality of the evidence you assemble and the way you incorporate it in your own writing will determine the success or failure of your documented essay.

Keep in mind that the reason most instructors assign research papers is to give you an opportunity to demonstrate how well you can analyze and evaluate source material, synthesize it, and use it to support your own conclusions about a subject. Very few research assignments require you simply to report other people's findings on a topic. Normally, you are expected to use your source material as evidence to support your thesis. Writing a documented essay requires the use of high-order thinking skills: interpreting, summarizing, analyzing, and evaluating. That is why a research paper or term paper so often serves as the culminating test of learning in college courses. Such papers are good practice for the world of work, too. The critical thinking skills required to produce a documented essay are the same skills required of professionals on the job.

1. Gathering the Evidence

Your first task is to find, evaluate, and make notes on source material that supports your thesis. Usually, you do this work in the library, using books, periodicals, or academic journals as your sources. CD-ROM searches and other computer-based research tools are also available. Your librarian will help you search for relevant, up-to-date information.

After you have found a number of promising-looking sources, your next task is to evaluate the material to see whether it really is appropriate for your paper. Inexperienced writers often get bogged down at this point, spending days or weeks reading each potential source in detail. A more efficient approach is to scan each work quickly to eliminate what is not current, relevant, or appropriate for your paper. Once you have identified enough solid supporting sources, read them carefully, using the reading and note-taking suggestions given on pages 1 to 5 (How to Read with Understanding). For every set of notes you make, be careful to record all the source information you need to document your paper accurately: author or editor, title, publisher, place and date of publication, and the page(s) on which you found the information you have noted. Keeping detailed and accurate bibliographical records as you read through your sources will save you hours of time and frustration later, when you come to document your paper and can't remember where a crucial piece of information came from. Accurate bibliographical records will also help keep you from falling into the trap of inadvertent plagiarism (more on this later).

2. Presenting the Evidence

Once your research notes are complete and you have begun your first draft, you need to know how to integrate the information you have found into your own writing. There are three methods you can choose from: summary, paraphrase, or direct quotation. A summary is a highly condensed version of another person's ideas or observations. A paraphrase is a longer summary. It could include, for example, the key idea and several supporting details, whereas a summary would present only the key idea. Whether you are summarizing or paraphrasing, however, you must *restate the source information in your own words*. If you use the actual words or phrases of the original, you are quoting, and you must signal that fact to the reader by using quotation marks.

A word about plagiarism. Everyone knows that plagiarism is using someone else's ideas and presenting them as your own. Submitting someone else's term paper or collecting material from various articles and passing it off as your own original thinking are clear examples of academic dishonesty. Not everyone realizes, however, that neglecting to identify your sources, even if the omission is unintentional, is also plagiarism. Whenever you use another writer's ideas in an essay, you need to let your reader know whose ideas they are and where you found them. Whether you are summarizing, paraphrasing, or quoting, you must acknowledge your sources. This process is called documentation. Careful documentation will not only ensure that you avoid plagiarism, it will also ensure that you are credited with the careful reading and research you have done.

To document the books, articles, or other information you have used in your paper, you need to follow an approved system of documentation. Two basic styles are used in most colleges and universities: the Modern Language Association (MLA) format, usually required in humanities courses, and the American Psychological Association (APA) format, commonly used in the social sciences. (Note that both these formats have abandoned the old-fashioned and cumbersome footnote system in favour of parenthetical referencing, which means indicating the source in parentheses immediately following the summary, paraphrase, or quotation.) The natural and physical sciences use a wide variety of documentation formats, and many colleges and universities publish their own style manuals for use in their courses. If your instructor requires a specific format, buy the appropriate handbook to guide you through the task of acknowledging source material. The style—including the order of information, capitalization, and punctuation—must be followed *exactly*. If your instructor leaves the choice of format up to you, try one of these style guides:

1. Gibaldi, Joseph, and Walter S. Achtert. *MLA Handbook for Writers of Research Papers*. 3rd ed. New York: Modern Language Association, 1988.
2. American Psychological Association. *Publication Manual of the American Psychological Association*. 3rd ed. Washington: American Psychological Association, 1983.

The two paragraphs that follow have been adapted from a documented essay written by Centennial College student Ken Horton. These paragraphs demonstrate how to incorporate short and long quotations into your own writing and also how to indicate that you have altered a quotation, either by leaving something out (use ellipses) or by adding or changing a word or phrase (use square brackets). Ken's documentation follows the MLA format.

title and author
of source are
identified

long quotation,
introduced by a
colon and set off
10 spaces from
the left margin

pages on which
the quotation
appears

The tone of "Behind the Formaldehyde Curtain" is savagely ironic. It is clear from the beginning of Mitford's essay that she is horrified by the practices of the funeral industry:

> [The body] is whisked off to a funeral parlor and is in short order sprayed, sliced, pierced, pickled, trussed, trimmed, creamed, waxed, painted, rouged and neatly dressed— transformed from a common corpse into a Beautiful Memory Picture. This process is ... so universally employed in the United States and Canada that the funeral director does it routinely, without consulting corpse or kin. (135–6)

short quotations, integrated into student's own sentences

quotation within a quotation

page reference

Throughout her essay, Mitford describes in stomach-churning detail the equipment, techniques, and results of the attentions inflicted on the hapless corpse, all in aid of making it fit to be "viewed" by relatives and friends of the deceased: "[r]agged edges are trimmed, and head joined to torso with a series of splints, wires and sutures" (139). As additional support for her thesis, Mitford quotes from *The Principles and Practices of Embalming*, which advises, for example, that "if Flextone [an embalming fluid] is used, it will produce a 'mild, flexible rigidity. The skin retains a velvety softness... [It is] ideal for women and children'" (138).

If you turn to the Further Suggestions for Writing on page 401, you will find a list of topics that will provide you with practice in writing documented essays based on the selections in this text.

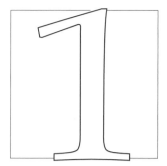

U N I T

Narration and Description: Explaining in Terms of Time and Space

What? The Definition

What does it look like? How did it happen? When you write a paper, or a part of one, that answers these questions for your readers, you are writing **description** and **narration**. Both are rhetorical modes, and each can be used as an end in itself: description to reconstruct for the reader how something or someone appears; narration to tell a story or re-create an event. More usually, however, they are found together, used in support of an expository or persuasive objective. And that is how we encourage you to use description and narration in your writing—as adjuncts, or helpers, to your explanation, analysis, or argument.

In its simplest terms, a narrative relates a sequence of events: it tells a story. Skilfully done, narration does not merely *tell* the readers what happened: it *re-creates* the experience for them so that they may see and hear and feel exactly what it was like. Story telling is one of humanity's oldest and most powerful arts. Just the phrase "Once upon a time..." is enough to capture almost everyone's attention. Novels and short stories are examples of narrative art, but they are based on fictional "events"—events that were created in the imagination of the writer. In this unit, we shall confine our attention to factual narration—events that actually happened in real life. We shall focus on the art of recounting a sequence of events in order to help explain or illustrate a point. In re-creating a series of events for the reader, good narration makes clear the causal connections between the stages of the action. The writer guides the reader through the story step by step. Process analysis and causal analysis (Unit Three and Unit Six) also involve narration in that they explain a chronological sequence of steps that result in a completed process.

If narration is organized in terms of time—"What happened next?"—description is organized in terms of space: "Where is it?" "What does it look (sound, smell, taste, or feel) like?" Good descriptive writing creates a verbal picture for the reader; it reconstructs an image of someone or something. Note that words do not restrict the writer to visual description alone. Truly vivid descriptive writing appeals to more than just the reader's sense of sight. Lorne Rubenstein's essay on golf, for example, evokes the sounds, the smells, and the feel of the game, as well as its visual appeal.

Descriptive writing may be **objective** or **subjective**. Objective description is purely factual; the writer's feelings do not enter into the written account. Lab reports and business proposals are examples of this kind of description. On the other hand, some descriptive writing is subjective or impressionistic; it creates a dominant impression based on the writer's values and feelings. For example, where a medical history would describe an Alzheimer's patient in objective terms, Michael Ignatieff's description of his afflicted mother is warm, personal, and deeply affecting.

Why? The Purpose

Narration and description are most often used to help explain a subject or develop a topic. Telling a story or creating a vivid sensory picture may be the most effective technique the writer can use to communicate clearly and memorably with the reader. For example, "Bush League Business" and "Growing Up Native" represent two very different pictures, two very different stories about life among First Nations peoples. But both Johnston and Geddes rely on narrative and description to convey to us their subject and their point of view. An essay on a very different subject, Harry Bruce's "The Softball Was Always Hard" (in Further Reading) employs narration and description almost exclusively to create for us the experience of children playing baseball with rough, outseam leather balls and no gloves, an experience not many of us have had the opportunity—or perhaps the inclination—to enjoy in real life. His account makes the experience vivid, memorable, and fun.

Occasionally, a writer may choose to use narration or description by itself as the organizing principle of an essay. More usually, however, the two are used together to support an expository purpose, as is the case in the selections we've chosen for this unit. The writers' primary intent in these essays is to explain a subject or argue an opinion by means of stories and verbal pictures. "Growing Up Native," for instance, recounts the experiences of an Indian child growing up in the Yukon; Geddes's purpose is to convey both the supportive warmth of her extended family and the ravages of racism on families and individuals.

Narration and description, then, can be used in two ways. First, they can be employed together with other rhetorical techniques, in an article, essay, or report, in support of an overall expository purpose. A descriptive paragraph or narrative segment may develop a point in a uniquely effective way. Second, an entire essay may be developed as a narrative or descriptive piece. In either case, the writer needs to know and apply a few structural principles on which effective narration and description depend.

How? The Technique

To write a good narrative, whether it's a single paragraph or an entire paper, keep the following principles in mind:

1. Select appropriate details. What you leave out is as important as what you put in. How do you decide what is or is not "appropriate"? Every story has a purpose; you are telling the story to illustrate that purpose. Only details that are clearly and directly related to your purpose should be included. In any story, there are dozens or hundreds of events and particulars that could form part of the sequence. For instance, a narrative focussing on the perils of drug abuse could recount an addict's tale of increasing dependence and eventual resort to crime. While the roots of the addiction perhaps lie in childhood deprivation or abuse, it is neither possible nor appropriate to narrate the entire story of the addict's life. Your first task is to be selective. With your purpose clearly in mind, choose only those details that contribute directly to your point. Put yourself in your reader's place as you consider what to include and what to leave out. Is a particular event or physical detail indispensable to your reader's understanding? Does it relate clearly to your main point and contribute directly to the overall effect you are aiming for? If in

doubt, leave it out. When you tell a story, economy is just as important as the use of precise, vigorous language. We've all been bored to stupefaction by storytellers who go on, and on, and on, delaying the point so long that by the time they do get to it—*if* they get to it—the listener's attention has long since wandered off in another direction.

2. Arrange the events of the story in the most effective time order. Once you've selected the significant details, consider how to arrange them to ensure maximum impact on the reader. How can you ensure the reader's interest right from the start? What should come first? What last? Is straight chronological order— a recounting of events in the order in which they occurred— called for? Or would the impact be greater if you began with an event that occurred in the middle of the chronological sequence, then introduced a flashback to fill in significant events that occurred before the point at which you began? This is the technique Michael Ignatieff chooses in "Deficits," for example. There is no single "best" arrangement of events in your story; once you've decided on the significant events you intend to include, experiment with a couple of different arrangements to determine which will produce the effect you're aiming for. Once you've settled on a time order, *stick to it*. Narratives usually rely on a certain amount of suspense to draw the readers through the story. Unless the time sequence is clear and logical, however, you're more likely to create confusion than suspense.

3. Use the same POINT OF VIEW (or angle of narration) throughout your paper. If an "I" is telling the story, don't shift in midstream to a "he" or a "she" or a "you." A consistent point of view is essential to the story's unity. Changing the point of view will only confuse your readers, who need to experience the story through a single narrative perspective.

4. Use TRANSITIONS to make your narrative coherent and to help your readers keep straight the relationships among events. Avoid stringing your sentences and paragraphs together with "and then … and then … and then," which will bore, if not annoy, your readers. Provide time markers that indicate where you are in the progression or development of the event: "after," "suddenly," "next," "as soon as," and "finally" are useful signals that help your readers keep on track.

Writing effective description also involves adhering to organizational principles that direct and shape your writing. Here are three to keep in mind:

1. Before you begin to write, decide on the purpose of your description. Is it your intention to create a factual, objective picture for your reader? Or do you wish to create a dominant impression that reflects your personal values and feelings? Clarifying your purpose is necessary before you can select appropriate key points and an effective structure.

2. Keeping your purpose in mind, select the physical details and words that will most effectively communicate the picture or impression you wish to convey. Good description evokes sensory impressions. You should include those features most likely to have a strong effect and memorable impact on your readers. Effective description often makes use of figurative language (see FIGURES OF SPEECH) to make the reader not only understand but also feel what the writer is describing.

3. Once you have selected the details you wish to include, your next task is to arrange them in the most appropriate order—an order that is either inherent in the subject or dictated by the context. To describe a person, for instance, you could move from head to toe (not very interesting), or from external features to internal character. Or you could provide an overview—a general impression—before concentrating on the features most significant to your purpose. For example, notice how George Galt organizes his description of the *Jefe* in "Night Pictures of Peru" (para. 20). Galt proceeds from his face, to his hands, to his paunch, to his uniform—for a purpose.

   If you were describing a photograph, you might introduce the details, in order, from left to right, or top to bottom, or from near to far—or vice versa. One pattern of organization is not necessarily better than another, although you are likely to have the greatest impact on your reader if you build from least important detail to the most important detail. (Just be sure your least important detail is described in language interesting enough to keep your reader awake!)

Writing narration and description may seem at first glance to be a relatively simple task. And it's true that you have probably had lots of experience with these forms in high school. Writing good narration and description—prose that has the intended effect on your readers—however, requires careful planning and close attention to detail. Mastering these rhetorical forms is well worth your time and effort, though, since most writing includes both narrative and descriptive passages. Because they answer the most fundamental questions readers ask—what is it like? what happened next?—narration and description are two of the most useful tools a writer can use to build understanding.

The essay below illustrates how narration and description can be used in combination to help communicate the writer's point.

New Year's in September

Introduction
(makes a general
statement about
a particular day)

New Year's Day is the day after Labour Day. Every teacher knows this; so does every student. It is a fact of life for all of us who have not yet graduated from school. On that day in early September, teachers and students are partners in their excitement—often cunningly disguised under a layer of cynical ennui—at the annual New Beginning. As full of potential as a brand new spiral-bound notebook or an unsharpened pencil or an uncluttered desk, we assemble, determined to do better this year.

Narrative begins
here with a
flashback to a
specific instance
of the general
statement in
paragraph 1

In the midst of this annual ritual, I find a moment to reflect on earlier first days, chosen from a staggering number now, since I have spent all but a handful of Labour Days in anticipation of school the next morning. Often my reflections fix on that day in 1971 when I faced my first class of college students. By that time, I'd had lots of first days: eight in primary school, five in high school, four in university, and two as a high school teacher. Many of them have been memorable, some pleasant, a few traumatic. But this first day in 1971 was the beginning of a new career: I was going to teach English to Theatre Arts students, and I was going to be great.

Aware that first impressions are all-important on these occasions, I pulled out all the stops and dressed resplendently in my green, double-breasted, pinstripe suit. This garment was my guarantee of a sensational start: the pants flared to a full twelve inches at the cuff (measurements in bell-bottomed

Description (note the use of precise details that enable the reader to "see" the writer)

Transition between descriptive passage and narrative

Narrative resumes here

Descriptive details appeal to several senses:

smell

hearing

sight

pants do not have metric equivalents); the lapels were knife-edged and came out to *here*, where the heavily padded shoulders took over. The vest was paisley satin; the belt almost three inches wide and trimmed with a silver buckle that weighed two pounds; and the tie ... is best left to your imagination. I finished off my ensemble with zippered boots that added a full inch to my 6'4" height. With my shiny new leather briefcase, recently trimmed shag haircut, and drooping Mexican bandit moustache, I presented the perfect picture of "with it" '70s professorial good taste. Those Theatre Arts students would be eating from my hand before I even began my carefully prepared introductory remarks.

The Theatre School was a drive across town, and I left very early so I would have time to explore my new environment. The Theatre School was a dingy and decrepit old church, long since deemed uninhabitable by a decent God-fearing congregation. Directed by a sign pointing me to the ancient parish hall, I pulled open the grimy door and was greeted by the heady scent of old building mixed with fibreglass resin, paint, glue, sawdust, and a potpourri of unidentifiable odours. Somewhere in the back of the building, a circular saw screamed frantically. I made my way along a bilious green hallway lined with brown lockers that looked as though they might have seen service in World War II. The glaring fluorescent lights, inches above my head, revealed the accumulated grime and abuse of many years. I crept past the woodshop where a set-building class was in progress. Banshees would have quailed before the agonized shrieks of that circular saw. What touch

Transition back to the narrative

Narrative resumes here

Descriptive details paint a picture of the class

Transition to narrative

Narrative continues and tension builds

were they cutting in there? At the end of the hall, I found my classroom and tentatively pushed open the scarred wooden door. Large drafting tables and high stools filled most of the space; a blackboard and battered wooden desk at the front were the only evidence of potential academic function. Swallowing my disappointment and determined to make the best of it, I sat down at the desk to look through my notes and await my students.

Mercifully, the circular saw wailed its last and expired. For a moment there was silence; then I heard the babble of excited voices. I stood and set my face in what I hoped was a stern but sympathetic expression, prepared to impress my class. They arrived in a clump, as motley and colourful a group as ever trod the planks of a pirate ship. Dressed in a mind-boggling variety of torn and tattered blue jeans, checkered bell-bottoms, bright miniskirts, flowing granny dresses, garishly-coloured shirts, bandannas, hats, scarves and bangles, they swarmed into the room. Shouting and hooting in high spirits, chattering with neighbours or singing loudly and unselfconsciously, they selected their tables and perched on the high stools like bright, raucous birds. Before long, someone noticed me, and word quickly spread through the flock. Soon the room was silent. We spent several long, anxious moments staring at each other in wonder. They apparently had never seen anything quite like my suit; I certainly had never experienced anything like this gypsy mob. The silence grew, none of us sure how to begin. It was like a first meeting between alien races. Finally a late arrival broke the ice. A long-haired girl sauntered through the door and down the aisle to the front of

Climactic incident breaks the ice— and the tension— with use of dialogue, the "punch line"

the class. She was dressed in faded overalls and a yellow T-shirt displaying what looked like a two-word obscenity (misspelled) across her chest. We eyed each other. She climbed onto a stool, grinned, and said "Hi, I'm Peggy. You speak English?"

Conclusion (brings together descriptive details of place, time, and characters)

I didn't wear my green doubled-breasted pinstripe to the Theatre School again. In return, I was accepted and allowed to teach ... so long as I didn't take myself too seriously. All in all, it was a happy arrangement—so happy, indeed, that I still think back on that long-abandoned old building with affection. Certainly, the structure was a fire trap and an eyesore, but somehow, despite—or maybe *because of*—their horrible environment, the students were among the most creative, the most dedicated, and the most fun I have experienced in my teaching career. They are scattered now all over the country, some of them probably still working in theatre. Wherever they are and whatever they are doing, they often get a quick and affectionate "Break a leg!" from a grateful teacher on our New Year's anniversary: the first Tuesday in September.

Last sentence echoes the introduction, contributing to unity

Night Pictures of Peru

GEORGE GALT

The overhead lights dimmed, then died. 1 My eyes tried to locate the small, dirt-smeared window onto the square, but couldn't: the streetlamps had gone dark, too. We were in a remote town high in the Peruvian Andes, eating unfamiliar

"Night Pictures of Peru" by George Galt. Originally appeared in *Writing Away* (McClelland & Stewart). Reprinted with the permission of the author.

food after sundown. Suddenly we couldn't see a thing, and for a few strange moments the noisy restaurant fell silent.

2   A thin white candle appeared up at the bar. Soon each table in the room had its own small yellow flame. Like everything else we'd seen that had been manufactured in Peru, the candles seemed badly made. They sputtered and threw weak pools of light, not illuminating the room so much as carving a maze of shadows.

3   We'd been told to be very careful up here on the *altiplano°*. By 1980, Peru had become dangerous. In the decade before our visit, tourists had been robbed, beaten, even killed. When we'd first arrived in Lima, we'd remarked on the poverty, the run-down buildings, the urban chaos. Don't leave your coats or bags untended in a public place, not even for half a minute, a guidebook had counselled. Every morning we strapped comfortable money belts onto our skin, went out with more cash than we'd ever carried before, and walked among the poorest people I'd ever seen. How to reconcile our wealth with their beggarhood? In Peru that large historical question lies compressed in rolled-up dollars tied around your waist. The question chafes°, but short of shedding your belt and becoming a beggar yourself, there's no quick answer.

4   That night in the semidarkness we took turns making our way to the dessert cooler. We were lightheaded from the altitude, and physically exhausted from the day's roller-coaster train ride up the steep mountains. From the station, we'd walked a long way with our bags through dusty streets to a hotel. And everywhere we'd gone, people had stared at our fair skin and good clothes. The restaurant was a welcome refuge. I remember feeling pleasantly tired when I came back from the dessert display with my pastry. But even in that thin light I sensed something on the table was wrong.

5   "Did you move your purse?" I asked.

6   The purse was gone. A few seconds earlier a man had tapped Fay's shoulder and asked her respectfully for the time. She'd turned for a moment to reply. And in that instant, from the other side, her bag had been snatched by the man's accomplice.

7   We exchanged pained looks. Our money and papers were strapped around our waists, but in the purse had been her camera with our roll of film from the Amazon: images of giant, magic-realist butterflies floating past psychedelic orchids.

8   I raged into the street. The sidewalk was a crush of brown faces. I could see them for about six feet around the restaurant doorway; beyond that darkness drew a curtain. The only lights were the glowing red dots of cigarettes hanging in the air. Around the doorway a few pairs of eyes noted me impassively°.

"Foreign aid," I shrugged, when I returned and reported the   9
hopelessness of giving chase. "They need the camera more than we
do." But we were both angry about the film.

The altitude, the adrenalin pumped up by a new place, the out-   10
rage at being so easily duped all got me going. I decided to do business with the police—an ill-conceived move. In Peru, as in many
Latin American countries, there are towns where the line dividing
criminals from law enforcers is very fine, and sometimes invisible.
But I was emboldened by the waiter in the restaurant. When I complained about the thief on the premises, he said to me in simple,
idiot-proof Spanish, "The police, they know who has your camera."

After several wrong turns in the blacked-out streets, I found the   11
police station, an old stone building. I had to bend to get through
the tiny doorway. In a corner of the windowless lobby stood a
wooden reception booth. There, a single candle fluttered, and a
man in a dirty uniform appeared to be sleeping on a stool.

"What do you want?" he growled, his eyes thin slits, his mouth   12
barely moving.

I explained that I wanted to see the *Jefe*° about a robbery. This   13
seemed to anger the drowsy guard. He opened his eyes, fired off a
volley of splenetic°-sounding Spanish that missed me, and waved
toward a diminutive° doorway covered by a black cloth.

"There?"   14

"*Si*," he snapped.   15

I ducked and brushed past the black material. The next room   16
had neither furniture nor candles. I could just make out two other
little portals°, each draped with the same black curtain. A second
policeman passed in the dark and eyed me disapprovingly.

"I want to see the chief," I said, not really believing myself any-   17
more. I didn't like this place, but doubted I could now turn tail. I
was a complainant, but in here I felt it would take only a whim to
turn me into a detainee.

The second officer led me through two more airless, lightless rooms   18
and left me sitting against a cold stone wall on a bench with several
other beleaguered° people. A faint wash of light leaked around the curtain hanging in the chief's doorway. I was now deep in the bowels of
the ancient station—wondering if and when I'd be getting out. Our
photographs of Amazonian butterflies suddenly seemed frivolous. I
was thinking more of Amnesty International's reports documenting torture, also about bad period movies with scenes set in watery dungeons.

One by one the people on the bench were ushered out of the   19
dark hallway and into the *Jefe*'s office. The woman beside me
sobbed quietly all the time we waited. When she'd gone through
the black curtain, I heard her wailing and a male voice shouting
back at her. Whatever the problem was, mine couldn't compare.

20   The *Jefe* sat by an old gas heater. Two candles burned on his battered table, illuminating a sleepy, flaccid°, moustachioed face. In the half-darkness, with his hands propped on the table and his ample girth bisected by a row of metal buttons, he looked like a large, upturned beetle—possibly poisonous. His uniform was cleaner, but his demeanour was consistent with that of his subordinates: bored, resentful, suspicious.

21   I recounted the tale of the theft. At my mention of the word "camera," his eyes flicked open and he shifted to look at me. What restaurant? he asked. I told him.

22   And how much money is the camera worth?

23   I tried to explain that it wasn't the camera so much as the film that concerned me.

24   Yes, but how much is the camera worth?

25   It had cost us a few hundred dollars, by Peruvian measure a huge sum. He eagerly made a note of this. Then his interest seemed to flag.

26   "The waiter in the restaurant," I continued, "told us you might be able to help get it back." As I struggled with these words in my deformed Spanish, they didn't come out sounding as innocuous as I'd intended. I stood there semi-paralyzed. Had I just made some sort of fateful accusation?

27   The chief turned a pair of disgusted eyes on me. *You utterly contemptible foreign scumbag*, said the eyes. *You presumptuous° gringo piece of shit*. He considered what I'd said for a few more nasty seconds.

28   "Perhaps it's not possible," I added, lamely.

29   "Listen, *señor*," he declaimed at last, addressing the dark air in the pompous tones of Peruvian officialdom. "It's a very difficult problem. Very difficult. To repossess your camera, you must go to the restaurant and speak again with your waiter. Your waiter knows who has your camera."

30   I walked back to the hotel, the black-out broken now by a starlit Andean sky. I was the only fair-skinned man in the streets, and the only pedestrian over five-foot-nine. It occurred to me that perhaps everyone here knew where our camera was, everyone but us. The police chief had instructed me to be sure to return in the morning to file a formal statement. But we decided to catch a bus to Ayacucho.

31   The thieves of Huancayo, were they simply petty criminals? Or proud avengers of the local culture that had been ravaged for more than 450 years by the Conquistadors° and their descendants?

32   Or are those even the right questions? Later we learned something new. As we continued overland towards Cuzco, the old Incan capital, other travellers told us that an unknown Maoist guerrilla group had claimed responsibility for blowing up a hydro tower

near Huancayo, disrupting power transmission for miles around. It was their first act of massive violence.

Later still I learned that the guerrillas called themselves the   33
Shining Path. Whenever I see their name in the press, where it has often appeared since, I think of that powerless night, the white candles, the black curtains, our never-developed blue-butterfly film, and all the eyes staring as we walked in and out of the town.

```
┌─────────────────────────┐
│                         │
│                         │
└─────────────────────────┘
```

GEORGE GALT

George Galt (b. 1938) is a Toronto journalist, critic, and editor. His books include two travel narratives, *A Journey through the Aegean Islands* and *Whistle Stop: A Journey across Canada*, and a collection of essays by Canadian writers, *The Thinking Heart*.

Words and Meanings

Paragraph

altiplano	high mountain plane	3
chafes	irritates, rubs	
impassively	without emotion	8
the *Jefe*	police chief	13
splenetic	angry	
diminutive	small	
portals	doorways	16
beleaguered	troubled	18
flaccid	limp, lacking in muscle tone	20
presumptuous	arrogant, pushy	27
Conquistadors	Spanish conquerors of Peru in 16th century	31

Structure and Strategy

1. Trace the incidents that make up the narrative. Where are the travellers? What is taken from them? What is their immediate reaction? Their subsequent actions? Indicate the paragraphs that detail each of the major events.
2. The dominant image of Galt's essay is darkness. Find at least five examples in which Galt uses the lack of light to contribute to the atmosphere of his essay.
3. What contrast does Galt introduce in paragraph 3? What relationship does this contrast have to the rest of the essay?

4. Paragraphs 20 to 29 describe the author's meeting with the *Jefe* (police chief). What senses does Galt appeal to in these paragraphs? How is the conflict between rich and poor reinforced in these paragraphs?

5. How do the questions in paragraph 31 reinforce the basic conflict around which Galt has structured the essay?

Content and Purpose

1. What angers the travellers after the theft and makes them take action?

2. Why does Galt change his mind and begin to see his complaint as "frivolous" (paragraph 18)?

3. What is the author's reaction to the incident he describes? What does he learn from this experience?

4. The darkness in Huancayo is caused by the blowing up of a power station by a guerrilla group known as the Shining Path (*Sendero Luminoso*). Whose rights would this group claim to support?

5. Consider the name of the guerrilla force. Does Galt intend it to be understood literally or ironically (see IRONY)? Explain how the contrasting points of view in the essay could support both interpretations.

Suggestions for Writing

Select one of these topics. Then review the principles outlined on pages 21 to 23 before you begin to write.

1. Have you ever been robbed or been the victim of some kind of crime? Write an essay that narrates the event and describe your reaction to it.

2. Write an essay that describes in convincing detail a particular place—city location, secluded spot—that evokes fear in the people who live or visit there.

Passion Play

LORNE RUBENSTEIN

1   he squishiness of the green, still sodden ground beneath my spiked feet; the earthy scent of the now-fertile soil and the spray of water as my club head contacts the ball; the

"Passion Play" from *Maclean's Magazine*, May 24, 1993 by Lorne Rubenstein. Reprinted with the permission of Maclean Hunter Ltd.

flight of the ball towards the green; or, often, its helter-skelter path, wind-borne, clasped to the welcome breezes blowing spring warmth onto the course. These are some of my impressions of early games of golf each spring. Every year for 30 years I have taken to the game anew, wondering what the season will bring. Still, the passion remains for a game that Winston Churchill once derided as being like "chasing a quinine pill around a cow pasture."

Ah, but Churchill was misguided. What did he know of the energizing feeling that courses through a golfer's body when he contacts the ball on the sweet spot of the club face? How could he even dare to speak so maliciously of a game in which even the most horrible hacker can sink a long putt across the hollows and humps of a tricky green, knowing for a moment that he or she is feeling just like Jack Nicklaus or Nancy Lopez? More golfers than ever are celebrating an illogical love of a game in which even the great Ben Hogan, master of the swing, said that he hits only a few shots each round that come off as he imagines.   2

Can so little success anywhere, on any field of play or in any walk of life, offer such rewards as a golf ball perfectly struck? Golfers know. And never mind the golfer's standard rueful lament. Asked after a round how he played, a golfer can quite rightly answer: "I didn't play my usual game today. Come to think of it, I never play my usual game."   3

But who needs "usual" games anyway? Golf, and especially late spring golf, when hope still is writ large in the golfer's mind, is about reaching for the unusual, the outer limits of what the golfer can do. We golfers are exhorted to "extend" the club head, to "swing to the target." Spring golf stretches our vision, pulls us out of our winter selves, huddled for warmth, at last. But winter also propels us forward for golf. The very hibernation it imposes makes the anticipation of a spring round keen indeed. Awakening, sensate° again, we believe in ourselves. Against common sense, encouraged by thoughts sharpened over many a winter's night, the golfer believes that he can still play to his potential. That is the promise of the game, the lure that brings the golfer out spring after spring. An odd round down south during the winter does not count. That's a holiday round. Now comes the real thing, in spring.   4

But what is the real thing? With no apologies to Churchill, or to George Bernard Shaw, who sneered that golf is "a typical capitalist lunacy of upper-class Edwardian England," the fact is that golf is not some backwater foolishness where only the lightweight, the fat cat and the dopey participate. Many golfers are fit, and more than a few read books, attend plays, keep up with the news and even make worthwhile contributions to society beyond advising fellow   5 golfers where to place their elbows on the backswing. There is high art and bizarre science enough in striking the ball to satisfy most anybody, and even to capture the imagination of people who, mistakenly thinking they are politically correct, call golf "an old man's game."

6   No, no, a thousand scorecards no. Think of something Brendan Gill wrote about his father in his memoir *Here At The New Yorker*. Gill's father was "a brilliant surgeon and physician.... He hunted, fished, hiked, chopped wood, planted trees, and painted houses, barns, sheds and every other surface a brush could reach. But his favorite outdoor activity was golf. The game amounted to a passion with him."

7   Passion. Now there's a word often heard in connection with golf. Go figure: "Passion," used to describe a game in which nobody even hits one another, or runs after a ball. The word means "strong emotion; outburst of anger; strong enthusiasm." Roget° comes up with such synonyms as "desire, distress, eloquence, fervor, mania, torment, zeal." Golf does inspire these feelings. It might seem crazy, but there's a fellow who shall go unnamed here who has said that his self-esteem rises and falls with his golf. He's an orthopedic surgeon whose family life and career are going beautifully. But he can't figure his golf game out. He can't play his "usual" game.

8   This fellow, and millions like him around the world, know what a gentleman named Douglas Bertram Watson meant when he titled his book *I'll Never Be Cured and I Don't Much Care: The History of an Acute Attack of Golf and Pertinent Remarks Relating to Various Places of Treatment*. Exactly. Who cares? Life is fraught with problems, so why should a golfer not be allowed the simple pleasure of an early evening on the course, alone or in company. How good it feels when a warm drizzling rain tickles one's head. The white flag on the green ahead may be barely discernible as it slaps the air in the dusk, but a shot hit just so will reach the green, and perhaps cuddle up to the flagstick. Is this a dream, only a dream? These spring rounds can make the dream real.

9   But perhaps it does not matter if the shot is good. Maybe the walk is what matters, the opportunity for silence, for reflection. A round of golf can be a communion with oneself and with nature. Truly, though, the game is rarely played this way nowadays. Most public courses are jammed, and buzz with carts. People accuse one another of playing too slowly. Golfers diligently add up their scores as if they are checking stock quotations; they are too concerned with their scores. The game becomes a sombre affair.

To care too much about score is to lose the rhythm of the game. 10
Judging our shots, we can miss the essential pliability of golf, the
way it bends us every which way. Golf is really not about judgment, but about acceptance. The essence of the game is that a player drives the ball in the middle of the fairway and lands in a deep,
ugly scar of a divot° left by a golfer ahead. Accept it. This is the
game: golf is played outdoors on grass. It is not possible to control
the environment. Let the pliability of the game encourage a supple-
ness° within yourself.

This is what the late George Knudson, Canada's deeply intro- 11
spective° and mightily gifted golfer, alluded to when he suggested
that the golfer "give up control to gain control." That is, the player
ought to stop thinking about what to do with the golf club at every
segment of its route away from and back to the ball. Said Knudson:
"Let yourself swing."

Perhaps that sounds too much like Zen golf. But we will risk 12
any accusation of limp thinking because we know that we find
almost an altered state when we bounce on the rolling turf, and
when we are aware of the high grass swaying in the rough and
when we wrap our fingers around a velvety grip and when we
swing the club to and fro and when we fall into the grace of the
game, an outing that sends us inward.

If we play sensibly, we can discover the sensuality that lurks 13
everywhere on the course. Thinking about slow play, Knudson
once said: "I don't know what all the concern is about. Slow play
just means that you're going to spend a longer time in a nice place."
Take a book along on the course, then. Read a poem. Chat with
your companions. Swing, swing, swing. Walk in the woods.

Knudson's comment can be a code for the game. Spring has 14
been here for weeks, but the season still feels fresh, and we are
renewed. As for me, I have scratched the itch long enough. I want
grass clippings stuck to the soles of my shoes, mud on my golf ball,
dirt on my club face, the club in my hand while I turn it round and
round until it feels right. Care to join me?

LORNE RUBENSTEIN

Lorne Rubenstein (b. 1948) lives in Toronto and travels widely in the world
of golf. A regular columnist for *The Globe and Mail* since 1980, he also contributes to a variety of international sports publications. His books include
The Natural Golf Swing (1988, with George Knudson), *Links: An Insider's
Tour through the World of Golf* (1990), and *Touring Prose* (1992).

Words and Meanings

4	sensate	able to feel
7	Roget	editor of *Roget's Thesaurus*, a dictionary of synonyms
10	divot	hole in the grass made by a clumsily swung golf club
	suppleness	flexibility
11	introspective	inward-looking, thoughtful

Structure and Strategy

1. In paragraph 1, identify descriptive details that appeal to at least three different senses.
2. Find examples of vivid sensory images in two other paragraphs.
3. An alliteration is a FIGURE OF SPEECH in which a sound, usually a consonant, is repeated at the beginning of words (for example, "Passion Play"). Find three examples of alliteration in paragraph 2. What effect do these alliterative phrases have?
4. Find three examples of points that Rubenstein supports by using quotations.

Content and Purpose

1. Is this essay an objective or a subjective description? Summarize Rubenstein's purpose in a sentence or two.
2. Paragraph 2 contains ALLUSIONS to one political figure and three athletes. Who are they? Can you understand the point of the paragraph without knowing the contributions these people have made to history or sport?
3. How does the appeal of golf differ from that of other sports, especially team sports? See paragraphs 8, 9, and 10.
4. Paragraph 5 challenges some of the myths about the image of golf held by non-golfers. What are these myths?
5. Explain in your own words what the author means when he describes a golf game as "an outing that sends us inward" (paragraph 12).
6. What does the game's "essential pliability" (paragraph 10) encourage in a golfer? What does it suggest about the possibility of controlling all the odds, all the good and bad bounces in one's life?

Suggestions for Writing

1. Write an essay describing your passion for playing a particular sport or performing some kind of physical activity.

2. Write an essay describing the changes that come with a new season of the year. Be careful to choose words as well as physical details that will support the dominant impression you wish to convey.

Black Rock

DAVID FENNARIO

A couple of years ago, I went down to St. 1 Gabriel's Church on Centre St. in Point St. Charles° and joined the members of various Irish societies in their annual march to the memorial stone marking the common grave of 6,000 immigrants who died here of typhoid fever back in 1847 when they fled the Great Famine in Ireland.

Wreaths were laid, speeches were made, but nobody cried 2 when the pipers played. After all, the last survivors of the famine had died over 60 years ago, but still, the feeling was there—a need to remember a tragedy that has been largely forgotten or ignored by most historians and politicians.

I first saw the Irish Stone back in the 1950s on one of the bicycle 3 trips I used to take with some friends of mine from the avenues in Verdun. Ten-year-olds pedalling our bikes along Bridge St. toward the Victoria Bridge in the heat and exhaust fumes of rush-hour traffic on a hot July day. We were heading down to the river to wash up before going home for supper, having gotten our jeans splotched with dirt from the old cattle pens near the Canada Packer's plant.

My friend Larry just wanted to go straight home because we 4 were already late, but we knew we had to get the smell of manure off us, otherwise our mothers would know we had been down to the slaughterhouse, a forbidden place.

Danny, who loves animals, had been upset by what we had seen 5 in the pens: cattle bellowing, pigs squealing, the stink and smell of shit and blood. He wanted to go tell the police all about it because he was sure they would close the place down. But my other friend Bob didn't agree. "I think the cops already know about it, Danny," he said.

I was wondering how I was going to explain my missing shoe 6 to my mother—already picturing in my mind the inevitable whack to the side of the head—when I saw Larry brake his bike to a halt on the sidewalk, about 100 feet away. He was yelling about something, but I couldn't hear him. Then I saw Danny pointing at what looked to be a huge black rock, stuck in the middle of a traffic islet that divides the left and right expressway lanes leading over the Victoria Bridge to the South Shore.

7   We stood there together, trying to read the inscription carved on the side of this strange-looking boulder. "To preserve from desecration°, the remains of 6,000 immigrants who died of ship fever, AD 1847. This stone is erected by the workmen of Peto, Brassey and Betts, employed in the construction of the Victoria Bridge, AD 1859."

8   Words like "desecration" and the AD's prefacing the dates had us a bit confused, but we did figure out that the great black rock was probably some kind of tombstone marking the grave of some 6,000 people. But who they were or where they came from or how they ever ended up being buried under an expressway was beyond our understanding.

9   Later, I went home with one shoe on, received the whack to the side of the head and had a nightmare in bed about that spooky black rock. Something about people getting slaughtered along with the cows and the pigs and nobody wanting to listen to me or Danny Casey when we tried to tell them what was happening down there on Bridge St.

10   Years later, I was to uncover the mystery of the black rock. I was in my teens, out of school, out of work and browsing around a lot of libraries because I like to read, especially history. Ever since I first asked my father where the sidewalks came from, I've always been curious about the past. Where did all this come from? But I didn't read much about Canadian history until I discovered the Salle Gagnon in the Cité de Montréal library, which specialized in Canadian history. Every day I'd sit there reading books about Montreal, instead of looking for a job, and I was surprised to see that my own community of Verdun-Point St. Charles got some mention in the records.

11   I discovered that the old legend I had heard about Griffintown being named after a guy who started a soap factory down there near the Lachine Canal was true. Then I came upon a book, *Loyola and Montreal,* by T.P. Slattery, published in 1962, which mentioned and even had a picture of the black rock.

12   Briefly, in a few pages, Slattery, whose family was from Griffintown, described the famine in Ireland brought on when the potatoes went bad two years in a row, with a million and a half peasants dying of disease and starvation between 1846 and 1851 and another million emigrating.

In 1847, 100,000 immigrants fled from Ireland to Canada on   13
board ships usually carrying lumber. "Coffin ships," the Irish called
them, because so many people died down in the holds from lack of
proper food and ventilation. Others died in the thousands that year
in quarantine at Gross Île, located about 40 miles east of Quebec
City, in the St. Lawrence. Those immigrants who could walk were
shipped further west up the river to Montreal where the city
fathers, worried about a possible epidemic, built some sheds to
house the Irish out in Point St. Charles.

A letter of this period relates that "after a few weeks' service,   14
these wooden structures contained colonies of bugs in every cran-
ny; the wool, the cotton, the wood were black with them. Hundreds
of the sick crowded upon straw; little children in the arms of their
dead mothers ... a chaos of suffering and evil odours."

Fifty to sixty died each day throughout the spring and summer of   15
1847 and were buried in a common pit lined with quicklime. A grave
that probably would have remained unmarked if the workers who
built the Victoria Bridge hadn't taken a boulder from one of the cribs in
the river and erected it on the site. Not a memory in granite or marble,
but a huge black rock that was pulled out of the water like a bad tooth.

Slattery, a successful lawyer and graduate of Montreal's Loyola   16
College, places no blame on anyone for the tragedy he wrote about
in his book. But other Irish writers and historians have pointed out
that the famine was not just the consequence of the potatoes going
bad; it was also a consequence of 700 years of British imperial rule
over Ireland. They point out that while the Irish people were dying
from starvation, food grown in Ireland continued to be exported
out of the country by the British landlords, under the protection of
British troops.

"During the winter of 1846–47," wrote Thomas Gallager in his   17
book *Paddy's Lament*, published in 1982, "while over 400,000 persons were dying of famine or famine-related disease, the British
government ... allowed 17 million pounds of sterling worth of
grain, cattle, pigs, flour, eggs and poultry to be shipped to
England—enough food to feed, at least during those crucial winter
months, twice the almost 6 million men, women and children who
composed the tenant-farmer and farmer-labourer population."

As I came across these facts during my reading at the Cité de   18
Montréal library, I began to realize that the nightmare I had when I
was 10 years old was not far from the truth. Horrible things have
happened to people and are still happening today, but nobody
seems to want to know about it. Too afraid or scared to admit
what's going on around them, because they think or feel they can't
do anything about it anyhow. Just like in a nightmare.

19   I wasn't sure then if I could do anything about changing the world when I was going through so many changes myself, but discovering what the Irish Stone was all about gave me reason for becoming a writer. It made me want to tell the story of my community, a community that had somehow been largely left out of history.

20   I'm still trying.

```
┌─────────────────────┐
│                     │
│                     │
└─────────────────────┘
```

DAVID FENNARIO

While still a student at Dawson College in Montreal, David Fennario was invited to become the Centaur Theatre's first playwright-in-residence. His plays include *On the Job* and *Nothing to Lose,* which toured the country in English translation. In 1979 he wrote *Balconville,* Canada's first bilingual play. Fennario still lives in Montreal's Verdun-Pointe Ste. Charles district, the setting for his article on the Black Rock.

Paragraph Words and Meanings

1   Point St. Charles   working-class district in Montreal

7   desecration   violation, sacrilegious treatment

Structure and Strategy

1. Identify the two contrasting narratives in paragraphs 1 to 9. How do the details of these narratives lead up to and prepare for the points that follow?
2. Underline five or six sentences containing descriptive details that you find particularly effective. What senses do they appeal to?
3. What is the function of the quotations Fennario introduces (see paragraphs 13, 14, and 17). How could Fennario have PARAPHRASED this information, and how would the effect on the reader be different?
4. Identify the sentence fragments in the essay. (Hint: check paragraphs 3, 15, and 18.) Are these "errors"? Or is there a stylistic reason for their inclusion?
5. Consider the simile (see FIGURES OF SPEECH) in the last sentence of paragraph 15. Why is it particularly effective?

Content and Purpose

1. Why do you think Fennario includes the story of his childhood adventure in the stockyards (paragraphs 3 to 9)? How does the experience affect him? Where else in the essay does he refer to the impact it had on him?

2. Where is the Black Rock? How did it get there? What does it commemorate?
3. What happened to the immigrants who are "buried under an expressway" (paragraph 8)? How does Fennario piece together their tragic story?
4. After describing the horrific conditions in which these Irish immigrants lived and died (paragraphs 13 to 15), the author makes some larger political points about Anglo-Irish relations. Summarize these points in your own words. Is it Fennario's intention in these paragraphs to be objective and analytical? Why?
5. What is Fennario's purpose in this article? Does he imply any connection between the Irish immigrants' experience and the experience of the Québécois?

Suggestion for Writing

Describe a public memorial with which you are familiar. It could be a statue, a grave marker, a memorial stone, or any other commemorative structure. Your essay should combine a clear description of what the monument looks like with a vivid impression of what it represents.

Growing Up Native
CAROL GEDDES

I remember it was cold. We were walking   1
through a swamp near our home in the Yukon bush. Maybe it was fall and moose-hunting season. I don't know. I think I was about four years old at the time. The muskeg° was too springy to walk on, so people were taking turns carrying me—passing me from one set of arms to another. The details about where we were are vague, but the memory of those arms and the feeling of acceptance I had is one of the most vivid memories of my childhood. It didn't matter who was carrying me—there was security in every pair of arms. That response to children is typical of the native community. It's the first thing I think of when I cast my mind back to the Yukon bush, where I was born and lived with my family.

2   I was six years old when we moved out of the bush, first to Teslin, where I had a hint of the problems native people face, then to Whitehorse, where there was unimaginable racism. Eventually I moved to Ottawa and Montreal, where I further discovered that to grow up native in Canada is to feel the sting of humiliation and the boot of discrimination. But it is also to experience the enviable security of an extended family and to learn to appreciate the richness of the heritage and traditions of a culture most North Americans have never been lucky enough to know. As a film-maker, I have tried to explore these contradictions, and our triumph over them, for the half-million aboriginals° who are part of the tide of swelling independence of the First Nations today.

3   But I'm getting ahead of myself. If I'm to tell the story of what it's like to grow up native in northern Canada, I have to go back to the bush where I was born, because there's more to my story than the hurtful stereotyping that depicts Indian people as drunken welfare cases. Our area was known as 12-mile (it was 12 miles from another tiny village). There were about 40 people living there—including 25 kids, eight of them my brothers and sisters—in a sort of family compound. Each family had its own timber plank house for sleeping, and there was one large common kitchen area with gravel on the ground and a tent frame over it. Everybody would go there and cook meals together. In summer, my grandmother always had a smudge fire going to smoke fish and tan moose hides. I can remember the cosy warmth of the fire, the smell of good food, and always having someone to talk to. We kids had built-in playmates and would spend hours running in the bush, picking berries, building rafts on the lake and playing in abandoned mink cages.

4   One of the people in my village tells a story about the day the old lifestyle began to change. He had been away hunting in the bush for about a month. On his way back, he heard a strange sound coming from far away. He ran up the crest of a hill, looked over the top of it and saw a bulldozer. He had never seen or heard of such a thing before and he couldn't imagine what it was. We didn't have magazines or newspapers in our village, and the people didn't know that the Alaska Highway was being built as a defence against a presumed Japanese invasion during the Second World War. That was the beginning of the end of the Teslin Tlingit people's way of life. From that moment on, nothing turned back to the way it was. Although there were employment opportunities for my father and uncles, who were young men at the time, the speed and force with which the Alaska Highway was rammed through the wilderness caused tremendous upheaval for Yukon native people.

It wasn't as though we'd never experienced change before. The   5
Tlingit Nation, which I belong to, arrived in the Yukon from the
Alaskan coast around the turn of the century. They were the middle-
men and women between the Russian traders and the Yukon inland
Indians. The Tlingit gained power and prestige by trading European
products such as metal goods and cloth for the rich and varied furs
so much in fashion in Europe. The Tlingit controlled Yukon trading
because they controlled the trading routes through the high mountain passes. When trading ceased to be an effective means of survival, my grandparents began raising wild mink in cages. Mink
prices were really high before and during the war, but afterwards
the prices went plunging down. So, although the mink pens were
still there when I was a little girl, my father mainly worked on highway construction and hunted in the bush. The Yukon was then, and
still is in some ways, in a transitional period—from living off the
land to getting into a European wage-based economy.

As a young child, I didn't see the full extent of the upheaval. I   6
remember a lot of togetherness, a lot of happiness while we lived in
the bush. There's a very strong sense of family in the native community, and a fondness for children, especially young children. Even today,
it's like a special form of entertainment if someone brings a baby to
visit. That sense of family is the one thing that has survived all the
incredible difficulties native people have had. Throughout a time of
tremendous problems, the extended family system has somehow lasted, providing a strong circle for people to survive in. When parents
were struggling with alcoholism or had to go away to find work,
when one of the many epidemics swept through the community, or
when a marriage broke up and one parent left, aunts, uncles, and
grandparents would try to fill those roles. It's been very important to
me in terms of emotional support to be able to rely on my extended
family. There are still times when such support keeps me going.

Life was much simpler when we lived in the bush. Although   7
we were poor and wore the same clothes all year, we were warm
enough and had plenty to eat. But even as a youngster, I began to
be aware of some of the problems we would face later on.
Travelling missionaries would come and impose themselves on us,
for example. They'd sit at our campfire and read the bible to us and
lecture us about how we had to live a Christian life. I remember
being very frightened by stories we heard about parents sending
their kids away to live with white people who didn't have any children. We thought those people were mean and that if we were bad,
we'd be sent away, too. Of course, that was when social workers
were scooping up native children and adopting them out to white
families in the south. The consequences were usually disastrous for

the children who were taken away—alienation, alcoholism and suicide, among other things. I knew some of those kids. The survivors are still struggling to recover.

8   The residential schools were another source of misery for the kids. Although I didn't have to go, my brothers and sisters were there. They told stories about having their hair cut off in case they were carrying head lice, and of being forced to do hard chores without enough food to eat. They were told that the Indian culture was evil, that Indian people were bad, that their only hope was to be Christian. They had to stand up and say things like "I've found the Lord," when a teacher told them to speak. Sexual abuse was rampant in the residential school system.

9   By the time we moved to Whitehorse, I was excited about the idea of living in what I thought of as a big town. I'd had a taste of the outside world from books at school in Teslin (a town of 250 people), and I was tremendously curious about what life was like. I was hungry for experiences such as going to the circus. In fact, for a while, I was obsessed with stories and pictures about the circus, but then when I was 12 and saw my first one, I was put off by the condition and treatment of the animals.

10   Going to school in Whitehorse was a shock. The clash of native and white values was confusing and frightening. Let me tell you a story. The older boys in our community were already accomplished hunters and fishermen, but since they had to trap beaver in the spring and hunt moose in the fall, and go out trapping in the winter as well, they missed a lot of school. We were all in one classroom and some of my very large teenage cousins had to sit squeezed into little desks. These guys couldn't read very well. We girls had been in school all along, so, of course, we were better readers. One day the teacher was trying to get one of the older boys to read. She was typical of the teachers at that time, insensitive and ignorant of cultural complexities. In an increasingly loud voice, she kept commanding him to "Read it, read it." He couldn't. He sat there completely still, but I could see that he was breaking into a sweat. The teacher then said, "Look, she can read it," and she pointed to me, indicating that I should stand up and read. For a young child to try to show up an older boy is wrong and totally contrary to native cultural values, so I refused. She told me to stand up and I did. My hands were trembling as I held my reader. She yelled at me to read and when I didn't she smashed her pointing stick on the desk to frighten me. In terror, I wet my pants. As I stood there fighting my tears of shame, she said I was disgusting and sent me home. I remember feeling this tremendous confusion, on top of my humiliation. We were always told the white teachers

knew best, and so we had to do whatever they said at school. And yet I had a really strong sense of receiving mixed messages about what I was supposed to do in the community and what I was supposed to do at school.

Pretty soon I hated school. Moving to a predominantly white 11 high school was even worse. We weren't allowed to join anything the white kids started. We were the butt of jokes because of our secondhand clothes and moose meat sandwiches. We were constantly being rejected. The prevailing attitude was that Indians were stupid. When it was time to make course choices in class—between typing and science, for example—they didn't even ask the native kids, they just put us all in typing. You get a really bad image of yourself in a situation like that. I bought into it. I thought we were awful. The whole experience was terribly undermining. Once, my grandmother gave me a pretty little pencil box. I walked into the classroom one day to find the word "squaw" carved on it. That night I burned it in the wood stove. I joined the tough crowd and by the time I was 15 years old, I was more likely to be leaning against the school smoking a cigarette than trying to join in. I was burned out from trying to join the system. The principal told my father there was no point in sending me back to school so, with a Grade 9 education, I started to work at a series of menial° jobs.

Seven years later something happened to me that would 12 change my life forever. I had moved to Ottawa with a man and was working as a waitress in a restaurant. One day, a friend invited me to her place for coffee. While I was there, she told me she was going to university in the fall and showed me her reading list. I'll never forget the minutes that followed. I was feeling vaguely envious of her and once again, inferior. I remember taking the paper in my hand, seeing the books on it and realizing, Oh, my God, I've read these books! It hit me like a thunderclap. I was stunned that books I had read were being read in university. University was for white kids, not native kids. We were too stupid, we didn't have the kind of mind it took to do those things. My eyes moved down the list, and my heart started beating faster and faster as I suddenly realized I could go to university, too!

My partner at the time was a loving supportive man who 13 helped me in every way. I applied to the university immediately as a mature student but when I had to write Grade 9 on the application, I was sure they'd turn me down. They didn't. I graduated five years later, earning a bachelor of arts in English and philosophy (with distinction)....

Today, there's a glimmer of hope that more of us native people 14 will overcome the obstacles that have tripped us up ever since we began sharing this land. Some say our cultures are going through a renaissance. Maybe that's true. Certainly there's a renewed interest in native dancing, acting and singing, and in other cultural traditions. Even indigenous° forms of government are becoming strong again. But we can't forget that the majority of native people live in urban areas and continue to suffer from alcohol and drug abuse and the plagues of a people who have lost their culture and have become lost themselves. And the welfare system is the insidious° glue that holds together the machine of oppression of native people.

15   Too many non-native people have refused to try to understand the issues behind our land claims. They make complacent pronouncements such as "Go back to your bows and arrows and fish with spears if you want aboriginal rights. If not, give it up and assimilate into white Canadian culture." I don't agree with that. We need our culture, but there's no reason why we can't preserve it and have an automatic washing machine and a holiday in Mexico, as well.

16   The time has come for native people to make our own decisions. We need to have self-government. I have no illusions that it will be smooth sailing—there will be trial and error and further struggle. And if that means crawling before we can stand up and walk, so be it. We'll have to learn through experience.

17   While we're learning, we have a lot to teach and give to the world—a holistic° philosophy, a way of living with the earth, not disposing of it. It is critical that we all learn from the elders that an individual is not more important than a forest; we know that we're here to live on and with the earth, not to subdue it.

18   The wheels are in motion for a revival, for change in the way native people are taking their place in Canada. I can see that we're equipped, we have the tools to do the work. We have an enormous number of smart, talented, moral Indian people. It's thrilling to be a part of this movement.

19   Someday, when I'm an elder, I'll tell the children the stories: about the bush, about the hard times, about the renaissance, and especially about the importance of knowing your place in your nation.

CAROL GEDDES

Carol Geddes is an Indian from the Tlingit Nation in the Yukon. She has a graduate degree in communications from McGill University and has made several films, including *Doctor, Lawyer, Indian Chief*, a National Film Board production about the struggles of native women.

Words and Meanings

muskeg	swamp, marshland	1
aboriginal	original or earliest known inhabitants of a region	2
menial	low-skilled	11
indigenous	aboriginal, belonging to the First Nations	14
insidious	treacherous	
holistic	believing in the oneness, the interconnectedness of the earth and all living things	17

Structure and Strategy

1. Geddes frequently uses ANECDOTES to convey or support her points. Look at paragraph 10. What does the anecdote in that paragraph tell you about the author? About her teacher? Find another anecdote in the essay that also illustrates the clash between two cultures.
2. What is the topic of paragraph 12?
3. What is the function of the concluding paragraph of this essay? How does it contribute to the UNITY of the piece? Why do you think it appears at the end rather than at the beginning of the essay?

Content and Purpose

1. The essay begins with one of the author's early childhood memories; it goes on to describe life in the remote bush culture. What is the dominant impression Geddes creates of life for children growing up in northern native communities? Contrast this way of life to that of children growing up in large urban centres.
2. Paragraphs 4 and 5 outline some of the changes in the native way of life that have taken place in this century. What were these changes? What caused them?
3. What were some of the negative influences that the dominant white culture had on native people both in the bush and in the cities of the North, as Geddes describes them?
4. What were the effects of school on the author? How did she overcome these effects?
5. What thematic connection is there between paragraph 1 and paragraph 17?
6. In Geddes's view, what does the non-native culture have to gain from native culture?

Suggestions for Writing

1. Discuss the effects of the educational system on students who do not come from the mainstream culture.
2. Explore the reasons for the growth of native militancy, with respect to land claims, self-government, and cultural survival.
3. In the last few years, the media have brought to public awareness evidence that the residential schools for native children were, as Geddes describes them, "a source of misery." After researching the topic, explain how these schools failed the children they were supposed to serve, and why.
4. Using this essay as a model, write your own autobiographical narrative entitled "Growing Up _____." Fill in the blank to reflect your heritage.

Bush League Business

BASIL JOHNSTON

1   At the end of March 1945, three months short of completing Grade 9, I dropped out of [school] to return to the sanctuary° and comfort of Cape Croker°.

2   In the fall of the same year, when my father left the reserve to seek his fortune in the lumber camps, I was left in sole possession and proprietorship of the family estate, which consisted of a log house, a log barn and a log privy situated on a parcel of land of twenty-five acres, more or less. Formerly my grandmother, Rosa, had owned it.

3   Upon my father's departure, survival—mine—became my first and only object in the sixteenth year of my life. With trout near extinction in Georgian Bay and pulp depleted, opportunities for survival were scarce for everyone but farmers. To go on "relief," as welfare was known in those days, was unthinkable. No man worthy of the name would ever think of asking for relief, and people at the Cape proudly boasted that only two people got relief during the Depression.

4   I would make the people of the Cape proud of me. In the waning days of August I began to assess the community's business needs, its resources and my expertise. In training I had Grade 8 and half of

Grade 9, which was of no value to anyone. According to my analysis there was one constant need in winter: fuel. And as far as my keen eye could see, the resources were limitless. All that was required in the way of capital expenditures was an axe. I already had an axe.

Before launching my timbering operation, I conducted a mental market-research survey, in accordance with the finest business and economic principles. There were Pulch (Mrs. Isadore Pitawaniquot), Meeks (Stanley McLeod, my uncle), Shabow (Mr. Francis Nadjiwon), Bee Dee (Peter Nadjiwon), Kitchi-Flossie (Mrs. William Akiwenzie), Chick (Walter Johnston, my uncle), Kitchi-Susan (Mrs. Susan Taylor), Shawnee (Charles Jones), Kitchi-Low See (Mrs. Lucy Nawash), Christine Keeshig (my grandmother's sister), Maggie (Mrs. Desjardins), Eezup (Andrew Akiwenzie), Pollock (Mrs. E. Akiwenzie), and many, many more.

Revenue! More than I had realized. I calculated that I could cut a load of poles every day. At three dollars a load, less a dollar to the teamster for delivery, that was sixty dollars a month—a handsome profit. I'd survive. More than survive! Except that there were Sundays and Saturdays, and that my potential customers would not burn a load of fuel each day. I reduced my estimates accordingly. Then I realized that many of my potential customers cut their own wood, and that I would be in direct competition with my uncle Stanley. There wasn't as much revenue in cutting wood as I had originally thought.

I needed advice. I went to my Uncle Stanley, who was an expert in survival. He suggested that I go into the fur industry, at the primary level, trapping or harvesting raccoons. And he showed me a price list issued by one of the fur buyers on Spadina Avenue in Toronto to illustrate how profitable the raccoon industry was: up to twenty-four dollars for a prime pelt. I panted and drooled. Uncle was willing to share both his expertise and his resources. There were more raccoons than my uncle and I together could harvest. All I needed was to kill one fat raccoon every day and I'd be in business.

Uncle was generous. He conceded° to me as my own hunting territory the ridge, a part of the Niagara Escarpment formation that extended from the Lighthouse to Cove of Cork, bending inward as it followed the contour of Little North Bay, outward to Benjamin's Point and then south-west until it sloped into the flat sedimentary rocks at Pine Tree Point. In addition, all the territory between was mine to hunt.

One of the advantages of this kind of enterprise is that little capital investment is required. My total capital equipment consisted of two enthusiastic but inexperienced dogs and an axe. But that was all that was needed for this kind of business.

After the trawling season was over it was my daily routine to set out with a lunch in an old army haversack, axe in hand and preceded by two exuberant dogs who raced ahead and ranged the bushes in search of any beast worth barking at: squirrels, rabbits, chipmunks, groundhogs, skunks, porcupines, foxes, partridge—anything, so long as it was alive. I had to investigate every round of barking, otherwise the dogs would not leave the quarry; or worse, they would mutiny and go home. Instead of walking ten to twelve miles, which would have constituted the whole round-trip distance of my beat, I frequently walked anywhere between twenty and twenty-five miles, often for nothing.

11   On returning home in the evening I had to cut wood, make a fire, cook a meal, and, if I had got a raccoon, skin and clean the beast and stretch the pelt on the roof or side of the barn. By the time I had completed these operations, I was ready for sleep.

12   My hunting technique was primitive and simple, but effective. If the dogs treed a raccoon, I'd chop the tree down and, if need be, two or three other trees. As soon as tree and quarry fell to earth my assistants would be instantly upon the raccoon, holding the victim for the coup de grâce°, which I delivered with the flat of my axe. If the dogs ran the raccoon into a cave or burrow, a torch made from a mixture of leaves and pine gum stuck at the end of a pole would flush it out. Once the raccoon emerged, my assistants would seize it and hold it fast in their jaws for execution. Once, as I delivered the fatal blow, my dog Chalk sprang at my victim for one extra bite. I hit Chalk instead of the raccoon. From the way my dog quivered and convulsed, I thought I had killed him.

13   Despite their numbers, I didn't kill as many raccoons as I expected. Nevertheless, I killed enough to cover the roof and sides of the barn with raccoon hides.

14   Only once did I kill more than two in a day; on that occasion I killed six in one cave. Killing an enormous moose or catching a net full of fish may be the dream of most hunters or fishermen, but the dream may turn into a bad dream. I killed the six raccoons at Benjamin's Point on my return patrol. I looked at my victims with the practised eye of a fur appraiser; at least fifty dollars. My energies were instantly restored. And even though my energies and strength could have borne the total weight of the six raccoons, I could no more carry six flopping raccoon corpses than I could carry two greased monkeys, no matter how I tried. I resorted to the simple expedient° of carrying forward three at a time for some distance, leaving them on the ground, and then returning for the other three. By this means I eventually arrived at the old Bert Ashkewe homestead and corner. It was already dark and I still had a mile to walk. Only the vision of fifty dollars sustained me. While I mentally caressed the bills I heard the snort of horses and the rumble of wagon wheels. It was Charles Jones, Jr., known as Shawnee in the village. I hitched a ride.

After I was done skinning the raccoons, I reviewed my produc- 15
tion and estimates of revenue for the coming winter—a market
forecast of sorts. Up to this point the raccoon division of my fur
operations was not yielding as much profit as I had originally antic-
ipated, and it would yield even less during the winter, that was
clear. I would have to diversify°.

Once more I studied the price list. The only fur bearer on the 16
list that inhabited our reserve in sufficient numbers to justify hunting was the squirrel: black, red, grey and flying. In fact, there was
an overpopulation of black squirrels, especially in Peter Nadjiwon's
sugar bush. At $1.25 for a prime black-squirrel pelt, there was a tidy
profit to be realized.

I diversified the very next morning. With only a slingshot I 17
blasted fifteen fat squirrels from the trees before half the afternoon
was over. Besides a handsome profit, there was meat.

At home I studied the deskinning manuals that my Uncle 18
Stanley had given to me. According to the instructions, squirrels
were to be unskinned from the ankles, then over the head, inside
out, in much the same way women remove their nightgowns. After
the squirrel is unskinned, the pelt should be sheathed inside-out
tightly over a pointed arched wooden frame, much as a dress is
slipped over a mannequin. Not only would I have to deskin the
squirrels, I would have to make the frames. Fortunately, across the
road, there was a cedar-rail fence; ample raw material for frames.

I couldn't wait to perform surgery; the manual, with its dia- 19
grams, made the operation look simple. All one had to do was to
follow instructions. Because I did not have the proper instruments,
I could not begin immediately....

... I went across the road to my neighbour, Francis Nadjiwon, 20
to borrow the proper surgical instrument.

With proper instruments and as directed by the diagrams, I cut 21
an incision from ankle to ankle, following, as it were, an invisible
inseam. Just as the manual had promised, it was easy. Step two was
to peel off said squirrel's hide down and over its arms and head. I
peeled, but the hide did not peel off as easily as promised in the
diagram. As I undressed my patient, tissue, sinew and fat clung to
the hide and would not let go. I consulted my manual, but it offered
no guidance on a method of removing skin from tough tissue, or of
pinning down a limp squirrel long enough to divest it of its skin. I
resolved this difficulty by tying the squirrel's hindpaws to a nail. At
least I had some control over the beast, and I peeled its pelt off as
far as the head where, in my haste, I peeled too indelicately; I tore
the skin. Discouraging as was the wasted work and the loss of profit, I consoled myself with the thought that at least I had the meat. I
could not indulge in self-pity too long. I had to go on.

22   I operated on the second squirrel without accident. By sawing, chopping, splitting, carving, whittling and shaving I eventually constructed a stretching frame. As gently as I could, I slipped the pelt over the frame, pulled and stretched downward. Either I pulled too hard, or the pelt was too thin; my squirrel pelt split.

23   Two gone and wasted; thirteen to go. It was now 9:30 P.M. As yet I had not eaten. At this rate of deskinning, I would not be done until noon the next day.

24   On I worked, resolved to deskin every little beast, even if I had to work through the night. I had to recover some of my invested time and effort. As a surgeon must take care not to skewer a patient during surgery, so did I operate on squirrel number three.

25   Afterward I mounted my patient on a frame. I felt proud as I earned $1.25, which had taken an hour and a half. By 3:00 A.M. I had deskinned two more.

26   Hungry, sleepy, cold and stiff-fingered, I decided there and then to close down my squirrel diversification program. To hell with squirrels; raccoons were easier.

27   Maybe it would be better to go back to school. I had heard vague rumours that Spanish° was offering a high-school program. If it were true, I would return. It was my only chance to escape a life of cutting wood.

28   Though raccoons were easier to harvest, they did not generate enough income to support even a marginal existence. To keep from starving and to uphold the image of being a man, capable of self-support, I undertook whatever work was available: trawling the waters of the Cape the entire summer, fishing with nets in the fall with Casimir Taylor, drawing water for Resime Akiwenzie and Herman Taylor during their hog-slaughtering sessions and, finally, working for Frank Nadjiwon as farm-hand. For Frank I made a crooked ladder and dismantled a bicycle I was unable to reassemble. I felled trees with style, dug post-holes with grace and spread manure with finesse. I also told Frank about the high-school program being offered at Spanish, and spoke of my intention to return to an institution to which I had not given a single thought since I left it.

29   Frank said, "Yes! You ought to go back, it's your only chance." I guess he knew better than I suspected that I was never going to be a carpenter, plumber, farmer, blacksmith, mechanic or any kind of tradesman. He knew from his experience in the army that no one ever got very far with only Grade 8, not even soldiers. Spanish, no matter how tough, could never be as bad as the army.

BASIL JOHNSTON

An Ojibwa writer born on Parry Island Sound Indian Reserve, Basil Johnston (b. 1929) is a lecturer in the Ethnology Department of the Royal Ontario Museum. An expert on the Ojibwa language, he is the author of many stories, essays, and books on First Nations' culture and history, including *Ojibway Heritage* (1976), *How the Birds Got Their Colours* (1978), and *Indian School Days* (1988), an autobiographical account of his childhood experiences at a residential school run by Jesuit priests in Spanish, Ontario.

Words and Meanings

Paragraph

sanctuary	safe place	1
Cape Croker	Ojibwa reserve on the Bruce Peninsula	
conceded	allotted, gave	8
coup de grâce	final blow	12
expedient	means, solution	14
diversify	branch out into other activities	15
Spanish	town north of Manitoulin Island, location of the residential school Johnston attended	27

Structure and Strategy

1. Assess the DICTION of this piece. How does Johnston's use of business jargon contribute to the TONE? For example, he uses phrases such as "capital expenditures" (paragraph 4), "market-research survey" (paragraph 5), and "diversify" (paragraph 15) to describe hunting in the northern Ontario bush. Identify other examples of this technique. What do they say about the author's attitude toward his subject?
2. Reread paragraph 6. Is it funny? Why?
3. To what does Johnston compare skinning and stretching a squirrel pelt in paragraph 18? What's the effect of this incongruous comparison?
4. What function do paragraph 12 and paragraphs 18 to 25 have in common? Why has Johnston included them?

Content and Purpose

1. Paragraphs 2 and 3 summarize the author's predicament. What was it? What choices did he have to solve it? Why didn't he go on welfare? Why didn't he turn to his community's traditional ways of earning a living, fishing and logging?
2. Paragraphs 9 to 13 narrate the events of a typical working day in the life of the young raccoon hunter. What strikes you about

the work involved? Identify four or five specific details that make the description effective and memorable.

3. What made Johnston decide to "diversify" into squirrel hunting? What does he learn from his decision?

4. This piece, taken from Johnston's autobiographical work, *Indian School Days*, is a mature adult's recollection of an experience he had when he was sixteen. Identify four or five passages that clearly relate adolescent experience from an adult's perspective. How would these events be described if they were told from the point of view of a teenager?

5. What decision does the narrator arrive at by the end of the piece? Does anyone support his decision? Why?

Suggestions for Writing

1. Write an essay narrating the story of your first job. What did you learn about the value, fun, or misery of "hard work"? Include a variety of descriptive details that not only communicate your experience but also convey to your readers your purpose in writing the essay.

2. Write an essay exploring some of the problems faced by First Nations peoples who attempt to maintain their traditional livelihood, hunting and trapping. Many native communities have been decimated by the decline of wildlife populations that sustained them for centuries. Another kind of pressure comes from animal-rights activists who object on principle to harvesting animals. Are trapping and hunting morally indefensible? What are the implications of banning these activities based on principles foreign to First Nations peoples?

Deficits

MICHAEL IGNATIEFF

1   t begins the minute Dad leaves the house.

2   "Where is George?"

3   "He is out now, but he'll be back soon."

4   "That's wonderful," she says.

About three minutes later she'll look puzzled: "But George..." 5
"He's away at work, but he'll be back later." 6
"I see." 7
"And what are you doing here? I mean it's nice, but..." 8
"We'll do things together." 9
"I see." 10

Sometimes I try to count the number of times she asks me these 11
questions but I lose track.

I remember how it began, five or six years ago. She was 66 12
then. She would leave a pot to boil on the stove. I would discover it
and find her tearing through the house, muttering, "My glasses, my
glasses, where the hell are my glasses?"

I took her to buy a chain so that she could wear her glasses around 13
her neck. She hated it because her mother used to wear *her* glasses on
a chain. As we drove home, she shook her fist at the windscreen.

"I swore I'd never wear one of these damned things." 14

I date the beginning to the purchase of the chain, to the silence 15
that descended over her as I drove her home from the store.

The deficits, as the neurologists call them, are localized. She can 16
tell you what it felt like when the Model T Ford ran over her at the
school gates when she was a girl of seven. She can tell you what her
grandmother used to say, "A genteel° sufficiency will suffice°,"
when turning down another helping at dinner. She remembers the
Canadian summer nights when her father used to wrap her in a
blanket and take her out to the lake's edge to see the stars.

But she can't dice an onion. She can't set the table. She can't 17
play cards. Her grandson is five, and when they play pairs with his
animal cards, he knows where the second penguin will be. She just
turns up cards at random.

He hits her because she can't remember anything, because she 18
keeps telling him not to run around quite so much.

Then I punish him. I tell him he has to understand. 19

He goes down on the floor, kisses her feet, and promises not to 20
hit her again.

She smiles at him, as if for the first time, and says, "Oh, your 21
kiss is so full of sugar."

After a week with him, she looks puzzled and says, "He's a nice 22
little boy. Where does he sleep? I mean, who does he belong to?"

"He's your grandson." 23

"I see." She looks away and puts her hand to her face. 24

My brother usually stays with her when Dad is out of town. 25
Once or twice a year, it's my turn. I put her to bed at night. I hand her
the pills—small green ones that are supposed to control her moods—
and she swallows them. I help her out of her bra and slip, roll down

her tights, and lift the nightie over her head. I get into the bed next to hers. Before she sleeps she picks up a Len Deighton and reads a few paragraphs, always the same paragraphs, at the place where she has folded down the page. When she falls asleep, I pick the book off her chest and I pull her down in the bed so that her head isn't leaning against the wall. Otherwise she wakes up with a crick in her neck.

26   Often when I wake in the night, I see her lying next to me, staring into the dark. She stares and then she wanders. I used to try to stop her, but now I let her go. She is trying to hold on to what is left. There is a method in this. She goes to the bathroom every time she wakes, no matter if it is five times a night. Up and down the stairs silently, in her bare feet, trying not to wake me. She turns the lights on and off. Smooths a child's sock and puts it on the bed. Sometimes she gets dressed, after a fashion, and sits on the downstairs couch in the dark, clutching her handbag.

27   When we have guests to dinner, she sits beside me at the table, holding my hand, bent forward slightly to catch everything that is said. Her face lights up when people smile, when there is laughter. She doesn't say much any more; she is worried she will forget a name and we won't be able to help her in time. She doesn't want anything to show. The guests always say how well she does. Sometimes they say, "You'd never know, really." When I put her to bed afterward I can see the effort has left her so tired she barely knows her own name.

28   She could make it easier on herself. She could give up asking questions.

29   "Where we are now, is this our house?"

30   "Yes."

31   "Where is our house?"

32   "In France."

33   I tell her: "Hold my hand, I'm here. I'm your son."

34   "I know."

35   But she keeps asking where she is. The questions are her way of trying to orient° herself, of refusing and resisting the future that is being prepared for her.

36   She always loved to swim. When she dived into the water, she never made a splash. I remember her lifting herself out of the pool, as sleek as a seal in a black swimsuit, the water pearling off her back. Now she says the water is too cold and taking off her clothes too much of a bother. She paces up and down the poolside, watching her grandson swim, stroking his towel with her hand, endlessly smoothing out the wrinkles.

37   I bathe her when she wakes. Her body is white, soft, and withered. I remember how, in the changing-huts, she would bend over as she slipped out of her bathing suit. Her body was young. Now I

see her skeleton through her skin. When I wash her hair, I feel her skull. I help her from the bath, dry her legs, swathe her in towels, sit her on the edge of the bath and cut her nails: they are horny and yellow. Her feet are gnarled°. She has walked a long way.

When I was as old as my son is now I used to sit beside her at 38 the bedroom mirror watching her apply hot depilatory° wax to her legs and upper lip. She would pull her skirt up to her knees, stretch her legs out on the dresser, and sip beer from the bottle, while waiting for the wax to dry. "Have a sip," she would say. It tasted bitter. She used to laugh at the faces I made. When the wax had set, she would begin to peel it off, and curse and wince, and let me collect the strips, with fine black hairs embedded in them. When it was over, her legs were smooth, silky to touch.

Now I shave her. I soap her face and legs with my shaving 39 brush. She sits perfectly still; as my razor comes around her chin we are as close as when I was a boy.

She never complains. When we walk up the hill behind the 40 house, I feel her going slower and slower, but she does not stop until I do. If you ask her whether she is sad, she shakes her head. But she did say once, "It's strange. It was supposed to be more fun than this."

I try to imagine what the world is like for her. Memory is what 41 reconciles° us to the future. Because she has no past, her future rushes toward her, a bat's wing brushing against her face in the dark.

"I told you. George returns on Monday." 42

"Could you write that down?" 43

So I do. I write it down in large letters, and she folds it in her white 44 cardigan pocket and pats it and says she feels much less worried.

In half an hour, she has the paper in her hand and is showing 45 it to me.

"What do I do about this?" 46

"Nothing. It just tells you what is going to happen." 47

"But I didn't know anything of this." 48

"Now you do," I say and I take the paper away and tear it up. 49

It makes no sense to get angry at her, but I do. 50

She is afraid Dad will not come back. She is afraid she has been 51 abandoned. She is afraid she will get lost and never be able to find her way home. Beneath the fears that have come with the forgetting, there lie anxieties for which she no longer has any names.

She paces the floor, waiting for lunch. When it is set before her, 52 she downs it before anyone else, and then gets up to clear the plates.

"What's the hurry?" I ask her. 53

She is puzzled. "I don't know," she says. She is in a hurry, and she 54 does not know why. She drinks whatever I put before her. The wine goes quickly.

55   "You'll enjoy it more if you sip it gently."

56   "What a good idea," she says and then empties the glass with a gulp.

57   I wish I knew the history of this anxiety. But I don't. All she will tell me is about being sprawled in the middle of Regent Street° amid the blood and shop glass during an air raid, watching a mother sheltering a child, and thinking: I am alone.

58   In the middle of all of us, she remained alone. We didn't see it. She was the youngest girl in her family, the straggler in the pack, born cross-eyed till they straightened her eyes out with an operation. Her father was a teacher and she was dyslexic°, the one left behind.

59   In her wedding photo, she is wearing her white dress and holding her bouquet. They are side by side. Dad looks excited. Her eyes are wide open with alarm. Fear gleams from its hiding place. It was her secret and she kept it well hidden. When I was a child, I thought she was faultless, amusing, regal. My mother.

60   She thinks of it as a happy family, and it was. I remember them sitting on the couch together, singing along to Fats Waller records. She still remembers the crazy lyrics they used to sing:

> There's no disputin'
> That's Rasputin
> The high-falutin loving man.

I don't know how she became so dependent on him, how she lost so many of the wishes she once had for herself, and how all her wishes came to be wishes for him.

61   She is afraid of his moods, his silences, his departures, and his returns. He has become the weather of her life. But he never lets her down. He is the one who sits with her in the upstairs room, watching television, night after night, holding her hand.

62   People say: it's worse for you, she doesn't know what is happening. She used to say the same thing herself. Five years ago, when she began to forget little things, she knew what was in store, and she said to me once, "Don't worry. I'll make a cheerful old nut. It's you who'll have the hard time." But that is not true. She feels everything. She has had time to count up every loss. Every night, when she lies awake, she stares at desolation.

63   What is a person? That is what she makes you wonder. What kind of a person are you if you only have your habits left? She can't remember her grandson's name, but she does remember to shake out her tights at night and she never lets a dish pass her by without trying to clean it, wipe it, clear it up, or put it away. The house is littered with dishes she is putting away in every conceivable cupboard. What kind of a person is this?

64   It runs in the family. Her mother had it. I remember going to see her in the house with old carpets and dark furniture on Prince Arthur

Avenue. The windows were covered with the tendrils of plants growing in enormous Atlas battery jars, and the parquet° floors shone with wax. She took down the giraffe, the water buffalo, and the leopard— carved in wood—that her father had brought back from Africa in the 1880s. She sat in a chair by the fire and silently watched me play with them. Then—and it seems only a week later—I came to have Sunday lunch with her and she was old and diminished and vacant, and when she looked at me she had no idea who I was.

I am afraid of getting it myself. I do ridiculous things: I stand on my head every morning so that the blood will irrigate my brain; I compose suicide notes, always some variant of Captain Oates's: "I may be gone for some time." I never stop thinking about what it would be like for this thing to steal over me. 65

She has taught me something. There are moments when her pacing ceases, when her hunted look is conjured° away by the stillness of dusk, when she sits in the garden, watching the sunlight stream through all the trees they planted together over 25 years in this place, and I see something pass over her face which might be serenity°. 66

And then she gets up and comes toward me looking for a glass to wash, a napkin to pick up, a child's toy to rearrange. 67

I know how the story has to end. One day I return home to see her and she puts out her hand and says: "How nice to meet you." She's always charming to strangers. 68

People say I'm already beginning to say my farewells. No, she is still here. I am not ready yet. Nor is she. She paces the floor, she still searches for what has been lost and can never be found again. 69

She wakes in the night and lies in the dark by my side. Her face, in profile, against the pillow has become like her mother's, the eye sockets deep in shadow, the cheeks furrowed° and drawn, the gaze ancient and disabused°. Everything she once knew is still inside her, trapped in the ruined circuits—how I was when I was little, how she was when I was a baby. But it is too late to ask her now. She turns and notices I am awake too. We lie side by side. The darkness is still. I want to say her name. She turns away from me and stares into the night. Her nightie is buttoned at the neck like a little girl's. 70

MICHAEL IGNATIEFF

Michael Ignatieff (b. 1947) is a Canadian writer and broadcaster. He won the Governor General's Award for *The Russian Album* in 1987. His other books include *A Just Measure of Pain* (1978), *The Needs of Strangers* (1985), and *Blood and Belonging: Journey into the New Nationalism* (1993).

Words and Meanings

Paragraph

16	genteel	polite, well-bred
	suffice	be enough, satisfy
35	orient	find her bearings; figure out where she is in time and space
37	gnarled	knobby, crooked
38	depilatory	hair remover
41	reconciles	makes us able to accept; resigns us
57	Regent Street	street in central London, England
58	dyslexic	having a reading disability
64	parquet	wood floor laid out in square design
66	conjured	made to disappear magically
	serenity	inner peace
70	furrowed	deeply wrinkled
	disabused	undeceived, under no illusion

Structure and Strategy

1. Look up the word "deficits" in a medical dictionary and in a good general dictionary. What meanings of the word apply to Ignatieff's title?
2. Using both narration and description, Ignatieff describes the effects of Alzheimer's disease on its victims, and on those who care for them. What function does the opening dialogue (paragraphs 1 to 11) serve?
3. This essay contains several passages of dialogue. Each is included because it supports in some way Ignatieff's thesis. Consider how each of the following passages contributes to the purpose or intended effect of the essay: paragraphs 28 to 35; paragraphs 42 to 49; paragraphs 52 to 56.
4. Paragraphs 37 and 38 present the ironic contrast between Ignatieff's boyhood relationship with his mother and their current relationship. Identify the specific details that you think are most effective in conveying this contrast.
5. How does the author's own fear of contracting Alzheimer's disease affect the TONE of the essay?

Content and Purpose

1. The thesis of Ignatieff's essay is implied rather than explicitly stated. Sum up the thesis in a one-sentence thesis statement.

2. What was the initial reaction of the mother when the first signs of the disease appeared? Does she maintain this feeling as her confusion and loss of memory increase?
3. Ignatieff includes a number of poignant descriptive details: the toenails, the gnarled feet, the depilatory wax, the bath. Why does he include these intimate aspects of his mother's life and condition? What emotional effect do they have on the reader?
4. What is the fundamental irony underlying the relationship between mother and son? Reread paragraphs 25, 27, and 70 for clues.
5. What experiences in the mother's life may be responsible for the "fear [that] gleams from its hiding place" in her eyes?
6. Is Ignatieff comfortable with the task of caring for his mother? Identify specific passages in the essay that point to the writer's personal conflict.

Suggestions for Writing

1. Modelling your essay on the combination of descriptive and narrative techniques that Ignatieff uses in "Deficits," write a paper on the physical and psychological impact of a serious illness on someone you know.
2. Using "Deficits" and "The Way of All Flesh" by Judy Stoffman (Unit Three) as background material, write an essay explaining how society can and must enable older people to live in dignity, despite physical or mental handicaps.
3. Traditional societies like the Chinese respect and venerate the old, but progressive western societies increasingly see the aged as an unwelcome burden. Write an essay in which you identify and explain two or three significant reasons why our society excludes or rejects the elderly.

The Rake

DAVID MAMET

There was the incident of the rake and there was the incident of the school play, and it seems to me that they both took place at the round kitchen table. 1

2   The table was not in the kitchen proper but in an area called "the nook," which held its claim to that small measure of charm by dint of a waist-high wall separating it from an adjacent area known as the living room.

3   All family meals were eaten in the nook. There was a dining room to the right, but, as in most rooms of that name at that time and in those surroundings, it was never used.

4   The round table was of wrought iron and topped with glass; it was noteworthy for that glass, for it was more than once and rather more than several times, I am inclined to think, that my stepfather would grow so angry as to bring some object down on the glass top, shattering it, thus giving us to know how we had forced him out of control.

5   And it seems that most times when he would shatter the table, as often as that might have been, he would cut some portion of himself on the glass, or that he or his wife, our mother, would cut their hands on picking up the glass afterward, and that we children were to understand, and did understand, that these wounds were our fault.

6   So the table was associated in our minds with the notion of blood.

7   The house was in a brand-new housing development in the southern suburbs. The new community was built upon, and now bordered, the remains of what had once been a cornfield. When our new family moved in, there were but a few homes in the development completed, and a few more under construction. Most streets were mud, and boasted a house here or there, and many empty lots marked out by white stakes.

8   The house we lived in was the development's Model Home. The first time we had seen it, it had signs plastered on the front and throughout the interior telling of the various conveniences it contained. And it had a lawn, and was one of the only homes in the new community that did.

9   My stepfather was fond of the lawn, and he detailed me and my sister to care for it, and one fall afternoon we found ourselves assigned to rake the leaves.

10   Why this chore should have been so hated I cannot say, except that we children, and I especially, felt ourselves less than full members of this new, cobbled-together° family, and disliked being assigned to the beautification of a home that we found unbeautiful in all respects, and for which we had neither natural affection nor a sense of proprietary° interest.

11   We went to the new high school. We walked the mile down the open two-lane road on one side of which was the just-begun suburban community and on the other side of which was the cornfield.

The school was as new as the community, and still under construction for the first three years of its occupancy. One of its innovations was the notion that honesty would be engendered° by the absence of security, and so the lockers were designed and built both without locks and without the possibility of attaching locks. And there was the corresponding rash of thievery and many lectures about the same from the school administration, but it was difficult to point with pride to any scholastic or community tradition supporting the suggestion that we, the students, pull together in this new, utopian° way. We were, in school, in an uncompleted building in the midst of a mud field in the midst of a cornfield. Our various sports teams were called The Spartans; and I played on those teams, which were of a wretchedness consistent with their novelty.

Meanwhile my sister interested herself in the drama society. The year after I had left the school she obtained the lead in the school play. It called for acting and singing, both of which she had talent for, and it looked to be a signal triumph for her in her otherwise unremarkable and unenjoyed school career.

On the night of the play's opening she sat down to dinner with our mother and our stepfather. It may be that they ate a trifle early to allow her to get to the school to enjoy the excitement of the opening night. But however it was, my sister had no appetite, and she nibbled a bit at her food, and then she got up from the table to carry her plate back to scrape it in the sink, when my mother suggested that she sit down, as she had not finished her food. My sister said she really had no appetite, but my mother insisted that, as the meal had been prepared, it would be good form to sit and eat it.

My sister sat down with the plate and pecked at her food and she tried to eat a bit, and told my mother that, no, really, she possessed no appetite whatever, and that was due, no doubt, not to the food, but to her nervousness and excitement at the prospect of opening night.

My mother, again, said that, as the food had been cooked, it had to be eaten, and my sister tried and said that she could not; at which my mother nodded. She then got up from the table and went to the telephone and looked the number up and called the school and got the drama teacher and identified herself and told him that her daughter wouldn't be coming to school that night, that, no, she was not ill, but that she would not be coming in. Yes, yes, she said, she knew that her daughter had the lead in the play, and, yes, she was aware that many children and teachers had worked hard for it, et cetera, and so my sister did not play the lead in her school play. But I was long gone, out of the house by that time, and well out of it. I heard that story, and others like it, at the distance of twenty-five years.

17   In the model house our rooms were separated from their room, the master bedroom, by a bathroom and a study. On some weekends I would go alone to visit my father in the city and my sister would stay and sometimes grow frightened or lonely in her part of the house. And once, in the period when my grandfather, then in his sixties, was living with us, she became alarmed at a noise she had heard in the night; or perhaps she just became lonely, and she went out of her room and down the hall, calling for my mother, or my stepfather, or my grandfather, but the house was dark, and no one answered.

18   And, as she went farther down the hall, toward the living room, she heard voices, and she turned the corner, and saw a light coming from under the closed door in the master bedroom, and heard my stepfather crying, and the sound of my mother weeping. So my sister went up to the door, and she heard my stepfather talking to my grandfather and saying, "Jack. Say the words. Just say the words…" And my grandfather, in his Eastern European accent, saying, with obvious pain and difficulty, "No. No. I can't. Why are you making me do this? Why?" And the sound of my mother crying convulsively.

19   My sister opened the door, and she saw my grandfather sitting on the bed, and my stepfather standing by the closet and gesturing. On the floor of the closet she saw my mother, curled in a fetal position, moaning and crying and hugging herself. My stepfather was saying, "Say the words. Just say the words." And my grandfather was breathing fast and repeating, "I can't. She knows how I feel about her. I can't." And my stepfather said, "Say the words, Jack. Please. Just say you love her." At which my mother would moan louder. And my grandfather said, "I can't."

20   My sister pushed the door open farther and said—I don't know what she said, but she asked, I'm sure, for some reassurance, or some explanation, and my stepfather turned around and saw her and picked up a hairbrush from a dresser that he passed as he walked toward her, and he hit her in the face and slammed the door on her. And she continued to hear "Jack, say the words."

21   She told me that on weekends when I was gone my stepfather ended every Sunday evening by hitting or beating her for some reason or other. He would come home from depositing his own kids back at their mother's house after their weekend visitation, and would settle down tired and angry, and, as a regular matter on those evenings, would find out some intolerable behavior on my sister's part and slap or hit or beat her.

22   Years later, at my mother's funeral, my sister spoke to our aunt, my mother's sister, who gave a footnote to this behavior. She said

when they were young, my mother and my aunt, they and their parents lived in a small flat on the West Side. My grandfather was a salesman on the road from dawn on Monday until Friday night. Their family had a fiction, and that fiction, that article of faith, was that my mother was a naughty child. And each Friday, when he came home, his first question as he climbed the stairs was, "What has she done this week...?" At which my grandmother would tell him the terrible things that my mother had done, after which she, my mother, was beaten.

This was general knowledge in my family. The footnote concerned my grandfather's behavior later in the night. My aunt had a room of her own, and it adjoined her parents' room. And she related that each Friday, when the house had gone to bed, she, through the thin wall, heard my grandfather pleading for sex. "Cookie, please." And my grandmother responding, "No, Jack." "Cookie, please." "No, Jack." "Cookie, please." 23

And once, my grandfather came home and asked, "What has she done this week?" and I do not know, but I imagine that the response was not completed, and perhaps hardly begun; in any case, he reached and grabbed my mother by the back of the neck and hurled her down the stairs. 24

And once, in our house in the suburbs there had been an outburst by my stepfather directed at my sister. And she had, somehow, prevailed. It was, I think, that he had the facts of the case wrong, and had accused her of the commission of something for which she had demonstrably had no opportunity, and she pointed this out to him with what I can imagine, given the circumstances, was an understandable, and, given my prejudice, a commendable degree of freedom. Thinking the incident closed she went back to her room to study, and, a few moments later, saw him throw open her door, bat the book out of her hands, and pick her up and throw her against the far wall, where she struck the back of her neck on a shelf. 25

She was told, the next morning, that her pain, real or pretended, held no weight, and that she would have to go to school. She protested that she could not walk, or, if at all, only with the greatest difficulty and in great pain; but she was dressed and did walk to school, where she fainted, and was brought home. For years she suffered various headaches; an X ray taken twenty years later for an unrelated problem revealed that when he threw her against the shelf he had cracked her vertebrae. 26

When we left the house we left in good spirits. When we went out to dinner, it was an adventure, which was strange to me, looking 27 back, because many of these dinners ended with my sister or myself being banished, sullen or in tears, from the restaurant, and told to wait in the car, as we were in disgrace.

28   These were the excursions that had ended, due to her or my intolerable arrogance, as it was then explained to us.

29   The happy trips were celebrated and capped with a joke. Here is the joke: My stepfather, my mother, my sister, and I would exit the restaurant, my stepfather and mother would walk to the car, telling us that they would pick us up. We children would stand by the restaurant entrance. They would drive up in the car, open the passenger door, and wait until my sister and I had started to get in. They would then drive away.

30   They would drive ten or fifteen feet, and open the door again, and we would walk up again, and they would drive away again. They sometimes would drive around the block. But they would always come back, and by that time the four of us would be laughing in camaraderie° and appreciation of what, I believe, was our only family joke.

31   We were raking the lawn, my sister and I. I was raking, and she was stuffing the leaves into a bag. I loathed the job, and my muscles and my mind rebelled, and I was viciously angry, and my sister said something, and I turned and threw the rake at her and it hit her in the face.

32   The rake was split bamboo and metal, and a piece of metal caught her lip and cut her badly.

33   We were both terrified, and I was sick with guilt, and we ran into the house, my sister holding her hand to her mouth, and her mouth and her hand and the front of her dress covered in blood.

34   We ran into the kitchen where my mother was cooking dinner, and my mother asked what happened.

35   Neither of us, myself out of guilt, of course, and my sister out of a desire to avert the terrible punishment she knew I would receive, neither of us would say what occurred.

36   My mother pressed us, and neither of us would answer. She said that until one or the other answered, we would not go to the hospital; and so the family sat down to dinner where my sister clutched a napkin to her face and the blood soaked the napkin and ran down onto her food, which she had to eat; and I also ate my food and we cleared the table and went to the hospital.

37   I remember the walks home from school in the frigid winter, along the cornfield that was, for all its proximity to the city, part of the prairie. The winters were viciously cold. From the remove of years, I

can see how the area might and may have been beautiful. One could have walked in the stubble of the cornfields, or hunted birds, or enjoyed any of a number of pleasures naturally occurring.

```
┌──────────────────────────┐
│                          │
│                          │
└──────────────────────────┘
```

DAVID MAMET

U.S. dramatist David Mamet (b. 1947) has taught theatre, founded theatre groups, and written numerous outstanding plays, including the award-winning *American Buffalo*, *Glengarry Glen Ross*, and *Oleanna*.

Words and Meanings

Paragraph

cobbled-together	makeshift, clumsily put together	10
proprietary	sense of ownership	
engendered	produced, encouraged	12
utopian	ideal, visionary	
camaraderie	sense of sharing, of friendship, in a group of people	30

Structure and Strategy

1. How does paragraph 1 set up the key events on which this narrative is based?
2. Why does the author spend so much time on the specific place these events occur (paragraphs 1 to 5)? What is the horrible IRONY in paragraph 6?
3. Identify the paragraphs that tell the stories of the two incidents referred to in the first paragraph.
4. Analyze the descriptive details that make up paragraphs 2, 3, 7, 11, and 12. How do these details contribute to the sense of unhappiness, even desperation, of the author's life and that of his sister?
5. What IRONY is there in the fact that the family lives in "the development's Model Home" (paragraph 8)? Where in the essay are you told how the children feel about the house?
6. The essay contains at least two short narratives besides those the author refers to in paragraph 1. Identify the stories and explain how they contribute to the author's THESIS. Could they have been omitted without affecting the dominant impression of this essay?
7. The concluding paragraph describes the place where the key events of this story occurred. What is implied by the details

Mamet includes in this paragraph? Is the CONCLUSION an effective ending to this disturbing essay? Why?

8. David Mamet is a renowned playwright. What characteristics or qualities do you see in "The Rake" that reveal his dramatic skills?

Content and Purpose

1. Why do you think Mamet has titled his essay "The Rake"?
2. Most analysis of abusive families suggests that violence runs in families, that violent parents breed violent children. How does "The Rake" support this thesis? How many generations are involved?
3. Why is the name of the sports teams in the author's high school particularly appropriate (paragraph 12)? What is the high school like? Is it the "new, utopian" school that it was designed to be?
4. Which specific episodes reveal most clearly the mother's rigidity, her failure to empathize with her children, especially her daughter? Why is it IRONIC that these episodes occur at the kitchen table?
5. The stepfather commits the most directly brutal acts against the children. Who is the primary victim of his rages? When do his rages occur? What triggers them?
6. In paragraphs 4 and 5, Mamet comments on the responsibility for violence—and the displacement of responsibility—that occurs in abusive families. Who appears to suffer as a result of the stepfather's rage? Who really suffers?
7. In paragraphs 29 and 30, the author describes their one family joke. Why do the children share in the laughter? What effect does the recounting of this "joke" have on the reader?
8. This essay is an adult's reflections on a very unhappy childhood. Find two incidents in which a child encounters something that she or he is unable to comprehend at the time. What details are added twenty-or-so years later? How do these details change the adult's understanding of the incidents?

Suggestions for Writing

1. Write an essay that tells a story from your own childhood (it need not be violent or sad—it could be a happy or humorous recollection). Your narrative should focus on a childhood experience that now, as an adult, you see differently.
2. Write an essay that narrates the effects of a family trauma or disruption on the children.

Men's Bodies,
Men's Selves

JOHN UPDIKE

Inhabiting a male body is much like hav-   1
ing a bank account: as long as it's healthy, you don't think much
about it. Compared with the female body, it is a low-maintenance
proposition: a shower now and then, trim the fingernails every ten
days, a haircut once a month. Oh yes, shaving—scraping or
buzzing away at your face every morning. Byron, in *Don Juan*°,
thought the repeated nuisance of shaving balanced out the periodic
agony, for females, of childbirth. Women are, his lines tell us,

> Condemn'd to child-bed, as men for their sins
> Have shaving too entail'd upon their chins,—
>
> A daily plague, which in the aggregate
> May average on the whole with parturition.

From the standpoint of reproduction, the male body is a deliv-   2
ery system, as the female body is a mazy device for retention. Once
the delivery is made, men feel a faint but distinct falling-off of
interest. Yet against the enduring female heroics of birth and nur-
ture should be set the male's superhuman frenzy to deliver his
goods: he vaults walls, skips sleep, risks wallet, health, and his
political future all to ram home his seed into the gut of the chosen
woman. The sense of the chase lives in him as the key to life. His
body is, like a delivery rocket that falls away in space, a disposable
means. Men put their bodies at risk to experience the release from
gravity.

When my tenancy of a male body was fairly new—of six or so   3
years' duration—I used to jump and fall just for the joy of it.
Falling—backwards or down stairs—became a specialty of mine,
an attention-getting stunt I was practicing into my thirties, at suburban parties. Falling is, after all, a kind of flying, though of briefer
duration than would be ideal. My impulse to hurl myself from
high windows and the edges of cliffs belongs to my body, not my
mind, which resists the siren call° of the chasm with all its might;
the interior struggle knocks the wind from my lungs and tightens

my scrotum and gives any trip to Europe, with its Alps, castle parapets°, and gargoyled cathedral lookouts, a flavor of night-mare. Falling, strangely, no longer figures in my dreams, as it often did when I was a boy and my subconscious was more honest with me. An airplane, that necessary evil, turns the earth into a map so quickly the brain turns aloof and calm; still, I marvel that there is no end of young men willing to become jet pilots.

4   Any accounting of male-female differences must include the male's superior recklessness, a drive not, I think, toward death, as the darker feminist cosmogonies° would have it, but to test the limits, to see what the traffic will bear—a kind of mechanic's curiosity. The number of men who do lasting damage to their young bodies is striking; war and car accidents aside, secondary-school sports, with the approval of parents and the encouragement of brutish coaches, take a fearful toll on skulls and knees. We were made for combat, back in the post-simian°, East African days, and the bumping, the whacking, the breathlessness, the pain-smother-ing adrenaline rush form a cumbersome and unfashionable bliss, but bliss nevertheless. Take your body to the edge, and see if it flies.

5   The male sense of space must differ from that of the female, who has such interesting, active, and significant inner space. The space that interests men is outer. The fly ball high against the sky, the long pass spiraling overhead, the jet fighter like a scarcely visi-ble pinpoint nozzle laying down its vapor trail at 40,000 feet, the gazelle haunch flickering just beyond arrow-reach, the uncountable stars sprinkled on their great black wheel, the horizon, the moun-taintop, the quasar—these bring portents with them and awaken a sense of relation with the invisible, with the empty. The ideal male body is taut with lines of potential force, a diagram extending out-ward; the ideal female body curves around centers of repose. Of course, no one is ideal, and the sexes are somewhat androgynous° subdivisions of a species: Diana° the huntress is a more trendy body-type nowadays than languid, overweight Venus°, and poly-morphous° Dionysus° poses for more underwear ads than Mars°. Relatively, though, men's bodies, however elegant, are designed for covering territory, for moving on.

6   An erection, too, defies gravity, flirts with it precariously. It extends the diagram of outward direction into downright detacha-bility—objective in the case of the sperm, subjective in the case of the testicles and penis. Men's bodies, at this juncture, feel only part-ly theirs; a demon of sorts has been attached to their lower torso, whose performance is erratic and whose errands seem, at times, ridiculous. It is like having a (much) smaller brother toward whom you feel both fond and impatient; if he is you, it is you in curiously

simplified and ignoble° form. This sense, of the male body being two, is acknowledged in verbal love play and erotic writing, where the penis is playfully given a pet name, an individuation not even the rarest rapture grants a vagina. Here, where maleness gathers to a quintessence° of itself, there can be no insincerity, there can be no hiding; for sheer nakedness, there is nothing like a hopeful phallus; its aggressive shape is indivisible from its tender-skinned vulnerability. The act of intercourse, from the point of view of a consenting female, has an element of mothering, of enwrapment, of merciful concealment even. The male body, for this interval, is tucked out of harm's way.

To inhabit a male body, then, is to feel somewhat detached from it. Our being seems to lie not in cells and muscles but in the traces our thoughts and actions inscribe on the air. The male body skims the surface of nature's deeps, wherein the blood and pain and mysterious cravings of women perpetuate the species. Participating less than the female body in nature's processes, the male body gives the impression—false—of being exempt from time. Its powers of strength and reach descend in early adolescence, along with acne and sweaty feet, and depart, in imperceptible increments, after thirty or so. It surprises me to discover, when I remove my shoes and socks, the same paper-white hairless ankles that struck me as pathetic when I observed them on my father. I felt betrayed when, in some tumble of touch football twenty years ago, I heard my tibia snap; and when, between two reading engagements in Cleveland, my appendix tried to burst; and when, the other day, not for the first time, there arose to my nostrils out of my own body the musty attic smell my grandfather's body had.

A man's body does not betray its tenant as rapidly as a woman's. Never as fine and lovely, it has less distance to fall; what rugged beauty it has is wrinkle-proof. It keeps its capability of procreation indecently long. Unless intense athletic demands are made on it, the thing serves well enough to sixty, which is my age now. From here on, it's chancy. There are no breasts or ovaries to admit cancer to the male body, but the prostate, that awkwardly located little source of seminal fluid, shows the strain of sexual function with fits of hysterical cell replication, and all that beer and potato chips adds up in the coronary arteries. A writer, whose physical equipment can be minimal as long as it gets him to the desk, the lectern, and New York City once in a while, cannot but be grateful to his body, especially to his eyes, those tender and intricate sites where the brain extrudes° from the skull, and to his hands, which hold the pen or tap the keyboard. His body has been not himself exactly, but a close pal, pot-bellied and balding like most of his other pals now. A man and his body are like a boy and the buddy who has a driver's license and the use of his father's car for the evening; one goes along, gratefully, for the ride.

JOHN UPDIKE

One of America's best-known and most prolific writers, John Updike (b. 1931) has lived and worked in Massachusetts for forty years. He has written numerous novels, essays, columns, and criticism. His most recent collection of non-fiction is *Odd Jobs*, and his most recent novel is *Memories of the Ford Administration*.

Words and Meanings

Paragraph

1	*Don Juan*	Lord Byron's mock-epic poem about male–female relationships, written 1818–23
3	siren call	the song of the mythological sirens was supposed to be irresistible to sailors, who were lured by its magic to their deaths
	parapets	low wall around the edge of the roof (that is, a very high and dangerous place)
4	cosmogonies	theories of the origin of the universe
	post-simian	the period of our evolutionary development that followed the ape stage
5	androgynous	having both male and female physical characteristics
	Diana	Roman goddess of the hunt; usually portrayed as strong, fit, physically active
	Venus	Roman goddess of love; usually portrayed as plump and relaxed, often reclining on a couch
	polymorphous	capable of changing form and shape
	Dionysus	god of fertility and wine; sometimes depicted as a mature, full-bearded man, sometimes as a beardless adolescent
	Mars	god of war; stern, tough, very muscular
6	ignoble	insignificant, dishonourable
	quintessence	most concentrated form, the essential part
8	extrudes	pushes out, sticks out from

Structure and Strategy

1. What is the central contrast introduced in paragraph 1? Why do you think Updike supports this contrast with the quotation from Byron's comic masterpiece? What is the TONE of this paragraph?

2. Throughout this essay, Updike writes of a man's relationship to his body in terms of a tenant inhabiting a property. Find three or four examples of this recurring metaphor (see FIGURES OF SPEECH). How does it relate to his THESIS?
3. Consider the development of paragraph 5. What two contrasts does Updike use to support his topic sentence? How are these contrasts related to one another? How do the mythological references help develop the topic?
4. Overall, the TONE of this essay is serious, but Updike enlivens the essay with humour. Identify four or five instances of Updike's sense of humour.
5. This essay is the work of a writer two generations removed from his childhood experiences. Identify two images in paragraph 7 that bring this fact to the reader's attention. Find three specific examples Updike uses to support the topic sentence in this paragraph.
6. What contrast does the author develop in the last paragraph? How does it bring the essay to a conclusion?
7. Consider the similes (see FIGURES OF SPEECH) in the first and last sentence of this piece. Are they effective? Why?

Content and Purpose

1. Why, according to paragraph 2, is a man's "sense of the chase … the key to life"? If the male body is "a disposable means," what is the "end" it serves?
2. How does the mature Updike's perception of falling through space differ from his childhood and early adult experiences? What is the "interior struggle" he refers to in paragraph 3?
3. Identify three basic differences between men and women that Updike develops in paragraphs 4, 5, and 6.
4. Does the essay maintain that sexual intercourse is an act of aggression on the part of the male? (See paragraphs 2 and 6.)
5. What attitude toward women does this essay reveal?

Suggestions for Writing

1. Do you think Updike accurately describes the way boys and men see the world and their role in it? Write an essay in response to the position he puts forward.
2. Consider the connection between the anatomical, biological realities of the female body and a woman's sense of herself in the world. In other words, write a descriptive essay entitled, "Women's Bodies, Women's Selves," along the lines of Updike's essay.

Additional Suggestions for Writing

NARRATION

Write a narrative essay based on one of the following topics. Your essay should support a generalization about the experience (a thesis), and it should be based on personal experience.

1. An embarrassing experience in your life
2. An act of courage that affected other people (something you did or saw someone else do)
3. The first day of a new activity (for example, school, job, marriage)
4. The birth of a child (or death of a parent, grandparent, or sibling)
5. An experience that led to success
6. An experience that led to failure
7. A journey that taught you something
8. A chance encounter that led to something significant
9. A memorable experience in your life
10. "We are all immigrants to this place, even if we were born here." (Margaret Atwood)
11. "The world is burdened with young fogeys." (Robertson Davies)

DESCRIPTION

Using a variety of sensory details, write a description of one of the following. Your description may be objective—in other words, entirely factual. Or it may be subjective, creating a dominant impression based on feelings.

1. The ugliest or most beautiful person you have ever known
2. Your closest friend (or your worst enemy)
3. A family holiday
4. A place that fills you with peace (or sorrow or dread)
5. Your favourite (or least favourite) restaurant
6. A dangerous spot that you've explored
7. A sporting event
8. An illness
9. One of your parents (or siblings or children)
10. A famous person whom you encountered face to face
11. Your favourite (or least favourite) space at school
12. The most spectacular scenery (or painting or music) you've ever experienced
13. With reference to a parent, grandparent, or other elderly person close to you, describe what Irving Layton means by "the inescapable lousiness of growing old."
14. "Less is a possibility." (Douglas Coupland)

Example: Explaining with Word Pictures

What? The Definition

If someone were to tell you that the Canadian music industry has made a major contribution to the third generation of rock 'n' roll, you would probably be puzzled—even if you think you really know the rock scene. However, your confusion would quickly evaporate if the speaker were to explain by using the kind of word pictures we call **examples**. For instance, Rush and The Tragically Hip are two examples of contemporary Canadian rock artists who have a creative, original style. The idea of rock's "third generation" becomes clear if you think of Elvis Presley as the father of the first generation and of The Beatles as the leaders of the second generation. These recognizable examples make the opening statement understandable to anyone who knows even a little about contemporary music.

An example is something selected from a class of things and used to show the character of all of them. Examples may be briefly stated instances of people, places, ideas, or things: three examples of German automobiles manufactured outside of Germany are BMW, Audi, and Mercedes-Benz. Examples may also be developed at greater length: an extended example is sometimes called an *illustration*—that is, it is a "word picture." Examples or illustrations are essential in effective writing because they enable the reader to visualize the concept you are explaining. Both are needed if you want to be clear—and, furthermore, they're interesting.

Why? The Purpose

Explaining a subject by offering examples of it is probably the simplest of the various strategies available to a writer. Example papers answer the question, "What are some significant examples of S?" By identifying and explaining a few significant examples of your subject, you ensure that your reader understands what you mean. The consequences of *not* including examples can be disastrous, especially when you are trying to explain a concept or principle.

Here's an example of what we mean: every student has, at one time or another, suffered through a course given by a "Droner." He's the instructor who, whether lecturing on the mysteries of quantum theory, the intricacies of accounting, or the subtleties of the semicolon, drones on and on, oblivious to the snores of his slumbering students. Often, the Droner has his material down cold; he knows all about physics, balance sheets, or punctuation—in theory, or what we call the ABSTRACT. But the Droner is unable or unwilling to relate these concepts to experiences that we can all understand. He cannot make the abstract principles CONCRETE for his listeners. His lectures lack specific examples that the students can picture in their minds or relate to their past experience to help them understand the concept he is trying so insensitively to explain.

Abstract words refer to ideas or qualities that we can't experience through our physical senses: words such as *respect, evil, truth, justice,* and *love.* Abstractions should be used cautiously in writing. Too many of them produce fuzzy generalities that explain little. Does the statement "Everyone needs love" refer to the "love" of a tender parent–child relationship or that of a torrid back-seat passion? Unless "love" is made concrete by the addition of examples or illustrations, the statement remains unclear. Your reader may well understand it to mean something quite different from what you intended. Good writing is a careful blend of abstract and concrete, general statement and specific examples. Thus, one important function of examples is to explain an abstraction or generality by providing vivid, familiar word pictures.

Another function of examples is to support or back up a statement, particularly a statement of your opinion about something. In this case, the use of examples becomes a persuasive strategy. If, for instance, you wanted to convince your reader that job prospects for college and university graduates are improving, you could provide statistical examples of increased hiring by major industries. Perhaps you might assemble instances of recent recruitment drives on campus by companies such as Bell Canada, Northern Telecom, and the Bank of Montreal. Again, you use examples to clarify ideas and help persuade your reader that your opinion is valid.

Thus, examples are valuable on two counts. First, they ground your abstract concepts in concrete reality that your reader can see and understand. Second, they lend substance and credibility to your THESIS, the point you are making in your paper. If you use examples well, you'll ensure that your words don't suffer the fate of the Droner's: lost to the ears of a snoring audience.

We expect to find vivid word pictures in good writing. Examples bring ideas to life, and, therefore, we find them not just in the kind of paper we've been discussing in this chapter, but in all kinds of writing. Writers of classification, process analysis, comparison, or any other rhetorical pattern often use examples to illustrate or emphasize important points. Adam Gopnik, for instance, uses examples to clarify his ideas in his comparison essay, "Quattrocento Baseball."

How? The Technique

Examples may be chosen from several sources: personal experience, the experience of others, quotations, statistics, or facts you've discovered through research. Whatever kinds of examples you choose to use, organizing and developing your paper require careful thought. The overall thesis must be clear and the scope of the examples appropriate to the thesis.

Your thesis statement will probably look something like this:

> Some examples of S are a, b, c....

Example: Three Canadian doctors who have made significant contributions to human welfare are Frederick Banting, Hans Selye, and Norman Bethune.

All you need to do now is develop each example in turn. At the end of this introduction, we've included a short essay based on this thesis statement so that you can see what the finished product looks like.

Examples are an all-purpose tool on the writer's workbench. They make your general ideas specific, your thesis convincing, and your communication interesting. Using a good example or two is also a sure-fire way to liven up an introduction or conclusion. Examples reach out and grab the reader's attention.

Now that you're aware of the usefulness of examples in your writing, you should know the three "safety rules" to follow when selecting them.

1. Make sure each example is *representative* of your subject. Eric Lindros is not a "typical hockey player," nor is Vancouver's West Point Grey your "average Canadian neighbourhood." The examples you choose must be typical enough to represent fairly the group or the idea you are explaining.

2. Make sure all examples are *pertinent*. They must be relevant, significant, and acceptable to your audience as examples of the quality or idea they've been chosen to illustrate. For instance, most readers would recognize Donald Sutherland as a Canadian actor who is a current international star. The same readers might not accept Kate Nelligan as an example of the same phenomenon, since it's debatable whether or not she is internationally renowned. And if you were to identify Madonna or John Candy as your example, your whole paper would be called into question, since the former is not Canadian, and the latter died in 1994.

3. Make sure the range and the number of your examples is *limited*. You're not writing the Sears catalogue, throwing in every colour and size in a jumbled and eventually overwhelming list. There is no set number of examples to include. How many you need depends on your purpose. The challenge is to be both selective and comprehensive, to include just enough examples to convey your idea clearly and forcefully.

Following the structural principles and the safety rules outlined here will ensure that your paper is soundly constructed and communicates exactly what you want it to, as the essay below demonstrates.

The Social Value of Education

Introduction

Most of us think of higher education as something we engage in because it will benefit us personally. We often overlook the fact that education does more than just develop the mind and spirit or prepare us for a career. The education we acquire for personal reasons also benefits the society in which we live, sometimes in surprising ways. Medical doctors, for example, are among our most highly educated citizens and are in a position to promote not only the health of their patients but also the well-being of our society. Three Canadian medical doctors who have made significant contributions to human welfare are Frederick Banting, Hans Selye, and Norman Bethune.

Thesis statement (S plus three examples)

Paragraph 2
develops first
example in thesis
statement

⟶ Frederick Banting (1891–1941) was born in Alliston, Ontario, and educated at the University of Toronto. He served in the Army Medical Corps in World War I. During the early 1920s, he joined a team of biochemical researchers at the University of Toronto. Along with physiologist Charles Best, Banting discovered the internal secretion of the pancreas, which they named "insulin." An insufficient supply of insulin causes the disease known as diabetes. The discovery and production of insulin made it possible to control the disease, thus saving or prolonging the lives of countless diabetics. Banting's contribution to this momentous medical achievement won him the Nobel Prize for Medicine and Physiology in 1923.

Paragraph 3
develops second
example

⟶ Hans Selye (1907–1983), a Vienna-born endocrinologist, was a physician who specialized in the study of the glands in the body that secrete hormones. After studying in Prague, Paris, and Rome, Selye joined the faculty of McGill University in 1932 and in 1945 became the first director of the Institute of Experimental Medicine and Surgery at the University of Montreal. Over the next three decades, Selye's research and publications made him the world's foremost expert on the effects of stress on the human body. Through his books and lectures, he popularized the notion that there are two kinds of stress. One, "eustress," is beneficial and leads to accomplishment and healing. The other, "distress," is the kind more familiar to us. It is destructive: it breaks down the body and leads to diseases such as high blood pressure, ulcers, mental illness, even cancer. Selye's work has thus contributed to our understanding of the effects of stress not only on the individual but also on society, since a general increase in frustration and anxiety may lead to an overall increase in the incidence of disease.

Paragraph 4 develops third example ⟶ Norman Bethune (1890–1939), who was born in Gravenhurst, Ontario, studied medicine in Toronto and in England. He had a strong social conscience and throughout his life used his medical knowledge and skill to relieve the suffering of the poor. After contracting tuberculosis in the 1920s, he moved to Quebec, where he experimented with various treatments of that disease. His research led to improvements in the technology and techniques of chest surgery. Meanwhile, Bethune's leftist political views prompted him to challenge the conservative Canadian medical establishment and eventually to join the Communist party. His political commitment led him in 1936 to fight in the Spanish Civil War. There he organized the first mobile blood-transfusion service, an innovation that saved thousands of lives. In 1938, Bethune's commitment to the anti-fascist cause took him to China, which was then defending itself against the Japanese invasion. In China he worked tirelessly to bring the benefits of modern medicine to a peasant people. Though Bethune died of blood poisoning after he had been in China only a year, his humanitarian efforts and devotion to the downtrodden made him a hero and enhanced the reputation of Canada among the Chinese people.

Conclusion ⟶ These three Canadian physicians are good examples of the social value of education. Whether a person is engaged in medicine or business, teaching or technology, the education he or she acquires helps others. Though our achievements may be less dramatic than those of Banting, Selye, or Bethune, what we learn will inevitably benefit not just ourselves but also the people around us, and, by extension, society as a whole.

Odd Enders

LARRY ORENSTEIN

Death is never funny. It is cancer, heart fail- 1
ure, stroke, clogged arteries, pneumonia, emphysema, asthma, bronchitis, choking, drowning, car accident. It is mostly quiet, conventional and inevitable.

But, in the twilight area between Dryden's "Death in itself is noth- 2
ing" and Kojak's "Death is dumb," there are "other causes." A man who stumbles during his morning constitutional°, bites his tongue and dies of gangrene—as Allan Pinkerton, head of the U.S. detective agency bearing his name, did in 1884—is a man who is checking out with a drum roll, a man who, in short, is joining the Club of Odd Ends.

Membership in the club sometimes requires the assistance of a 3
sponsor. In 1977, a 36-year-old San Diego woman decided to murder her 23-year-old husband, a U.S. Marine drill instructor, to collect his $20,000 in life insurance. First, she baked him a blackberry pie containing the venom sac of a tarantula. But he ate only a few pieces. She then tried to (1) electrocute him in the shower, (2) poison him with lye, (3) run him over with a car, (4) make him hallucinate while driving by putting amphetamines in his beer, and (5) inject an air bubble into his veins with a hypodermic needle. Finally, dispensing with subtlety, she and an accomplice, a 26-year-old woman, beat him over the head with a metal weight while he slept. This worked.

In 1978, a Parisian grocer stabbed his wife to death with a 4
wedge of parmesan cheese. In 1984, a New Zealand man killed his wife by jabbing her repeatedly in the stomach with a frozen sausage.

In April, 1984, a 41-year-old Pennsylvania man was asphyxiat- 5
ed after his 280-pound wife sat on his chest during an argument. Nine months later, a 41-year-old Indiana woman beat her male

companion to death by repeatedly dropping a bowling ball on his head while he lay on the floor in front of a television set.

6   Last summer, a man in Sao Paulo, Brazil, caught his wife in bed with her lover, and glued her hands to the man's penis. Doctors separated the two, but the man died from toxic chemicals absorbed through his skin. In Prague, a woman jumped out of a third-story window after learning her husband had been unfaithful. She landed on the husband, who was entering the building at that moment. He died instantly; she survived.

7   A despondent° Los Angeles man put a gun to his head and pulled the trigger. The bullet passed through his head, ricocheted off a water heater and struck his female companion between the eyes.

8   Some people, of course, discover the Club of Odd Ends on their own and sign their membership cards with a flourish. An Italian man set himself on fire, apparently had second thoughts and died falling off a cliff trying the beat out the flames. Last fall, a 26-year-old computer specialist died near Bristol apparently after tying one end of a rope to a tree and the other around his neck, getting into his car and driving off.

9   In 1971, a Shrewsbury man killed himself by drilling into his skull eight times with an electric power drill. Sixteen years later, a Chichester man who could no longer bear the pain from angina killed himself by drilling a hole in his heart.

10   Some people become Odd Enders by accident. In 1947, an eccentric U.S. recluse°, while carrying food to his equally reclusive brother, tripped a burglar trap in his house and was crushed to death under bundles of old newspapers, three breadboxes, a sewing machine and a suitcase filled with metal. His brother starved to death.

11   In 1982, a 27-year-old man fired two shotgun blasts at a giant saguaro cactus in the desert near Phoenix. The shots caused a 23-foot section of the cactus to fall and crush him to death. That same year, an elderly Louisiana man with ailing kidneys was waving a gun at quarrelling relatives when it went off. The bullet severed a tube from his dialysis machine°, and he bled to death.

12   In 1983, the assistant manager of a topless night club in San Francisco was crushed to death between the ceiling and a trick piano rigged to rise 12 feet above the club's stage. When the club was opened in the morning, the man's 240-pound body was found draped over his naked, intoxicated girl friend, who survived apparently by kicking a switch to stop the cables hoisting the piano.

13   In November, 1985, a flight attendant with three months of experience survived the hijacking of an Egyptian airliner that left 60 people dead in Malta. She was killed seven months later when her plane crashed in a sandstorm near Cairo.

In April, an award-winning astronomer at the University of   14
Arizona was crushed to death between a door and a 150-ton revolving telescope dome. In June, a man demonstrating electrical currents to his children in Orillia, Ont., was electrocuted when an experiment backfired. A California woman taking pictures of a glacier in Alaska was killed when a 1,000-pound chunk of ice broke free and fell on her.

A 22-year-old Peruvian woman died of septicemic poisoning° in   15
June after the rusty padlock on the leather chastity belt that her jealous husband forced her to wear dug into her flesh and caused an infection.

In 1980, the 70-year-old mayor of a Maryland town who was   16
checking a sewage-treatment plant slipped on a catwalk°, fell into a tank of human waste and drowned. In July, a retired barman in Northern Ireland was buried alive when he fell into a grave being dug for his brother.

The Club of Odd Ends, however, does not accept all applicants. A   17
Brazilian public servant lost an arm last summer when he stuck it into a lion's cage "to test God's power." One night in 1982, an Ohio bachelor awoke, thought he saw a prowler at the foot of his bed, reached for his gun, fired into the darkness and shot himself in the penis.

Some people, of course, are destined to become Odd Enders no   18
matter what they do. In May, a Louisiana lawyer stood in the stern of his new boat, raised his hands skyward and said: "Here I am." He was killed by a bolt of lightning.

[ ]

LARRY ORENSTEIN

Larry Orenstein is an assistant foreign editor at *The Globe and Mail* and is a member of the Crime Writers of Canada.

Words and Meanings

Paragraph

constitutional	a brisk walk taken for healthy exercise	2
despondent	feeling hopeless, depressed	7
recluse	someone who lives in isolation, avoiding the company of others	10
dialysis machine	machine used for patients with severe kidney disease; it removes waste products from the blood	11
septicemic poisoning	bacterial infection of the blood	15
catwalk	narrow bridge or scaffolding	16

Structure and Strategy

1. Why has Orenstein written this piece in such short paragraphs? Who are his intended readers?
2. Orenstein identifies people who suffer bizarre deaths as belonging to the "Club of Odd Ends." Into what three categories of membership does he group his examples? (See paragraphs 3, 8, and 10.)
3. In the introduction to this unit, we identify three "safety rules" to follow when selecting examples to support a thesis. Does Orenstein follow these rules? If not, which one(s) do you think "Odd Enders" violates?
4. "Odd Enders" contains many examples of situational IRONY, such as the example given in paragraph 2, where the head of a famous detective agency dies after biting his own tongue. Explain the irony of this example, and find at least three more examples of situational irony in the article.
5. How does the concluding paragraph contribute to the UNITY of the article?

Content and Purpose

1. What is the thesis of Orenstein's article? Can you state it in one sentence?
2. What was your reaction to "Odd Enders"? Do you think your response was what the author intended?

Suggestion for Writing

Some of the examples in "Odd Enders" are similar to stories found in tabloid newspapers such as the *National Enquirer*. Write a short essay explaining the appeal of these kinds of papers. Why do people enjoy reading about strange murders, film star scandals, aliens, and Elvis sightings?

Seeing Red

MARGARET VISSER

1   Shaking a blue rag at a bull enrages the bull—as would shaking a green rag, a yellow rag, or a brown one.

When we wish to infuriate bulls, however, we shake *red* flags, or red-lined matadors' capes, because we think red is the appropriately irritating colour. Bulls themselves are indifferent to colour, and just hate the flapping.

Human beings have endowed° the colour red with more connotations° than any other colour. Indeed, red used to be really the only colour. Before the discovery of the spectrum in the seventeenth century, all other colours tended to be considered variations of either black (brown, blue, green, violet) or white (yellow). Our colour range therefore was black—red—white. "Red" included orange and pink; copper tones, and often gold, also counted as red (hence Red Indian, and "not a red cent").

In several tongues "coloured" means only "red," like *colorado* in Spanish. Many languages use surprisingly few colour terms, but all of them include black and white, and nearly all have red. In English, only three colours become verbs by adding -en: blacken, redden, whiten. Wine and grape language also preserves the three-term range: there are all the different "reds" (rosé is a recent appellation°); but "white" wine is actually yellow; and "black" grapes are not really black.

Red is most fundamentally associated with blood and with fire, and each of those mighty preoccupations can be either terrifying or a basic good—so that the ramifications° of red, both positive and negative, are extraordinarily complex and resonant. Red is alive, and vibrant. Angry people go red in the face; embarrassment causes us to blush (a word linked with "blaze": red as both blood and fire). Artists know that red looks warm, present, and near; it attracts.

It also marks things out, and has therefore become an internationally agreed signal of danger and of prohibition: stop signs, red pencils, being in debt or "in the red." Red as "blood" is for war and wounds (the Red Cross), crime and criminals (caught "red-handed"), and also Christ's redeeming blood. Christian liturgical° red means the blood of martyrs, and the fiery Holy Spirit. Fire engines and fire extinguishers are—obviously—red.

The dynamism of red, together with its warnings of blood and fire, make it the colour of revolutions, angry people on the march—and finally of Communism and the Left generally. Canada's Liberal Party, like Toronto's York University, uses red mostly by default: calm, status-quo blue, the modern West's favourite colour, is bespoken° by the opposition. Yet in adopting red for their colour both institutions place themselves, however slightly, left of conservative.

Red is the colour of passion: hearts, sentiment (the red, red rose); and of eroticism, sexual transgression, prostitution. It riots in red-light

districts, red underwear, lipstick, and rouge. Red, like ripe fruit, arous-
es the appetite: gules, the heraldic term for red, is related to "gullet°."

8   For at least 3,000 years red was also the most fast° and successful
dye. Red clothes made their wearers stand out in a crowd. The
famous imperial purple of ancient Rome was usually an oxblood or
porphyry red. Greek *porphyreos*, the colour of the stone porphyry,
gave us the word "purple" (which has come to mean violet). The dye
itself came from a Mediterranean shellfish. Another great red was
kermes, made from an insect that lives on a species of oak. Ancient
Sanskrit had one word for both "worm" and "insect": both "kermes"
and "crimson" came via Arabic from the Sanskrit word that gave us
"worm," and so did vermilion, "little worm." Mexico later gave the
world cochineal, from the bodies of insects found on cactuses.

9   Red dresses and shawls, red shirts and cummerbunds were for
"best" wear, and for feasts. (Scarlet was originally a superb woollen
cloth, so expensive that it was often dyed red: the colour took the
name of the cloth.) Wedding dresses, until well into the nineteenth
century in Europe, were usually red. The festive meaning makes
red one of the two Christmas colours, favoured for balloons, paper
hats, candies, decorations—but also there is fire (warmth in the
depth of winter), new life (in the "death" of darkness), love (the
main Christian message), and even eroticism, for the rubicund°
Santa Claus is a fertility figure, and grossly phallic°.

MARGARET VISSER

Born in South Africa in 1940, Margaret Visser is a professor of Classics at
York University and a well-known writer, columnist, and speaker. Her books
include *Much Depends on Dinner* (1986), *The Rituals of Dinner* (1991), and
The Way We Are (1994).

Paragraph | ## Words and Meanings

Paragraph		
2	endowed	given
	connotations	see List of Useful Terms
3	appellation	name, class description
4	ramifications	associations, connotations
5	liturgical	associated with religious meaning and ritual
6	bespoken	already spoken for, taken
7	gullet	the inside of the throat (esophagus)

fast	long-lasting, not fading after repeated washings	8
rubicund	red-faced	9
phallic	image related to the penis	

Structure and Strategy

1. What strategy does Visser use in her INTRODUCTION?
2. This essay is developed through numerous examples of the meanings of the colour red. Into what categories does Visser group her examples?
3. How does the first sentence of paragraph 6 link its content with that of paragraphs 4 and 5?
4. What two functions does the concluding sentence serve? How does it contribute to the UNITY of the essay?

Content and Purpose

1. Visser's title is a pun (see FIGURES OF SPEECH). Is it effective? What does "seeing red" mean?
2. Why do you think Visser chose to explore the meanings of the colour red? What is it about this colour that attracts her interest?
3. What are two contradictory associations of the colour red? (See paragraphs 4 and 5.) Cite three specific examples that Visser uses to support these associations.
4. From what cultures does Visser take most of her examples?

Suggestion for Writing

Write an essay exploring the associations of some other colour in a specific culture or cultures; for example, green, blue, yellow, purple, or those "non-colours," black and white. Develop a thesis about the colour's meanings, and support the thesis with a wide variety of examples.

Being at Home
MERRILY WEISBORD

My companion's father has just died. He has hardly any family left alive. He lies in the tub, soaking and talking

"Being at Home" from *Boundaries of Identity: A Quebec Reader* by Merrily Weisbord. Copyright by Merrily Weisbord. Reprinted with the permission of the author.

out the sadness. His parents, who came to Quebec from Poland and Germany via Belgium, France, and Italy, lie buried east of Mirabel, past St. François, in the snow-covered fields of Quebec. Far, it seems to him, from where they began.… And yet, the sanctity of the burial place goes back to Homer, says my friend, searching for his connection to his parents, to his destiny, to life itself.

2   My father's father was a blacksmith who came to Quebec to avoid conscription in the Czar's army. My great-grandfather, on my mother's side, was the chief Rabbi of Quebec City. My father grew up in St. Sophie and my mother on Bagg Avenue. They joined the Communist Party during the Spanish Civil War, and I had no religious training. I was brought up to believe in the Brotherhood of Man.

        The other day I was swimming at the Polyvalent in St. Jerome. A little girl, shivering, grumped and grepsed° as her mother rushed
3   to dry her off. Beside us, on the bench, a pregnant woman watched. After much rubbing, the kid, warm enough to look around, said prophetically, "C'est dur d'avoir un enfant."

        "Tu as raison," I said to the kid. "Comme tu es intelligente."
4   The kid looked at me, looked at me again and whooped in surprise, "Mama, c'est une anglaise."

        My daughter, Anna, 15, sings, loves and perhaps most amaz-
5   ingly, dreams in English and French. She should be fêted° but instead she feels like she is on both sides of the fence:

> Having gone to French classical lycée, I was attacked for not understanding the French grammatical accords, and got the genuine French versus English line, 'Ah, t'es Anglais!' shot back at me every time the feminine double e came around. I was a bloke.
>
>   Now, in English school, I am a pepper. Accused of speaking the Dreaded Language of French and having, uh, French friends. Personally, I think the French can have our precious English slang, and we their French clichés, as long as I get to belong to one side or the other. Being neither a "bloke" or a "pepper," I've been left out in the cold, or should I say froid—the linguistic nightmare of this super cool province.

When my older daughter, Kim, went to Polyvalent St. Jerome, she often overheard, "Fais pas ton juif°." She was brave enough to say she was Jewish and to ask her friends to restrain themselves. When she went to her friends' homes for dinner, their parents would say, "Fais pas ton juif" and her friends would spring to her defense with, "Fais pas ça, c'est une juive, elle."

6   Now, Kim, 25, trained in St. Hyacinthe, a doctor of veterinary medicine, lives with "un Québécois pure laine°," and hangs out with her highschool gang of Louise, Claudie, Lorrain and the two

Pierres. She works at a clinic in St. Sauveur where she has established close professional ties with many animal lovers. The other day, a woman whose animals she routinely treats, came in with a difficult case. Kim cajoled the dog and reassured the woman. Together, they lifted the dog up on the table. The dog peed, and the woman yelled, "Mon petit juif."

In the 30s, the Anglo establishment had a quota system for the number of Jews they allowed to attend their elite universities. My mother made it in but her brother didn't. Clubs, schools, and resorts were closed to my parents because they were *not* Anglo, English, Canadian Canadians.   7

Now, in the current reductionist environment, I am an Anglo. Or even worse, an Anglophone, probably one of the least euphonic° words in the lexicon° of divisionist [jargon]. But this is not me. I can't identify with simplistic categories—middle-age, pre-menopausal, old, intellectual, anglophone....   8

I voted "Oui" in the referendum because I thought that a new Quebec would be committed to social justice, embracing all people as equals. Now, too often, I recall Montreal poet, A.M. Klein's phrase, "the body-odour of race," a phrase representing an attitude not particular to Quebec, but unworthy of it.   9

Today, Kim tells me she has been accepted to do her postdoctoral residency at Guelph. She sits in the big chair in the living room, her legs apart, remembering Ontario with trepidation°: "Nowhere have I felt so Québécois. They don't laugh out loud in movies. They don't drive fast. They don't speak French. They don't kiss in public. They don't sit with their legs apart, not even the men."   10

Who is Québécois? How big is Quebec's heart and imagination? My children are the flowers of this potential fecund° soil. Yet there is no word to describe them as, I think, no one word can describe me. We live here, in the case of my family, tied to the soil, having, for better or for worse, taken root.   11

MERRILY WEISBORD

A member of Quebec's Anglophone writing community, Merrily Weisbord lives in the Laurentian mountains north of Montreal. Her books include *The Strangest Dream: Canadian Communists, the Spy Trials and the Cold War* and *Our Future Selves: Love, Life, Sex and Aging*. She is also the co-author of *The Valour and the Horror: The Untold Story of Canadians in the Second World War*. Her piece "Being at Home" originally appeared in French in a special edition of *Liberté* devoted to Quebec's English-language writing community.

Words and Meanings

Paragraph

3	grepsed	griped, complained
5	fêted	celebrated
	Fais pas ton juif	"Quit acting like a Jew."
6	pure laine	literally means "pure wool"; metaphorically refers to the direct descendants of French colonists, the "true Québécois"
8	euphonic	pleasant-sounding
	lexicon	glossary, word-list
10	trepidation	concern, fear
11	fecund	fertile, productive, rich

Structure and Strategy

1. How does the opening ANECDOTE contribute to the rest of the essay? Does the title accurately reflect the author's THESIS?
2. Weisbord uses four illustrations to develop her thesis. Identify the paragraphs that make up each illustration.
3. Identify the quotations Weisbord uses to support her points (paragraph 3 to 4, 5, and 6). Why didn't she simply PARA-PHRASE her family's various experiences with "the language question in Quebec"? How would paraphrasing change the effect?

Content and Purpose

1. What is the THESIS of the essay? Summarize it in a single sentence.
2. Are Weisbord and her children "Anglophones"? Why or why not?
3. The title of this piece can be interpreted several ways. What does it mean to you?
4. What IRONY do paragraphs 7 and 8 point to?
5. What Anglo-Canadian markers does Weisbord's daughter identify? (See paragraph 10.) Do you agree with her perceptions? What effect does her "thumbnail sketch" of les Anglais have on the reader?

Suggestion for Writing

Write an essay illustrating by means of well-chosen examples significant differences between two geographical or cultural groups (for example, Canadians and Americans, Ontarians and Maritimers, Torontonians and Vancouverites).

No Wonder They Call Me a Bitch

ANN HODGMAN

I've always wondered about dog food. Is a Gaines-burger really like a hamburger? Can you fry it? Does dog food "cheese" taste like real cheese? Does Gravy Train actually make gravy in the dog's bowl, or is that brown liquid just dissolved crumbs? And exactly what *are* by-products?

Having spent the better part of a week eating dog food, I'm sorry to say that I now know the answers to these questions. While my dachshund, Shortie, watched in agonies of yearning, I gagged my way through can after can of stinky, white-flecked mush and bag after bag of stinky, fat-drenched nuggets. And now I understand exactly why Shortie's breath is so bad.

Of course, Gaines-burgers are neither mush nor nuggets. They are, rather, a miracle of beauty and packaging—or at least that's what I thought when I was little. I used to beg my mother to get them for our dogs, but she always said they were too expensive. When I finally bought a box of cheese-flavored Gaines-burgers— after twenty years of longing—I felt deliciously wicked.

"Dogs love real beef," the back of the box proclaimed proudly. "That's why Gaines-burgers is the only beef burger for dogs with real beef and no meat by-products!" The copy was accurate: meat by-products did not appear in the list of ingredients. Poultry by-products did, though—right there next to preserved animal fat.

One Purina spokesman told me that poultry by-products consist of necks, intestines, undeveloped eggs and other "carcass remnants," but not feathers, heads, or feet. When I told him I'd been eating dog food, he said, "Oh, you're kidding! Oh, *no!*" (I came to share his alarm when, weeks, later, a second Purina spokesman said that Gaines-burgers *do* contain poultry heads and feet—but *not* undeveloped eggs.)

Up close my Gaines-burger didn't much resemble chopped beef. Rather, it looked—and felt—like a single long, extruded° piece of redness that had been chopped into segments and formed into a patty. You could make one at home if you had a Play-Doh Fun Factory.

7   I turned on the skillet. While I waited for it to heat up I pulled out a shred of cheese-colored material and palpated° it. Again, like Play-Doh, it was quite malleable°. I made a little cheese bird out of it; then I counted to three and ate the bird.

8   There was a horrifying rush of cheddar taste, followed immediately by the dull tang of soybean flour—the main ingredient in Gaines-burgers. Next I tried a piece of red extrusion. The main difference between the meat-flavored and cheese-flavored extrusions is one of texture. The "cheese" chews like fresh Play-Doh, whereas the "meat" chews like Play-Doh that's been sitting out on a rug for a couple of hours.

9   Frying only turned the Gaines-burger black. There was no melting, no sizzling, no warm meat smells. A cherished childhood illusion was gone. I flipped the patty into the sink, where it immediately began leaking rivulets of red dye.

10   As alarming as the Gaines-burgers were, their soy meal began to seem like an old friend when the time came to try some *canned* dog foods. I decided to try the Cycle foods first. When I opened them, I thought about how rarely I use can openers these days, and I was suddenly visited by a long-forgotten sensation of can-opener distaste. *This* is the kind of unsavory place can openers spend their time when you're not watching! Every time you open a can of, say, Italian plum tomatoes, you infect them with invisible particles of by-product.

11   I had been expecting to see the usual homogeneous° scrapple° inside, but each can of Cycle was packed with smooth, round, oily nuggets. As if someone at Gaines had been tipped off that a human would be tasting the stuff, the four cycles really were different from one another. Cycle-1, for puppies, is wet and soyish. Cycle-2, for adults, glistens nastily with fat, but it's passably edible—a lot like some canned Swedish meatballs I once got in a Care package at college. Cycle-3, the "lite" one, for fatties, had no specific flavor; it just tasted like dog food. But at least it didn't make me fat.

12   Cycle-4, for senior dogs, had the smallest nuggets. Maybe old dogs can't open their mouths as wide. This kind was far sweeter than the other three Cycles—almost like baked beans. It was also the only one to contain "dried beef digest," a mysterious substance that the Purina spokesman defined as "enzymes" and my dictionary defined as "the products of digestion."

13   Next on the menu was a can of Kal Kan Pedigree with Chunky Chicken. Chunky *chicken?* There were chunks in the can, certainly— big, purplish-brown chunks. I forked one chunk out (by now I was becoming more callous°) and found that while it had no discernible° chicken flavor, it wasn't bad except for its texture—like meat loaf with ground-up chicken bones.

In the world of canned dog food, a smooth consistency is a sign 14
of low quality—lots of cereal. A lumpy, frightening, bloody, stringy
horror is a sign of high quality—lots of meat. Nowhere in the world
of wet dog foods was this demonstrated better than in the fanciest I
tried—Kal Kan's Pedigree Select Dinners. These came not in a can
but in a tiny foil packet with a picture of an imperious° Yorkie°.
When I pulled open the container, juice spurted all over my hand,
and the first chunk I speared was trailing a long grey vein. I
shrieked and went instead for a plain chunk, which I was able to
swallow only after taking a break to read some suddenly fascinating office equipment catalogues. Once again, though, it tasted no
more alarming than, say, canned hash.

Still, how pleasant it was to turn to *dry* dog food! Gravy Train 15
was the first I tried, and I'm happy to report that it really does
make a "thick, rich, real beef gravy" when you mix it with water.
Thick and rich, anyway. Except for a lingering rancid°-fat flavor, the
gravy wasn't beefy, but since it tasted primarily like tap water, it
wasn't nauseating either.

My poor dachshund just gets plain old Purina Dog Chow, but 16
Purina also makes a dry food called Butcher's Blend that comes in
Beef, Bacon & Chicken flavor. Here we see dog food's arcane semi-
otics° at its best: a red triangle with a 7 stamped into it is supposed
to suggest beef; a tan curl, chicken; and a brown *S*, a piece of bacon.
Only dogs understand these messages. But Butcher's Blend does
have an endearing slogan: "Great, Meaty Tastes—without bothering the Butcher!" *You know, I wanted to buy some meat, but I just could-
n't bring myself to bother the butcher...*

Purina O.N.E. ("Optimum Nutritional Effectiveness") is target- 17
ed at people who are unlikely ever to worry about bothering a
tradesperson. "We chose chicken as a primary ingredient in Purina
O.N.E. for several reasonings," the long, long essay on the back of
the bag announces. Chief among these reasonings, I'd guess, is the
fact that chicken appeals to people who are—you know—*like us*.
Although our dogs do nothing but spend eighteen-hour days alone
in the apartment, we still want them to be *premium* dogs. We want
them to cut down on red meat, too. We also want dog food that
comes in a bag with an attractive design, a subtle typeface, and no
kitschy° pictures of slobbering golden retrievers.

Besides that, we want a list of the Nutritional Benefits of our 18
dog food—and we get it on O.N.E. One thing I especially like about
this list is its constant references to a dog's "hair coat," as in "Beef
tallow° is good for the dog's skin and hair coat." (On the other
hand, beef tallow merely provides palatability, while the dried beef
digest in Cycle provides palatability *enhancement*.)

19   I hate to say it, but O.N.E. was pretty palatable. Maybe that's because it has about 100 percent more fat than, say, Butcher's Blend. Or maybe I'd been duped by the packaging; that's been known to happen before.

20   As with people food, dog snacks taste much better than dog meals. They're better looking too. Taste Milk-Bone Flavor Snacks. The loving-hands-at-home prose describing each flavor is colorful; the writers practically choke on their own exuberance. Of bacon they say, "It's so good, your dog will think it's hot off the frying pan." Of liver: "The only taste your dog wants more than liver—is even more liver!" Of poultry: "All those farm fresh flavors deliciously mixed in one biscuit. Your dog will bark with delight!" And of vegetable: "Gardens of taste! Specially blended to give your dog that vegetable flavor he wants—but can rarely get!"

21   Well, I may be a sucker, but advertising *this* emphatic just doesn't convince me. I lined up all seven flavors of Milk-Bone Flavor Snacks on the floor. Unless my dog's palate is a lot more sensitive than mine—and considering that she steals dirty diapers out of the trash and eats them, I'm loath to think it is—she doesn't detect any more difference in the seven flavors than I did when I tried them.

22   I much preferred Bonz, the hard-baked, bone-shaped snack stuffed with simulated marrow. I liked the bone part, that is; it tasted almost exactly like the cornmeal it was made of. The mock marrow inside was a bit more problematic: in addition to looking like the sludge that collects in the treads of my running shoes, it was bursting with tiny hairs.

23   I'm sure you have a few dog food questions of your own. To save us time, I've answered them in advance.

24   *Q. Are those little cans of Mighty Dog actually branded with the sizzling word* BEEF, *the way they show in the commercials?*

25   A. You should know by now that that kind of thing never happens.

26   *Q. Does chicken-flavored dog food taste like chicken-flavored cat food?*

27   A. To my surprise, chicken cat food was actually a little better—more chickeny. It tasted like inferior canned pâté.

28   *Q. Was there any dog food that you just couldn't bring yourself to try?*

29   A. Alas, it was a can of Mighty Dog called Prime Entree with Bone Marrow. The meat was dark, dark brown, and it was surrounded by gelatin that was almost black. I knew I would die if I tasted it, so I put it outside for the raccoons.

ANN HODGMAN

U.S. writer and editor Ann Hodgman writes a food column for *Eating Well* and is a regular contributor to *Spy* magazine. She has written more than twenty books for children and is the author of several humour books including *Tiny Tales of Terror* and *My Babysitter Is a Vampire*.

Words and Meanings

Paragraph

extruded	pushed out	6
palpated	handled, squeezed	7
malleable	squishy	
homogeneous	looking alike, the same in appearance	11
scrapple	scraps of leftovers, combined, sliced, and fried (like burgers)	
callous	insensitive	13
discernible	noticeable	
imperious	haughty, arrogant, bossy	14
Yorkie	Yorkshire terrier	
rancid	rotten, disgusting smell of food gone bad	15
arcane semiotics	study of hidden meanings of words and pictures	16
kitschy	"cutesy"	17
tallow	fat	18

Structure and Strategy

1. How would you describe the TONE of this essay? (Hint: the title provides a clue.)
2. What is the organizing principle of this essay? Are the examples arranged randomly, or are they grouped into identifiable categories?
3. Identify three different senses that the author appeals to in her description of Gaines-burgers in paragraphs 7, 8, and 9.
4. Hodgman's humour depends to a large degree on her DICTION. What effect do phrases such as "stinky, white-flecked mush" (paragraph 2), "leaking rivulets of red dye" (paragraph 9), and "glistens nastily with fat" (paragraph 11) have on the reader?
5. Why do you think the essay concludes with a question-and-answer format? Is it effective or not?

Content and Purpose

1. What did you think when you first saw the title of this essay? Were you prepared for what you read? Why do you think Hodgman chose this title?

2. The first two paragraphs set up the terms of Hodgman's "experiment." What does she do? Whatever for?
3. What is the PURPOSE of this essay? Sum up Hodgman's argument in a thesis statement.
4. What are the ominously named "by-products"? What is Hodgman's favourite dog food?
5. In paragraphs 16–18, Hodgman shifts from a description of the appearance and flavour of dog food to the significance of the design and wording on dog food packages. Who or what is she SATIRIZING in these paragraphs? What do the packages she describes say about the people who buy these products?

Suggestions for Writing

1. Write an essay about pets: what does the choice of pet tell us about its owner? What kind of person would choose to care for a lizard, for example, or tropical fish, or a poodle, or a mutt?
2. Write an essay the thesis of which is developed by examples of the kinds of subtle promises that commercials or product packaging conveys to consumers. Cosmetics, sports apparel, fitness apparatus, travel brochures, and liquor ads are good places to start.

Canadian Women over Four Centuries

DIANE THOMPSON

1   In the drama of Canada's history, women have generally been credited with minor roles or behind-the-scenes chores. Most historians have concentrated on the hero, showing how the "great man" has always been at centre stage, shaped by his times and yet influencing them; history = biography = history. This historical approach is not so satisfactory with women, for although there were certainly outstanding women in our past, their greatest contributions have been made collectively. In some instances, the women belonged to a formal organization with explicit aims, such

as the Ursuline Order°. In other cases, a number of women worked separately but to a common end, as the writers on early English Canada have added greatly to our understanding of that era. Finally, there were women who fought their individual battles for entry into the various professions; their individual successes eventually combined to effect a change in the nature of Canadian society.

Recently, Canadian historians have turned to writing "social history," which focuses on the daily struggles of ordinary men, women and children. Perhaps now women will receive more attention—and perhaps people will discover that many of these "ordinary women" were in fact quite extraordinary and deserving of acclaim. 2

This neglect of the woman's role has been partially due to the fact that many of the earliest women arriving in Canada, women quite worthy to be called heroic, were associated with religious orders. To become a nun is to become virtually anonymous; one working for the glory of God does not seek recognition from mankind. And so these women, humble and self-effacing, were accepted at their own valuation and remained in history, as they did in the society of early Quebec, in the background. It is surely time to lift the veil. 3

Prominent among these women was Madame de la Peltrie, a wealthy widow who, despite family objections, came to Quebec in 1639. She brought with her Mère Marie de l'Incarnation and two other nuns, and established a branch of the Ursuline Order in New France. Together, these indomitable° women founded a convent for Indian children.... They lived in wretched surroundings, worked to exhaustion and struggled in any spare moments to learn the Indian language. The letters of Mère Marie tell a great deal about these early days. Many of her letters were to wealthy women in France. Although some responded, there was never enough money for the nuns to live at more than a bare subsistence level. 4

But Madame de la Peltrie yearned for even greater hardships than these. She appealed to go into the Huron mission field, perhaps to seek the martyrdom that came to Pères Lalement, Jogues and several others, but the Jesuits refused her services. So Madame de la Peltrie was at Quebec to meet Jeanne Mance when she arrived. This beautiful young woman had been determined from an early age to become a missionary in Canada, and she eagerly joined Maisonneuve's expedition to found a mission at Montreal. The project was strongly opposed by the governor of Quebec, because the site for the new mission was deep in Iroquois territory. However, the small group, containing a handful of women, could not be deterred—nor could Madame de la Peltrie, who was determined to 5 join in this adventure. Despite the governor's forebodings, they arrived safely at Montreal. The women immediately raised an altar and a Mass of thanksgiving was celebrated.

6   A habitation, including a chapel, was built before winter. The next year Jeanne Mance's hospital was built—*outside* the walls of the fort, for lack of space within. It was, of course, vulnerable to attacks, which came often and supplied her with patients.

7   In 1660, despite poor health, Jeanne Mance undertook the oner-ous° trip back to France to seek badly-needed funds. She went to the rich widow who had subsidized her first journey to Quebec, spoke movingly of the needs of the colony and received another substantial donation. She left most of the money to be invested by a French nobleman of her acquaintance, keeping only enough for the most pressing needs at Montreal. She spent some time gathering new recruits, then met with her "banker" just before her ship sailed. When he was questioned about his investment plans, the gentle-man assured her, "My daughter, God will provide for you." In fact, he had applied the money to his own debts and never repaid it.

8   Another of the nuns was Marguerite Bourgeoys, who came to establish the first girls' school in Montreal. All four of these women—Jeanne Mance, Madame de la Peltrie, Mère Marie and Marguerite Bourgeoys—seemed to thrive on hardship and depriva-tion. The "delicate" Jeanne Mance died first, at age 67, and Marguerite Bourgeoys lived to be 80. During her long life she also founded a religious order, The Sisters of the Congregation, and acted as chaperone to the King's Daughters.

9   The King's Daughters—these women played a more traditional role. In pioneering times there is always a shortage of marriageable women, and the gap is filled in various ways. The early fur traders, both French and Scottish, often took Indian wives. The women served the men faithfully, showing them how to live off the land, acting as their translators, bearing their children, but were frequent-ly abandoned. Intendant Jean Talon wanted French brides for the colonists establishing their seigneuries° along the St. Lawrence in the 1660s. The parish priests in France found these brides, who were sent off to the New World in several shiploads, carefully supervised at all times. Many were wards of the state, and all were given the customary dowry by the King when they were married; hence, the name of King's Daughters. Naturally, most of these girls found husbands almost immediately and received their dowry, generally consisting of an ox, a cow, two chickens, two barrels of salt meat, two pigs and eleven crowns. The few girls who went unclaimed usually chose to enter a convent rather than return, humiliated, to their home parish.

Life for those who married may well have been better than   10
what they left behind, but it was far from easy. Buxom, healthy-
looking women were the first to be chosen, for they were expected
to bear numerous children (the first "family allowance" went to
parents who reared ten or more children!) and put in a hard day's
work. A Swedish traveller of about this time wrote that the woman
of New France "has a hard life full of suffering, especially among
the working classes. She is always to be seen in the fields, the
meadows or in the stables, there is no form of work to which she
does not turn her hand." In addition to all this, a woman with any
education was expected to teach both her children and her husband
how to read and write. This situation continued far into the future;
more than a century later, Governor Simcoe's wife noted in her
diary that, "The Canadian Women are better educated than the
Men, who take care of their Horses and attend little to anything
else, leaving the management of their Affairs to the women."

... [T]here were "brideships" in English Canada as well. There   11
was a dearth of women in early British Columbia about the time of
the Gold Rush, and the Columbia Emigration Society of London
came to the rescue. Groups of prospective brides were sent on at
least three ships arriving in Victoria in the 1860s. It appears that
these women too had their pick of suitors—though, regrettably, a
few discovered that the miners would pay handsomely for their
favours, and simply couldn't resist this more lucrative way of life.

We learn something about life in early Quebec from the letters   12
of the Ursulines, but we learn much more about life in Upper
Canada from the books produced by women there. Most of those
who left written records came from the British upper classes and
were quite accustomed to analysing and describing the society in
which they moved. As a result, we find that the first Canadian
novel was written by an Englishwoman, Mrs. Frances Brooke. She
spent five years in Quebec, where her husband was chaplain to the
garrison in the 1760s. *The History of Emily Montague*, published in
1769, is a spirited account of the life and amusements in a garrison-
based society. But the realistic descriptions of life in Upper Canada
are far more valuable for sociological purposes, and at the top of
the list are those by Susanna Moodie and her sister Catherine Parr
Traill.

These women were well-educated, literate, and almost the   13
same age; both came with their husbands to pioneer in Canada in
1832. Here the similarities end. Their personalities could hardly
have been more different: in a word, Catherine was optimistic,
while Susanna was pessimistic. Yet, when one learns of Susanna's
experiences, her attitude is easy to understand. Nothing in her

background nor her husband's had prepared them for life in the backwoods, and they did not make a success of it. Colonel Moodie proved quite incapable of adequately supporting his large family. He was away for long stretches of time, serving in the militia or seeking the position that he considered his due; he was, after all, a "gentleman." Susanna used her pen to supplement the family income and attempt to pay off their debts. She wrote novels that were published in England and short stories for an early Canadian magazine, the *Literary Garland*. This intellectual activity, after a hectic day of housekeeping and farm chores, also helped her to keep a sense of humour in spite of everything. (Incredibly, she could laugh when, their first night in a new cabin, "a countless swarm of mice … scampered over our pillows, and jumped upon our faces, squeaking and cutting a thousand capers over the floor"!)

14   Most of her writing has been long neglected; Susanna Moodie lives for us because of one book, *Roughing It in the Bush*. This was published in England in 1852, after the Moodies had been in Upper Canada for twenty years, but its harsh criticism of Canadian life prevented its publication here until 1871. Critical it certainly was, but it was also a very realistic account of the rigours of pioneering life, a life for which many aspirants° were unsuited. Witness the Moodies themselves. And so Susanna produced this book—which is still very entertaining reading—with a very firm purpose, as expressed in her final paragraph:

> If these sketches should prove the means of deterring one family from sinking their property and shipwrecking all their hopes, by going to reside in the backwoods of Canada, I shall consider myself repaid for revealing the secrets of the prison-house, and feel that I have not toiled and suffered in the wilderness in vain.

15   How different was sister Catherine's attitude! *Her* book was entitled *The Canadian Settler's Guide*, and her aim was not to deter settlers but to assist them to be successful pioneers—as she and her husband were. This very practical book, published in 1854, was useful to both males and females, whose roles often overlapped in pioneering situations. She told them what to bring, how to build a log cabin, gave them recipes for such local delicacies as maple wine and Indian pound cake and remedies for such ailments as ague and dysentery. Catherine was fascinated by all aspects of her new country. A keen naturalist, she studied the unfamiliar plants and produced *Canadian Wild Flowers* (1869) and *Studies of Plant Life in Canada* (1885)....

16   Anna Jameson, wife of the Attorney General of Upper Canada, spent only eight months in Canada, yet she managed to travel to

areas where no [European] women had been before. In 1837, she took a lengthy, rigorous trip by canoe and steamship, making long portages and sleeping on the ground when necessary. In this manner, she travelled the length of Lake Huron and attended an Indian Council on Manitoulin Island. *Winter Studies and Summer Rambles in Canada* contains her perceptive comments on all she viewed and experienced, with particular attention to the role of women. For example, "I have not often in my life met with contented and cheerful-minded women, but I never met with so many repining and discontented women as in Canada. I never met with *one* woman recently settled here, who considered herself happy in her new home and country.... Those born here, or brought here early by their parents or relations, seemed to me very happy, and many of them had adopted a sort of pride in their new country, which I liked much." She herself was determined to be fair to the young country and so, for example, she noted that Toronto was "like a fourth- or fifth-rate provincial town with the pretensions of a capital city," yet hastened to add that she "cannot but see that good spirits and corrective principles are at work; that progress is making."

As a final example, there is Anne Langton, who came out to 17 stay with her brother on his farm near Peterborough. Her journal, also addressed to friends back home, and later published under the title *A Gentlewoman in Upper Canada*, tells of the little school she ran for neighbouring children. She too gives us many homely details of life in the backwoods. On a typical winter's day, the temperature in her bedroom was 29 degrees Fahrenheit below freezing, but when she tried to block off the drafts, her elderly mother chided her, "saying it was ridiculous for people to come to Canada and not be able to bear a breath of air." Although she seldom complained, one of her remarks echoes those made about the women of New France: "I have sometimes thought, and I may as well say it, now that it is grumbling day—woman is a bit of a slave in this country."

Certainly the women of the prairies did not lead an easy life 18 either. There, even more than in eastern Canada, it was difficult to distinguish between "women's work" and "men's work." Women often worked on the farm as well as in the farmhouse, helping out at harvest time and taking full charge during long winter periods when the men were away working in the bush or in the towns. Many women felt that if they bore men's responsibilities, they should have men's rights and privileges as well. Hence the drive for suffrage° and equal rights was spearheaded by western women.

One of the most prominent of these women was Nellie 19 McClung of Winnipeg. She, like many of her fellow suffragettes, was also active in the Women's Christian Temperance Union, believing a world where liquor was banished and women sat in Parliament was bound to be a better place. From 1912 to 1916, the Winnipeg Political Equality Group campaigned vigorously, using such ingenious methods as a theatrical production of a mock sitting of the legislature. Nellie, playing the part of the premier, met a delegation of men seeking "votes for men" from an all-woman parliament. She satirized Sir Rodmond Roblin, the Conservative premier of the time, unmercifully—and effectively. When the Liberals won the next election, in 1916, they passed a bill granting suffrage to women. But Nellie didn't get her vote then; she and her husband had moved to Edmonton, and she was busy organizing the Alberta women. Following Manitoba's lead, most of the other provinces granted the vote to women in the next few years, although Quebec held out until 1940.

20   Most women gained their federal vote almost concurrently with their provincial vote. In the wartime election of 1917, Prime Minister Robert Borden campaigned on the issue of conscription°. Knowing full well that women with close relatives in the armed forces would support his conscription policy, he shrewdly allowed these women to vote. Borden won the election and when the war ended the following year, the franchise was extended to all women.

21   This was a giant step forward for women, but they were still far from their goal of complete political equality. Enter Emily Murphy of Alberta, to take up where Nellie McClung left off. In 1916 Emily was appointed a magistrate, the first woman in the entire British Empire to hold such a position. A lawyer appearing before her challenged her qualifications on the grounds that a woman is not legally a "person" under the BNA Act°. The Alberta Supreme Court ruled that she was eligible to hold her position, but that was only the beginning of a long-drawn-out issue known as the Persons Case.

22   Women across Canada were urging the appointment of a woman to the Senate, and in 1921, the Montreal Women's Club specifically requested that Emily Murphy be named a Senator. Prime Minister Borden and his successor Arthur Meighen both refused, on the now-familiar grounds that a woman was not a "person" within the meaning of the BNA Act and only "persons" could be appointed to the Senate. When the Liberal Prime Minister Mackenzie King responded the same way, Emily Murphy tried a new approach.

23   There is a provision of the Supreme Court Act that allows a group of citizens to seek an interpretation on a constitutional point. Emily was joined by four other prominent western women (Nellie McClung, Henrietta Muir Edwards, Irene Parlby and Louise McKinney) and the group was henceforth known as "the Alberta Five." Their petition

was presented in 1927, and the case was argued in the Supreme Court of Canada the following year. All provinces were invited to send lawyers, but only two did; Alberta argued on behalf of the women's case, Quebec opposed it. The decision was that women were not qualified to enter the Senate; that in fact, according to the constitution, women were not persons. The female reaction can be summed up by a quotation from a contemporary newspaper article: "The iron dropped into the souls of women in Canada when we heard that it took a man to decree that his mother was not a person."

The Alberta Five were not finished yet. They petitioned that the   24 case be taken to the Privy Council in London (at that time the highest court of appeal). In 1929 the case was argued there, Quebec withdrew its opposition, and the decision of the Canadian Supreme Court was reversed. The judgement stated that, "Their lordships have come to the conclusion that the word persons includes members of the male and female sex ... and that women are eligible to become members of the Senate of Canada." Emily Murphy had won the *right* to enter the Senate, but she was never summoned....

Nor did entry into the professions come easily. Women have tra-   25 ditionally been the custodians° of culture and learning, responsible for training and educating children. It was a logical step for women, who were expected to teach their own children at home, to become teachers in state or private schools. It was, of course, only unmarried women who taught for a living; once married, a woman's place could only be in the home. A teacher's pay was low—another reason why the job so often went to a woman—and she was usually expected to board with a local family and always to be a perfect model of decorum° and respectability. These women had a minimum of formal training, at most a term in a Normal School, for women were long denied the right to enter university. It was 1875 before a woman received a degree from a Canadian university. Grace Anne Lockhart earned a Bachelor of Science degree from Mount Allison University in Sackville, N.B., and that university also awarded the first Arts degree to a woman, Harriet Stewart, in 1882.

Medical schools held out even longer. Emily Stowe, unable to   26 train as a doctor in Canada, went to study in New York. She obtained her degree in 1867, and returned to set up practice in Toronto. Again she was thwarted; new regulations required American graduates to attend a series of lectures in an Ontario medical school, and none of them would accept her. She practised illegally, despite being fined, until she was finally allowed to attend lectures at the Toronto School of Medicine. Her daughter, Augusta, equally determined, succeeded in becoming the first woman graduate from a Canadian medical school and went on to post-graduate work and a distinguished career.

27   Another formidable combination consisted of the MacGill mother and daughter. Mother Helen received the first Bachelor of Music degree given to a Canadian woman and went on to gain the first Bachelor of Arts given to a female graduate of Trinity College. Later, she worked as a journalist in the United States, where news-paperwomen were more readily accepted. She developed a strong concern for prison reform which stayed with her on her return to Canada. In 1917 she became a Judge of the Juvenile Court in Vancouver. Her biography, *My Mother, the Judge*, was written by her daughter Elsie, who was the first woman graduate in Engineering at the University of Toronto....

28   The reasons for barring women from these fields usually stressed the need to "protect" women from the seamier° aspects of life. Nor could they be expected to withstand pressures, long hours and hard work that men had to endure. These arguments were thrust aside during World War I, when there was a severe shortage of male labour. Women were quickly pressed into ser-vice, not just in the professions, but in jobs which would never have been thought of only a few years before. They served over-seas as ambulance drivers, and at home drove streetcars, acted as crew on tugboats and fishing boats, worked in banks, offices and stores, and as "farmerettes," helping to bring in the prairie wheat harvest. Above all, they worked in munitions factories, 35,000 women in Quebec and Ontario alone. In the widespread unem-ployment that followed the war, most women returned home willingly, but turned out again during the Second World War. By 1943, one-third of the labour force was women and they welded 6500 tanks and assembled 244,000 machineguns. Once again, women thankfully left these arduous jobs when peace came, but they had certainly proved their strength, endurance and resilience.

29   After the war, many women retreated to the life in suburbia so amply documented in recent literature. Others, however, continued to work, though in the more traditional jobs, and each census revealed that a higher proportion of the labour force was female. With the increasing momentum of the Women's Movement in the late '60s and the '70s, women turned at last to the world of business and finance.

30   Yet here too acceptance comes slowly. As late as 1976, Earle McLaughlin, then chairman of the Royal Bank, told a reporter that it was impossible to find a woman qualified to sit on the bank's Board of Directors. When the storm of indignation subsided, it was

seen that this bank and the other four major banks had each hastily discovered at least one suitable woman. Even so, by 1979 women made up 30% of the work force, but still constituted less than 1% of directors and company officers....

From the Ursulines to the Women's [Christian Temperance   31 Union to the Alberta Five, women have traditionally worked] together in groups. Yet, to concentrate exclusively on these collective contributions is to ignore the outstanding individuals, the "great women" of our past. There have been women of exceptional courage, such heroines as Laura Secord, Madame de La Tour and Madeleine de Verchères. There have been distinguished writers, artists and athletes. It seems almost unfair to write a paper on Canadian women without including Emily Carr, Pauline Johnson and L.M. Montgomery. These women have, however, received a certain amount of attention over the years: they will surely not object now to standing in the shadows while the light shines on their lesser-known compatriots°.

DIANE THOMPSON

A native of New Brunswick, Diane Thompson (1941–83) began teaching English and humanities in 1974 at Vancouver Community College, where she also served as department head. In addition, Ms. Thompson worked with CUSO, teaching in Trinidad and Tanzania, and co-edited *Canadian Viewpoints: An Anthology of Canadian Writing.*

Words and Meanings

Paragraph

Ursuline Order	Roman Catholic religious order for women, named for its patron, St. Ursula, active in missionary work in early Canada	1
indomitable	strong, resourceful, determined	4
onerous	difficult, burdensome, hard to bear	7
seigneuries	originally referred to lands granted to colonists by the King of France and later came to mean the power and authority of the *seigneurs* (landowners)	9
aspirants	persons who try something in the hope of success	14
suffrage	the right to vote	18
conscription	compulsory military service	20

21	the BNA Act	the British North America Act, which provided for the federation of Canada in 1867; repatriated in 1982 under the name Constitution Act
25	custodians	promoters and guardians
	decorum	etiquette, good manners
28	seamier	unpleasant
31	compatriots	fellow citizens

Structure and Strategy

1. With what metaphor (see FIGURES OF SPEECH) does Thompson introduce this essay? Where does she extend this metaphor? How does it contribute to the UNITY of the piece?
2. Identify the thesis statement in paragraph 1. How does it set up the essay as a whole?
3. Consider Thompson's use of TRANSITIONS in paragraphs 1, 2, and 8. How do they contribute to COHERENCE?
4. Which paragraphs focus on the examples of the collective contributions of women who "belonged to a formal organization with explicit aims" (paragraph 1)?
5. On what pattern of development is paragraph 13 based? Paragraph 16?
6. How many examples of writers does Thompson use to develop her second major point (paragraphs 12 to 17)? How many examples of individual efforts by women who were active in politics (paragraphs 18 to 24)? Do you think Thompson's examples satisfy the three "safety rules" outlined on pages 77 to 78?
7. Which paragraphs develop the third main point of the essay, "women who fought their individual battles for entry into the various professions" (paragraph 1)?
8. What concluding strategy does Thompson employ (paragraph 31)? Is it effective?

Content and Purpose

1. According to the author, why have men played such prominent roles in history while little or no attention has been paid to the contributions made by women? (See paragraphs 1 to 3, 10, and 28.) Does the author feel that this imbalance is changing? Why?
2. Who were Madame de la Peltrie, Mère Marie, Jeanne Mance, and Marguerite Bourgeoys? What did they contribute to early Canada? What seemed to motivate them?
3. Who were the King's Daughters? How did they get their name? What did they contribute to Lower Canada?

4. Summarize the differences between the writings of early Upper Canada immigrant sisters Susanna Moodie and Catherine Parr Traill (paragraphs 13 to 15).
5. What was Anna Jameson's view of immigrant versus native-born women in the colony of Upper Canada? Do you think this contrast in attitude still holds true today?
6. From which regions of Canada does Thompson draw her examples? Why?
7. Summarize the events that led to women's obtaining the right to vote (suffrage) in 1918.
8. What were the implications of the celebrated "Persons Case"? Where was the matter decided? Why?
9. What were the reasons usually given for barring women from professions such as medicine and law (paragraph 28)? What historical events revealed the silliness of these rationalizations?

Suggestions for Writing

1. Do some research into the life of one of the women discussed in this essay. Write an essay that provides more details of the path her life took and the obstacles she faced. Use this person's life as an example of the kind of contribution our society needs if it is to develop and grow.
2. Write an essay of example based on two women not mentioned in this essay who have accomplished something significant for women or for our society generally.

The End of the Wild

WADE DAVIS

ome time ago at a symposium° in 1 Barbados, I was fortunate to share the podium with two extraordinary scientists. The first to speak was Richard Leakey, the renowned anthropologist who with his mother and father drew from the dust and ashes of Africa the story of the birth of our species. The meeting concluded with astronaut Story Musgrave, the first physician to walk in space. It was an odd and moving juxtaposition of the end-points of the human experience. Dr. Musgrave recognized the irony and it saddened him. He told of what it had been like to know the beauty of the earth as seen from the heavens. There he was, suspended 200 miles above the earth, travelling 18,000 miles per hour with the golden visor of his helmet illuminated by a single sight, a small and fragile blue planet enveloped in a veil of clouds, floating, as he recalled, "in the velvet void of space." To have experienced that vision, he said, a sight made possible only by the brilliance of human technology, and to remember the blindness with which we as a species abuse our only home, was to know the purest sensation of horror.

2   Many believe that this image of the Earth, first brought home to us but a generation ago, will have a more profound impact on human thought than did the Copernican revolution of the 16th century, which transformed the philosophical foundations of the western world by revealing that the planet was not the center of the universe. From space, we see not a limitless frontier nor the stunning products of man, but a single interactive sphere of life, a living organism composed of air, water, and earth. It is this transcendent vision which, more than any amount of scientific data, teaches us the Earth is a finite place that can endure our foolish ways for only so long.

3   In light of this new perspective, this new hope, the past and present deeds of human beings often appear inconceivably cruel and sordid. Shortly after leaving Barbados, while lecturing in the midwest of the United States, I visited two places that in a different, more sensitive world would surely be enshrined as memorials to the victims of the ecological catastrophes that occurred there. The first locality was the site of the last great nesting flock of passenger pigeons, a small stretch of woodland on the banks of the Green River near Mammoth Cave, Ohio. This story of extinction is well known. Yet until I stood in that cold, dark forest, I had never sensed the full weight of the disaster, the scale and horror of it.

4   At one time passenger pigeons accounted for 40% of the entire bird population of North America. In 1870, at a time when their numbers were already greatly diminished, a single flock a mile wide and 320 miles long containing an estimated 2 billion birds passed over Cincinnati on the Ohio River. Imagine such a sight. Assuming that each bird ate half a pint of seeds a day, a flock that size must have consumed each day over 17 million bushels of grain. Such sightings were not unusual. In 1813, James Audubon° was travelling in a wagon from his home on the Ohio River to Louisville, some sixty miles away, when a flock of passenger pigeons filled the sky so that the "light of noonday sun was obscured as by an eclipse." He reached Louisville at sunset and the

birds still came. He estimated that the flock contained over 1 billion birds, and it was but one of several columns of pigeons that blackened the sky that day.

Audubon visited roosting and nesting sites to find trees two feet in diameter broken off at the ground by the weight of birds. He found dung so deep on the forest floor that he mistook it for snow. He once stood in the midst of a flock when the birds took flight and then landed. He compared the noise and confusion to that of a gale, the sound of their landing to thunder.   5

It is difficult now to imagine the ravages of man that over the course of half a century destroyed this creature. Throughout the 19th century, pigeon meat was a mainstay of the American diet and merchants in the eastern cities sold as many as 18,000 birds a day. Pigeon hunting was a full time job for thousands of men. The term "stool pigeon" derives from a standard killing technique of the era. A hunter would sew shut the eyes of a living bird, bind its feet to a pole driven into the ground, and wait in the surrounding grass for the flocks to respond to its cry. When the birds came, they arrived in such numbers that the hunter could simply bat them out of the air with a club. The more affluent classes slaughtered birds for recreation. It was not unusual for shooting clubs to go through 50,000 birds in a weekend competition; hundreds of thousands of live birds were catapulted to their death before the diminishing supply forced skeet shooters to turn to clay pigeons.   6

By 1896, a mere 50 years after the first serious impact of man, there were only some 250,000 birds left. In April of that year, the birds came together for one last nesting flock in the forest outside of Bowling Green, Ohio. The telegraph wires hummed with the news and the hunters converged. In a final orgy of slaughter over 200,000 pigeons were killed, 40,000 mutilated, 100,000 chicks destroyed. A mere 5,000 birds survived. The entire kill was to be shipped east but there was a derailment on the line and the dead birds rotted in their crates. On March 24, 1900 the last passenger pigeon in the wild was shot by a young boy. On September 1, 1914, as the Battle of the Marne consumed the flower of European youth, the last passenger pigeon died in captivity.   7

When I left the scene of this final and impossible slaughter, I travelled west to Sioux City, Iowa to speak at Buena Vista College. There I was fortunate to visit a remnant patch of tall grass prairie, a 180-acre preserve that represents one of the largest remaining vestiges of an ecosystem that once carpeted North America from southern Canada to Texas. Again it was winter, and the cold wind blew through the coneflowers and the dozens of species of grass. The young biology student who was with me was familiar with   8 every species in that extraordinary mosaic—they were like old friends to him. Yet as we walked through that tired field my thoughts drifted from the plants to the horizon. I tried to imagine buffalo moving through the grass, the physics of waves as millions of animals crossed that prairie.

9   As late as 1871 buffalo outnumbered people in North America. In that year one could stand on a bluff in the Dakotas and see nothing but buffalo in every direction for thirty miles. Herds were so large that it took days for them to pass a single point. Wyatt Earp described one herd of a million animals stretched across a grazing area the size of Rhode Island. Within nine years of that sighting, buffalo had vanished from the Plains.

10   The destruction of the buffalo resulted from a campaign of biological terrorism unparalleled in the history of the Americas. U.S. government policy was explicit. As General Philip Sheridan wrote at the time, "The buffalo hunters have done in the past two years more to settle the vexed Indian Question than the regular army has accomplished in the last 30 years. They are destroying the Indians' commissary°. Send them powder and lead, and let them kill until they have exterminated the buffalo." Between 1850 and 1880 more than 75 million hides were sold to American dealers. No one knows how many more animals were slaughtered and left on the prairie. A decade after native resistance had collapsed, Sheridan advised Congress to mint a commemorative medal, with a dead buffalo on one side, a dead Indian on the other.

11   I thought of this history as I stood in that tall grass prairie near Sioux City. What disturbed me the most was to realize how effortlessly we have removed ourselves from this ecological tragedy. Today the people of Iowa, good and decent folk, live contentedly in a landscape of cornfields that is claustrophobic in its monotony. For them the time of the tall grass prairie, like the time of the buffalo, is as distant from their immediate lives as the fall of Rome or the battle of Troy. Yet the destruction occurred but a century ago, well within the lifetime of their grandfathers.

12   This capacity to forget, this fluidity of memory, is a frightening human trait. Several years ago I spent many months in Haiti, a country that as recently as the 1920s was 80% forested. Today less than 5% of the forest cover remains. I remember standing with a Vodoun priest on a barren ridge, peering across a wasteland, a desolate valley of scrub and half-hearted trees. He waxed eloquent as if words alone might have squeezed beauty from that wretched sight. He could only think of angels, I of locusts. It was amazing. Though witness to an ecological holocaust that within this century had devastated his entire country, this man had managed to endure without

losing his human dignity. Faced with nothing, he adorned his life with his imagination. This was inspiring but also terrifying. People appear to be able to tolerate and adapt to almost any degree of environmental degradation. As the farmers of Iowa today live without wild things, the people of Haiti scratch a living from soil that will never again know the comfort of shade.

From a distance, both in time and space, we can perceive these   13
terrible and poignant events as what they were—unmitigated ecological disasters that robbed the future of something unimaginably precious in order to satisfy the immediate and often mundane needs of the present. The luxury of hindsight, however, does nothing to cure the blindness with which today we overlook deeds of equal magnitude and folly.

As a younger man in Canada I spent a long winter in a logging   14
camp on the west coast of Haida Gwaii, or the Queen Charlotte Islands as they were then commonly known. It was a good life and it put me through school. I was a surveyor, which meant that I spent all of my time far ahead of the loggers in the dense uncut forest, laying out the roads and the falling boundaries, determining the pattern in which the trees would come down. At the time I had already spent more than a year in the Amazon and I can tell you that those distant forests, however immense and mysterious, are dwarfed by the scale and wonder of the ancient temperate rainforests of British Columbia. In the valleys and around the lakes, and along the shore of the inlet where the soil was rich and deep, we walked through red cedar and sitka spruce, some as tall as a 25 storey building, many with over 70 million needles capturing the light of the sun. Miracles of biological engineering, their trunks stored thousands of gallons of water and could be twenty feet or more across at the base. Many of them had been standing in the forest for more than a thousand years, the anchors of an extraordinarily complex ecosystem° of mountains and rain, salmon and eagles, of squirrels that fly, fungi that crawl, and creatures that live on dew and never touch the forest floor. It is a world that is far older, far richer in its capacity to produce the raw material of life, and far more endangered than almost any region of the Amazon.

To walk through these forests in the depths of winter, when the   15
rain turns to mist and settles softly on the moss, is to step back in time. Two hundred million years ago vast coniferous° forests formed a mantle across the entire world. Then evolution took a great leap and the flowers were born. The difference between the two groups of plants involves a mechanism of pollination and fertilization that changed the course of life on earth. In the case of the more primitive conifers, the plant must produce the basic food for

the seed with no certainty that it will be fertilized. In the flowering plants, by contrast, fertilization itself sparks the creation of the seed's food reserves. In other words, unlike the conifers, the flowering plants make no investment without the assurance that a viable seed will be produced. As a result of this and other evolutionary advances, the flowering plants came to dominate the earth in an astonishingly short period of time. Most conifers went extinct and those that survived retreated to the margins of the world, where a small number of species managed to maintain a foothold by adapting to particularly harsh conditions. Today, at a conservative estimate, there are over 250,000 species of flowering plants. The conifers have been reduced to a mere 700 species and in the tropics, the hotbed of evolution, they have been almost completely displaced.

16   On all the earth, there is only one region of any size and significance where, because of unique climatic conditions, the conifers retain their former glory. Along the northwest coast of North America the summers are hot and dry, the winters cold and wet. Plants need water and light to create food. Here in the summer there is ample light for photosynthesis, but not enough water. In the winter, when both water and light are sufficient, the low temperatures cause the flowering plants to lose their leaves and become dormant. The evergreen conifers, by contrast, are able to grow throughout the long winters and since they use water more efficiently than broad leafed plants, they also thrive during the dry summer months. The result is an ecosystem so rich, so productive, that the biomass° in the best sites is easily four times as great as that of any comparable area of the tropics.

17   Inevitably there was, at least for me, an almost surrealistic quality to life in our remote camp where men lived away from their families and made a living cutting down in minutes trees that had taken a thousand years to grow. The constant grinding of machinery, the disintegration of the forest into burnt slash and mud, the wind and sleet that froze on the rigging and whipped across the frozen bay, etched patterns into the lives of the men. Still, no one in our camp had any illusions about what we were doing. All the talk of sustained yield and overmature timber, decadent and normal forests we left to the government bureaucrats and the company PR hacks. We used to laugh at the little yellow signs stuck on the sides of roads that only we would ever travel, that announced that twenty acres had been replanted, as if it mattered in a clearcut that stretched to the horizon....

18   Everyone knew, of course, that the ancient forests would never come back. One of my mates used to say that the tangle of half-hearted trees that grew up in the slash no more resembled the forest

he'd cut down, than an Alberta wheatfield resembled a wild prairie meadow. But nobody was worried about what they were doing. It was work, and living on the edge of that immense forest, they simply believed that it would go on forever.

If anyone in the government had a broader perspective, we never heard about it. Our camp was nineteen miles by water across an inlet from a backroad that ran forty miles to the nearest forestry office. The government had cut back on overtime pay, and, what with the statutory coffee and lunch breaks, the forestry fellows couldn't figure out how to get to our camp and back in less than seven and a half hours. So they didn't try. The bureaucracy within the company wasn't much better. The mills down south kept complaining that our camp was sending them inferior grades of Douglas fir, which was surprising since the species doesn't grow on the Charlottes.

There were, of course, vague murmurs of ecological concern that filtered through to our camp. One morning in the cookhouse I ran into a friend of mine, a rock blaster named Archie whose voice had been dusted by ten thousand cigarettes and the dirt from a dozen mine failures. Archie was in a particularly cantankerous mood. Clutching a donut he'd been marinating in caffeine, he flung a three day old newspaper onto the table. The headline said something about Greenpeace.

"Fucking assholes," he critiqued.

"What's wrong, Arch?" I asked.

"Sons of bitches don't know a damn thing about pollution," he said. Archie then proceeded to tell me about working conditions in the hard rock uranium mines of the Northwest Territories shortly after the Second World War. The companies, concerned about the impact of radioactivity, used to put the workers, including Archie, into large sealed chambers and release a gas with suspended particles of aluminum in it. The idea being that the aluminum would coat the lungs and, at the end of the shift, the men would gag it up, together with any radioactive dust.

"Now that," growled Archie, "was environmental pollution."

In truth, it is difficult to know how much the forest destruction actually affected the men. Some clearly believed blindly in the process and were hardened by that faith. Others were so transient, moving from camp to camp, sometimes on a monthly basis, that they never registered the full measure of the impact of any one logging show. Some just didn't care. The entire industry was so itinerant° than no one ever developed a sense of belonging to a place. There was no attachment to the land, nor could there be given what we were doing. In the slash° of the clearcuts, there was little room for sentiment.

26   I knew of a veteran faller who, having cut down thousands of trees, finally came upon one giant cedar that was simply too magnificent to be felled. When he refused to bring it down, the bullbucker° threatened to fire him. The faller felt he had no choice. He brought it down and then, realizing what he had done, he sat on the stump and began to weep. He quit that afternoon and never cut another tree.

27   Like everyone else in our camp, I was there to make money. On weekends, when our survey crew was down, I picked up overtime pay by working in the slash as a chokerman°, wrapping the cables around the fallen logs so the yarders° could drag them to the landings° where they were loaded onto the trucks. Setting beads° is the most miserable job in a logging show, the bottom rung of the camp hierarchy.

28   One Saturday I was working in a setting high up on the mountain that rose above the camp. It had been raining all day and the winds were blowing from the southeast, dragging clouds across the bay and up the slope, where they hung up in the tops of giant hemlocks and cedars that rose above the clearcut. We were working the edge of the opening, but the landing was unusually close by. It took no time at all for the mainline to drag the logs in, and for the haulback° to fling the chokers° back to us. We'd been highballing° all day and both my partner and I were a mess of mud, grease and tree sap. He was a native boy, a Nisga'a from New Aiyansh on the Nass River, but that's all I knew about him.

29   Late in the afternoon, something got fouled up on the landing, and the yarder shut down. Suddenly it was quiet and you could hear the wind that had been driving the sleet into our faces all day. My partner and I abandoned the slash for the shelter of the forest. We found a dry spot out of the wind in a hollow at the base of an enormous cedar and waited for the yarder to start up. We didn't speak. He kept staring off into the forest. All hunched up with the cold, we looked the same—orange hardhats, green-black rain gear, rubber corkboots. We shared a cigarette. I was watching his face as he smoked. It struck me as strange that here we were, huddled in the forest in silence, two young men from totally different worlds. I tried to imagine what it might have been like had we met but a century before, I perhaps a trader, he a shadow in the wet woods. His people had made a home in the forest for thousands of years. I thought of what this country must have been like when my own grandfather arrived. I saw in the forest around us a world that my own children might never know, that Nisga'a children would never know. I turned to my partner. The whistle blew on the landing.

30   "What the hell are we doing?" I asked.

31   "Working," he said. I watched him as he stepped back into the clearcut, and then I followed. We finished the shift and, in the

falling darkness, rode back to camp together in the back of the company crummy. That was the last I saw of him.

Fifteen years have passed since I left that camp and I've often wondered what became of the Nisga'a boy. It's a good bet he's no longer working as a logger. Natives rarely get promoted beyond the landing and, what's more, over the last decade a third of all logging jobs have been lost. The industry keeps saying that environmentalists are to blame, but in reality all the conservation initiatives of the last ten years in B.C. have not cost the union more than a few hundred jobs, if that. Automation and dwindling timber supplies have put almost 20,000 people out of work in this province alone. And still we keep cutting. In Oregon, Washington and California only 10% of the original coastal rainforest remains. In British Columbia roughly 60% has been logged, largely since 1950. In the mere 15 years since I stood in the forest with that Nisga'a boy, over half of all timber ever extracted from the public forests of British Columbia has been taken. At current rates of harvest, the next 20 years will see the destruction of every valley of ancient rainforest in the province.

We are living in the midst of an ecological catastrophe every bit as tragic as that of the slaughter of the buffalo and the passenger pigeon. Our government policies are equally blind, our economic rationales equally compelling. Until just recently, forestry policy in British Columbia explicitly called for the complete eradication of the old growth forests. The rotation cycle, the rate at which the forests were to be cut across the province, and thus the foundation of sustained yield forestry, was based on the assumption that all of these forests would be eliminated and replaced with tree farms. In other words, consideration of the intrinsic value of these ancient rainforests had no place in the calculus of forestry planning. Like the buffalo and the passenger pigeon, these magnificent forests were considered expendable°.

But while the passenger pigeons are extinct, and the buffalo reduced to a curiosity, these forests still stand. They are as rare and spectacular as any natural feature on the face of the earth, as biologically significant as any terrestrial ecosystem that has ever existed. If, knowing this, we still allow them to fall, what will it say about us as a people? What will be the legacy of our times?

The truth is, in an increasingly complex and fragmented world we need these ancient forests, alive and intact. For the children of the Nisga'a they are an image of the dawn of time, a memory of an era when raven emerged from the shadow of the cedar and young boys went in search of spirits at the north end of the world. For my own two young girls these forests echo with a shallow history, but one that is nevertheless rich in the struggles of their great grandparents, men and women who travelled halfway around the world to live in this place. Today all peoples in this land are drawn together by a single thread of destiny. We live at the edge of the clearcut, our hands will determine the fate of these forests. If we do nothing, they will be lost within our lifetimes and we will be left to explain our inaction. If we preserve these ancient forests they will stand apart for all generations and for all time as symbols of the geography of hope.

WADE DAVIS

A native of British Columbia, Wade Davis has worked as a logger, park ranger, forestry engineer, researcher, writer, and environmental activist. He is an anthropologist, biologist, plant explorer, and photographer whose books include *Passage of Darkness, The Serpent and the Rainbow,* and *Shadows in the Sun.* He is also host and co-writer of "Earthguide," a television series on the environment.

Paragraph	**Words and Meanings**	
1	symposium	academic conference
4	Audubon	Haitian-born U.S. scientist and artist who painted all the species of birds known in the United States in the early nineteenth century
10	commissary	food supply
14	ecosystem	interdependent network of all living things
15	coniferous	evergreens that reproduce by cones, not seeds
16	biomass	weight (density) of all living things in a given area
25	itinerant	travelling from place to place
25 to 28		The terms in these paragraphs are loggers' jargon to describe the act of getting trees out of the bush (slash). The foreman (bullbucker) supervises the workers who hook the logs onto a cable (choker) that is operated by machine (yarder). Once the logs reach the "landing," the site from which they are loaded onto trucks, another line (the haulback) returns the empty chokers (or beads) to the site to be re-set. Performing these activities at top speed to ensure maximum production is "highballing."

expendable   something we can use up for short-term gain   33
                              without serious consequences

Structure and Strategy

1. Davis introduces his essay with examples of two scientists who spoke, along with the author, at an international conference. Why did he choose to begin with Leakey and Musgrave? What is the "odd and moving juxtaposition" these two men represent?
2. What is the THESIS of this essay? Which sentence in paragraph 3 most clearly expresses it?
3. Which paragraphs detail the extinction of the passenger pigeon? Which deal with the decimation of the plains buffalo herds? What is the third ILLUSTRATION of Davis's point? In what ORDER has he arranged these three main sections of his essay?
4. Identify vivid descriptive details in paragraphs 5, 14, and 17. What is the purpose of the ANECDOTE in paragraph 26?
5. Identify the TOPIC SENTENCES in paragraphs 6, 10, 12, and 16; then determine what kind of support the author uses to develop his topic in each of these paragraphs.
6. How is the topic of paragraph 7 developed? Find another paragraph in the essay that uses the same kind of support to develop the topic. What effect do these paragraphs have on the reader?
7. What is the TONE of paragraph 19? How does the tone contribute to your understanding of the author's opinion of the government?
8. Why does Davis elaborate his third point in such detail, including dialogue and characterization?
9. Besides EXPOSITION, what other rhetorical mode does Davis employ in "The End of the Wild"?
10. Who is the audience for this piece? What is its overall TONE?

Content and Purpose

1. According to the essay, what does the earth look like from space? (See paragraph 2.) What IRONY is explored in paragraphs 2 and 3? What, according to Davis, should we have learned from the image of earth as seen by space travellers?
2. What was the passenger pigeon population in North America in 1870? What happened to them? How? Why?
3. What is a "stool pigeon" (paragraph 6)? What is the meaning of the idiom today?
4. What has North America lost along with the buffalo? (See paragraphs 8, 10, and 11). How do these paragraphs reinforce Davis's thesis?

5. Explain in your own words the political purpose of the U.S. government in promoting the slaughter of the buffalo that makes this "biological terrorism" (paragraph 10) so horrific.
6. Why, according to Davis, are the rainforests of British Columbia even more remarkable and more endangered than those of the Amazon? (See paragraphs 14 to 16.)
7. What, according to the essay, are the attitudes of the loggers, the logging companies, the government, and the Native peoples to clearcutting the rainforest?
8. Why do you think Davis includes the narrative involving "a rock blaster named Archie" (paragraph 20) and "a native boy, a Nisga'a from New Aiyansh" (paragraph 28)? What effect do these narratives have on the reader?
9. Summarize what has happened in the fifteen years since the author worked in the logging industry (see paragraph 32).
10. How does Davis unify his essay in the CONCLUSION (paragraphs 33 to 35)? How does he connect his three examples? Why does he want to preserve the rainforests?

Suggestion for Writing

Using an example from the natural environment (avoid pigeons, buffaloes, and rainforests), write an essay illustrating the interdependence of humanity and the rest of the ecosystem. What, for example, has happened to the groundfish stocks in the North Atlantic? What has caused the depletion and how has it affected the people of Atlantic Canada?

Lost in Translation

EVA HOFFMAN

1   Every day I learn new words, new expressions. I pick them up from school exercises, from conversations, from the books I take out of Vancouver's well-lit, cheerful public library. There are some turns of phrase to which I develop strange allergies. "You're welcome," for example, strikes me as a gaucherie°, and I can hardly bring myself to say it—I suppose because it implies that there's something to be thanked for, which

in Polish would be impolite. The very places where the language is at its most conventional, where it should be most taken for granted, are the places where I feel the prick of artifice°.

Then there are words to which I take an equally irrational lik- 2 ing, for their sound, or just because I'm pleased to have deduced their meaning. Mainly they're words I learn from books, like "enig-matic" or "insolent"—words that have only a literary value, that exist only as signs on the page.

But mostly, the problem is that the signifier has become severed 3 from the signified. The words I learn now don't stand for things in the same unquestioned way they did in my native tongue. "River" in Polish was a vital sound, energized with the essence of river-hood, of my rivers, of my being immersed in rivers. "River" in English is cold—a word without an aura. It has no accumulated associations for me, and it does not give off the radiating haze of connotation°. It does not evoke°.

The process, alas, works in reverse as well. When I see a river 4 now, it is not shaped, assimilated by the word that accommodates it to the psyche—a word that makes a body of water a river rather than an uncontained element. The river before me remains a thing, absolutely other, absolutely unbending to the grasp of my mind.

When my friend Penny tells me that she's envious, or happy, or 5 disappointed, I try laboriously to translate not from English to Polish but from the word back to its source, to the feeling from which it springs. Already, in that moment of strain, spontaneity° of response is lost. And anyway, the translation doesn't work. I don't know how Penny feels when she talks about envy. The word hangs in a Platonic° stratosphere, a vague prototype° of all envy, so large, so all-encompassing that it might crush me—as might disappoint-ment or happiness.

I am becoming a living avatar° of structuralist° wisdom; I can- 6 not help knowing that words are just themselves. But it's a terrible knowledge, without any of the consolations that wisdom usually brings. It does not mean that I'm free to play with words at my wont°; anyway, words in their naked state are surely among the least satisfactory play objects. No, this radical disjoining between word and thing is a desiccating° alchemy°, draining the world not only of significance but of its colors, striations, nuances—its very existence. It is the loss of a living connection.

The worst losses come at night. As I lie down in a strange bed in a 7 strange house—my mother is a sort of housekeeper here, to the aging Jewish man who has taken us in return for her services—I wait for that spontaneous flow of inner language which used to be

my nighttime talk with myself, my way of informing the ego°
where the id° had been. Nothing comes. Polish, in a short time, has
atrophied, shriveled from sheer uselessness. Its words don't apply
to my new experiences; they're not coeval° with any of the objects,
or faces, or the very air I breathe in the daytime. In English, words
have not penetrated to those layers of my psyche from which a private conversation could proceed. This interval before sleep used to
be the time when my mind became both receptive and alert, when
images and words rose up to consciousness, reiterating what had
happened during the day, adding the day's experiences to those
already stored there, spinning out the thread of my personal story.

8   Now, this picture-and-word show is gone; the thread has been
snapped. I have no interior language, and without it, interior
images—those images through which we assimilate the external
world, through which we take it in, love it, make it our own—
become blurred too. My mother and I met a Canadian family who
live down the block today. They were working in their garden and
engaged us in a conversation of the "Nice weather we're having,
isn't it?" variety, which culminated in their inviting us into their
house. They sat stiffly on their couch, smiled in the long pauses
between the conversation, and seemed at a loss for what to ask.
Now my mind gropes for some description of them, but nothing
fits. They're a different species from anyone I've met in Poland, and
Polish words slip off them without sticking. English words don't
hook on to anything. I try, deliberately, to come up with a few. Are
these people pleasant or dull? Kindly or silly? The words float in an
uncertain space. They come up from a part of my brain in which
labels may be manufactured but which has no connection to my
instincts, quick reactions, knowledge. Even the simplest adjectives
sow confusion in my mind; English kindliness has a whole system
of morality behind it, a system that makes "kindness" an entirely
positive virtue. Polish kindness has the tiniest element of irony.
Besides, I'm beginning to feel the tug of prohibition, in English,
against uncharitable words. In Polish, you can call someone an idiot
without particularly harsh feelings and with the zest of a strong
judgment. Yes, in Polish these people might tend toward "silly" and
"dull"—but I force myself toward "kindly" and "pleasant." The cultural unconscious is beginning to exercise its subliminal° influence.

9   The verbal blur covers these people's faces, their gestures with a
sort of fog. I can't translate them into my mind's eye. The small event,
instead of being added to the mosaic of consciousness and memory,
falls through some black hole, and I fall with it. What has happened
to me in this new world? I don't know. I don't see what I've seen,
don't comprehend what's in front of me. I'm not filled with language

anymore, and I have only a memory of fullness to anguish me with the knowledge that, in this dark and empty state, I don't really exist....

My voice is doing funny things. It does not seem to emerge from the same parts of my body as before. It comes out from somewhere in my throat, tight, thin, and mat—a voice without the modulations, dips, and rises that it had before, when it went from my stomach all the way through my head. There is, of course, the constraint and the self-consciousness of an accent that I hear but cannot control. Some of my high school peers accuse me of putting it on in order to appear more "interesting." In fact, I'd do anything to get rid of it, and when I'm alone, I practice sounds for which my speech organs have no intuitions, such as "th" (I do this by putting my tongue between my teeth) and "a," which is longer and more open in Polish (by shaping my mouth into a sort of arrested grin). It is simple words like "cat" or "tap" that give me the most trouble, because they have no context of other syllables, and so people often misunderstand them. Whenever I can, I do awkward little swerves to avoid them, or pause and try to say them very clearly. Still, when people—like salesladies—hear me speak without being prepared to listen carefully, they often don't understand me the first time around. "Girls' shoes," I say, and the "girls" comes out as a sort of scramble. "Girls' shoes," I repeat, willing the syllable to form itself properly, and the saleslady usually smiles nicely, and sends my mother and me to the right part of the store. I say "Thank you" with a sweet smile, feeling as if I'm both claiming an unfair special privilege and being unfairly patronized.

It's as important to me to speak well as to play a piece of music without mistakes. Hearing English distorted grates on me like chalk screeching on a blackboard, like all things botched and badly done, like all forms of gracelessness. The odd thing is that I know what is correct, fluent, good, long before I can execute° it. The English spoken by our Polish acquaintances strikes me as jagged and thick, and I know that I shouldn't imitate it. I'm turned off by the intonations I hear on the TV sitcoms—by the expectation of laughter, like a dog's tail wagging in supplication, built into the actors' pauses, and by the curtailed, cutoff rhythms. I like the way Penny speaks, with an easy flow and a pleasure in giving words a fleshly fullness; I like what I hear in some movies; and once the Old Vic° comes to Vancouver to perform *Macbeth*, and though I can hardly understand the particular words, I am riveted by the tones of sureness and command that mold the actors' speech into such majestic periods.°

Sociolinguists° might say that I receive these language messages as class signals, that I associate the sounds of correctness with the social status of the speaker. In part, this is undoubtedly true. The class-linked notion that I transfer wholesale from Poland is that belonging to a "better" class of people is absolutely dependent on speaking a "better" language. And in my situation especially, I know that language will be a crucial instrument, that I can overcome the stigma° of my marginality°, the weight of presumption against me, only if the reassuringly right sounds come out of my mouth.

13   Yes, speech is a class signifier. But I think that in hearing these varieties of speech around me, I'm sensitized to something else as well—something that is a matter of aesthetics°, and even of psychological health. Apparently, skilled chefs can tell whether a dish from some foreign cuisine is well cooked even if they have never tasted it and don't know the genre of cooking it belongs to. There seem to be some deep-structure qualities—consistency, proportions of ingredients, smoothness of blending—that indicate culinary achievement to these educated eaters' taste buds. So each language has its own distinctive music, and even if one doesn't know its separate components, one can pretty quickly recognize the propriety of the patterns in which the components are put together, their harmonies and discords. Perhaps the crucial element that strikes the ear in listening to living speech is the degree of the speaker's self-assurance and control.

14   As I listen to people speaking that foreign tongue, English, I can hear when they stumble or repeat the same phrases too many times, when their sentences trail off aimlessly—or, on the contrary, when their phrases have vigor and roundness, when they have the space and the breath to give a flourish at the end of a sentence, or make just the right pause before coming to a dramatic point. I can tell, in other words, the degree of their ease or disease, the extent of authority that shapes the rhythms of their speech. That authority—in whatever dialect, in whatever variant of the mainstream language—seems to me to be something we all desire. It's not that we all want to speak the King's English, but whether we speak Appalachian or Harlem English, or Cockney, or Jamaican Creole, we want to be at home in our tongue. We want to be able to give voice accurately and fully to ourselves and our sense of the world. John Fowles, in one of his stories in *The Ebony Tower*, has a young man cruelly violate an elderly writer and his manuscripts because the legacy of language has not been passed on to the youthful vandal properly. This seems to me an entirely credible premise. Linguistic dispossession° is a sufficient motive for violence, for it is close to the dispossession of one's self. Blind rage, helpless rage is rage that has no words— rage that overwhelms one with darkness. And if one is perpetually without words, if one exists in the entropy° of inarticulateness°,

that condition itself is bound to be an enraging frustration. In my New York apartment, I listen almost nightly to fights that erupt like brushfire on the street below—and in their escalating fury of repetitive phrases ("Don't do this to me, man, you fucking bastard, I'll fucking kill you"), I hear not the pleasures of macho toughness but an infuriated beating against wordlessness, against the incapacity to make oneself understood, seen. Anger can be borne—it can even be satisfying—if it can gather into words and explode in a storm, or a rapier-sharp attack. But without this means of ventilation, it only turns back inward, building and swirling like a head of steam—building to an impotent, murderous rage. If all therapy is speaking therapy—a talking cure—then perhaps all neurosis° is a speech dis-ease.

> [blank box]

EVA HOFFMAN

Eva Hoffman (b. 1945) emigrated with her family from Poland to Canada in 1959. She lived and went to school in Vancouver, British Columbia, and then studied at Harvard University, where she completed a Ph.D. in English. Now living in New York, Hoffman is an editor for *The New York Times*.

Words and Meanings

		Paragraph
gaucherie	awkward, boorish expression	1
artifice	effort, the "work" of crafting something carefully	
connotation	see List of Useful Terms	3
evoke	produce or call to mind (connotations)	
spontaneity	immediacy, quickness	5
Platonic	developed by the Greek philosopher Plato (c. 427–347 B.C.)	
prototype	the first, primary model of something; the original from which copies are made	
avatar	incarnation; an idea given bodily form	6
structuralist	structuralism is a theory of language that emphasizes form (the words) over function (the meaning)	
wont	habit	
desiccating	intellectually and emotionally drying up; the opposite of nourishing	
alchemy	power that can (or claims to) transform one thing into something else (for example, copper into gold, words into meaning)	

7	ego	in Freudian theory, the part of the personality that governs rational, realistic behaviour
	id	in Freudian theory, the unconscious part of the personality that supplies energy to the other parts of the psyche and demands immediate gratification
	coeval	co-existent; occurring at the same time as
8	subliminal	subconscious; hidden below the surface of consciousness
11	execute	do, perform, carry out
	Old Vic	theatre company from England
	periods	in the sixteenth and seventeenth centuries, a period was a long, complex sentence composed of perfectly balanced main and subordinate clauses
12	sociolinguists	those who study the relationship between language and the way people are organized into social groups
	stigma	mark or sign that indicates some shameful behaviour
	marginality	living life on the sidelines, unable to become integrated into mainstream culture
13	aesthetics	having to do with what is beautiful, as distinct from what is useful, functional, etc.
14	linguistic dispossession	the experience of having lost (or never had) mastery over one's own language
	entropy	tendency to increasing disorder, chaos
	inarticulateness	the inability to express thoughts and feelings effectively in words
	neurosis	psychological disorder or illness

Structure and Strategy

1. Which sentence in the first part of this essay (paragraphs 1 to 6) sums up the problem Hoffman is struggling with? What examples does she choose to illustrate her point?

2. Consider the DICTION of this essay. Identify three or four examples of complex, ABSTRACT vocabulary followed by CONCRETE examples or an illustration that clarifies the author's meaning.

3. Paragraphs 8 and 9 introduce a short narrative to illustrate the difficulties the author experienced living in the "empty state" (paragraph 9) between Polish and English. What makes this illustration particularly effective?

4. What examples does the essay use to show the reader the sounds and rhythms of spoken language? (See paragraph 11.)

5. What is the topic of paragraph 14? Which sentence in that paragraph most clearly sums up the topic?

Content and Purpose

1. Identify examples of the words and phrases Hoffman has problems with as she attempts to make the transition between Polish and English.
2. In paragraph 3, Hoffman says "the problem is that the signifier has become severed from the signified." Explain in your own words what she means by this.
3. What does Hoffman mean when she says, "I don't really exist" (paragraph 9)? What is the connection between language and identity?
4. In paragraph 10, the focus of the essay changes from the problems of thinking in a new language to the difficulties of speaking an unfamiliar language. What examples does Hoffman provide to illustrate her personal linguistic difficulties and how she felt about them?
5. Hoffman is concerned with more than just the "correctness" of her pronunciation. What is her larger concern? (See paragraphs 11 to 13.) What ANALOGY does she use in paragraph 13 to illustrate her point?
6. What, according to the essay, is the link between "linguistic dispossession" and violence? (See paragraph 14.)

Suggestions for Writing

1. Have you ever tried to learn a new language? Write an essay based on your experience. Provide examples of the kinds of difficulties that you encountered while learning to speak, listen to, read, and/or write a new language.
2. Write an essay that shows how cultural assumptions and expectations are embodied in the idiom of a language. Show by examples how certain words or phrases simply do not translate from one language to another.
3. Write an essay in which you explain by means of examples how your use of language changes depending on the person(s) you are talking to, and what these differences might signify.

Additional Suggestions for Writing: Example

Choose one of the topics below and write a thesis statement based on it. Expand your thesis statement into an essay by selecting specific examples from your own experience, current events, or your studies to develop the main points.

1. Fast food is becoming a gastronomic way of life.
2. People are not always what they appear to be.
3. Recent ecological disasters show how little we care for the environment that sustains us.
4. Popular tourist attractions share certain characteristics.
5. Television commercials reveal some significant characteristics of our culture.
6. A good novel is a wonderful way to escape from everyday cares.
7. Choosing a spouse is easy if one knows what to look for.
8. "Good fences make good neighbours." (Robert Frost)
9. Faith is a source of strength in one's personal life.
10. "Religion is the opiate of the masses." (Karl Marx)
11. Through travel, we learn about ourselves as well as about other people.
12. A good teacher is concerned for students' personal well-being as well as for their intellectual development.
13. You are (or are not) what you wear.
14. Films aimed at those between 15 and 22 share certain characteristics.
15. "The love of money is the root of all evil." (I Timothy 6:10)
16. "Money is indeed the most important thing in the world; and all sound and successful personal and national morality should have this fact for its basis." (George Bernard Shaw)
17. "Manners are more important than laws." (Edmund Burke)
18. "Feeling godless, what we have done is made technology God." (Woody Allen)
19. "Power corrupts. Absolute power corrupts absolutely." (Lord Acton)
20. Are you optimistic or pessimistic about the human condition as we approach the end of the twentieth century? Write an essay defending your point of view and include two or three well-chosen illustrations to support your thesis.

Process Analysis: Explaining "How"

What? The Definition

The next time you find yourself sitting in a dentist's waiting room, pick up a copy of one of the women's magazines—*Chatelaine, Good Housekeeping*, or *Ladies' Home Journal*, for instance. In the table of contents, you'll find a wealth of articles that are examples of process analysis: "Lose Ten Pounds in Ten Days," "Bake the Ultimate Chocolate Cheesecake," or "Raising the Perfect Child." Many of the articles in men's magazines are no different in form, only in content. Their readers learn how to choose a sports car, make a killing in the stock market, tie a Windsor knot, or meet the perfect mate. Across the land, bookstores abound with do-it-yourself manuals on fitness, beauty, computer programming, weight control, financial planning, home renovations, and gourmet cooking. These examples of writing, all intended to teach us how to do something, attest to our interest in self-improvement and our fascination with figuring out how something is done. **Process analysis** is the kind of writing that explains how the various steps of a procedure lead to its successful accomplishment.

Why? The Purpose

Process analysis is used for two different purposes that lead to two different kinds of papers or reports. The first kind is the strictly "how-to" paper that gives the reader directions to follow. A **directional process analysis** answers one of two questions:

1. How do you do S?
2. How do you make S?

Students often need to write a direction process analysis on exams or in assignments. For example, how do you debug a C++ program? How does a paramedic prepare an accident report? What are the essential steps in assembling a hydraulic valve? In directional process analysis, you are writing for the do-it-yourselfer. You must make the instructions clear so that your readers can follow along, step by step. Directions that are vague or incomplete will infuriate them. Remember the Christmas you spent struggling to assemble your supercharged, battery-operated UltraZapMobile? Remember the hopelessly confusing directions provided: "Insert Tab Square B2 firmly into Slot 5A3 while simultaneously sliding the grommet-blaster into the rotating webfork..."? No mere mortal could possibly comprehend such GOBBLEDYGOOK.

The second kind of process analysis answers these questions:

1. How does S work?
2. How does S happen?
3. How is S done?

These questions lead to **informational process analysis**. Its purpose is to explain to your reader how something is, or was, accomplished. Your readers simply want to be informed about the subject; they don't necessarily want to do the task themselves. Jessica Mitford's "Behind the Formaldehyde Curtain" is a fascinating example of informational process analysis. The subject is a process about which everyone should be informed, but few would care to try out at home. Topics such as how holes in the ozone layer develop, how Newfoundland entered Confederation, how a cell divides, how a corporate merger occurs, or how the Alberta Badlands were formed would all require the writer to produce informational process analyses.

How? The Technique

Writing a process analysis that will direct or inform your readers rather than confuse or infuriate them is not difficult if you follow these six steps:

1. Think through the whole process carefully and write down, in order, an outline of all the steps involved. If you are describing a complex process, break down each step in the sequence into substeps and group them CHRONOLOGICALLY.

2. Now write your thesis statement. Here's the formula for a thesis statement for a *directional* paper:

> To do (or make) S, you first a, then b, and finally c.

Example: To fail your year in the grand style, you must antagonize your teachers, disdain your studies, and cheat on your work.

The thesis statement for an *informational* paper also identifies the steps or stages of the process you are explaining:

> S works (or occurs or is done) by a, b, c....

Example: Speech is produced by breathing, phonation, resonation, and articulation.

3. Check to be sure you have included any preparatory steps or special equipment the reader should know about before beginning, as in this example: "Make sure you have your pliers, screwdriver, table saw, and bandages handy."

4. Define any specialized or technical terms that may be unfamiliar to your reader. If you need to use words like "phonation," "resonation," or "articulation"—as we did in the example above—you must explain clearly what the terms mean. Underline the mystery words in your outline, so you'll remember to define them as you write the paper. (See Unit Seven for instructions on how to write simple sentence definitions.)

5. Write your first draft. Be sure to use TRANSITIONS, or time-markers, to indicate the progression through the steps or stages. A variety of transitional words and phrases will help smooth your reader's path through your explanation of the process, as these examples illustrate:
   "*First*, assemble your tools...."
   "*Next*, the legal assistant must...."
   "*After* the Conservative regime was defeated,..."
   "The sound is *then* shaped by the tongue, lips, and teeth...."
   "*Finally*, Brascan's takeover of Genstar was approved by the shareholders...."

6. Revise your draft carefully. What may seem like a simple procedure to you, since you know it so well, can bewilder someone who knows little about it. Ask a friend to read through your process analysis. If it's as clear to her as it is to you, you're done—congratulations! If it isn't clear to her, back to the drawing board. Clarify any steps that caused confusion and revise until the whole paper is both clear and interesting to whoever reads it.

   The essay below, written with tongue firmly in cheek, illustrates the form and development of a directional process paper.

Flunking with Style

Introduction
(challenges widely
held opinion)

People often remark that succeeding in school takes plenty of hard work. The remark implies that failure is a product of general idleness and zero motivation. This is an opinion I'd like to challenge. My long and checkered past in numerous educational institutions has taught me that to fail grandly, to fail extravagantly, to go down in truly blazing splendour, requires effort and imagination. To fail your year in the grand style, you must antagonize your teachers, disdain your studies, and cheat on your work. Keep the following guidelines in mind.

Thesis statement

First step (developed by example)

The first step, antagonizing your teachers, isn't difficult if you keep in mind what it is that teachers like: intelligent, interested, even enthusiastic faces in front row centre. Show that you're bored before the class begins by slouching in a desk at the back of the room. Wear your Walkman, and don't forget to turn up the volume when that teacher starts to talk. Carry on running conversations with your seatmates. Aim an occasional snort or snicker in the teacher's direction when she's putting a complex point on the board. Above all, never volunteer an answer and respond sullenly with an "I dunno" if the teacher has the nerve to ask you a question. Before long, you'll have that teacher bouncing chalk stubs off your head. Once you've earned the loathing of all your instructors, you'll be well on your way to a truly memorable failure.

Second step
(note the enumerated transitions)

The second step, disdaining your studies, is easy to master; they're probably B-O-R-I-N-G anyway. First, don't buy your books until close to midterm and keep them in their original condition; don't open, read, or note anything in them. Better yet, don't buy your texts at all. Second, never attempt to take notes in class. Third, stop going to class completely, but have lots of creative excuses for missed assignments: "My friend's aunt died"; "My gerbil's in a coma"; "My boyfriend was in another car wreck"; "My dog ate the lab report"; "I've got mono." You can bet your teachers will be really amused by these old stand-bys. By now, you are well on your way to disaster.

Third step (more examples)

The third step, cheating, will deliver the coup de grâce to your academic career. Should an instructor be so sadistic as to assign a research paper, just copy something out of a book that the librarian will be happy to find for you. Your instructor will be astonished at the difference between the book's polished, professional prose and your usual halting scrawls; you're guaranteed a zero. During your exams, sit at the back and crane your neck to read your classmate's paper. Roll up your shirt-sleeves to reveal the answers you've tattooed all over your forearms. Ask to be excused three or four times during the test so you can consult the notes you've stashed in the hall or the washroom. Be bold! Dig out your old wood-burning kit and emblazon cheat notes on the desk. If you want to ensure not just failure but actual expulsion, send in a ringer—a look-alike to write the exam for you!

Conclusion (issues a challenge)

If you follow these guidelines, you will be guaranteed to flunk your year. Actively courting failure with verve, with flair, and with a sense of drama will not only ensure your status as an academic washout but will also immortalize you in the memories of teachers and classmates alike. The challenge is yours! Become a legend—pick up the torch and fall with it!

And the Best Damn Stew-Maker Too

PETER GZOWSKI

1   One of the nicest things about growing up is the way you can enjoy all the foods you turned your nose up at as a kid.... The greatest treat of all among the foods I once disdained is stew.

2   Stew was my mother's admission she'd run out of either ideas or money, a kind of dinner-hour equivalent of—and about as tasty as—the Red River Cereal she tried to convince me to eat in the mornings.

3   For the grown-up me, stew has become a source of sheer pleasure. I like eating it, spearing the tenderest cubes of nut-brown meat, savouring the gay orange carrots and pale parsnips—*parsnips?* my mother's halo just clattered to heaven's floor—and sopping up the last rivulets of dark gravy with chunks of fresh bread. I *love* cooking it, and in the long cold winter there is no happier way for me to spend a late Friday afternoon than to follow the ritual I am pleased to share with you now. The quantities, I should tell you, are for two people, though there'll be enough extra if someone drops in or, failing that, for a reheated (and delicious) Saturday lunch.

4   At the liquor store, get a bottle of dark, fairly dry sherry. Make sure they put it in a brown paper bag. (This may not help your reputation in a strange town, but be brave.)

5   At the butcher's, get a pound and a quarter of lean stewing beef, cut into inch-and-a-half cubes.

6   At the grocer's, pick up some leeks, cooking onions, a few carrots and parsnips, a tin of beef stock, a nineteen-ounce tin of tomatoes and a tin of whole, peeled potatoes. From a guy who likes things simple and old-fashioned, I know, this last suggestion will surprise you. But experience has taught me that even the best potatoes, cooked from scratch in a stew, get just a bit starchier than those little ones they put in the cans.

7   If you don't have butter, olive oil, flour, pepper (beef stews need no salt), garlic and other spices at home, pick those up, too. Oh, what the heck, get another couple of heads of garlic anyway.

And from your favourite bakery, get a fresh baguette.   8

If you have a fireplace, begin by lighting a fire to take the   9
chill from the fading day. Then open your sherry and pour yourself a small glass—the shopping was cold, after all. Put a sinfully
thick slice of butter and about a quarter cup of your best olive oil
into a generously sized saucepan or soup kettle, and turn the heat
to medium-high. While the butter melts and blends with the
golden oil, take the paper bag from the booze store, put a cup of
flour into it and grind some pepper on top. Throw the cubes of
meat in the bag and shake it vigorously. Pick the meat out by
hand—the way the flour coats every piece evenly is surely one of
the great miracles of the kitchen—and put it in the pan. As it
browns, chop three or four peeled onions into eighths, and the
white parts of the same number of leeks into inches. Chop a *lot* of
garlic—I use about five cloves, but you can never have too
much—and scrape everything in with the meat. Reduce the heat,
have a sip of sherry and take a moment to enjoy the seductive
smell rising from the pan. Stir from time to time with a wooden
spoon.

When the meat is brown, splash in about a cup—who   10
measures?—of the sherry and the tin of beef stock. Add a sprinkle
of oregano, if it pleases you, or a bit of sweet basil. Lower the heat a
notch (you don't want to *boil* it), and savour the smell again as you
open the tin of tomatoes. This is a good time to cut up the carrots
and parsnips, as well—I peel the parsnips but just scrape the
roughest skin off the carrots. Try to get all your pieces roughly the
size of Brazil nuts.

You can slow down now, while your stew simmers. In another   11
twenty minutes or so, add the tomatoes, liquid and all, and root
veggies, and, half an hour after that, the tinned potatoes. Give it
another ten or fifteen minutes—there's no rush, you know—while
you put out some bowls, forks and spoons. You can rip up the
baguette by hand.

The result, like youth itself, would be wasted on kids anyway.   12

PETER GZOWSKI

Born in Toronto in 1934, Peter Gzowski is a broadcaster, journalist, literacy promoter, and golf addict. He is the regular host of the CBC radio program "Morningside" and the author or editor of numerous books including *Spring Tonic*, *The Game of Our Lives*, and *Canadian Living*, a collection of his columns from one of Canada's most popular magazines.

Structure and Strategy

1. Is this essay an example of directional or informational process analysis?
2. List, in order, the steps to follow to produce Gzowski's stew.
3. Identify the words and phrases Gzowski uses to establish TRANSITION and create COHERENCE.
4. How do the INTRODUCTION and CONCLUSION tie the piece together?

Content and Purpose

1. Why do you think Gzowski organizes the first step, assembling the ingredients, by taking the reader from store to store to procure the necessary foods? (See paragraphs 4 to 7.)
2. Why does Gzowski invite the reader to "begin by lighting a fire to take the chill from the fading day" and "have a sip of sherry" as the stew simmers? What kind of atmosphere is he attempting to create?

Suggestion for Writing

Do you have a special recipe that satisfies not only the body but also the spirit? Write an essay telling your reader how to create the dish? In your conclusion, explain why you think this dish is food for the soul as well as the body.

Desperation Writing
PETER ELBOW

1   I know I am not alone in my recurring twinges of panic that I won't be able to write something when I need to, I won't be able to produce coherent° speech or thought. And that lingering doubt is a great hindrance° to writing. It's a constant fog or static that clouds the mind. I never got out of its clutches till I discovered that it was possible to write something—not something great or pleasing but at least something usable, workable—when my mind is out of commission. The trick is that you have to do all your cooking out on the table: your mind is incapable of

"Desperation Writing" from *Writing without Teachers* by Peter Elbow. Copyright 1973 by Oxford University Press, Inc. Reprinted by permission.

doing any inside. It means using symbols and pieces of paper not as a crutch but as a wheel chair.

The first thing is to admit your condition: because of some mood or event or whatever, your mind is incapable of anything that could be called thought. It can put out a babbling kind of speech utterance, it can put a simple feeling, perception, or sort-of-thought into understandable (though terrible) words. But it is incapable of considering anything in relation to anything else. The moment you try to hold that thought or feeling up against some other to see the relationship, you simply lose the picture—you get nothing but buzzing lines or waving colors.

So admit this. Avoid anything more than one feeling, perception, or thought. Simply write as much as possible. Try simply to steer your mind in the direction or general vicinity of the thing you are trying to write about and start writing and keep writing.

Just write and keep writing. (Probably best to write on only one side of the paper in case you should want to cut parts out with scissors—but you probably won't.) Just write and keep writing. It will probably come in waves. After a flurry°, stop and take a brief rest. But don't stop too long. Don't think about what you are writing or what you have written or else you will overload the circuit again. Keep writing as though you are drugged or drunk. Keep doing this till you feel you have a lot of material that might be useful; or, if necessary, till you can't stand it any more—even if you doubt that there's anything useful there.

Then take a pad of little pieces of paper—or perhaps 3 x 5 cards—and simply start at the beginning of what you were writing, and as you read over what you wrote, every time you come to any thought, feeling, perception, or image that could be gathered up into one sentence or one assertion°, do so and write it by itself on a little sheet of paper. In short, you are trying to turn, say, ten or twenty pages of wandering mush into twenty or thirty hard little crab apples. Sometimes there won't be many on a page. But if it seems to you that there are none on a page, you are making a serious error—the same serious error that put you in this comatose° state to start with. You are mistaking lousy, stupid, second-rate, wrong, childish, foolish, worthless ideas for no ideas at all. Your job is not to pick out *good* ideas but to pick out ideas. As long as you were conscious, your words will be full of things that could be called feelings, utterances, ideas—things that can be squeezed into one simple sentence. This is your job. Don't ask for too much.

After you have done this, take those little slips or cards, read through them a number of times—not struggling with them, simply wandering and mulling through them; perhaps shifting them around and looking through them in various sequences. In a sense these are cards you are playing solitaire with, and the rules of this particular game permit shuffling the unused pile.

7   The goal of this procedure with the cards is to get them to distribute themselves in two or three or ten or fifteen different piles on your desk. You can get them to do this almost by themselves if you simply keep reading through them in different orders; certain cards will begin to feel like they go with other cards. I emphasize this passive, thoughtless mode because I want to talk about desperation writing in its pure state. In practice, almost invariably at some point in the procedure, your sanity begins to return. It is often at this point. You actually are moved to have thoughts or—and the difference between active and passive is crucial here—to *exert* thought; to hold two cards together and *build* or *assert* a relationship. It is a matter of bringing energy to bear.

8   So you may start to be able to do something active with these cards, and begin actually to think. But if not, just allow the cards to find their own piles with each other by feel, by drift, by intuition, by mindlessness.

9   You have now engaged in the two main activities that will permit you to get something cooked out on the table rather than in your brain: writing out into messy words, summing up into single assertions, and even sensing relationships between assertions. You can simply continue to deploy these two activities.

10   If, for example, after that first round of writing, assertion-making, and pile-making, your piles feel as though they are useful and satisfactory for what you are writing—paragraphs or sections or trains of thought—then you can carry on from there. See if you can gather each pile up into a single assertion. When you can, then put the subsidiary° assertions of that pile into their best order to fit with that single unifying one. If you *can't* get the pile into one assertion, then take the pile as the basis for doing some more writing out into words. In the course of this writing, you may produce for yourself the single unifying assertion you were looking for; or you may have to go through the cycle of turning the writing into assertions and piles and so forth. Perhaps more than once. The pile may turn out to want to be two or more piles itself; or it may want to become part of a pile you already have. This is natural. This kind of meshing into one configuration, then coming apart, then coming together and meshing into a different configuration°—this is growing and cooking. It makes a terrible mess, but if you can't do it in your head, you have to put up with a cluttered desk and a lot of confusion.

11   If, on the other hand, all that writing *didn't* have useful material in it, it means that your writing wasn't loose, drifting, quirky, jerky, associative enough. This time try especially to let things simply remind you of things that are seemingly crazy or unrelated. Follow these odd associations. Make as many metaphors as you can—be as nutty as possible—and explore the metaphors themselves—open them out. You may have all your energy tied up in some area of your experience that you are leaving out. Don't refrain from writing about whatever else

is on your mind: how you feel at the moment, what you are losing your mind over, randomness that intrudes itself on your consciousness, the pattern of the wallpaper, what those people you see out the window have on their minds—though keep coming back to the whateveritis you are supposed to be writing about. Treat it, in short, like ten-minute writing exercises. Your best perceptions and thoughts are always going to be tied up in whatever is really occupying you, and that is also where your energy is. You may end up writing a love poem—or a hate poem—in one of those little piles while the other piles will finally turn into a lab report on data processing or whatever you have to write about. But you couldn't, in your present state of having your head shot off, have written that report without also writing the poem. And the report will have some of the juice of the poem in it and vice versa.

$$\boxed{}$$

PETER ELBOW

Peter Elbow (b. 1935) is an influential teacher of writing in the United States. His works include *Writing without Teachers* (1973) and *Writing with Power* (1981).

Words and Meanings

		Paragraph
coherent	see COHERENCE in the List of Useful Terms	1
hindrance	something that gets in the way	
flurry	short, intense burst of activity	4
assertion	statement, sentence that is to be proved	5
comatose	in a deep sleep, incapable of moving	
subsidiary	subordinate, supporting	10
configuration	combination of parts into a whole	

Structure and Strategy

1. For whom is Elbow writing this essay? Who is his AUDIENCE?
2. Throughout the essay, Elbow speaks directly to his readers, addressing them as "you." What is the effect of this technique? How would the essay be different if it had been written in the third person? Try rewriting paragraph 2 in the third person to see the difference (for example, "The first thing writers must do is to admit their condition....").
3. Identify the main steps into which Elbow breaks down the process of "desperation writing."
4. What is the function of paragraph 9? How does it help the reader follow the process?

5. Elbow recommends that desperate writers should "make as many metaphors as [they] can ... and explore the metaphors themselves." Identify three metaphors Elbow uses in this essay. (See paragraphs 1, 4, and 6. For a definition of metaphor, see FIGURES OF SPEECH.) Are they effective? Why?

Content and Purpose

1. How does the author describe the confusion that clouds the minds of people when they know they have to write something, but feel blocked? Do you ever have this feeling, and if so, how do you deal with it?
2. What kind of advice does Elbow provide to help people get something, anything, on paper? What does the "desperate writer" then do with the material that is generated?
3. In paragraph 9, Elbow describes the "two main activities" that will eventually lead to coherent writing. Is there any similarity between the strategies he recommends and the organizational strategies for writing a thesis statement that this text recommends?
4. Paragraph 11 deals with the "drifting, quirky, jerky, associative" writing that the desperate writer produces. What is the relationship between this tapping of the unconscious mind and the conscious mind's shaping of the material into coherent writing?

Suggestions for Writing

1. "A man may write at anytime, if he will set himself doggedly to it," wrote Samuel Johnson in 1750. Explain the process that you go through when faced with a writing assignment.
2. Write a brief process analysis outlining how you approach a necessary task that you do not want to do; for example, filing your income tax return, cleaning the house, disciplining a child, working out, studying for a final exam.

Home Ice

PAUL QUARRINGTON

1   Think of it as wintry gardening. Better yet, think of it as nocturnal thaumaturgy°. Focus on the magical aspects,

for on a more worldly level, we are about to discuss standing outside on the most bitter of nights with a spurting garden hose in
your hand, likely frozen there forever. We are about to discuss making a backyard skating rink.

It seems to me that the backyard rink ranks right up there with   2
frozen duck ponds and ice-locked rivers. Which is to say, they have
a home not only on the earth but also in our frostbitten imagina-
tions. Dreams of Stanley Cups and figure-skating championships
are born there. Local arenas are nice enough places, I suppose, but
the important thing is the sense of community. When I think of local
arenas, I think of the benches, the snack bars, the people huddled
together eating cold hot dogs and blowing on cups of hot chocolate.
The ice itself is nothing special—it is quiet and subdued, not like the
unruly ice you find in the backyard rink. Curlers and assorted Celts
call the outdoor variety "roaring ice." The blades of skates produce
sharp-edged howls. The ice of a backyard rink is welted and scarred
and unable to smooth the wrinkled face of the planet. It is elemen-
tal, having as much claim to the land as rocks or wind.

That is why the process is not really so much "making" or   3
"constructing" a backyard rink; it is more along the lines of allow-
ing one to come into being, a sort of shivering midwifery. Some
people conceive of the process as imposing the rink on the ground,
which results in that most mundane and dreary objection to the
backyard skating rink: it will ruin the grass. That is not true. You
don't have to take my word for it. I went and asked Peter Hayward,
a landscaper/gardener here in Orillia, Ontario, where the back-
yards are huge and backyard rinks commonplace. "No, it won't
ruin the grass," he assured me, although after a moment of judi-
cious and professional musing, he added, "Might make it grow a
bit *funny*." What he meant was that the grass may grow in opposing directions in the spring—but only for a time.

Funny grass is a small price to pay. This is something you can   4
do for your children, something meaningful. The magic will not be
lost upon them. They will be delighted that a field of ice has
bloomed during the night. They will stare at it and think, "Geez,
Dad [or Mom] must have frozen his [or her] butt off!" They will be
right. There is little point sugarcoating this truth. If you can't stand
the cold, stay in the kitchen.

I propose to pass on the recipe for the definitive, the quintessen-   5
tial, the perfect backyard skating rink. I did not arrive at such a
recipe without a lot of help. I turned to my friend Peter Hayman
(not to be confused with Peter Hayward, although this, perhaps,
cannot be helped), a Toronto filmmaker and father of three young
boys. He was led to make a rink mostly because he remembered one

from his childhood: "Also, there's a rink at the end of our street that the city is supposed to keep up, and, of course, they never do. A little thaw, and it's wiped out." I have skated on Hayman's rink and know it to be first-class. (I have a simple test: any ice that does not immediately flip me onto my dustcover is first-class.) I also received a lot of information from Ronn Hartviksen, an art teacher who lives in Thunder Bay. Hartviksen is the creator of perhaps the most ambitious and beautiful backyard rink in the world, a huge thing (about 65 by 110 feet) that has achieved almost legendary status in the hockey-playing community. The rink is called the "Bean Pot," a nod to Boston and the Boston Bruins, Hartviksen's favourite hockey team. An ice artist, he has put the team's distinctive "B" at centre ice.

6   When Dave King was preparing the Canadian team for the 1988 Olympics, he made sure the players found time to visit Hartviksen's place and skate on the Bean Pot. Similarly, he had the team skate on the Ottawa Canal. Coach King, a man who takes pains to seem reasonable and sedate°, sometimes talks about "the romance of the backyard rink" and hints there is something very important to be discovered out on that ice.

7   "The indoor rink," opines King, "is a good place to develop technical skills. But the outdoor rink is the place to acquire a real love for the game. In the new generation of hockey players, this is missing." Despite unpredictable chinooks° in Calgary, where King lives, he continues to make his own backyard rink. Lastly, I went to the guru of the backyard rink, the man who made what is surely the most famous backyard rink in the world, Walter Gretzky.

8   If you are going to make a backyard rink, decide early in the season, well before winter is actually in sight. This is the easy part, walking outside and choosing the likeliest site. It may be that you have a smallish backyard and are therefore simply going to flood the whole thing. Others may be faced with a larger expanse and should select some portion of it. The guiding principle should arise from the fact that you are going to have to shovel, resurface and otherwise groom your backyard rink, so you should keep it to a manageable size. Twenty by forty feet seems reasonable: large enough for skaters to manoeuvre, even to play a spirited, if congested, game of shinny, but small enough to care for.

9   A prime consideration is flatness. It is not necessary that the ground be perfectly smooth (you will be surprised at how hilly and full of cavities your lawn really is), but there is no getting around the fact that it must be level. Some depressions can, of course, be built up with snow, and small rises will just become part of the rink (I can recall a section of a rink long ago that would supply me with a quick burst of speed, alarming, not to mention astounding, everyone else

on the ice), but a slope, even a gentle one, will undermine all your best efforts.

The last consideration is proximity° to a water source. Tapping into an inside source is best. If you can run a hose into the basement, for example, and hook up with the washing-machine taps, you will reap a number of benefits. Remember that no nozzle/hose connection is perfect, and imagine some of the nasty things that could happen at an outside connection—such as finding the thing encased in a block of ice. Even if you avoid nightly chipping and hacking, any outside terminal is going to require a bucket or two of hot water just to get the tap cranked. So if you can get to the water inside, so much the better, especially because, in the maintenance stages, you can employ the hot water for resurfacing, a technique I call "the poor man's Zamboni" (a machine used to resurface the ice in arenas). My own experience has taught me the value of hot water to promote a smooth ice surface. Curiously, none of the authorities I talked to used the method.

But let's not worry about maintenance right now; let's get the thing started. Just a couple of quick points here: you probably lack enough hose, because you are used to pulling it up the centre of the lawn. It is now necessary to pull the hose around the outside of a 20-by-40-foot rectangle (you must be able to stand at any point around the perimeter°, hose in hand), so go out and buy another section. It must be a good-quality, thick, heavy rubber hose, because plastic ones are likely to crack open when the world is hung about with ice spikes.

Having selected the site, make sure the ground is properly tended, which means mowing and raking. If you don't, you might face what proved to be the bane of my childhood backyard rinks: errant° blades of grass popping through the ice surface. I know this does not seem likely or even possible, but believe me, little green Ninjas will sprout up and flip you onto your backside. So give your lawn a marine cut late in the fall.

Here is an optional step, depending on where you live. Ronn Hartviksen—who, you will recall, resides in Thunder Bay—says that sometimes in late fall, he will hose down the naked earth. It's cold enough to freeze, and he has a layer of black ice for his rink's foundation. In other, more southerly places, watering your lawn late fall serves no purpose except to demonstrate to your neighbours that you are fairly strange, so they will not think twice the first time you are out there at midnight and 40 below.

Now you wait.

You wait for cold temperatures. "It would be lovely to do all this, say, over the Christmas holidays," says Hayman, "but that's usually just not possible here in Toronto. You're more likely going to have to wait until the middle of January." So you wait for the requisite cold temperatures, and you wait for snow. Wait until there is a whole lot of snow, maybe two or three good dumpings. Then clear some of it away from your rectangle, leaving behind anywhere from four to six inches. This clearing supplies you with a little border, something to aid in water retention while flooding. It also gives a comfortable sense of containment and might even keep a puck on the ice, although you and I both know that the puck will hit your little ridge of snow, pick up torque° and be gone into the neighbour's yard.

16   It is best to flatten the snow. Hartviksen sends out a troop of kids to play what he calls "boot hockey." He also possesses a heavy piece of wood that he can drag behind him, smoothing the surface. This is not as crucial a step as some people believe. I recall from childhood when someone—I think maybe Mr. Michaels (the kind of man who locked his garage doors)—rented one of those huge industrial drum rollers. The problem is that snow sticks to things like that; also, those rollers are fairly useless unless you fill them with water, which can cause problems. For instance, it can deprive you of your coffee breaks, lest the water inside the drum freeze. The process of backyard rink building raises the market value of coffee breaks considerably; they soon seem as important as reaching Base Camp while scaling K2.

17   The foundation of the base is snow. Snow plus water and the chilly, chilly air. I am going to advocate the "slush" approach to base building, which differs slightly from, say, Hartviksen's "sugar-cube" approach. (Hartviksen's approach is really more of an aid to visualization. He gives the snow a heavy watering and imagines each section of snow as a large sugar cube. The darkening on the surface gives a good indication of the degree of saturation.)

18   I am a proponent of the most active sort of base building, getting out there with a hose and creating slush, which is then smoothed flat. You want the slush to be more solid than a Slurpee, just watery enough that snowball construction is out of the question. Do small sections at a time. Hayman's technique is effective here: water the ground, work it into slush with a snow shovel, use the back of the snow shovel to smooth it out, move along, do it again. Work lanes, walking backward across the rink-to-be. Once you get that done, have someone carry you inside to thaw you out in a dry, warm corner.

19   In the morning, it will be slightly hilly—well, let's face it, your rink at this point would baffle most topographical° mapmakers. But that's all right. You have done most of the heavy human work now;

it is time to turn things over to Mother Nature and let her smooth everything out. The next night ... oh, let's clear that up. It is not absolutely necessary to do this at night, although a fierce sun can slow things down even on the coldest day. In my experience, however, backyard rink building is always done at night for various practical reasons (a job being the chief one) and for one very impractical one: Did the elves ever show up at the shoemaker's before midnight?

The next night, go out there armed with your hose. Just the 20 hose, no fancy nozzles or sprayers: you have to have the open-ended hose because you want to get as much water on the ground in as short a time as possible. "People are always offering me gadgets to put on the end of my hose," says Hartviksen, "but I find they clog and drip and freeze my pant legs. I always end up with just the hose and my thumb. I alternate thumbs. I'm thinking of getting them insured." You should be able to hit most places without stepping on the ice surface, but if you can't, go ahead and step on it. Your foot will go through, but the footprints will be filled in as you build layer by layer, and that is a better option than depriving your rink-to-be of an even flooding. Depending on how cold it is, you might be able to do two, even three, floodings that first night. When you have finished do yourself an enormous favour: coil the hose up, and take it inside the house with you.

The next morning, you will find a vaguely flat sheet of ice, 21 although it might be alarmingly pitted, cracked and ravined. Now, in Peter Hayman's words, you "make like a referee." No, he doesn't mean that you get small-minded and petty and order your children to bed early for no good reason (just joking); he means that you get out there on hands and knees—as referees often do during games—grab handfuls of snow and start stuffing the cracks and holes. Stuffing and tamping, tamping and stuffing. It's amazing how much snow even the smallest crack can hold, so don't imagine this is the work of a few moments. However, the more patching you do, the better your rink is going to be.

Now, the ice might look uniformly strong, but it is very doubt- 22 ful that it is. The roll of the lawn has a lot of influence here, and usually, there are air pockets undermining the structure. I hold to the view that it is best to know about them at this stage of the game—when they can be corrected. So as you do your flood that evening, get out there. Flood the rink, drink cognac and wait until it freezes, flood the rink, drink cognac, drink cognac....

In the morning, you have something that looks like a skating 23 rink. This cheers you up, because you drank too much cognac the night before and are feeling a little poorly. There is still some patching to do, but it seems less fundamental—more like polishing than anything else—and after another couple of floodings that evening, you will have, if not a proper skating rink, what Hayman refers to with caution as "a skateable situation."

24   Put the lightest family member out there. Hold your breath. Watch as he or she makes a couple of circuits around the outer edges. There will be some creaking, maybe a little cracking—make like a referee, and flood again that evening. And the next. And the next. You need an ice thickness of perhaps six inches to survive sudden thaws. If it should snow, it must be cleared away almost immediately, because a thick blanket can result in an ice-snow commingling° that will ruin the surface.

25   In time, you will not have to flood every night, or even every other night, but many nights will find you out there, hose in hand, practising a little wintry gardening, a little nocturnal thaumaturgy.

PAUL QUARRINGTON

Novelist, playwright, screenwriter, journalist, and critic, Paul Quarrington (b. 1953) is one of Canada's most versatile writers. A former rock 'n' roll artist, he writes song lyrics as well as fiction, non-fiction, theatre, and films. His most recent works include *Whale Music* (1989) and *Civilization and Its Part in My Downfall* (1994).

Paragraph **Words and Meanings**

Paragraph		
1	nocturnal thaumaturgy	night-time magic
6	sedate	calm, composed, thoughtful, steady
7	chinooks	warm winter winds that blow eastward across the Rocky Mountains into Alberta and Saskatchewan
10	proximity	closeness
11	perimeter	outer boundary, the edge around the rink
12	errant	uncontrolled, growing in all directions
15	torque	speed and spin
19	topographical	showing the surface features of a place or region; for example, mountains, rivers, etc.
24	commingling	mixture, blending together

Structure and Strategy

1. What metaphor (see FIGURES OF SPEECH) does the author use in the opening paragraph? Does it recur later in the essay? (Hint: are there any other references to magic?) Why does the author choose such sophisticated DICTION ("nocturnal thaumaturgy") to identify his subject?
2. Paragraph 2 is based on a contrast. What is it and why does the author introduce it here? (See paragraph 3.)
3. After the introduction (paragraphs 1 to 4), Quarrington moves to the preparation stage (paragraphs 5 to 7). What three "experts" did the author consult? What are their qualifications to act as authorities on this subject?
4. In which paragraph does Quarrington's process analysis actually begin? Trace the ten steps involved in creating a backyard rink. Are the author's instructions clear and easy to follow? Do they adhere to the principles described in the introduction to this unit?
5. Quarrington employs several FIGURES OF SPEECH to develop his ideas; for example, "more solid than a Slurpee" (paragraph 18), and "make like a referee" (paragraph 21). Find other examples of figurative language. (Hint: look first at the title.)
6. What is the function of paragraphs 17 and 19?
7. Quarrington tries to encourage his readers by using humour to modify the impression that making a backyard rink is a long, tedious, and even painful process. Identify three or four examples of humour in this essay.

Content and Purpose

1. What objection to backyard rink building does paragraph 3 refute? What objection cannot be refuted and how does the author suggest the reader deal with it (paragraph 4)?
2. Identify three significant reasons why anyone would go through the trouble and discomfort of making a backyard rink.
3. The first step in the process, deciding where to put the rink, depends on what three factors? (See paragraphs 8 to 10.)
4. How does the author suggest you check to see whether your rink is ready for skating?

Suggestion for Writing

Write a directional process analysis for a multistep project; for instance, wallpapering a room, detailing a car, creating a garden, decorating a cake, surfing the Internet, making sushi, refinishing an antique. Make sure that your essay not only explains how to complete the process but also suggests why the process is worthwhile.

The Way of All Flesh: The Worm Is at Work in Us All

JUDY STOFFMAN

1   When a man of 25 is told that aging is inexorable°, inevitable, universal, he will nod somewhat impatiently at being told something so obvious. In fact, he has little idea of the meaning of the words. It has nothing to do with him. Why should it? He has had no tangible evidence yet that his body, as the poet Rilke said, enfolds old age and death as the fruit enfolds a stone.

2   The earliest deposits of fat in the aorta, the trunk artery carrying blood away from the heart, occur in the eighth year of life, but who can peer into his own aorta at this first sign of approaching debility°? The young man has seen old people but he secretly believes himself to be the exception on whom the curse will never fall. "Never will the skin of my neck hang loose. My grip will never weaken. I will stand tall and walk with long strides as long as I live." The young girl scarcely pays attention to her clothes; she scorns makeup. Her confidence in her body is boundless; smooth skin and a flat stomach will compensate, she knows, for any lapses in fashion or grooming. She stays up all night, as careless of her energy as of her looks, believing both will last forever.

3   In our early 20s, the lung capacity, the rapidity of motor responses and physical endurance are at their peak. This is the athlete's finest hour. Cindy Nicholas of Toronto was 19 when she first swam the English Channel in both directions. The tennis star Bjorn Borg was 23 when he triumphed this year at Wimbledon for the fourth time.

4   It is not only *athletic* prowess° that is at its height between 20 and 30. James Boswell, writing in his journal in 1763 after he had finally won the favors of the actress Louisa, has left us this happy description of the sexual prowess of a 23-year-old: "I was in full flow of health and my bounding blood beat quick in high alarms. Five times was I fairly lost in a supreme rapture. Louisa was madly fond of me; she declared I was a prodigy°, and asked me if this was extraordinary in human nature. I said twice as much might be, but

this was not, although in my own mind I was somewhat proud of my performance."

In our early 30s we are dumbfounded to discover the first grey hair at the temples. We pull out the strange filament and look at it closely, trying to grasp its meaning. It means simply that the pigment has disappeared from the hair shaft, never to return. It means also—but this thought we push away—that in 20 years or so we'll relinquish° our identity as a blonde or a redhead. By 57, one out of four people is completely grey. Of all the changes wrought by time this is the most harmless, except to our vanity.

In this decade one also begins to notice the loss of upper register hearing, that is, the responsiveness to high frequency tones, but not all the changes are for the worse, not yet. Women don't reach their sexual prime until about 38, because their sexual response is learned rather than innate. The hand grip of both sexes increases in strength until 35, and intellectual powers are never stronger than at that age. There is a sense in the 30s of hitting your stride, of coming into your own. When Sigmund Freud was 38 an older colleague, Josef Breuer, wrote: "Freud's intellect is soaring at its highest. I gaze after him as a hen at a hawk."

Gail Sheehy in her book *Passages* calls the interval between 35 and 45 the Deadline Decade. It is the time we begin to sense danger. The body continually flashes us signals that time is running out. We must perform our quaint deeds, keep our promises, get on with our allotted tasks.

Signal: The woman attempts to become pregnant at 40 and finds she cannot. Though she menstruates each month, menstruation being merely the shedding of the inner lining of the womb, she may not be ovulating regularly.

Signal: Both men and women discover that, although they have not changed their eating habits over the years, they are much heavier than formerly. The man is paunchy around the waist; the woman no longer has those slim thighs and slender arms. A 120-pound woman needs 2,000 calories daily to maintain her weight when she is 25, 1,700 to maintain the same weight at 45, and only 1,500 calories at 65. A 170-pound man needs 3,100 calories daily at 25, 300 fewer a day at 45 and 450 calories fewer still at 65. This decreasing calorie need signals that the body consumes its fuel ever more slowly; the cellular fires are damped and our sense of energy diminishes.

In his mid-40s the man notices he can no longer run up the stairs three at a time. He is more easily winded and his joints are not as flexible as they once were. The strength of his hands has declined somewhat. The man feels humiliated: "I will not let this happen to me. I will turn back the tide and master my body." He starts going to the gym, playing squash, lifting weights. He takes up jogging. Though he may find it neither easy nor pleasant, terror drives him past pain. A regular exercise program can retard some of the symptoms of aging by improving the circulation and increasing the lung capacity, thereby raising our stamina and energy level, but no amount of exercise will make a 48-year-old 26 again. Take John Keeley of Mystic, Connecticut. In 1957, when he was 26, he won the Boston marathon with a time of 2:20. [In 1979,] fit and 48, [he was] as fiercely competitive as ever, yet it took him almost 30 minutes longer to run the same marathon.

11   In the middle of the fourth decade, the man whose eyesight has always been good will pick up a book and notice that he is holding it farther from his face than usual. The condition is presbyopia, a loss of the flexibility of the lens which makes adjustment from distant to near vision increasingly difficult. It's harder now to zoom in for a closeup. It also takes longer for the eyes to recover from glare; between 16 and 90, recovery time from exposure to glare is doubled every 13 years.

12   In our 50s, we notice that food is less and less tasty; our taste buds are starting to lose their acuity°. The aged Queen Victoria was wont to complain that strawberries were not as sweet as when she was a girl.

13   Little is known about the causes of aging. We do not know if we are born with a biochemical messenger programmed to keep the cells and tissues alive, a messenger that eventually gets lost, or if there is a "death hormone," absent from birth but later secreted by the thymus or by the mysterious pineal gland, or if, perhaps, aging results from a fatal flaw in the body's immunity system. The belief that the body is a machine whose parts wear out is erroneous, for the machine does not have the body's capacity for self-repair.

14   "A man is as old as his arteries," observed Sir William Osler. From the 50s on, there's a progressive hardening and narrowing of the arteries due to the gradual lifelong accumulation of calcium and fats along the arterial walls. Arteriosclerosis eventually affects the majority of the population in the affluent countries of the West. Lucky the man or woman who, through a combination of good genes and good nutrition, can escape it, for it is the most evil change of all. As the flow of blood carrying oxygen and nutrients to the muscles, the brain, the kidneys and other organs diminishes, these organs begin to starve. Although all aging organs lose weight, there is less shrinkage of organs such as the liver and kidneys, the cells of which regenerate, than there is shrinkage of the brain and the muscles, the cells of which, once lost, are lost forever.

For the woman it is now an ordeal to be asked her age. There is a fine tracery of lines around her eyes, a furrow in her brow even when she smiles. The bloom is off her cheeks. Around the age of 50 she will buy her last box of sanitary pads. The body's production of estrogen and progesterone which govern menstruation (and also help to protect her from heart attack and the effects of stress) will have ceased almost completely. She may suffer palpitations°, suddenly break into a sweat; her moods may shift abruptly. She looks in the mirror and asks, "Am I still a woman?" Eventually she becomes reconciled to her new self and even acknowledges its advantages: no more fears about pregnancy. "In any case," she laughs, "I still have not bad legs."

The man, too, will undergo a change. One night in his early 50s he has some trouble achieving a complete erection, and his powers of recovery are not what they once were. Whereas at 20 he was ready to make love again less than half an hour after doing so, it may now take two hours or more; he was not previously aware that his level of testosterone, the male hormone, has been gradually declining since the age of 20. He may develop headaches, be unable to sleep, become anxious about his performance, anticipate failure and so bring on what is called secondary impotence—impotence of psychological rather than physical origin. According to Masters and Johnson, 25 percent of all men are impotent by 65 and 50 percent by 75, yet this cannot be called an inevitable feature of aging. A loving, undemanding partner and a sense of confidence can do wonders. "The susceptibility° of the human male to the power of suggestion with regard to his sexual prowess," observe Masters and Johnson, "is almost unbelievable."

After the menopause, the woman ages more rapidly. Her bones start to lose calcium, becoming brittle and porous. The walls of the vagina become thinner and drier; sexual intercourse now may be painful unless her partner is slow and gentle. The sweat glands begin to atrophy° and the sebaceous glands that lubricate the skin decline; the complexion becomes thinner and drier and wrinkles appear around the mouth. The skin, which in youth varies from about one-fiftieth of an inch on the eyelids to about a third of an inch on the palms and the soles of the feet, loses 50 percent of its thickness between the ages of 20 and 80. The woman no longer buys sleeveless dresses and avoids shorts. The girl who once disdained cosmetics is now a woman whose dressing table is covered with lotions, night creams and makeup.

Perhaps no one has written about the sensation of nearing 60 with more brutal honesty than the French novelist Simone de Beauvoir: "While I was able to look at my face without displeasure,

I gave it no thought. I loathe my appearance now: the eyebrows slipping down toward the eyes, the bags underneath, the excessive fullness of the cheeks and the air of sadness around the mouth that wrinkles always bring.... Death is no longer a brutal event in the far distance; it haunts my sleep."

19   In his early 60s the man's calves are shrunken, his muscles stringy looking. The legs of the woman, too, are no longer shapely. Both start to lose their sense of smell and both lose most of the hair in the pubic area and the underarms. Hair, however, may make its appearance in new places, such as the woman's chin. Liver spots appear on the hands, the arms, the face; they are made of coagulated melanin, the coloring matter of the skin. The acid secretions of the stomach decrease, making digestion slow and more difficult.

20   Halfway through the 60s comes compulsory retirement for most men and working women, forcing upon the superannuated worker the realization that society now views him as useless and unproductive. The man who formerly gave orders to a staff of 20 now finds himself underfoot as his wife attempts to clean the house or get the shopping done. The woman fares a little better since there is a continuity in her pattern of performing a myriad of essential household tasks. Now they must both set new goals or see themselves wither mentally. The unsinkable American journalist I.F. Stone, when he retired in 1971 from editing *I.F. Stone's Weekly*, began to teach himself Greek and is now reading Plato in the original. When Somerset Maugham read that the Roman senator Cato the Elder learned Greek when he was 80, he remarked: "Old age is ready to undertake tasks that youth shirked° because they would take too long."

21   However active we are, the fact of old age can no longer be evaded from about 65 onward. Not everyone is as strong minded about this as de Beauvoir. When she made public in her memoirs her horror at her own deterioration, her readers were scandalized. She received hundreds of letters telling her that there is no such thing as old age, that some are just younger than others. Repeatedly she heard the hollow reassurance, "You're as young as you feel." But she considers this a lie. Our subjective reality, our inner sense of self, is not the only reality. There is also an objective reality, how we are seen by society. We receive our revelation of old age from others. The woman whose figure is still trim may sense that a man is following her in the street; drawing abreast, the man catches sight of her face—and hurries on. The man of 68 may be told by a younger woman to whom he is attracted: "You remind me of my father."

22   Madame de Sévigné, the 17th-century French writer, struggled to rid herself of the illusion of perpetual youth. At 63 she wrote: "I have been dragged to this inevitable point where old age must be

undergone: I see it there before me; I have reached it; and I should at least like so to arrange matters that I do not move on, that I do not travel further along this path of the infirmities, pains, losses of memory and the disfigurement. But I hear a voice saying: 'You must go along, whatever you may say; or indeed if you will not then you must die, which is an extremity from which nature recoils.'"

Now the man and the woman have their 70th birthday party. It is a sad affair because so many of their friends are missing, felled by strokes, heart attacks or cancers. Now the hands of the clock begin to race. The skeleton continues to degenerate from loss of calcium. The spine becomes compressed and there is a slight stoop nothing can prevent. Inches are lost from one's height. The joints may become thickened and creaking; in the morning the woman can't seem to get moving until she's had a hot bath. She has osteoarthritis. This, like the other age-related diseases, arteriosclerosis and diabetes, can and should be treated, but it can never be cured. The nails, particularly the toenails, become thick and lifeless because the circulation in the lower limbs is now poor. The man has difficulty learning new things because of the progressive loss of neurons from the brain. The woman goes to the store and forgets what she has come to buy. The two old people are often constipated because the involuntary muscles are weaker now. To make it worse, their children are always saying, "Sit down, rest, take it easy." Their digestive tract would be toned up if they went for a long walk or even a swim, although they feel a little foolish in bathing suits.

In his late 70s, the man develops glaucoma, pressure in the eyeball caused by the failure of aqueous humour° to drain away; this can now be treated with a steroid related to cortisone. The lenses in the eyes of the woman may thicken and become fibrous, blurring her vision. She has cataracts, but artificial lenses can now be implanted using cryosurgery°. There is no reason to lose one's sight just as there's no reason to lose one's teeth; regular, lifelong dental care can prevent tooth loss. What can't be prevented is the yellowing of teeth, brought about by the shrinking of the living chamber within the tooth which supplies the outer enamel with moisture.

Between 75 and 85 the body loses most of its subcutaneous fat. On her 80th birthday the woman's granddaughter embraces her and marvels: "How thin and frail and shrunken she is! Could this narrow, bony chest be the same warm, firm bosom to which she clasped me as a child?" Her children urge her to eat but she has no enjoyment of food now. Her mouth secretes little saliva, so she has difficulty tasting and swallowing. The loss of fat and shrinking muscles in the 80s diminish the body's capacity for homeostasis, that is, righting any physiological imbalance. The old man, if he is cold, can barely shiver (shivering serves to restore body heat). If he lives long enough, the man will have an enlarged prostate which causes the urinary stream to slow to a trickle. The man and the woman probably both wear hearing aids now; without a hearing aid, they hear vowels clearly but not consonants; if someone says "fat," they think they've heard the word "that."

26   At 80, the speed of nerve impulses is 10 percent less than it was at 25, the kidney filtration rate is down by 30 percent, the pumping efficiency of the heart is only 60 percent of what it was, and the maximum breathing capacity, 40 percent.

27   The old couple is fortunate in still being able to express physically the love they've built up over a lifetime. The old man may be capable of an erection once or twice a week (Charlie Chaplin fathered the last of his children when he was 81), but he rarely has the urge to climax. When he does, he sometimes has the sensation of seepage rather than a triumphant explosion. Old people who say they are relieved that they are now free of the torments of sexual desire are usually the ones who found sex a troublesome function all their lives; those who found joy and renewal in the act will cling to their libido°. Many older writers and artists have expressed the conviction that continued sexuality is linked to continued creativity: "There was a time when I was cruelly tormented, indeed obsessed by desire," wrote the novelist André Gide at the age of 73, "and I prayed, 'Oh let the moment come when my subjugated° flesh will allow me to give myself entirely to....' But to what? To art? To pure thought? To God? How ignorant I was! How mad! It was the same as believing that the flame would burn brighter in a lamp with no oil left. Even today it is my carnal self that feeds the flame, and now I pray that I may retain carnal desire until I die."

28   Aging, says an American gerontologist°, "is not a simple slope which everyone slides down at the same speed; it is a flight of irregular stairs down which some journey more quickly than others." Now we arrive at the bottom of the stairs. The old man and the old woman whose progress we have been tracing will die either of a cancer (usually of the lungs, bowel or intestines) or of a stroke, a heart attack or in consequence of a fall. The man slips in the bathroom and breaks his thigh bone. But worse than the fracture is the enforced bed rest in the hospital which will probably bring on bed sores, infections, further weakening of the muscles and finally, what Osler called "an old man's best friend": pneumonia. At 25 we have so much vitality that if a little is sapped by illness, there is still plenty left over. At 85 a little is all we have.

And then the light goes out.   29
The sheet is pulled over the face.   30

In the last book of Marcel Proust's remarkable work *Remembrance of*   31
Things Past, the narrator, returning after a long absence from Paris,
attends a party of his friends throughout which he has the impression of being at a masked ball: "I did not understand why I could not
immediately recognize the master of the house, and the guests, who
seemed to have made themselves up, in a way that completely
changed their appearance. The Prince had rigged himself up with a
white beard and what looked like leaden soles which made his feet
drag heavily. A name was mentioned to me and I was dumbfounded
at the thought that it applied to the blonde waltzing girl I had once
known and to the stout, white haired lady now walking just in front
of me. We did not see our own appearance, but each like a facing mirror, saw the other's." The narrator is overcome by a simple but powerful truth: the old are not a different species. "It is out of young men
who last long enough," wrote Proust, "that life makes its old men."

The wrinkled old man who lies with the sheet over his face was   32
once the young man who vowed, "My grip will never weaken. I
will walk with long strides and stand tall as long as I live." The
young man who believed himself to be the exception.

JUDY STOFFMAN

Judy Stoffman, currently book review editor of *The Toronto Star*, was born
in Budapest, Hungary, and came to Vancouver as a refugee in 1957. She
has degrees in English from the University of British Columbia and from
Sussex University in England. She has also lived and studied in Aix-en-
Provence, France. She has worked for CBC Radio and TV, and as an editor for *Canadian Living Magazine*, *The Globe and Mail*, and *Weekend* magazine, where "The Way of All Flesh" originally appeared.

Words and Meanings

Paragraph

inexorable	relentless, unstoppable	1
debility	weakness	2
prowess	courage, skill	4
prodigy	person capable of extraordinary achievement	
relinquish	give up	5
acuity	sharpness	12

15	palpitations	irregular heartbeats
16	susceptibility	sensitiveness, impressibility
17	atrophy	wither
20	shirked	neglected
24	aqueous humour	fluid in the interior chamber of the eyeball
	cryosurgery	surgical technique involving freezing of the tissues
27	libido	sexual desire
	subjugated	conquered, subdued
28	gerontologist	expert on aging

Structure and Strategy

1. How does the first paragraph reinforce the title and subtitle of this essay?
2. Into how many stages does Stoffman divide the aging process? Identify the paragraphs that describe each stage.
3. Why do you think Stoffman uses so many direct quotations in an essay on the subject of aging? Select two of these direct quotations and explain why they are particularly effective.
4. How does the last paragraph unify or bring together the whole essay? Why do you think Stoffman ends her essay with a sentence fragment?

Content and Purpose

1. The title of this essay is a biblical ALLUSION ("I am going the way of all the earth...." 1 Kings 2:2). Why do you think Stoffman chose this title?
2. What is "the worm" referred to in the subtitle?
3. Summarize the changes, both internal and external, that occur during one's fifties (paragraphs 12 to 17).
4. On his eightieth birthday, Morley Callaghan, the celebrated Canadian novelist, declared that "everyone wants to live to be 80, but no one wants to *be* 80." Do you think Stoffman would agree or disagree with Callaghan?
5. As a result of the Charter of Rights and Freedoms in Canada, many vigorous 65-year-olds are challenging the principle of compulsory retirement. Do you agree or disagree that workers should be required to retire at 65? Why?

Suggestions for Writing

1. Write a directional process essay explaining how to enjoy the experience of aging.

2. Write a directional process essay explaining how to put off the aging process for as long as possible.

Behind the Formaldehyde° Curtain

JESSICA MITFORD

The drama begins to unfold with the arrival of the corpse at the mortuary.

Alas, poor Yorick°! How surprised he would be to see how his counterpart of today is whisked off to a funeral parlor and is in short order sprayed, sliced, pierced, pickled, trussed, trimmed, creamed, waxed, painted, rouged and neatly dressed—transformed from a common corpse into a Beautiful Memory Picture. This process is known in the trade as embalming and restorative art, and is so universally employed in the United States and Canada that the funeral director does it routinely, without consulting corpse or kin. He regards as eccentric those few who are hardy enough to suggest that it might be dispensed with. Yet no law requires embalming, no religious doctrine commends it, nor is it dictated by considerations of health, sanitation, or even of personal daintiness. In no part of the world but in Northern America is it widely used. The purpose of embalming is to make the corpse presentable for viewing in a suitably costly container; and here too the funeral director routinely, without first consulting the family, prepares the body for public display.

Is all this legal? The processes to which a dead body may be subjected are after all to some extent circumscribed by law. In most states, for instance, the signature of next of kin must be obtained before an autopsy may be performed, before the deceased may be cremated, before the body may be turned over to a medical school for research purposes; or such provision must be made in the decedent's° will. In the case of embalming, no such permission is required nor is it ever sought. A textbook, *The Principles and Practices of Embalming*, comments on this: "There is some question regarding the legality of much that is done within the preparation room." The author points out that it would be most unusual for a responsible member of a bereaved family to instruct the mortician, in so many words, to *"embalm"* the body of a deceased relative. The very term "embalming" is so seldom used that the mortician must rely upon custom in the matter. The author concludes that unless the family specifies otherwise, the act of entrusting the body to the care of a funeral establishment carries with it an implied permission to go ahead and embalm.

4   Embalming is indeed a most extraordinary procedure, and one must wonder at the docility° of Americans who each year pay hundreds of millions of dollars for its perpetuation, blissfully ignorant of what it is all about, what is done, how it is done. Not one in ten thousand has any idea of what actually takes place. Books on the subject are extremely hard to come by. They are not to be found in most libraries or bookshops.

5   In an era when huge television audiences watch surgical operations in the comfort of their living rooms, when, thanks to the animated cartoon, the geography of the digestive system has become familiar territory even to the nursery school set, in a land where the satisfaction of curiosity about almost all matters is a national pastime, the secrecy surrounding embalming can, surely, hardly be attributed to the inherent gruesomeness of the subject. Custom in this regard has within this century suffered a complete reversal. In the early days of American embalming, when it was performed in the home of the deceased, it was almost mandatory° for some relative to stay by the embalmer's side and witness the procedure. Today, family members who might wish to be in attendance would certainly be dissuaded° by the funeral director. All others, except apprentices, are excluded by law from the preparation room.

6   A close look at what does actually take place may explain in large measure the undertaker's intractable reticence° concerning a procedure that has become his major *raison d'être*. Is it possible he fears that public information about embalming might lead patrons to wonder if they really want this service? If the funeral men are loath to discuss the subject outside the trade, the reader may, understandably, be equally loath to go on reading at this point. For those who have the stomach for it, let us part the formaldehyde curtain....

7   The body is first laid out in the undertaker's morgue—or rather, Mr. Jones is reposing in the preparation room—to be readied to bid the world farewell.

8   The preparation room in any of the better funeral establishments has the tiled and sterile look of a surgery, and indeed the embalmer-restorative artist who does his chores there is beginning to adopt the term "dermasurgeon" (appropriately corrupted by

some mortician-writers as "demi-surgeon") to describe his calling. His equipment, consisting of scalpels, scissors, augers, forceps, clamps, needles, pumps, tubes, bowls and basins, is crudely imitative of the surgeon's, as is his technique, acquired in a nine- or twelve-month post-highschool course in an embalming school. He is supplied by an advanced chemical industry with a bewildering array of fluids, sprays, pastes, oils, powders, creams, to fix or soften tissue, shrink or distend it as needed, dry it here, restore the moisture there. There are cosmetics, waxes and paints to fill and cover features, even plaster of Paris to replace entire limbs. There are ingenious aids to prop and stabilize the cadaver: a Vari-Pose Head Rest, the Edwards Arm and Hand Positioner, the Repose Block (to support the shoulders during the embalming), and the Throop Foot Positioner, which resembles an old-fashioned stocks°.

Mr. John H. Eckels, president of the Eckels College of Mortuary   9
Science, thus describes the first part of the embalming procedure: "In the hands of a skilled practitioner, this work may be done in a comparatively short time and without mutilating the body other than by slight incision—so slight that it scarcely would cause serious inconvenience if made upon a living person. It is necessary to remove the blood, and doing this not only helps in the disinfecting, but removes the principal cause of disfigurements due to discoloration."

Another textbook discusses the all-important time element: 10
"The earlier this is done, the better, for every hour that elapses between death and embalming will add to the problems and complications encountered...." Just how soon should one get going on the embalming? The author tells us, "On the basis of such scanty information made available to this profession through its rudimentary and haphazard system of technical research, we must conclude that the best results are to be obtained if the subject is embalmed before life is completely extinct—that is, before cellular death has occurred. In the average case, this would mean within an hour after somatic° death." For those who feel that there is something a little rudimentary°, not to say haphazard, about his advice, a comforting thought is offered by another writer. Speaking of fears entertained in early days of premature burial, he points out, "One of the effects of embalming by chemical injection, however, has been to dispel fears of live burial." How true; once the blood is removed, chances of live burial are indeed remote.

To return to Mr. Jones, the blood is drained out through the   11
veins and replaced by embalming fluid pumped in through the arteries. As noted in *The Principles and Practices of Embalming*, "every operator has a favorite injection and drainage point—a fact which becomes a handicap only if he fails or refuses to forsake his favorites when conditions demand it." Typical favorites are the

carotid artery, femoral artery, jugular vein, subclavian vein. There are various choices of embalming fluid. If Flextone is used, it will produce "mild, flexible rigidity. The skin retains a velvety softness, the tissues are rubbery and pliable. Ideal for women and children." It may be blended with B. and G. Products Company's Lyf-Lyk tint, which is guaranteed to reproduce "nature's own skin texture … the velvety appearance of living tissue." Suntone comes in three separate tints: Suntan; Special Cosmetic Tint, a pink shade "especially indicated for young female subjects"; and Regular Cosmetic Tint, moderately pink.

12   About three to six gallons of a dyed and perfumed solution of formaldehyde, glycerin, borax, phenol, alcohol and water is soon circulating through Mr. Jones, whose mouth has been sewn together with a "needle directed upward between the upper lip and gum and brought out through the left nostril," with the corners raised slightly "for a more pleasant expression." If he should be buck-toothed, his teeth are cleaned with Bon Ami and coated with colorless nail polish. His eyes, meanwhile, are closed with flesh-tinted eye caps and eye cement.

13   The next step is to have at Mr. Jones with a thing called a trocar. This is a long, hollow needle attached to a tube. It is jabbed into the abdomen, poked around the entrails and chest cavity, the contents of which are pumped out and replaced with "cavity fluid." This done, and the hole in the abdomen sewn up, Mr. Jones's face is heavily creamed (to protect the skin from burns which may be caused by leakage of the chemicals), and he is covered with a sheet and left unmolested for a while. But not for long—there is more, much more, in store for him. He has been embalmed, but not yet restored, and the best time to start the restorative work is eight to ten hours after embalming, when the tissues have become firm and dry.

14   The object of all this attention to the corpse, it must be remembered, is to make it presentable for viewing in an attitude of healthy repose. "Our customs require the presentation of our dead in the semblance of normality … unmarred by the ravages of illness, disease or mutilation," says Mr. J. Sheridan Mayer in his *Restorative Art*. This is rather a large order since few people die in the full bloom of health, unravaged by illness and unmarked by some disfigurement. The funeral industry is equal to the challenge: "In some cases the gruesome appearance of a mutilated or disease-ridden subject may be quite discouraging. The task of restoration may seem impossible and shake the confidence of the embalmer. This is the time for intestinal fortitude° and determination. Once the formative work is begun and affected tissues are cleaned or removed, all doubts of success vanish. It is surprising and gratifying to discover the results which may be obtained."

The embalmer, having allowed an appropriate interval to   15
elapse, returns to the attack, but now he brings into play the skill
and equipment of sculptor and cosmetician. Is a hand missing?
Casting one in plaster of Paris is a simple matter. "For replacement
purposes, only a cast of the back of the hand is necessary; this is
within the ability of the average operator and is quite adequate." If
a lip or two, a nose or an ear should be missing, the embalmer has
at hand a variety of restorative waxes with which to model replace-
ments. Pores and skin texture are simulated by stippling with a little
brush, and over this cosmetics are laid on. Head off? Decapitation
cases are rather routinely handled. Ragged edges are trimmed, and
head joined to torso with a series of splints, wires and sutures. It is a
good idea to have a little something at the neck—a scarf or a high
collar—when time for viewing comes. Swollen mouth? Cut out tissue as needed from inside the lips. If too much is removed, the surface contour can easily be restored by padding with cotton. Swollen
necks and cheeks are reduced by removing tissue through vertical
incisions made down each side of the neck. "When the deceased is
casketed, the pillow will hide the suture incisions ... as an extra
precaution against leakage, the suture may be painted with liquid
sealer."

The opposite condition is more likely to present itself—that of   16
emaciation. His hypodermic syringe now loaded with massage
cream, the embalmer seeks out and fills the hollowed and sunken
areas by injection. In this procedure the backs of the hands and fingers and the under-chin area should not be neglected.

Positioning the lips is a problem that recurrently challenges the   17
ingenuity of the embalmer. Closed too tightly, they tend to give a
stern, even disapproving expression. Ideally, embalmers feel, the
lips should give the impression of being ever so slightly parted, the
upper lip protruding slightly for a more youthful appearance. This
takes some engineering, however, as the lips tend to drift apart. Lip
drift can sometimes be remedied by pushing one or two straight
pins through the inner margin of the lower lip and then inserting
them between the two front upper teeth. If Mr. Jones happens to
have no teeth, the pins can just as easily be anchored in his
Armstrong Face Former and Denture Replacer. Another method to
maintain lip closure is to dislocate the lower jaw, which is then held
in its new position by a wire run through holes which have been
drilled through the upper and lower jaws at the midline. As the
French are fond of saying, *il faut souffrir pour être belle°*.

If Mr. Jones has died of jaundice, the embalming fluid will very   18
likely turn him green. Does this deter the embalmer? Not if he has
intestinal fortitude. Masking pastes and cosmetics are heavily laid
on, burial garments and casket interiors are color-correlated with

particular care, and Jones is displayed beneath rose-colored lights. Friends will say "How *well* he looks." Death by carbon monoxide, on the other hand, can be rather a good thing from the embalmer's viewpoint: "One advantage is the fact that this type of discoloration is an exaggerated form of a natural pink coloration." This is nice because the healthy glow is already present and needs but little attention.

19   The patching and filling completed, Mr. Jones is now shaved, washed and dressed. Cream-based cosmetic, available in pink, flesh, suntan, brunette and blond, is applied to his hands and face, his hair is shampooed and combed (and, in the case of Mrs. Jones, set), his hands manicured. For the horny-handed son of toil° special care must be taken; cream should be applied to remove ingrained grime, and the nails cleaned. "If he were not in the habit of having them manicured in life, trimming and shaping is advised for better appearance—never questioned by kin."

20   Jones is now ready for casketing (this is the present participle of the verb "to casket"). In this operation his right shoulder should be depressed slightly "to turn the body a bit to the right and soften the appearance of lying flat on the back." Positioning the hands is a matter of importance, and special rubber positioning blocks may be used. The hands should be cupped slightly for a more lifelike, relaxed appearance. Proper placement of the body requires a delicate sense of balance. It should lie as high as possible in the casket, yet not so high that the lid, when lowered, will hit the nose. On the other hand, we are cautioned, placing the body too low "creates the impression that the body is in a box."

21   Jones is next wheeled into the appointed slumber room where a few last touches may be added—his favorite pipe placed in his hand or, if he was a great reader, a book propped into position. (In the case of little Master Jones a Teddy bear may be clutched.) Here he will hold open house for a few days, visiting hours 10 A.M. to 9 P.M.

22   All now being in readiness, the funeral director calls a staff conference to make sure that each assistant knows his precise duties. Mr. Wilber Kriege writes: "This makes your staff feel that they are a part of the team, with a definite assignment that must be properly carried out if the whole plan is to succeed. You never heard of a football coach who failed to talk to his entire team before they go on the field. They have drilled on the plays they are to execute for hours and days, and yet the successful coach knows the importance of making even the bench-warming third-string substitute feel that he is important if the game is to be won." The winning of *this* game is predicated upon glass-smooth handling of the logistics°. The funeral director has notified the pallbearers whose names were furnished by the family, has arranged for the presence of clergyman,

organist, and soloist, has provided transportation for everybody, has organized and listed the flowers sent by friends. In *Psychology of Funeral Service* Mr. Edward A. Martin points out: "He may not always do as much as the family thinks he is doing, but it is his helpful guidance that they appreciate in knowing they are proceeding as they should.... The important thing is how well his services can be used to make the family believe they are giving unlimited expression to their own sentiment."

The religious service may be held in a church or in the chapel of   23
the funeral home; the funeral director vastly prefers the latter arrangement, for not only is it more convenient for him but it affords him the opportunity to show off his beautiful facilities to the gathered mourners. After the clergyman has had his say, the mourners queue up to file past the casket for a last look at the deceased. The family is *never* asked whether they want an open-casket ceremony; in the absence of their instruction to the contrary, this is taken for granted. Consequently well over 90 per cent of all American funerals feature the open casket—a custom unknown in other parts of the world. Foreigners are astonished by it. An English woman living in San Francisco described her reaction in a letter to the writer:

> I myself have attended only one funeral here—that of an elderly fellow worker of mine. After the service I could not understand why everyone was walking towards the coffin (sorry, I mean casket), but thought I had better follow the crowd. It shook me rigid to get there and find the casket open and poor old Oscar lying there in his brown tweed suit, wearing a suntan makeup and just the wrong shade of lipstick. If I had not been extremely fond of the old boy, I have a horrible feeling that I might have giggled. Then and there I decided that I could never face another American funeral—even dead.

The casket (which has been resting throughout the service on a   24
Classic Beauty Ultra Metal Casket Bier) is now transferred by a hydraulically operated device called Porto-Lift to a balloon-tired, Glide Easy casket carriage which will wheel it to yet another conveyance, the Cadillac Funeral Coach. This may be lavender, cream, light green—anything but black. Interiors, of course, are color-correlated, "for the man who cannot stop short of perfection."

At graveside, the casket is lowered into the earth. This office,   25
once the prerogative° of friends of the deceased, is now performed by a patented mechanical lowering device. A "Lifetime Green" artificial grass mat is at the ready to conceal the sere° earth, and overhead, to conceal the sky, is a portable Steril Chapel Tent ("resists the intense heat and humidity of summer and the terrific storms of winter ... available in Silver Grey, Rose or Evergreen"). Now is the

time for the ritual scattering of earth over the coffin, as the solemn words "earth to earth, ashes to ashes, dust to dust" are pronounced by the officiating cleric. This can today be accomplished "with a mere flick of the wrist with the Gordon Leak-Proof Earth Dispenser. No grasping of a handful of dirt, no soiled fingers. Simple, dignified, beautiful, reverent! The modern way!" The Gordon Earth Dispenser (at $5) is of nickel-plated brass construction. It is not only "attractive to the eye and long wearing"; it is also "one of the 'tools' for building better public relations" if presented as "an appropriate non-commercial gift" to the clergyman. It is shaped something like a saltshaker.

26   Untouched by human hand, the coffin and the earth are now united.

27   It is in the function of directing the participants through this maze of gadgetry that the funeral director has assigned to himself his relatively new role of "grief therapist." He has relieved the family of every detail, he has revamped° the corpse to look like a living doll, he has arranged for it to nap for a few days in a slumber room, he has put on a well-oiled performance in which the concept of *death* has played no part whatsoever—unless it was inconsiderately mentioned by the clergyman who conducted the religious service. He has done everything in his power to make the funeral a real pleasure for everybody concerned. He and his team have given their all to score an upset victory over death.

> [ ]

JESSICA MITFORD

Essayist Jessica Mitford was born to a prominent family at Batsford Mansion, England, in 1917, and settled in the United States in 1939. Mitford began her writing career in the 1950s; among her best known works are *Hons and Rebels, The Trial of Dr. Spock,* and *Kind and Unusual Punishment.*

Paragraph
Words and Meanings

	formaldehyde	chemical used to embalm bodies
2	Alas, poor Yorick	famous line from Shakespeare's *Hamlet*, addressed to a skull
3	decedent	dead person
4	docility	lamblike trust and willingness
5	mandatory	necessary
	dissuaded	persuaded against

intractable reticence	unwillingness to discuss	6
stocks	wooden shackles used to punish offenders	8
somatic	bodily	10
rudimentary	basic	
intestinal fortitude	"guts," courage	14
il faut souffrir pour *être belle*	French for "you have to suffer to be beautiful"	17
horny-handed son of toil	cliché for a labourer	19
logistics	arrangements	22
prerogative	privilege	25
sere	dry	
revamped	altered	27

Structure and Strategy

1. Consider the title and first paragraph of this essay. What ANALOGY is introduced? How does the analogy help establish Mitford's TONE?
2. Look at the last paragraph. How is the analogy introduced in paragraph 1 reinforced in the conclusion? What words specifically contribute to the analogy?
3. The process of preparing a corpse for burial involves two main procedures: embalming and restoration. Identify the paragraphs in which Mitford explains these two procedures.
4. Identify the substeps that make up the final stage in the burial process (paragraphs 20 to 25).

Content and Purpose

1. In paragraphs 2 and 8, without saying so directly, how does Mitford imply that she disapproves of embalming? Can you find other examples of her implied disapproval?
2. What medical justification for embalming is offered in paragraph 10? How does Mitford undercut this argument?
3. Why does Mitford refer to the corpse as "Mr. Jones"?
4. What reason does Mitford suggest is behind the "secrecy surrounding embalming"? If the details of the procedure were common knowledge, what do you think the effect would be on the mortuary business?
5. What was your reaction to Mitford's essay? Do you think your response was what the author intended?

Suggestions for Writing

1. Mitford's essay explains the funeral director's job as a process. Write a process analysis explaining a job or task with which you are familiar.
2. Research another means of disposing of the dead, such as cremation (burning a dead body) or cryonics (freezing a dead, diseased body in the hope of restoring it to life when a cure has been found). Write an informational process paper explaining it.
3. Write an informational process analysis explaining the ceremony or ritual behaviour associated with the birth of a baby, a child's birthday, or the initiation of a child into the religious community (such as a bar mitzvah or confirmation).

Additional Suggestions for Writing: Process Analysis

I. Choose one of the topics below and develop it into an informational process analysis.

1. How a computer (or any other electronic device) works
2. How a child is born
3. How a particular rock group, sports personality, or political figure appeals to the crowd
4. How a bill is passed in Parliament
5. How a company plans the marketing of a new product
6. How a particular chemical reaction takes place
7. How alcohol (or any other drug) affects the body
8. How microwaves cook food
9. How learning takes place
10. How a particular process in nature occurs—for example, how coral forms, a spider spins a web, salmon spawn, lightning happens, or a snowflake forms

II. Choose one of the topics below and develop it into a directional process analysis.

1. How to buy (or sell) something: a used car, a house, a piece of sports equipment, a stereo system, junk
2. How to perform a particular life-saving technique—for example, mouth-to-mouth resuscitation or the Heimlich manoeuvre
3. How to play roulette, blackjack, poker, or some other game of chance
4. How to get attention
5. How to prepare for a job interview
6. How to choose a mate (or roommate, friend, or pet)
7. How to make or build something—for example, beer, a kite, a radio transmitter, bread
8. How to survive English (or any other subject that you are studying)
9. How to get your own way
10. How to talk your way out of a traffic ticket, a failing grade, a date, a conversation with a bore, a threatened punishment, or keeping a promise

U N I T

Classification and Division: Explaining Kinds and Parts

What? The Definition

In **analysis**, we separate something into its parts in order to determine their essential features and study their relationship to each other. A research chemist, for example, analyzes a substance by breaking it down into its component elements. We speak of trying to "analyze someone's motives" in an effort to understand what prompts a person to behave in a certain way. Some people undergo years of psychoanalysis in an attempt to identify and explore their unconscious mental processes. In Unit Three, we used the term *process analysis* to describe a writing pattern in which the subject is divided into steps or stages: the steps involved in making stew or in embalming a body, for instance. In Unit Six, we will look at subjects that are analyzed in terms of their causes or effects, an organizational pattern called *causal analysis*. The subjects of this unit, **classification** and **division**, are also forms of analysis.

The various kinds of analysis all involve sorting or dividing—breaking a complex whole into its categories or parts.

In the rhetorical pattern called **classification**, the subject is a group of things, and the writer's task is to sort the group into classes or categories on the basis of some shared characteristic. For example, fast-food hamburgers can be classified according to the chains that serve them: McDonald's, Wendy's, Harvey's, and Burger King. Then the writer would explain the distinctive features of the burgers in each category. Newspapers can be classified into tabloids like *The Toronto Sun*, which aim for a working-class audience; broad-based, general circulation papers like *The Toronto Star*, which aim for a middle-class audience; and upscale, business-oriented papers like *The Globe and Mail*, which appeal to professional, upper-middle-class readers. Singles could be classified into the kinds of dates they represent: divine, dull, or disastrous.

Classification is a familiar strategy. It is used so often that there is even an old joke that relies on popular knowledge of the technique for its point: "There are two kinds of people in the world—those who sort the world into two kinds of people and those who don't."

In **division**, on the other hand, a single subject is divided into its component parts. For example, a Big Mac consists of two all-beef patties, special sauce, pickles, cheese, lettuce, and onions on a sesame seed bun. A newspaper can be divided into its various sections: news, sports, features, entertainment, and classified ads. In one of the reading selections that follows, Martin Luther King, Jr., divides a "complete life" into three dimensions: length, breadth, and height. In division, the subject is always a single entity: one hamburger, one newspaper, or one life. The writer's task is to identify and explain the parts that make up the whole.

Why? The Purpose

Division and classification are methods by which we can isolate, separate, and sort things. They are essential ways of making sense out of the world around us. Both strategies appeal to the reader's need for order in the way information is presented.

Classification, as we've seen, is a sorting mechanism. It is the pattern to choose when you find yourself writing a paper that answers the question, "What are the main kinds or types of S?"

Classification is useful when you need to examine a group of similar things with meaningful differences between them. You could classify colleges: CEGEPs in Quebec, CAATs in Ontario, and university-transfer institutions in British Columbia. You could classify people: various kinds of musicians or actors or athletes, for example. In one of the essays in this unit, Erika Ritter, based on her experience as a radio broadcaster, classifies all the people of the world into two types: AM and FM. Ideas (such as economic theories), places (such as resorts, slums, amusement parks), and events (such as golf tournaments, weddings, elections) can all be sorted into kinds and explained in terms that your readers will find informative, useful, and even—when appropriate—entertaining.

A *division paper* usually answers one of two questions:

1. What are the component parts of S?
2. What are the important characteristics or features of S?

Once you have reduced the subject to its constituent parts, you can examine each part in turn to discover its distinctive features and its function within the whole. Division can be used to explore and clarify many kinds of subjects. You can analyze an organization (a college, for instance), a geographical location (such as the city of Winnipeg), a musical group (perhaps a rock band), an idea (equal pay for work of equal value), or a part of the body (such as the digestive system) by dividing it into its parts.

Classification and division are used to give shape and order to the welter of information that surrounds us. In the business world, for example, papers and reports are too often a hodgepodge of data or opinion that fails to provide the reader with an orderly explanation of the subject. Dividing or classifying the material organizes it into logically related units that the reader can grasp and understand.

Besides giving form and focus to shapeless chunks of information, division and classification are useful for evaluation purposes. A real estate company might divide a city into its residential areas so that prospective home buyers can choose where they want to live. Consumers' magazines classify different kinds of dishwashers, stereo turntables, automobiles, or dandruff shampoos, in order to recommend which brand is the best buy. Whether the writer's purpose is to organize a mass of data or to evaluate the relative merits of several items or ideas, classification and division can help to ensure a clear, coherent piece of communication.

How? The Technique

Writing a good *classification paper* involves three steps. To begin with, make sure your classification is both complete and logical. For instance, classifying the Romance languages (those descended from Latin since A.D. 800) into French, Italian, and Portuguese would be incomplete because there are many more Romance languages than these three. However, if your purpose were to classify the Romance languages most frequently spoken in Canada today, the list above would be complete.

Your classification will be logical as long as your categories do not overlap: they must all be different from each other. To test your classification for logical soundness, check to be sure that no example can be included under more than one category. For instance, if you were to classify your favourite kinds of movies into the categories of science fiction, comedy, and war films, where would you put *Catch-22*, a comic film about war, or *Star Wars*?

Of course, a classification paper must be based on a clear thesis statement:

> The kinds (or categories) of S are a, b, c, and d.

Example: Most teachers fit into one of three categories: Bumblers, Martinets, and Pros.

Writing a good *division paper* involves similar steps: first, you clarify the principle of division; second, you identify the appropriate components of the subject; and third, you construct a clear thesis statement.

Most subjects can be divided in a number of different ways. For instance, you could divide a college into its physical areas: classrooms, offices, cafeteria, recreational facilities, and plant services. Or you could divide a college into its human components: faculty, students, administrators, and support staff. How you choose to divide something will determine the parts that you analyze and the relationship between those parts that you explore. Choose your dividing principle carefully, keeping your audience in mind: what specific aspects of your subject do you want your readers to know more about?

Next, decide whether your division is to be *exhaustive* (that is, to include *all* the component parts of the subject) or *representative* (to include a *few* of the major component parts). Sometimes, the nature of your subject determines which approach you will take: if there are only two or three component parts, for example, it makes good sense to include them all. But if there are a dozen or more, a carefully chosen representative sampling will give your readers the information they require without trying their patience in the process.

Finally, include a thesis statement that maps out the scope and arrangement of your paper. It will probably look something like this:

> The component parts of S are a, b, c, and d.

Example: Blood is made up of plasma, red cells, white cells, and platelets.

On the other hand, it may read like this:

> The significant characteristics of S are a, b, and c.

Example: A good business letter is one that is concise, clear, and courteous.

Classification and division are useful rhetorical strategies by themselves, but they can be used together effectively, too. In "What I

Have Lived For," for example, Bertrand Russell divides his life's purpose, his reason for living, into what he calls "three passions": the longing for love, the search for knowledge, and pity for the suffering of mankind. Then he classifies his search for knowledge into the three kinds of knowledge he sought: the social sciences, the natural sciences, and mathematics.

Whether you choose to apply them separately or together, classification and division are two of the most useful strategies you can use to explain a complex subject to your readers. They can help you create order out of chaos in many different situations. Both strategies have practical and professional applications. Division is used on the job in organizational analyses, cost breakdowns, and technical reports. Classification is frequently the logical pattern on which performance appraisals, market projections, or product assessments are based. The ability to analyze through division and classification is obviously a useful skill for any writer to acquire.

The sample essay below is a paper that classifies into three categories a subject dear to the hearts of all students: teachers.

Bumblers, Martinets, and Pros

Introduction (uses quotations)

The playwright George Bernard Shaw provided us with the memorable definition, "Those who can, do. Those who can't, teach." The film director Woody Allen took the definition one step farther, "Those who can't teach, teach gym." At one time or another, most of us have suffered these truisms. We've all encountered teachers who fit Shaw's definition, as well as some who manage to do their

Thesis statement — jobs successfully, even cheerfully. Overall, most teachers fit into one of three categories: Bumblers, Martinets, and Pros.

First category (developed with descriptive details)

Every student gets a Bumbler at least once. She's the teacher who trips over the doorjamb as she makes her first entrance. She looks permanently flustered, can't find her lesson plan, and dithers as she scrambles through her mess of books and papers. The Bumbler can't handle the simplest educational technologies: chalk self-destructs in her fingers, overhead projectors blow up at her touch, and filmstrips snap if she so much as looks in their direction. Organization isn't Ms. Bumbler's strong point, either. She drifts off in mid-sentence, eyes focused dreamily out the window. Students can easily derail her with off-topic questions. She'll forget to collect assignments or to give the test that everyone has studied for. The Bumbler is an amiable sort, but her mind is on a perpetual slow boat to nowhere. Students can learn in her class, but only if they are willing to take a great deal of initiative.

Second category (note the definition of an unfamiliar term)

Martinet was the name of a seventeenth-century French general who invented a particularly nasty system of military drill. Thus, the word itself has come to mean a strict disciplinarian, a stickler for the rules, a tough "drill sergeant." As a teacher, the Martinet is an uptight, rigid authoritarian who sends shivers down students' spines. He rarely smiles, certainly not during the first month. His voice is harsh, biting, and he specializes in the barbed response and the humiliating putdown. His classes unfold in a precise and boring manner. Each minute is accounted for, as he scouts the room for any disruptive or slumbering captives to be brought to heel. He tolerates no searching questions or interesting digressions. His assignments are lengthy and tedious; his tests are notoriously fearsome. Instead of the critical inquiry into ideas, rote learning takes place in the Martinet's classroom. And it takes place at the expense of the patience and self-esteem of his students.

Third category (note the implied contrast to the previous two categories)

Every once in a while, a student is blessed with the teacher who can be described as a Professional. The Pro is characterized by a genuine liking and respect for students and is motivated by enthusiasm for the subject matter. This teacher is organized enough to present lessons clearly, but not so hidebound as to cut off questions or the occasional excursion along an interesting sideroad of learning. The Pro's classroom is relaxed, friendly, yet stimulating enough to keep students concentrating on the task at hand. Assignments are designed to enhance learning; tests are rigorous but fair. Landing in the Pro's class is a stroke of luck. Such a teacher is a gift, for the Pro imparts the desire and ability to learn to the students he or she encounters.

These characterizations of the Bumbler, the Martinet, and the Pro are, of course, extreme portraits of some of the worst and best qualities a teacher can possess. Indeed, some teachers, in Jekyll-and-Hyde fashion, display characteristics of two or more types, sometimes in a single class period! In an ideal world and a perfect course, the student would be given a choice of instructors. Who would opt for a Bumbler or a Martinet, given the chance to sign up for a Pro?

Speak Low when You Speak FM

ERIKA RITTER

In recent years, a lot of attention—too 1 *much* attention, if you ask me—has been paid to the concept of personality types "A" and "B". The way the story goes, you are either a classic Type A (over-achieving, twitchy, driven to succeed) or a

From *Ritter in Residence* by Erika Ritter. Copyright 1987. Used by permission of the Canadian publishers, McClelland & Stewart, Toronto.

Type B—which means you are phlegmatic°, unmotivated, and, to put it bluntly, the sort who needs to be ordered in out of the rain.

2   If only the whole thing were as simple as that. While it's absolutely true that there *are* two basic personality types, that "A" and "B" business is strictly for blood groups. The two *real* personality categories, subtle, complex, and essentially incompatible, can be more accurately delineated as AM and FM.

3   You have to trust me on this one. See, I've worked in radio, and I can appreciate these distinctions. In fact, it was when I made the transition from an FM program in stereo to hosting an AM radio show that I began to understand what a wide chasm I was attempting to vault°.

4   The problem was, I spoke only FM. I was the type who referred to "a recent reissue of a fine old Angel recording", instead of "a golden oldie", as an AM announcer is required by broadcast law to say. The composers I'd mentioned on FM as "hearkening to the inspiration of a rollicksome Muse", had to become "good old boys" over on the AM dial. Indeed, my complete fluency in the AM tongue was indisputably established only when I discarded phrases like "a variegated repertoire for your audial delectation", in favour of "good-lookin' music comin' at ya".

5   And the linguistic distinctions go far beyond mere musical vocabulary. FM types speak of "data that can be delineated without a major assault on veracity°", at the same time as native speakers of AM talk about "the straight poop".

6   Well, you don't have to be a genius (sorry, AMers, I mean "a brain") to perceive that the development of these separate languages stems from the need to express utterly different personalities and to embrace a myriad (i.e., a whole bunch) of opposing characteristics that go far beyond the two major frequency bands on most radios.

7   Not only do FM people speak FM, they lead FM lives. For example, in order to unwind at the end of a hectic day in the library stacks, a typical FMer enjoys a long bath scented with some herbal fragrance purchased on that hiking trip through the Lake District° two summers ago. The AM personality, on the other hand, enjoys a vigorous shower with a loofah°—one of the few foreign-sounding words he permits into his vocabulary or his life.

8   While the FM personality prefers to travel around town by streetcar, clutching a volume of Henry James and a paper twist full of winegums, the AM type still owns that Volkswagen beetle he acquired in a swap for the complete works of Alan Watts and two joints back at Berkeley, where he took a summer course one time. The beetle is named Stokely—for reasons the AMer can no longer remember.

By now, you're getting the idea, I'm sure. But just in case you   9
aren't yet absolutely positive of what properly constitutes AM and
FM, here is a quick checklist of some of the major differences:

FM	AM
alfalfa sprouts in a pita	Big Mac
pleated wool skirt in clan tartan	faded denim culottes
Alistair Cooke	Bob Barker
Abyssinian cat named Haile Selassie	bull terrier named Deputy Dawg
rambling old cottage up on Georgian Bay	Club Med
Rainer Werner Fassbinder	Steven Spielberg
Dorothy L. Sayers	Raymond Chandler
"The Birds" by Respighi	"The Byrds' Greatest Hits"
Dubonnet	Upper Canada Lager
wire whisk	blender
Pierre Trudeau	Garry Trudeau

Classifying your friends according to type is easy, of course.   10
Those who are brisk but not boorish, somewhat American-oriented
in personality, sensual, and basically comfortable with the status
quo are natural AMers. Those who are retiring, convoluted°, Britishy
(regardless of racial inheritance), and altogether a tad twee°, belong
in the FM column in the ledger of life.

Things get trickier, however, when you attempt to work out which   11
pigeonhole you yourself belong in by right. After all, who of us isn't a
bit old-fashioned in some moods, fanciful and dreamy and nostalgic
for seminars in English Literature? While at other moments straight-
ahead, desperately modern, and so relaxed with the culture we live in
that we can actually take a coolerful of beers to the beach, string up a
net, and play volleyball with a bevy of suntanned companions.

We are, of course, much more complex than our easily assigned   12
friends, and contain within us the seeds of both the AM and FM
types. Roughly translated, this means we have the capacity to
regard a "traditional Christmas" as one spent either with Bing
Crosby or with the Early Music Consort. How these warring internal elements may be successfully resolved is, alas, material for
another discussion altogether.

ERIKA RITTER

Playwright, columnist, and radio broadcaster, Erika Ritter was born in
Regina, Saskatchewan. Her most recent publications include the play *Murder*

at McQueen (1986) and two collections of commentaries on urban trends and preoccupations, *Urban Scrawl* (1985) and *Ritter in Residence* (1987).

Paragraph

Words and Meanings

1	phlegmatic	calm, cool
3	vault	jump over
5	veracity	truth
7	Lake District	region of England made famous by nineteenth-century Romantic poets such as Wordsworth and Coleridge
	loofah	dried pod of a plant used as a bath brush
10	convoluted	indirect, not straightforward
	a tad twee	affected, pretentious

Structure and Strategy

1. What strategy does Ritter use in her INTRODUCTION (paragraphs 1 and 2)? How does she use this strategy to set up the classification on which the essay is based?
2. Consider the DICTION of this essay. Is it formal or informal? What is the effect of beginning sentences with words such as "See" (paragraph 3) and "Well" (paragraph 6)? How does Ritter's diction contribute to the TONE of the piece?
3. Which paragraphs outline the "linguistic distinctions" between AM and FM people? Underline three or four examples that Ritter uses to support her point about the different ways these two groups speak.
4. Is Ritter's classification complete and logical? (See the introduction to this unit.) What are the two points on which the author bases her classification (see paragraphs 4 and 5 and 7 and 8)? What is the function of paragraph 6?
5. How do paragraphs 11 and 12 contribute to the UNITY of Ritter's essay?

Content and Purpose

1. Into what two basic categories does Ritter classify people? What personal experience has she had that qualifies her to be an authority on this subject?
2. Look at the checklist in paragraph 9. How could you classify it into categories that distinguish AM people from FM people? (Hint: the first two are "favourite food" and "favourite outfit.")
3. According to the author, it's easy to divide all the people in the world into two groups. Who cannot be so easily classified? Why? (See paragraphs 10 and 11.)

Suggestions for Writing

1. Are you an AM person or an FM person—or both? Write an essay explaining which of the categories you fit into, and support your thesis with a variety of specific examples.
2. Write an essay classifying people according to what television stations they watch, or what newspapers they read, or how they spend their leisure time, or any other basis of classification that interests you. Be sure your classification is both complete and logical. (You might also want to make it humorous.)

Sit Down and Shut Up or Don't Sit by Me

DENNIS DERMODY

All right, I admit it: I'm a tad neurotic   1
when it comes to making it to the movies on time. I have to be there at least a half hour before the feature begins. Not that I'm worried about long lines at the box office, either. The movies I rush off to see are generally so sparsely attended you can hear crickets in the audience. It's just a thing I do.

Of course, sitting for 30 minutes watching a theater fill up is   2
pretty boring, but through the years I've amused myself with a Margaret Mead°-like study of the way people come in and take their seats and their antics during a movie. I felt I should share my impressions lest you find yourself succumbing to these annoying traits.

Right off the bat: Leave the kids at home. We're not talking   3
about *Aladdin* or *Home Alone 2*—that I understand—but recently I went to see *Body of Evidence*, and it looked like a day-care center in the theater. Strollers were flying down the aisle, children were whining for candy, restless and audibly bored (especially during the hot-wax-dripping sequence), and eventually the day-care atmosphere caused fights among the adults. "Shut your kid up!" prompted a proud parent to slug a fellow patron, and before you knew it there were angry skirmishes all over the theater and the police had to be brought in. So either leave them at home with a sitter or tie them up to a fire hydrant outside the theater.

4   For some people, choosing a seat takes on moral and philosophical implications. Sometimes they stand in the middle of the
aisle juggling coats, popcorn, and Cokes, seemingly overwhelmed
by the prospect of choice. Should I sit down front, or will that be
too close? Is this too far back? That man seems awfully tall, I bet I
couldn't see the movie if I sat behind him. I'd love to sit somewhere
in the middle but would I be too close to that group of teenagers
shooting heroin into their necks? If I sit on this side, will the angle
be too weird to watch the movie? Is that seat unoccupied because
it's broken? Good Lord, the lights are dimming and I haven't made
up my mind and now I won't be able to see where I'm going.

5   Many, upon choosing their seats, find they are unsatisfied and
have to move. I've watched many couples go from one spot to
another more than a dozen times before settling down—it's like
watching a bird testing different spots to build a nest.

6   As the lights begin to dim and the annoying theater-chain logo
streaks across the screen, lo and behold, here come the *latecomers*!
Their eyes unaccustomed to the dark, in a panic they search for
friends, for assistance, for a lonely seat. Just the other day, I
watched an elderly woman come into the darkened theater 10
minutes after the movie had begun and say out loud, "I can't see
anything!" She then proceeded to inch her way down the aisle,
grabbing onto what she thought were seats but were actually people's heads. I saw her sit down right in the lap of someone who
shrieked in shock. After the woman stumbled back into the aisle,
chattering wildly, someone mercifully directed her to an empty
seat. Then, after a great flourish of getting out of her bulky coat,
she asked spiritedly of the grumbling souls around her, "What did
I miss?"

7   I also must address the behavior of people *during* the movie.
The *chatterers* comment blithely on everything that is happening on
the screen. Like Tourette's syndrome° sufferers unable to control
what they blurt out, these people say anything that comes into their
heads. "What a cute puppy," they say when they spy an animal
ambling off to the side of the frame. "I have that lamp at home,"
they exclaim. And add, five minutes later, "But mine is red."

8   The *krinklers* wander down the aisle with a million shopping
bags and wait for a key sequence, then begin to forage° in their
bags for the perfect and most annoying plastic wrap, which they
use to make noise with sadistic relish. You try to focus on the screen
but the racket starts up again with a wild flourish. I've seen grown
men leap to their feet with tears streaming down their face and
scream, "Will you stop shaking that motherfucking bag!"

9   The *unending box of popcorn people* sit directly behind you and
start masticating during the opening credits. It's bad enough having

the smell of cooked corn wafting around you, but the sound is enough to drive you mad. You tell yourself that eventually they'll finish, but they never do. They keep chewing and chewing and chewing and you're deathly afraid that next they'll start on a four-pound box of malted milk balls.

So in summary: Get to the movie theater early and scout out   10
the territory. It's a jungle in there, filled with a lot of really stupid animals. Know the telltale signs and act accordingly. And then sit down and shut up.

DENNIS DERMODY

U.S. writer Dennis Dermody is the film critic for *Paper* magazine and a contributor to *Mirabella*, *Film Threat*, and *Details* magazines. For the past 12 years, he has been nanny to the son of actor Willem Dafoe. His forthcoming book, a collection of film essays, is entitled *How to Cook and Eat Macaulay Culkin*.

Words and Meanings

Paragraph

Margaret Mead	U.S. anthropologist famous for her studies of people's behaviour in various "exotic" cultures	2
Tourette's syndrome	hereditary disease that causes uncontrollable physical twitching and bursts of speech in its sufferers	7
forage	search for food	8

Structure and Strategy

1. What is the function of paragraph 3? After all, not all movie-goers bring their children to the theatre.
2. Identify three similes (see FIGURES OF SPEECH) in paragraphs 3, 5, and 7. How would the impact of this essay be lessened if the author had not included these figures of speech?
3. When Dermody uses phrases such as "tie them up to a fire hydrant" (paragraph 3) or "teenagers shooting heroin into their necks" (paragraph 4), he obviously does not mean to be taken seriously. Identify two or three other examples of this kind of exaggeration and consider how it affects the TONE of the essay.
4. What metaphor (see FIGURES OF SPEECH) does Dermody use in the conclusion of this piece? How does it contribute to the UNITY of the essay?

Content and Purpose

1. What does Dermody mean when he admits, in his opening sentence, that he is a "tad neurotic"? How does this confession affect the reader's response to the judgments that follow?
2. What is the author's PURPOSE (see paragraph 2)? Do you think he achieves it?
3. This essay classifies movie-goers according to their pre-movie and during-movie behaviours. Identify the six categories of the author's classification system.
4. Would you like to go to a movie with the author? Why?

Suggestions for Writing

1. Write an essay in which you classify party-goers, friends, relatives, neighbours, children, workers, bosses, students, or any other group of people you choose. Be sure your classification is logical and consistent, and that the purpose of your classification is clear to your reader.
2. How do you spend your time? Write an essay identifying the categories into which you divide your time each week. Do you learn anything about yourself from this exercise?

Toothpaste

DAVID BODANIS

1   nto the bathroom [we go], and after the most pressing need is satisfied it's time to brush the teeth. The tube of toothpaste is squeezed, its pinched metal seams are splayed, pressure waves are generated inside, and the paste begins to flow. But what's in this toothpaste, so carefully being extruded° out?

2   Water mostly, 30 to 45 per cent in most brands: ordinary, everyday simple tap water. It's there because people like to have a big gob of toothpaste to spread on the brush, and water is the cheapest stuff there is when it comes to making big gobs. Dripping a bit from the tap onto your brush would cost virtually nothing; whipped in with the rest of the toothpaste the manufacturers can sell it at a neat

and accountant-pleasing $2 per pound equivalent. Toothpaste manufacture is a very lucrative occupation.

Second to water in quantity is chalk: exactly the same material that schoolteachers use to write on blackboards. It is collected from the crushed remains of long-dead ocean creatures. In the Cretaceous° seas chalk particles served as part of the wickedly sharp outer skeleton that these creatures had to wrap around themselves to keep from getting chomped by all the slightly larger other ocean creatures they met. Their massed graves are our present chalk deposits.

The individual chalk particles—the size of the smallest mud particles in your garden—have kept their toughness over the aeons°, and now on the toothbrush they'll need it. The enamel outer coating of the tooth they'll have to face is the hardest substance in the body—tougher than skull, or bone, or nail. Only the chalk particles in toothpaste can successfully grind into the teeth during brushing, ripping off the surface layers like an abrading wheel grinding down a boulder in a quarry.

The craters, slashes, and channels that the chalk tears into the teeth will also remove a certain amount of built-up yellow in the carnage, and it is for that polishing function that it's there. A certain amount of unduly enlarged extra-abrasive chalk fragments tear such cavernous pits into the teeth that future decay bacteria will be able to bunker down there and thrive; the quality control people find it almost impossible to screen out these errant super-chalk pieces, and government regulations allow them to stay in.

In case even the gouging doesn't get all the yellow off, another substance is worked into the toothpaste cream. This is titanium dioxide. It comes in tiny spheres, and it's the stuff bobbing around in white wall paint to make it come out white. Splashed around onto your teeth during the brushing it coats much of the yellow that remains. Being water soluble it leaks off in the next few hours and is swallowed, but at least for the quick glance up in the mirror after finishing it will make the user think his teeth are truly white. Some manufacturers add optical whitening dyes—the stuff more commonly found in washing machine bleach—to make extra sure that the glance in the mirror shows reassuring white.

These ingredients alone would not make a very attractive concoction°. They would stick in the tube like a sloppy white plastic lump, hard to squeeze out as well as revolting to the touch. Few consumers would savor rubbing in a mixture of water, ground-up blackboard chalk and the whitener from latex paint first thing in the morning. To get around that finicky distaste the manufacturers have mixed in a host of other goodies.

8   To keep the glop from drying out, a mixture including glycerine glycol—related to the most common car anti-freeze ingredient—is whipped in with the chalk and water, and to give *that* concoction a bit of substance (all we really have so far is wet colored chalk) a large helping is added of gummy molecules from the seaweed *Chondrus Crispus*. This seaweed ooze spreads in among the chalk, paint and anti-freeze, then stretches itself in all directions to hold the whole mass together. A bit of paraffin oil (the fuel that flickers in camping lamps) is pumped in with it to help the moss ooze keep the whole substance smooth.

9   With the glycol, ooze and paraffin we're almost there. Only two major chemicals are left to make the refreshing, cleansing substance we know as toothpaste. The ingredients so far are fine for cleaning, but they wouldn't make much of the satisfying foam we have come to expect in the morning brushing.

10   To remedy that, every toothpaste on the market has a big dollop of detergent added, too. You've seen the suds detergent will make in a washing machine. The same substance added here will duplicate that inside the mouth. It's not particularly necessary, but it sells.

11   The only problem is that by itself this ingredient tastes, well, too like detergent. It's horribly bitter and harsh. The chalk put in toothpaste is pretty foul-tasting too for that matter. It's to get around that gustatory° discomfort that the manufacturers put in the ingredient they tout° perhaps the most of all. This is the flavoring, and it has to be strong. Double rectified peppermint oil is used—a flavorer so powerful that chemists know better than to sniff it in the raw state in the laboratory. Menthol crystals and saccharin or other sugar simulators are added to complete the camouflage operation.

12   Is that it? Chalk, water, paint, seaweed, anti-freeze, paraffin oil, detergent and peppermint? Not quite. A mix like that would be irresistible to the hundreds of thousands of individual bacteria lying on the surface of even an immaculately cleaned bathroom sink. They would get in, float in the water bubbles, ingest the ooze and paraffin, maybe even spray out enzymes to break down the chalk. The result would be an uninviting mess. The way manufacturers avoid that final obstacle is by putting something in to kill the bacteria. Something good and strong is needed, something that will zap any accidentally intrudant bacteria into oblivion. And that something is formaldehyde—the disinfectant used in anatomy labs.

13   So it's chalk, water, paint, seaweed, anti-freeze, paraffin oil, detergent, peppermint, formaldehyde and fluoride (which can go some way towards preserving children's teeth)—that's the usual mixture raised to the mouth on the toothbrush for a fresh morning's

clean. If it sounds too unfortunate, take heart. Studies show that thorough brushing with just plain water will often do as good a job.

```
┌──────────────────────┐
│                      │
│                      │
└──────────────────────┘
```

DAVID BODANIS

David Bodanis is a science writer who publishes in newspapers both in the United States and in England, where he now lives. He is the author of *The Body Book: A Fantastic Voyage to the World Within* and *The Secret House: 24 Hours in the Strange and Unexpected World in which We Spend Our Nights and Days.*

Words and Meanings
Paragraph

extruded	pushed	1
Cretaceous	one of the periods of the Mesozoic era (70 million years ago)	3
aeons	ages, an immensely long time	4
concoction	mixture	7
gustatory	having to do with taste	11
tout	advertise; promote aggressively in order to attract customers	

Structure and Strategy

1. This essay analyzes toothpaste by dividing it into its component parts. Identify each ingredient and the paragraph(s) in which it is described.
2. What is the function of paragraph 7? Paragraph 9? Paragraph 13?
3. Underline six or seven examples of the author's use of vivid description to help communicate key points.
4. Part of the effect of this essay depends on the author's description of toothpaste. He uses words that are very different from those we are familiar with in television commercials to describe the same product. For example, in paragraph 8 we read, "seaweed ooze spreads in among the chalk, paint and anti-freeze." Find other examples of Bodanis's use of language that you would never hear in a product advertisement. What effect does the author's DICTION have on the reader?

Content and Purpose

1. What is toothpaste's main ingredient and what is its primary function? What is the purpose of the simile (see FIGURES OF SPEECH) used in paragraph 4 to describe this function?

2. What's the function of glycol in toothpaste? The seaweed and paraffin? The detergent? The formaldehyde?
3. Explain the IRONY in the last paragraph.
4. Did you have any idea what toothpaste was made of before you read this essay? Did any of the ingredients surprise you? Revolt you? Why?

Suggestions for Writing

1. Does David Bodanis's analysis of toothpaste make you wonder about the composition of other familiar products? What, for instance, goes into margarine? Lipstick? Kraft Dinner? A hot dog? Write an essay that identifies the surprising elements of a common substance.
2. Write an essay in which you classify the different kinds of grooming aids available to assist us in making ourselves irresistible (or at least attractive) to others.

Why I Want a Wife

JUDY BRADY

1   I belong to that classification of people known as wives. I am A Wife. And, not altogether incidentally, I am a mother.

2   Not too long ago a male friend of mine appeared on the scene fresh from a recent divorce. He had one child, who is, of course, with his ex-wife. He is looking for another wife. As I thought about him while I was ironing one evening, it suddenly occurred to me that I, too, would like to have a wife. Why do I want a wife?

3   I would like to go back to school so that I can become economically independent, support myself, and, if need be, support those dependent upon me. I want a wife who will work and send me to school. And while I am going to school I want a wife to take care of my children. I want a wife to keep track of the children's doctor and dentist appointments. And to keep track of mine, too. I want a wife to make sure my children eat properly and are kept clean. I want a wife who will wash the children's clothes and keep them mended. I want a wife who is a good nurturant° attendant to my children,

who arranges for their schooling, makes sure that they have an adequate social life with their peers, takes them to the park, the zoo, etc. I want a wife who takes care of the children when they are sick, a wife who arranges to be around when the children need special care, because, of course, I cannot miss classes at school. My wife must arrange to lose time at work and not lose the job. It may mean a small cut in my wife's income from time to time, but I guess I can tolerate that. Needless to say, my wife will arrange and pay for the care of the children while my wife is working.

I want a wife who will take care of *my* physical needs. I want a wife who will keep my house clean. A wife who will pick up after my children, a wife who will pick up after me. I want a wife who will keep my clothes clean, ironed, mended, replaced when need be, and who will see to it that my personal things are kept in their proper place so that I can find what I need the minute I need it. I want a wife who cooks the meals, a wife who is a *good* cook. I want a wife who will plan the menus, do the necessary grocery shopping, prepare the meals, serve them pleasantly, and then do the cleaning up while I do my studying. I want a wife who will care for me when I am sick and sympathize with my pain and loss of time from school. I want a wife to go along when our family takes a vacation so that someone can continue to care for me and my children when I need a rest and change of scene.

I want a wife who will not bother me with rambling complaints about a wife's duties. But I want a wife who will listen to me when I feel the need to explain a rather difficult point I have come across in my course of studies. And I want a wife who will type my papers for me when I have written them.

I want a wife who will take care of the details of my social life. When my wife and I are invited out by my friends, I want a wife who will take care of the babysitting arrangements. When I meet people at school that I like and want to entertain, I want a wife who will have the house clean, will prepare a special meal, serve it to me and my friends, and not interrupt when I talk about things that interest me and my friends. I want a wife who will have arranged that the children are fed and ready for bed before my guests arrive so that the children do not bother us. I want a wife who takes care of the needs of my guests so that they feel comfortable, who makes sure that they have an ashtray, that they are passed the hors d'oeuvres, that they are offered a second helping of the food, that their wine glasses are replenished° when necessary, that their coffee is served to them as they like it. And I want a wife who knows that sometimes I need a night out by myself.

I want a wife who is sensitive to my sexual needs, a wife who makes love passionately and eagerly when I feel like it, a wife who makes sure that I am satisfied. And, of course, I want a wife who will not demand sexual attention when I am not in the mood for it. I want a wife who assumes the complete responsibility for birth control, because I do not want more children. I want a wife who will remain sexually faithful to me so that I do not have to clutter up my intellectual life with jealousies. And I want a wife who understands that *my* sexual needs may entail more than strict adherence° to monogamy°. I must, after all, be able to relate to people as fully as possible.

8   If, by chance, I find another person more suitable as a wife than the wife I already have, I want the liberty to replace my present wife with another one. Naturally, I will expect a fresh, new life; my wife will take the children and be solely responsible for them so that I am left free.

9   When I am through with school and have a job, I want my wife to quit working and remain at home so that my wife can more fully and completely take care of a wife's duties.

10   My God, who *wouldn't* want a wife?

> [blank box]

JUDY BRADY

Judy Brady (b. 1937) first published this article under her married name, Syfers, in *Ms.* magazine. "Why I Want a Wife" is one of the best-known feminist essays written in the last twenty years. Now divorced, Brady is a feminist and activist who writes on topics such as union organizing, abortion, and women's role in society.

Words and Meanings

Paragraph

3	nurturant	providing care, food, and training
6	replenished	filled
7	adherence	constancy, sticking to
	monogamy	custom of marrying, being faithful to only one mate

Structure and Strategy

1. What is the function of the first two paragraphs? What TONE do they establish?
2. Into what main functions does Brady divide the role of a wife? Identify the paragraph(s) that focus on each. Then write a thesis statement for this essay.

3. Why does Brady never use the pronouns "she" or "her" to refer to a wife? Is the frequent repetition of the word "wife" awkward? Or does it serve a particular purpose?
4. What is the effect of having so many sentences begin with the words "I want"?

Content and Purpose

1. What is Brady's attitude to the roles traditionally assigned to men and to women in our society? Identify two or three passages that clearly convey her feelings.
2. Consider the degree to which Brady's portrayal of male and female roles is an accurate reflection of our society's expectations. Who or what is responsible for these expectations?
3. Can you identify any contradictions between the duties that "a wife" would be required to perform and the actions of "the husband" who benefits from her care?
4. What would be the effect of this essay if it had been written by a man? How would the readers respond?

Suggestions for Writing

1. Write an essay organized, like Brady's, on the principle of division. Your first paragraph should contain the sentence, "I want a husband."
2. Write an essay in which you classify types of wives or husbands (or mothers, or fathers, or children).
3. In a short paper, identify and explain the differences in spousal (or parental) roles between your parents' generation and the family you have (or plan to have).

What I Have Lived For

BERTRAND RUSSELL

Three passages, simple but overwhelmingly strong, have governed my life: the longing for love, the search for knowledge, and unbearable pity for the suffering of mankind. These passions, like great winds, have blown me hither and thither, in a wayward° course, over a deep ocean of anguish, reaching to the very verge° of despair.

2   I have sought love, first, because it brings ecstasy°—ecstasy so great that I would often have sacrificed all the rest of life for a few hours of this joy. I have sought it, next, because it relieves loneliness— that terrible loneliness in which one shivering consciousness looks over the rim of the world into the cold unfathomable lifeless abyss°. I have sought it, finally, because in the union of love I have seen, in a mystic miniature, the prefiguring° vision of the heaven that saints and poets have imagined. This is what I sought, and though it might seem too good for human life, this is what—at last—I have found.

3   With equal passion I have sought knowledge. I have wished to understand the hearts of men. I have wished to know why the stars shine. And I have tried to apprehend the Pythagorean° power by which number holds sway above the flux°. A little of this, but not much, I have achieved.

4   Love and knowledge, so far as they were possible, led upward toward the heavens. But always pity brought me back to earth. Echoes of cries of pain reverberate° in my heart. Children in famine, victims tortured by oppressors, helpless old people a hated burden to their sons, and the whole world of loneliness, poverty, and pain make a mockery of what human life should be. I long to alleviate° the evil, but I cannot, and I too suffer.

5   This has been my life. I have found it worth living, and would gladly live it again if the chance were offered me.

BERTRAND RUSSELL

Bertrand Russell (1872–1970), the philosopher, mathematician, and social reformer, was awarded the Nobel Prize for Literature in 1950. His progressive views on the liberalization of sexual attitudes and the role of women led to his dismissal from the University of California at Los Angeles in the 1920s. Russell was a leading pacifist and proponent of nuclear disarmament. Among his many books are *Principia Mathematica*, *Why I Am Not a Christian*, and *History of Western Philosophy*.

Paragraph   ## Words and Meanings

1	wayward	unpredictable, wandering
	verge	edge, brink
2	ecstasy	supreme joy
	abyss	bottomless pit, hell
	prefiguring	picturing to oneself beforehand

Pythagorean	relating to the Greek philosopher Pythagoras and his theory that through mathematics one can understand the relationship between all things and the principle of harmony in the universe	3
flux	continual motion, change	
reverberate	echo	4
alleviate	relieve, lessen	

Structure and Strategy

1. Identify Russell's thesis statement and the topic sentences of paragraphs 2, 3, and 4.
2. How does the structure of the second sentence in paragraph 1 reinforce its meaning?
3. The number three is the basis for the structure of Russell's essay. Three is an ancient symbol for unity and completeness and for the human life cycle: birth, life, death. Find as many examples as you can of Russell's effective use of three's. (Look at paragraph and sentence structure as well as content.)
4. What is the function of the first sentence of paragraph 4?
5. How does Russell's concluding paragraph contribute to the UNITY of the essay?
6. Refer to the introduction of this unit and show how paragraph 1 sets up a division essay and how paragraph 4 is actually a classification.
7. Analyze the order in which Russell explains his three passions. Do you think the order is chronological, logical, climactic, or random? Does the order reflect the relative importance or value that Russell ascribes to each passion? How?

Content and Purpose

1. Love, to Bertrand Russell, means more than physical passion. What else does he include in his meaning of love (paragraph 2)?
2. What are the three kinds of knowledge Russell has spent his life seeking?
3. Which of Russell's three "passions" has he been least successful in achieving? Why?

Suggestions for Writing

1. What goals have you set for yourself for the next ten years? Write a short paper in which you identify and explain two or three of your goals.

2. In what ways are you different from other people? Write a short paper in which you identify and explain some of the qualities and characteristics that make you a unique human being.
3. Imagine that you are 75 years old. Write a short paper explaining what you have lived for.

The Dimensions of a Complete Life

MARTIN LUTHER KING, JR.

1   Many, many centuries ago, out on a lonely, obscure island called Patmos°, a man by the name of John° caught a vision of the new Jerusalem descending out of heaven from God. One of the greatest glories of this new city of God that John saw was its completeness. It was not partial and one-sided, but it was complete in all three of its dimensions. And so, in describing the city in the twenty-first chapter of the book of Revelation, John says this: "The length and the breadth and the height of it are equal." In other words, this new city of God, this city of ideal humanity, is not an unbalanced entity but it is complete on all sides.

2   Now John is saying something quite significant here. For so many of us the book of Revelation° is a very difficult book, puzzling to decode. We look upon it as something of a great enigma° wrapped in mystery. And certainly if we accept the book of Revelation as a record of actual historical occurrences it is a difficult book, shrouded with impenetrable mysteries. But if we will look beneath the peculiar jargon of its author and the prevailing apocalyptic° symbolism, we will find in this book many eternal truths which continue to challenge us. One such truth is that of this text. What John is really saying is this: that life as it should be and life at its best is the life that is complete on all sides.

3   There are three dimensions of any complete life to which we can fitly give the words of this text: length, breadth, and height. The length of life as we shall think of it here is not its duration or its longevity, but it is the push of a life forward to achieve its personal

ends and ambitions. It is the inward concern for one's own welfare. The breadth of life is the outward concern for the welfare of others. The height of life is the upward reach for God.

These are the three dimensions of life, and without the three 4 being correlated, working harmoniously together, life is incomplete. Life is something of a great triangle. At one angle stands the individual person, at the other angle stand other persons, and at the top stands the Supreme, Infinite Person, God. These three must meet in every individual life if that life is to be complete.

Now let us notice first the length of life. I have said that this is 5 the dimension of life in which the individual is concerned with developing his inner powers. It is that dimension of life in which the individual pursues personal ends and ambitions. This is perhaps the selfish dimension of life, and there is such a thing as moral and rational self-interest. If one is not concerned about himself he cannot be totally concerned about other selves.

Some years ago a learned rabbi, the late Joshua Liebman, wrote a 6 book entitled *Peace of Mind*. He has a chapter in the book entitled "Love Thyself Properly." In this chapter he says in substance that it is impossible to love other selves adequately unless you love your own self properly. Many people have been plunged into the abyss° of emotional fatalism° because they did not love themselves properly. So every individual has a responsibility to be concerned about himself enough to discover what he is made for. After he discovers his calling he should set out to do it with all of the strength and power in his being. He should do it as if God Almighty called him at this particular moment in history to do it. He should seek to do his job so well that the living, the dead, or the unborn could not do it better. No matter how small one thinks his life's work is in terms of the norms of the world and the so-called big jobs, he must realize that it has cosmic significance if he is serving humanity and doing the will of God.

To carry this to one extreme, if it falls your lot to be a street- 7 sweeper, sweep streets as Raphael painted pictures, sweep streets as Michelangelo carved marble, sweep streets as Beethoven composed music, sweep streets as Shakespeare wrote poetry. Sweep streets so well that all the host of heaven and earth will have to pause and say, "Here lived a great street-sweeper who swept his job well." In the words of Douglas Mallock:

If you can't be a highway, just be a trail;
If you can't be the sun, be a star
For it isn't by size that you win or you fail—
Be the best of whatever you are.

When you do this, you have mastered the first dimension of life—the length of life.

8   But don't stop here; it is dangerous to stop here. There are some people who never get beyond this first dimension. They are brilliant people; often they do an excellent job in developing their inner powers; but they live as if nobody else lived in the world but themselves. There is nothing more tragic than to find an individual bogged down in the length of life, devoid of the breadth.

9   The breadth of life is that dimension of life in which we are concerned about others. An individual has not started living until he can rise above the narrow confines of his individualistic concerns to the broader concerns of all humanity.

10   You remember one day a man came to Jesus and he raised some significant questions. Finally he got around to the question, "Who is my neighbor?" This could easily have been a very abstract question left in mid-air. But Jesus immediately pulled that question out of mid-air and placed it on a dangerous curve between Jerusalem and Jericho. He talked about a certain man who fell among thieves. Three men passed; two of them on the other side. And finally another man came and helped the injured man on the ground. He is known to us as the good Samaritan. Jesus says in substance that this is a great man. He was great because he could project the "I" into the "thou."

11   So often we say that the priest and the Levite were in a big hurry to get to some ecclesiastical meeting and so they did not have time. They were concerned about that. I would rather think of it another way. I can well imagine that they were quite afraid. You see, the Jericho road is a dangerous road, and the same thing that happened to the man who was robbed and beaten could have happened to them. So I imagine the first question that the priest and the Levite asked was this: "If I stop to help this man, what will happen to me?" Then the good Samaritan came by, and by the very nature of his concern reversed the question: "If I do not stop to help this man, what will happen to him?" And so this man was great because he had the mental equipment for a dangerous altruism°. He was great because he could surround the length of his life with the breadth of life. He was great not only because he had ascended to certain heights of economic security, but because he could condescend° to the depths of human need.

12   All this has a great deal of bearing in our situation in the world today. So often racial groups are concerned about the length of life, their economic privileged position, their social status. So often nations of the world are concerned about the length of life, perpetuating their nationalistic concerns, and their economic ends. May it not be that the problem in the world today is that individuals as well as nations have been overly concerned with the length of life, devoid of the breadth? But there is still something to remind us that

we are interdependent°, that we are all involved in a single process, that we are all somehow caught in an inescapable network of mutuality. Therefore whatever affects one directly affects all indirectly.

As long as there is poverty in the world I can never be rich, [13] even if I have a billion dollars. As long as diseases are rampant and millions of people in this world cannot expect to live more than twenty-eight or thirty years, I can never be totally healthy even if I just got a good check-up at Mayo Clinic. I can never be what I ought to be until you are what you ought to be. This is the way our world is made. No individual or nation can stand out boasting of being independent. We are interdependent. So John Donne placed it in graphic terms when he affirmed, "No man is an island entire of itself. Every man is a piece of the continent, a part of the main." Then he goes on to say, "Any man's death diminishes me because I am involved in mankind, and therefore never send to know for whom the bell tolls; it tolls for thee." When we discover this, we master the second dimension of life.

Finally, there is a third dimension. Some people never get [14] beyond the first two dimensions of life. They master the first two. They develop their inner powers; they love humanity, but they stop right here. They end up with the feeling that man is the end of all things and that humanity is God. Philosophically or theologically, many of them would call themselves humanists°. They seek to live life without a sky. They find themselves bogged down on the horizontal plane without being integrated on the vertical plane. But if we are to live the complete life we must reach up and discover God. H.G. Wells was right: "The man who is not religious begins at nowhere and ends at nothing." Religion is like a mighty wind that breaks down doors and makes that possible and even easy which seems difficult and impossible.

In our modern world it is easy for us to forget this. We so often [15] find ourselves unconsciously neglecting this third dimension of life. Not that we go up and say, "Good-by, God, we are going to leave you now." But we become so involved in the things of this world that we are unconsciously carried away by the rushing tide of materialism° which leaves us treading in the confused waters of secularism°. We find ourselves living in what Professor Sorokin of Harvard called a sensate° civilization, believing that only those things which we can see and touch and to which we can apply our five senses have existence.

Something should remind us once more that the great things in [16] this universe are things that we never see. You walk out at night and look up at the beautiful stars as they bedeck the heavens like swinging lanterns of eternity, and you think you can see all. Oh, no. You can never see the law of gravitation that holds them there. You walk around this vast campus and you probably have a great esthetic experience as I have had walking about and looking at the beautiful buildings, and you think you see all. Oh, no. You can never see the mind of the architect who drew the blueprint. You can never see the love and the faith and the hope of the individuals who made it so. You look at me and you think you see Martin Luther King. You don't see Martin Luther King; you see my body, but, you must understand, my body can't think, my body can't reason. You don't see the me that makes me me. You can never see my personality.

17   In a real sense everything that we see is a shadow cast by that which we do not see. Plato° was right: "The visible is a shadow cast by the invisible." And so God is still around. All of our new knowledge, all of our new developments, cannot diminish his being one iota°. These new advances have banished God neither from the microcosmic compass of the atom nor from the vast, unfathomable ranges of interstellar space. The more we learn about this universe, the more mysterious and awesome it becomes. God is still here.

18   So I say to you, seek God and discover him and make him a power in your life. Without him all our efforts turn to ashes and our sunrises into darkest nights. Without him, life is a meaningless drama with the decisive scenes missing. But with him we are able to rise from the fatigue of despair to the buoyancy of hope. With him we are able to rise from the midnight of desperation to the daybreak of joy. St. Augustine was right—we were made for God and we will be restless until we find rest in him.

19   Love yourself, if that means rational, healthy, and moral self-interest. You are commanded to do that. That is the length of life. Love your neighbor as you love yourself. You are commanded to do that. That is the breadth of life. But never forget that there is a first and even greater commandment, "Love the Lord thy God with all thy heart and all thy soul and all thy mind." This is the height of life. And when you do this you live the complete life.

20   Thank God for John who, centuries ago, caught a vision of the new Jerusalem. God grant that those of us who still walk the road of life will catch this vision and decide to move forward to that city of complete life in which the length and the breadth and the height are equal.

MARTIN LUTHER KING, JR.

Dr. Martin Luther King, Jr. (1929–68), the American civil rights leader, was a Baptist minister who advocated racial equality and non-violent resistance against discriminatory laws and practices. He was awarded the Nobel Prize for Peace in 1964. In 1968, he was assassinated in Memphis, Tennessee.

Words and Meanings

John of Patmos	Christian saint, author of the book of Revelation	1
the book of Revelation	last book of the New Testament, concerned with the end of the world and other mysteries	2
enigma	puzzle, mystery	
apocalyptic	concerned with the Apocalypse, the last day	
abyss	bottomless pit, hell	6
fatalism	belief that a predetermined fate rules our lives	
altruism	selfless concern for others	11
condescend	stoop, bend down to	
interdependent	dependent on each other	12
humanists	people interested in human nature and concerns	14
materialism	concern only for the goods of this world	15
secularism	social and non-religious concern for the world	
sensate	perceived by the senses	
Plato	ancient Greek philosopher, idealist	17
iota	smallest particle	

Structure and Strategy

1. What ANALOGY are paragraphs 1 and 2 based on? What analogy is introduced in paragraph 4?
2. Identify King's thesis statement. What question of division does it answer? (See the introduction to this unit.)
3. What is the function of paragraph 3? How does King begin to develop his three points in this paragraph?
4. Identify the paragraphs that develop each of the three dimensions of life. In what ORDER has King arranged his points?
5. How does paragraph 8 contribute to COHERENCE? Paragraphs 9 and 14?
6. Paragraphs 19 and 20 form the conclusion of this piece. What is the function of paragraph 20? How does it round off or conclude the essay effectively?
7. Writers and speakers often use PARALLEL STRUCTURE to emphasize key ideas. King's thesis statement is, of course, an example of parallelism, but there are other examples. Identify parallel structures in paragraphs 7 and 18. What do they emphasize? How effective are they? (Hint: read the paragraphs aloud.)

Content and Purpose

1. King originally wrote "Dimensions" as a speech. As you read through the piece, what clues can you find that indicate it was designed to be heard rather than read?
2. King regards the length of life as "selfish," but, nevertheless, the basis of the other dimensions of life. How does King convince the reader that this "selfishness" is a positive rather than a negative quality?
3. What is a parable? What is the purpose of the parable in paragraphs 10 and 11?
4. King's purpose in this piece is to demonstrate that the complete life is one in which the personal, social, and spiritual dimensions are integrated. Study King's development of one of these dimensions and show how he has carefully selected his examples to reinforce his thesis.

Suggestions for Writing

1. Write an essay of division in which you analyze your own vision of the complete life. What will bring you happiness and satisfaction?
2. Though it lasted only 39 years, King's own life fulfilled the dimensions of a "complete life." After doing some research, write a short paper describing his accomplishments.
3. Think of someone you know or have read about and write a paper explaining how that person's life satisfies King's criteria for completeness.

Additional Suggestions for Writing: Classification and Division

Use classification or division, whichever is appropriate, to analyze one of the topics below into its component parts, or characteristics, or kinds. Write a thesis statement based on your analysis and then develop it into a detailed, interesting essay.

part-time jobs	advice
marriages	morality
films	friendship
pop singers	an unforgettable event
computer games	parenting
popular novels	a winning team
radio stations	a short story, poem, or play
TV talk shows	shopping malls
families	a religious or social ritual (such
dreams	as a wedding, funeral, bar/bat
college students	mitzvah, birthday celebration)
cameras	

Comparison and Contrast: Explaining Similarities and Differences

What? The Definition

Why does a person choose to go to college rather than look for a full-time job? How does that same person choose between attending Douglas College and B.C. Institute of Technology in Vancouver, or between Laurentian University and the Haileybury School of Mines in Sudbury? Which Canadian hockey team deserves the title of dynasty: the Vancouver Canucks or the Montreal Canadiens? Who will be remembered as the better prime minister: Pierre Trudeau or Jean Chrétien? What's for lunch: chicken wings and potato skins, or a plate of nachos and a wet burrito? Every day of our lives, we are called upon to make choices, to evaluate alternatives. Sometimes, as in the "what's-for-lunch?" question, the decision may have few consequences (other than indigestion). But sometimes our decisions have far-reaching effects, as in the college-or-job dilemma. Fortunately, our minds quite naturally work in a way that helps us to assess the options and to choose between the alternatives.

First, we consider what the two subjects we are comparing have in common; in other words, how are they alike? The Jets and the Canadiens both skate, shoot, and occasionally score, and both teams have illustrious pasts. Then we consider how the two teams are different; in other words, what distinguishes one from the other? Montreal has good scouting, consistent coaching, and solid ownership. The Jets? Well, perhaps the less said, the better.

Pointing out similarities is called **comparing**; pointing out differences is called **contrasting**. When we assess both similarities and differences, we are engaging in **comparison and contrast**. Often, however, people use the term "comparison" to mean comparing, or contrasting, or both. In this chapter, we will use *comparison* to cover all three approaches.

Why? The Purpose

Comparison is a natural mental process; it's something we do, consciously or unconsciously, all the time. In writing, we use comparison to answer three questions:

1. What are the main similarities between S_1 and S_2?
2. What are the main differences between S_1 and S_2?
3. What are the main similarities and differences between S_1 and S_2?

Using such a pattern in written communication can be useful in several ways. First, an essay or report structured to compare various items can be highly informative. It can explain two subjects clearly by putting them alongside each other. Second, a comparison paper can evaluate as well as inform. It can assess the relative merits of two subjects and provide reasons on which a reader can base a judgment, or reasons to explain the writer's preference for one item over the other.

In school, you use the comparison pattern for both purposes: to *inform* and to *evaluate*. An exam may ask, "What similarities and differences are there between OS/2 and Microsoft Windows?" A research paper, on the other hand, may require you to focus on the parallels and divergences between health-insurance plans in Nova Scotia and Alberta, while a test question may take the comparison a step further by requiring you to evaluate the merits of the two health-care plans. Your field placement, for instance, may require a judgment about the overall competence of two engineering firms. Each case calls for a *comparison*. It serves as the structural principle of your exam answer, your paper, or your report.

How? The Technique

Organizing a paper according to the principle of comparison isn't difficult if you approach the task by asking three questions. First: are the two items really comparable? Second: what are the terms of comparison? Third: what is the most appropriate pattern of organization to use?

Comparing Wayne Gretzky to Dolly Parton has, at first glance, at least comic potential. It's true they are both high-paid entertainers. But there is no sustained or significant basis for drawing a comparison between them because their talents are just too different. The writer of a comparison, then, must be sure that a meaningful similarity exists between the two subjects. They must have something *significant* in common. For instance, Wayne Gretzky could be compared in an interesting manner to another hockey legend like Bobby Orr. Dolly Parton would best be compared to another high-camp vamp of the silver screen—Mae West, perhaps—or another country singer such as k.d. lang.

After deciding that your two subjects are comparable in a meaningful way, you should then carefully consider the terms of the comparison. If, for instance, you were asked to assess two engineering firms, it would make little sense to compare the management structure and computer systems of one firm to the washrooms and cafeteria food of the other. Resemblances and differences must be assessed in the same terms or categories. Your report should be organized to assess both firms in identical terms: management structure, computer systems, and employee facilities, for example.

Your final step is to decide on an appropriate structure for your comparison. There are two effective patterns to choose from: subject-by-subject and point-by-point. Like pineapples, comparison papers can be processed into *chunks* or *slices*. (Pineapples also come crushed, but this form is the one you're trying to avoid.)

Structuring a comparison according to the *chunk* pattern involves separating the two subjects and discussing each one separately, under the headings or categories you've chosen to consider. If you were asked, for example, to compare the novel and film versions of Margaret Laurence's *The Diviners*, you might decide to focus your analysis on the characters, the setting, and the plot of the two versions. You would first discuss the novel in terms of these three points, then you would do the same for the film. Here is a sample chunk outline for such an essay:

Paragraph 1 Introduction and thesis statement
Paragraph 2 S₁ Novel
            a. characters in the novel
            b. setting of the novel
            c. plot of the novel

Paragraph 3 S_2 Film
                 a. characters in the film
                 b. setting of the film
                 c. plot of the film
Paragraph 4   Conclusion summarizing the similarities and differences and possibly stating your preference

The chunk pattern does not rule out a discussion of the two subjects in the same paragraph. In this example, particularly in your analysis of the film, some mention of the novel might be necessary. However, the overall structure of the chunk comparison should communicate the essentials about Subject 1, then communicate the essentials about Subject 2.

The chunk style works best with fairly short papers (essay questions on exams, for instance) where the reader does not have to remember many intricate details about Subject 1 while trying to assimilate the details of Subject 2.

Structuring a comparison according to the *slice* pattern involves setting out the terms or categories of comparison, then discussing both subjects under each category heading. *The Diviners* essay structured in slices could communicate the same information as the chunked paper, yet its shape and outline would be quite different:

Paragraph 1   Introduction and thesis statement
Paragraph 2   Characters
                 S_1 in the novel
                 S_2 in the film
Paragraph 3   Setting
                 S_1 in the novel
                 S_2 in the film
Paragraph 4   Plot
                 S_1 in the novel
                 S_2 in the film
Paragraph 5   Conclusion with, perhaps, a statement of your preference

The slice pattern makes the resemblances and differences between the two subjects more readily apparent to the reader. It's the type of structure that is ideally suited to longer reports and papers, where the terms of comparison are complex and demand high reader recall.

Because comparing and contrasting is a natural human thought process, organizing written communication in this pattern is not very difficult. It does, however, require clear thinking and preparation. Before you even begin to write, you need to study the subjects themselves, decide on the terms of comparison, and choose the appropriate structure.

A good thesis statement is essential to a well-written comparison paper (as it is, indeed, to any piece of writing). Because comparison involves considering two different items in terms of several aspects, writing the thesis statement presents an interesting challenge.

Here are three models for you to choose from in drafting thesis statements for comparison papers.

> S_1 and S_2 can be compared in terms of a, b, and c.

Example: Chrétien and Trudeau can be compared in terms of their power bases, religious backgrounds, and family ties.

> S_1 and S_2 can be contrasted in terms of a, b, and c.

Example: College and university can be contrasted in terms of cost, instruction, and orientation.

> Although S_1 and S_2 are different in terms of a, b, and c, they are alike in terms of d.

Example: Although Canada and Scotland are different in size, geography, and culture, they are alike in their relationship with their southern neighbours.

Be prepared to spend time shaping and perfecting your thesis statement. The effort you invest at this stage will pay off by providing a solid framework on which you can construct and then communicate what it is you want to say.

Here is a comparison essay that illustrates the slice pattern of organization, based on the second example above.

College or University?

In the United States, the word "college" is used to designate all formal education that takes place after high school.

Introduction
(makes use of a
contrast)

Whether people attend a local two-year junior college or a university as renowned as Harvard, they are described as "going to college." In Canada, however, the word "college" is contrasted with the word "university." Here, "going to college" denotes a different educational experience from that of "going to university." The college experience and the university experience in Canada can be contrasted in terms of cost, instruction, and orientation.

Thesis statement

First point
(developed with
examples and
statistics)

A college education is less costly than a university education, partly because it takes less time to complete. For instance, a student can complete an engineering technology program at most community colleges in three years; the technician's program takes only two. An engineering degree from a university requires an investment of four years, or in some cases even five, if the particular institution offers a co-op program. Each extra year in school costs the student money in lost wages as well as in living expenses and tuition. Tuition is, of course, another reason for the difference in cost. By and large, university fees are about three times as high as those of a college. Although statistics indicate that the average university graduate earns, over a lifetime, approximately twice as much as the average college graduate, going to university costs considerably more than going to a community college.

Second point
(again, note the
well-chosen
examples)

The methods of instruction are different at university and college. At many universities, especially in the first two years, students attend large lecture classes for their introductory courses. They may participate in smaller seminar groups led by graduate students, yet the fundamentals of the undergraduate curriculum, whether in mathematics, psychology, or literature, are often presented in classes containing hundreds of people. Colleges offer a more "hands-on" approach and smaller-group interaction between students and instructors. Students who require psychology to complete a correctional worker program, for instance, will probably find themselves in a small class in which dialogue between students and teacher is encouraged.

The transition here connects the first and second points to the third point—the topic of this paragraph

→ The above example points to the third and most important difference between university and college: their orientation toward career learning. Though professional studies—those aimed at a particular career—may be part of a university education, the curriculum is largely based on theoretical learning—learning for its own sake. Often a student must complete postgraduate work in order to qualify for a particular profession, such as law, teaching, or medicine. Universities aim at providing students with a background in arts, sciences, and languages in addition to their chosen discipline. Colleges, on the other hand, are usually oriented toward providing a career education that will prepare students for jobs in such fields as data processing, recreation leadership, or fashion design. Hence, while there is an element of general education in most college programs, much of the learning is practical and job-specific.

Conclusion (restates the thesis in different words)

Canadian students interested in post-secondary education thus have an important choice to make. After considering the differences in time and cost and weighing the advantages of the broader academic study

offered by a university as opposed to
the more career-specific training provided by a college, they can decide
which kind of institution best suits
their needs, aptitudes, and goals.

Edmonton vs. Calgary: The Whole Truth

RON MARKEN

1   nyone east of Lloydminster or west of
Canmore will not know Alberta's two most burning questions:
"How much is left in the Heritage Fund?" and "Which is the better
city, Calgary or Edmonton?" Rumor has it that the United Nations
General Assembly intends to settle the second of these earth-shaking
issues in its next session. Until then, here are the facts.

2   Edmonton has been ticked off for fifty years because all the
world knows the magic words "Calgary Stampede," but thinks
Edmonton is a military outpost in Latvia. It was for this reason—
rather than to honor the Royal visit of King George VI in 1938 as
officials claimed—that Edmonton started a rivalry between the two
cities. "I am the best!" bleated Edmonton into the ear of a bemused°
and indifferent monarch. Calgary was not informed.

3   Ten years later, Calgary learned of the debate and, to prove
their superiority, knocked down six old buildings and knocked up
ten office towers. Edmonton writhed with jealousy because its
biggest building was the MacDonald Hotel. So, Edmonton leveled
Jasper Avenue. No one was watching, though.

4   What irritated Edmonton the most was that it had the legislature, was the capital city, and was home to the provincial university.
Still, no one beyond Wainwright had heard of it. Meanwhile,
Calgary was famous as far as Fort Worth. Even Montrealers knew
of its existence; they thought men wearing high heels and big white
hats were chic.

5   Edmonton had no choice. It poked holes in every acre of land
for fifty miles around (using Oklahoma and Texas money) and

struck natural gas. Then it struck oil! Finally its time had come; it was the Oil Capital of Canada.

The mayor of Calgary lazily swung his cowboy boots off his desk and sent a telegram to J.R. Ewing. Ten minutes later, all the world's oil companies had built their head offices in Calgary (a city whose total oil production rivals that of Cambridge, England). Calgary called Edmonton and said, in a friendly voice with just a trace of an Oklahoma accent, "You might be the Oil Capital of Canada, sweetie, but down here, we *own* the oil." 6

Edmonton writhed again. So it bought fifty-five young Americans, called them "Eskimos," and used them to beat up on the rest of Canada all through the '50s. (There are no real Eskimos in Edmonton, of course, but the name suggested it was cold as hell in Edmonton and therefore Edmonton was really tough.) Although Calgary didn't really want to, it also bought fifty-five young Americans with some petty cash from Standard°. They were called the "Stampeders" (naturally). They proceeded to lose all their games—with style. Everyone still loved Calgary. 7

Desperate by now, Edmonton went all the way. It tried to rival the Calgary Stampede with a forced extravaganza called "Klondike Days." The real Klondike, in the Yukon, thought it was pretty ridiculous, and Calgary ignored it completely. It was too busy putting on the one show that every man, woman, and child on earth wants to see: the Calgary Stampede. 8

One February day, Edmonton's phone rang. "Howdy, sweetie." It was Calgary. "How's the weather up there? We're havin' us a chinook° and I'm in my swimmin' pool." In Edmonton, the mercury hovered around minus fifty, but Edmonton (unable to buy a chinook for love or oily money) now bragged about being *hardier* than that candy-assed Calgary. No one believed that. Edmonton got so angry it bought fifteen Quebecers, ten Saskatchewanians, and a gawky kid from Ontario°. 9

"See, here!" shouted Edmonton into the phone. "I've got you at last! I have an NHL team and they are goin' ta kick the ass of everyone on this continent. No one can say, 'Where's Edmonton?' now. I'll show you!" Calgary, puzzled by this challenge, absentmindedly bought an entire NHL team from Atlanta, Georgia (famous for its hockey players), and continues a losing sports tradition. 10

But still, the world loves Calgary and hates Edmonton. It will never change. And even Edmonton's latest boast—"I have the longest street full of churches in all of Christendom and the biggest shopping mall in the entire galaxy!"—somehow fails to electrify. 11

Calgary got more attention by going broke. Edmonton writhes again. See you at the Stampede.

RON MARKEN

Ron Marken describes himself as follows: "Native to Alberta, teacher to Saskatchewan, husband to one and father to five. Professor of Irish literature, playwright, writer of fact and fiction, trained in both academic and lucid prose. Never lived in Manitoba." His play, *Dancing in Poppies,* has recently been adapted for television.

Words and Meanings

Paragraph		
2	bemused	a little puzzled, confused
7	Standard	Standard Oil (now Exxon)
9	chinook	warm winter wind that blows in from the Pacific Ocean across the Rocky Mountains into Alberta
	gawky kid from Ontario	Wayne Gretzky

Structure and Strategy

1. What points of contrast does Marken identify between Edmonton and Calgary? Do the two cities have anything in common?
2. Is this essay structured according to the *chunk* or the *slice* pattern?
3. What is personified in the essay? (See FIGURES OF SPEECH.)
4. What descriptive details contribute to the humour in paragraph 6?

Content and Purpose

1. What is the basis for Edmonton's supposed resentment of Calgary?
2. Explain the IRONY involved in the sports teams that the two cities imported.
3. Where are Lloydminster, Canmore, Wainwright, and Fort Worth? Why does the reader need to know?
4. Does the author have a preference for either Edmonton or Calgary? Support your answer by referring to specific details in the essay.

Suggestion for Writing

Compare and/or contrast two cities with which you are familiar. Without stating your preference directly, make sure your reader can identify which of the two you prefer.

Should Morality Be a Struggle? Ancient vs. Modern Ideas about Ethics

THOMAS HURKA

Imagine that two accountants do similar 1
jobs for similar companies. One day they make the same discovery:
with almost no chance of getting caught, they can embezzle a large
sum from their employers. They can both use the money, to pay off
debts or buy a new car.

The first accountant right away says to himself, "It's wrong to 2
steal," and never considers the matter again. But the second
accountant is torn. She, too, knows stealing is wrong, but she's
tempted and at first decides to go ahead. Then she decides she
won't, and then that she will. Finally, after weeks of agonizing, she
decides not to embezzle. Who is the morally better person?

My fellow students and I were asked this at the start of an 3
undergraduate seminar on Aristotle. The point wasn't that there
was a single right answer we had to give; it was to highlight differences between ancient and modern views of ethics.

Aristotle and most other Greek philosophers would have said 4
the first accountant is better, because he has a harmonious personality. He has correct beliefs about what's right and no appetites or
impulses that conflict with them. He's integrated, stable, at one
with his moral convictions.

Aristotle thought this kind of harmony was essential to true 5
virtue. The virtuous person would, for example, be moderate about
sensual pleasures, but he wouldn't find this difficult. He would dislike the taste of rich or unhealthy foods; he'd get no enjoyment
from adultery even if he happened to try it.

The Greeks could value inner harmony because they assumed 6
that morality and self-interest go hand in hand. The second accountant is tempted to embezzle the money because she thinks this will
benefit her. But Aristotle would say this is a mistake. What's really
in your interest is leading the best life, which is a life of virtue and
excludes stealing. To be tempted is to be confused.

7   Modern ethics is more sympathetic to the second accountant. We doubt whether virtue in Aristotle's sense is attainable; we think of morality as a struggle against evil or selfish impulses that we can't get rid of but can only restrain. (Think of dieting as portrayed in the "Cathy" comic strip. It's a battle against cravings for chocolate, ice cream, and the like. Wrongdoing strikes us as similarly delicious.)

8   This modern picture has partly religious origins. The Christian doctrine of original sin says that, after the fall in the Garden of Eden, all humans are corrupted. We have within us tendencies to evil that cannot be eliminated ("the old Adam") and against which we must constantly struggle. As St. Paul said, "The flesh lusteth against the spirit," and the best we can do is lust back against it.

9   But there are secular° versions of the same idea. Our twentieth-century psychologies teach us that we have inborn tendencies, the products now of biology rather than divinity, to pleasure, aggression, or dominance. They're the nasty, uncivilized part of our nature, and though they can be diverted, sublimated, or restrained, they can't be eliminated. The moral life, again, is a struggle against oneself.

10   Like the Greek picture, this modern one is tied to beliefs about morality and self-interest. But where the Greeks assume that doing what's right is the same as benefiting yourself, we think the two clash. Morality involves a sacrifice of your interests for other people's, and that's what makes it hard.

11   This makes us suspicious of the first accountant. Doesn't his easy virtue look like a mindless following of rules whose costs he doesn't really understand? Morality does require giving up your interests, and the second accountant's struggle reflects this. But the first accountant seems to ignore this, or to be missing some basic drives.

12   Our modern picture of morality is grim, in contrast with the light, harmonious picture Aristotle paints. But sometimes reality is more hard than beautiful. The German philosopher G.W.F. Hegel said that Greek civilization expressed a beautiful naïveté°, treating as in simple harmony what we see as opposed. You can see this in Greek ethics. There virtue is effortless because it's good for you— but we find it a struggle.

THOMAS HURKA

Thomas Hurka (b. 1952) teaches philosophy at the University of Calgary. He also writes a weekly column for *The Globe and Mail* through which he has introduced many Canadians to the relevance of ethics to everyday life. In 1994 Professor Hurka published *Principles: Short Essays on Ethics*, a collection of his *Globe and Mail* columns organized around such topics as abortion, war, capital punishment, and the environment.

Words and Meanings

Paragraph

secular	worldly, not religious or sacred	9
naïvete	simplicity, lack of sophistication	12

Structure and Strategy

1. What INTRODUCTION strategy does Hurka use to set up his THESIS?
2. What is the principal contrast on which this essay is based? What other contrasts are presented, and what is their function in the piece?
3. Which paragraphs explore the ancient view of morality? Which deal with the modern?
4. What functions do the two accountants serve in this essay?
5. What example does paragraph 7 use to illustrate the modern view? Do you think the example is effective?

Content and Purpose

1. Summarize what Hurka means by the ancient and modern views of morality. Identify three essential differences between them. What similarity is there between the ancient Greeks and ourselves?
2. According to the author, what major influences have shaped the modern view of morality? Can you think of others that have contributed to our contemporary notions of ethical behaviour?
3. Which view of morality—ancient or modern—do you think Hurka adheres to? What details in the essay led you to this conclusion?

Suggestions for Writing

1. Write an essay that answers the dilemma posed by the anecdote of the two accountants. Who is the more "moral" person: the one who would never consider stealing or the one who rejects the idea after considerable soul-searching?
2. Are there any circumstances under which it is permissible to steal? Write an essay in which you contrast "ethical" and "unethical" situations in which one might take what belongs to someone else.

3. Think of another moral dilemma (one that has nothing to do with stealing). Introduce the dilemma, outline two different courses of action to deal with it, and indicate what you think is the right response, the ethical response, to the predicament.

Patriotism Redux°

DOUGLAS COUPLAND

1   In a bookstore a few days ago, I was riffling through a pile of old Canadian magazines from the late '60s and early '70s. All of them were chock-full of a certain type of Canadian boosterist imagery particular to that era: lady Canadians in miniskirts and odd makeup, ecstatic at the thought of futuristic pod architecture (*Let's go, Canada!*); gentleman Canadians in mutton-chop sideburns and cable-knit sweaters, no doubt contemplating Marshall McLuhan (*Canada, this is our century!*). Wheat fields everywhere, swooping ultramodern buildings, a neo-utopia° of living rooms decorated with "mod" brown and orange stripes, avocado green appliances lurking in the kitchen awaiting instructions to cook a meat loaf recipe from *Chatelaine*. Standing there in the bookstore, I was amazed to remember just how potent° the notion was back then of Canada as a sexy, groovy, happening place.

2   Values drip from these photos: earnestness, a gleeful grasping of the future, the willful rejection of everything that's tired and old and worn-out, a determination to invent ourselves as a nation as we go along, a love of flared pants.

3   But of course, like virtually all imagery from that centennial era, most of it now seems pretty sad and silly and lost and almost heart-breakingly innocent—fodder for videotape loops at some of the hipper dance clubs. Our world since then seems to have become less interested in visions of nationalistic perkiness. Or so it would seem at first glance. But then I got to thinking more deeply about these pictures and what they meant to me and to Canada.

4   It was a quiet rainy day outside. The bookstore was empty. I sat on a stack of old atlases, and I looked at these old magazine photos further, inhaling their old-magazine smell. I realized, well ... I realized that these cheesy '70s photos inspired in me more love for Canada than they did laughs. They made me feel oddly protective;

they inspired a tug of patriotism I have never received from traditional history books. They made me remember that the Canadian values of 1971 (the values I was raised with) are still, in [the '90s], our exact same Canadian values: earnestness, a willingness to experiment with new ideas, a refusal to let the past control us (there is so little past here) and even (oh, Lord) flared pants. These are values most other countries don't have—can't have. And it is precisely because of these values that our nation will neither fade away nor rip itself apart: we'll be too busy coming up with a fresh new groovy idea to experiment with.

Sure, we like to think we're hip and cool and above corny nationalistic imagery, but deep down, we're all in flared pants. I bought a stack of magazines (three for $2) and I walked out of the store with less worry for Canada than when I had entered. Thinking of all those maxiskirted flag-waving models and those studly Lee-panted groovsters, I was thinking that we may laugh at them, but they, in the best sense, are still *us*.

5

DOUGLAS COUPLAND

A native of Vancouver, B.C., novelist Douglas Coupland (b. 1962) is the author of *Shampoo Planet* (1992) and *Life after God* (1994) as well as the groundbreaking novel *Generation X* (1991).

Words and Meanings

Paragraph

redux	Latin word, here meaning revived, restored	
neo-utopia	modern "perfect" world, a social and political paradise that could exist only in the imagination ("neo" means "new")	1
potent	powerful	

Structure and Strategy

1. Coupland begins his comparison with a contrast between Canada of the '60s and '70s and Canada now. What is the function of the descriptive details he includes of the images he finds in old magazines?
2. What is the basis of the comparison Coupland develops? What sentence most clearly summarizes it?
3. Consider the DICTION of this essay. How do phrases such as "Canada as a sexy, groovy, happening place" (paragraph 1) and "studly Lee-panted groovsters" (paragraph 5) affect the TONE?

Content and Purpose

1. What causes Coupland to be "amazed" (paragraph 1) as he looks at the old magazines? What image of centennial-era Canada do they present?
2. What typical values does Coupland identify in the Canada of the '60s and '70s? Are these values seen to be like or unlike Canadian values in the '90s?
3. What feelings about his country do the "cheesy '70s photos" evoke in Coupland? Why do you think these old pictures affected him in a way that traditional history books could not?

Suggestions for Writing

1. Find three or four old photographs. They could be from magazines, or newspapers, or perhaps pictures of your parents when they were young. Write an essay in which you contrast the styles and values of that time with those of the current era.
2. Do you agree with Coupland that the spirit of the '90s is similar to the optimistic, earnest, innovative spirit of the '60s? Write an essay that either supports or challenges this thesis, based on your own experience.

A Stranger in a Strange Land

AUSTIN CLARKE

1   One thing … I have been thinking of for the past few days: I have no real, true friends in this country, even after all these years; for those persons I hold dear are all in Barbados, or are scattered throughout the other West Indian countries.

2   Those are the persons who grew up with me; went to the same schools, were in the same choir; in the same cadet corps; the same scout troop, the 23rd Barbados; who attended St. Matthias Anglican church, for matins, Sunday school and evensong and service, from the age of 6 until I left Barbados in 1955; who were with me on picnics, outings and excursions; who attended cadet and scout camps

up in the country; who were prefects and head boys at Combermere School for Boys, and at Harrison College (also for boys, until recently when it become co-educational); persons with whom I could, and did, discuss the most personal things—joys and sorrows, the insoluble and very important crises of growing up.

I cannot pick one person in this country, my new "home," with whom I am free to share these confidences. And I am not speaking about the trust a man should put in a woman. I am talking about male children, who grow with you into boys, and eventually into men. A significant part of my history and development ended when I set foot in Toronto. This certainly must be the meaning of alienation, if not of rootlessness. It can manifest° itself in what the host society rushes to label as delinquent behaviour. No doubt much of the criminal behaviour of immigrant youths, and not only West Indian youths, may be ascribed° to this absence of roots and ruins.

The roots I call the mores°, and the ruins, the statues and the buildings of glass, steel and concrete, and the sensibility of our new friends of our transplanted "home," which is not always uniformly consistent with the way we see ourselves. This is the only meaning of the statement that, "immigrants behave differently from Canadians."

Individually, it is the difference between acquaintanceship and friendship. Metaphorically, it explains the immigrant's reliance upon materialistic accomplishments: large house, loud behaviour, conspicuous tastes. All this to the detriment, perhaps the inability, of transposing the roots and the ruins of the country of birth and of breeding.

In Barbados, I breathe in the smell of the soil, I taste the scandals of the landscape. The mud through which I trample and the sand that pours through my fingers are the roots and ruins I spoke about. It does tend to make my tentative accomplishment in this country empty, and at the same time, over-important and inflated.

> We are the hollow men.
> We are the stuffed men.
> Leaning together
> Headpiece filled with straw. Alas!
> Our dried voices, when
> We whisper together
> Are quiet and meaningless
> As wind in dry grass
> or rats' feet over broken glass
> In our dry cellar.

8   It took T.S. Eliot, himself an outsider in England, to grasp this essence of alienation, even though he may have had other personal crises in mind when he wrote this poem. We do know, however, that he was never accorded his wish to be an Englishman, even though he tried to be one, even though he is known as an English author; and this denial came in spite of the posture of snobbish Britishness he himself affected.

9   By nuance° and by innuendo°, and in crude sections of English society, he was not permitted to forget that The Dry Salvages (a poem that described his background in the United States) was not London. "I do not know much about gods." I would paraphrase his words to read, "I do not know much about Toronto's gods." In Toronto, I forget that back in Barbados are those ruins, roots and mud essential to my mental health, as "that river is a strong brown god"; and in forgetting of this part of Barbados now that I am here in the developed country, "the brown god is almost forgotten by the dwellers in cities." I forget them to the detriment° of my psychical° well-being.

10   So you see my dear, the reason for my silence, my reticence°, sometimes my petulant° reticence about things that normally summon passion. You see also, why we are the hollow men, and why our "voices when we whisper together are quiet and meaningless."

11   I stay awake at night, afraid to accept the reward of my toils during the day, because the night is a conspirator for "death's other kingdom" so I remain awake, alone at an hour when I am trembling with the tenderness of nostalgia, for those broken ruins and roots of Barbados. Awake, trying to delay and to postpone the inevitable behaviour of "dwellers in cities": that for the softest desire, I must face an institution, for relief from stress, I must face an institution, for the solution of a problem of passion, I must face an institution, because there are no persons, no friends of childhood.

12   [T]his is not my cynicism, nor my vengeance upon you because you were born here, it is simply a benediction°, and my recognizing your blessed advantage that you are able to sleep with your ruins and your "river," which are as comforting as they tell me a water bed is.

AUSTIN CLARKE

Novelist, journalist, and spokesperson for the black community, Austin Clarke was born in Barbados in 1932. He came to Canada in 1955 and worked as a reporter and broadcaster before turning to full-time writing. His books include two collections of fiction, *When Women Rule* (1985) and

Nine Men who Laughed (1986), and a memoir, *Growing Up Stupid under the Union Jack* (1980).

Words and Meanings

Paragraph

manifest	show	3
ascribed	to belong to, be caused by	
mores	customs, traditional ways	4
nuance	suggestion, shade of meaning	9
innuendo	an indirect hint or reference	
detriment	injury, damage, harm	
psychical	emotional, mental	
reticence	unwillingness to talk about, tendency to say little	10
petulant	irritable, sulky, a little bad-tempered	
benediction	blessing, mercy	12

Structure and Strategy

1. What is the ALLUSION in the title? What is the rest of the biblical passage? Why is it appropriate for this essay?
2. Paragraph 2 consists of a number of examples. What are they intended to illustrate?
3. Paragraph 7 is a quotation from T.S. Eliot's famous poem about twentieth-century alienation, "The Hollow Men." Why does Clarke place the quotation where he does? How does it provide an effective TRANSITION between paragraphs 6 and 8?
4. This essay contains many images that deepen the reader's understanding of Clarke's feelings of alienation as an immigrant living in Canada. Identify three of these images, and indicate how they contribute to the emotional impact of the essay.
5. Whom is Clarke addressing in this piece? (Hint: see paragraphs 3, 10, and 12 for clues.) What is the TONE of the essay?

Content and Purpose

1. What contrast lies at the heart of this essay? How does it relate to the contrast between acquaintance and friendship described in paragraph 5?
2. What does Clarke mean by "roots and ruins" (paragraphs 3 to 5)? How does this concept relate to his THESIS?
3. Paragraph 3 suggests a causal relationship that is not the main point of the essay but is nevertheless an interesting comment on the interaction between immigrants and their adopted country. What is this potential cause-and-effect relationship? Do you think Clarke's point is valid?

4. Do you agree with the author's observations about "the immi-grant's reliance upon materialistic accomplishments"? What does Clarke think causes this behaviour?
5. What is the "river" that Clarke refers to, and what does it repre-sent in his consciousness? How does it symbolize what he feels he has lost by leaving Barbados?
6. What do you think Clarke means by his "reticence" and fear of "accept[ing] the reward of my toils" (paragraphs 10 and 11)? Explain in your own words the reasons for his feelings. (Pay particular attention to the last sentence in paragraph 11.)

Suggestions for Writing

1. Write an essay contrasting the friends of your childhood with those of your adult years. What do friends offer or mean to us at these two stages of life?
2. Explore the differences between acquaintanceship and friend-ship. Choose your examples carefully to make the contrast clear to your reader.
3. If you have come to Canada from another country, write an essay that compares and contrasts your original home with your adopted home. Clarify what you feel you have lost as well as what you have gained in making the difficult transition from one culture to another.

Quattrocento° Baseball

ADAM GOPNIK

1   I am by vocation a student of fifteenth-century Italian art and a fan of the Montreal Expos. It is a mixture of callings that provokes more indulgent smiles than raised eye-brows, as though my penchant for wearing my Expos cap, peak backward, to seminars at the Institute of Fine Arts were a kind of sophisticated joke, a put-on—as though I were simply one more pop ironist "thoroughly bemused by the myths of popular culture," as Hilton Kramer puts it, "but differentiated from the mass audi-ence by virtue of [a] consciousness of [his] own taste." This kind of well-meaning misunderstanding has led me to brood a great deal

on the relationship of the one passion to the other, and, more generally, on what I suppose I have to call the aesthetics° of sport, and of
baseball in particular. I have tried to imagine a pasture on the
slopes of Parnassus° where Bill Lee° plays pepper with Giorgione°,
and Fra Filippo Lippi° calls off Warren Cromartie°.

To be sure, it has been submitted by a few nearsighted   2
observers that I admire the Expos precisely because they are *not* like
Carpaccio° or Sassetta°, because they "provide an outlet" for my
need to be attached to something that is neither Catholic nor half a
millennium away. It has occurred to others—for example, to my
wife, whom I met in a Verrocchio° seminar—that I am attracted to
the Expos because participation in their cult provides a very close
modern equivalent of the kind of communal involvement with
spectacle which was so crucial a part of the original experience of
fifteenth-century Italian art. My passion for the Expos, she argues,
is at heart a way of re-creating an essential piece of the
Quattrocento aesthetic—fellowship achieved through a formal
object—which the passage of time has replaced with one or another
kind of detached and devitalized "appreciation." It is a nice theory,
and may go a long way toward explaining my nearly equal passion
for the Montreal Canadiens, but I don't think it has much to say
about the Expos. In 1981, the Expos won their division and partici-
pated in the Championship Series for the first time, and surely, if my
wife's theory is correct, this should have been sheer epiphany° for
me; I should have felt as the people of Siena felt when they marched
through the streets with Duccio's "Maestà." Yet, while I found that
series by turns elating and heartbreaking, I was struck most by how
different, how disagreeably different, it was from my everyday, high-
summer experience of watching the Expos play. By the sixth inning
of the final match, my "involvement" with the destiny of the Expos
had become so intense that I no longer took any pleasure in the
game. I wanted only a climax, a *result*—my triumph or my doom. It
was, in short, sport deprived of anything like a detached aesthetic
experience—or anything like the pleasurably removed delight I take
in a Carpaccio or a Giorgione—and I sensed, suddenly, that it is precisely the kinship of my normal experience of baseball with my normal experience of Italian painting that has held me, and this suggested, in turn, that there must be some substratum° of pure aesthetic experience, divorced from symbolism or civic feeling, that can
account for the curious twinning of my obsessions....

"In its special mode of handling its given material, each art may be   3
observed to pass into the condition of some other art," writes Pater°
in the most famous passage on aesthetic transferal. Baseball, I believe,

aspires to the condition of painting. The blank, affectless° description of any particular moment in the game has in common with great painting a certain puzzling first-glance banality°. A child sits on the lap of a woman who sits on a rock. A very old man is seen against a neutral background in dim light. A fuzzy black square rests on a fuzzy maroon rectangle against a blood-red background. Now baseball: A man stands, stares, rocks, and throws a ball—almost too quickly to be seen—at a second man. The second actor, frozen in place, lunges at the near-invisible object with a club. Two other men, one dressed in formal clothes, squat and watch them. We see this action repeated, unchanged, again and again. Surely this sounds more like what goes on in a performance space in SoHo° on an off night ... than like a public spectacle that could become the national obsession of a restless and impatient people. Baseball can't be grasped by a formalist aesthetic; the appeal of the game can't be understood by an analysis of its moments. As in painting, the expressive effect, the spell, of baseball depends on our understanding of context, of the way what is being made now collects its meaning from what has gone before and what may come next. E.H. Gombrich has championed this view of how the meanings of pictures must be understood—not as a series of acts but as a series of choices within a context, an organized medium. The weight of Giotto becomes apparent only against the weightlessness of Duccio; the humidity of Giorgione becomes apparent only against the clarity of Mantegna. And just as Masaccio comes to alter irrevocably our understanding of Giotto, so each inning alters irrevocably the meaning of every inning that has preceded it: Henry Aaron's° first at-bat in 1974, as he approaches Babe Ruth's° record, suddenly lends an entirely new meaning, an unlooked-for centrality, to some nearly forgotten Aaron home run back in 1959. The significance of every action in the game depends entirely on its place within a history, on our recognition of it as one possibility, one choice, within a series of alternatives. The batter swings freely, the way the painter paints, but the swing itself is bound about by the ghosts of every other swing.

4   Just as painting, then, seems able to be better grasped by a historical than by a purely critical imagination, so baseball's most inspired observers are essentially historians, and do their best work at a distance. Baseball inspires reminiscence not because of the sentiment of its devotees° but, rather, because the meaning of its forms—of a crucial lapse, a fabled stat—can only be clarified by time. Statistics, like the best kind of art history, are not basically an attendant° or peripheral° activity. They are the means by which the act becomes articulate°. And in baseball, as in painting, the presence

of history—of the weight of tradition—is both bequest° and burden. Each game, each season must recapitulate all the cycles of the
larger history, from nascent° opportunity to exhaustion. Spring is
the time of Giotto, where there is an April freshness and the rebirth
of miraculous possibility. July is the Quattrocento, where history
begins to give shape to that possibility, to set problems without pre-
cluding° any outcome. August is baroque°: the weight of history, of
the season's corrosive and insistent patterns, demands an inflation
of effects and complicated new forms—shuffled rotations, patched
lineups, gimmicky plays. September is wholly modern: the presence of tradition becomes oppressive and begins to generate anxiety; we turn self-conscious, pray that nerve and daring, the bravura
gesture°, alone may see us through.

October, my memory and my father remind me, was once both   5
climax and renewal. The World Series celebrated our escape from
history, and held out the promise of another spring, as though we
would applaud Frank Stella and then begin all over again with the
Arena Chapel. Now we escape from the context of the season only
to enter the horrible context of prime-time entertainment, as if, just
as in much contemporary art, there were nothing left for us at the
end but an extended mockery of the same values that our calling
once upheld. There was a time, just a few years ago, when the World
Series was dominated by the Dodgers and the Yankees. No accident,
it seems to me, for these two teams have precisely the kind of smug,
sneering hardiness that I associate with much postmodern art and
architecture. The Dodgers seem like a Robert Venturi version of a
Monticello house: a familiar vernacular° form like team spirit, which
was once touching in its innocence and good cheer, is transformed by
the Dodgers into an effect to be cultivated and exploited. The tastes
of the fan, of the gallery-goer, are jeered at and gratified at the same
time. The Yankees, too, seem to me to operate by taking an archetyp-
al° bit of folklore—the interfering owner meets the prima-donna
player—and turning it into something rigged and artificial, mechanical in its self-consciousness. (Think of how natural and funny this
trope seemed just a few years ago in Oakland!) Steinbrenner's°
exploitation of the Yankees' tradition is exactly like Michael Graves'
exploitation of classical architectural form: not an imaginative extension but a cynical appropriation. October these days seems to share
the central miserable feature of postmodernism—the displacement of
the vernacular into a mode of irony.

Am I so bitter about October because of the continuing   6
failures—once last-minute, now apparently sealed by the third
week of the season—of my Expos over the past few years?
Perhaps—although the Expos, with their prolific, uncynical energy,

did seem to promise precisely the kind of natural, eager, unforced voice that art and baseball alike demand at the moment. Of course, a few turncoat Expos fans have now placed their aesthetic bets on the increasingly successful Toronto Blue Jays. I don't know; the Blue Jays seem to me suspiciously skilled at embodying the virtues of their city: dogged adherence to a goal and the subordination of the individual to a team ethic. I feel about the Torontonians' methodical approach to the pennant more or less the way that the Sienese° painters' guild must have felt about the Florentine° discovery of linear perspective—that this is precisely the kind of depressing gimmick you would expect from a town like that. The difference between the Expos' André Dawson, who many people came to think was the best player in baseball simply because he *looked* like the best player in baseball (he never really was), and, say, the Blue Jays' Jesse Barfield, is precisely the difference between a Sassetta saint and a Masaccio saint. Their guys are probably a lot closer to the real thing, but ours look more holy.

7   If I can find any consolation in recent Octobers, it is this: while meaning in baseball depends on context, perhaps only part of that context is provided by public history, by the official chronicle of box scores and All-Star ballots. For each game belongs to a private chronicle, too. Perhaps there is somewhere a fan who sees the Yankees or the Dodgers not in the context of the history of the game but in the context of his own history, whose real unhappiness ennobles their squabbling, and whose rituals (the cap worn just so, the radio placed just so), unknown to them, guarantee their victories. If he exists, then there is hope for rebirth in April after all.

ADAM GOPNIK

Canadian-born Adam Gopnik is a staff writer and art critic for *The New Yorker* magazine. In 1990 he organized with Kirk Varnedoe a controversial exhibition on art and popular culture at the Museum of Modern Art in New York. Also with Varnedoe, Gopnik wrote *High and Low: Modern Art and Popular Culture* (1990) and edited *Modern Art and Popular Culture: Readings in High and Low Art.*

Paragraph   **Words and Meanings**

Quattrocento	the fifteenth century in Italian art—a period of stylistic revolution characterized by interest in anatomy, proportion and perspective, combined with a new sense of human worth and dignity

aesthetics	the theory and study of beauty, usually in art or nature	1
Parnassus	a mountain in southern Greece, supposed in ancient times to be the sacred place where poets and other artists would go after death	
Bill Lee, Warren Cromartie	baseball stars of the 1970s	
Giorgione, Fra Filippo Lippi	Quattrocento painters	
Carpaccio, etc.	Quattrocento painters	2
epiphany	revealing or displaying a divine being	
substratum	underground layer, foundation, basis	
Pater	Walter Pater, nineteenth-century English art historian and critic	3
affectless	without emotion or feeling	
banality	triviality; something common, unexceptional	
SoHo	trendy theatre district in New York	
Henry (Hank) Aaron	the only player to eclipse Ruth's home run record	
Babe Ruth	legendary baseball hero of the 1920 and 30s	
devotees	fans	4
attendant	accompanying	
peripheral	on the fringes, not central	
articulate	expressed, put into words (in this case, numbers)	
bequest	legacy, something left by one generation for the next	
nascent	just beginning to exist, grow, or develop	
precluding	making impossible, preventing	
baroque	very ornate and elaborate style of art and architecture that prevailed in Europe from mid sixteenth to late eighteenth centuries	
bravura gesture	showing off; a gesture calculated to bring acclaim or applause	
vernacular	popular, common	5
archetypal	original, basic	
(George) Steinbrenner	the outspoken and highly controversial owner of the New York Yankees	
Sienese, Florentine	the Italian city-states Siena and Florence were rivals in Renaissance art; cf. the baseball rivalry between Toronto and Montreal today	6

Structure and Strategy

1. Is this essay based on a comparison or a contrast? Between what two things? Where is the author's THESIS introduced to the reader?
2. What INTRODUCTORY strategy has Gopnik used in this essay? What is the function of the last sentence in paragraph 1?

3. Underline a number of descriptive details in paragraph 3 that enable you to "see" paintings or baseball moves that you may not be familiar with.

4. How does the author move smoothly from his explanation of "context" in paragraph 3 to his discussion of statistics and the baseball season in paragraph 4? Identify the TRANSITIONS in these paragraphs.

5. What idea unifies paragraphs 5, 6, and 7? How do these paragraphs relate to the author's THESIS?

6. Contrast the length and complexity of the sentences and paragraphs in "Quattrocento Baseball" with those in "Edmonton vs. Calgary." What do the different STYLES imply about the audiences for whom these essays were written?

7. According to Gopnik, the month of October was once "both climax and renewal" (paragraph 5). Now, however, the baseball season ends quite differently: instead of a "renewal," we are confronted with "horrible prime-time entertainment." Similarly, painting has degenerated into "an extended mockery of [our] values." By studying the examples the author uses to illustrate this change, trace the development of the ideas in paragraph 5.

8. Given that Gopnik's essay is about art history, you might expect a serious tone; insofar as it is about baseball, you might expect a light, amusing tone. How would you characterize its actual TONE? What is Gopnik's attitude toward his subject? Toward his readers?

Content and Purpose

1. The second paragraph suggests two reasons for the author's unusual "twin obsessions." What are they? What does Gopnik realize about these theories that serves as the THESIS stated at the end of the paragraph?

2. What similarity between baseball and painting does the essay explore in paragraph 3? What does the author mean by "context"? What examples does he use to clarify how both painting and baseball rely on context for their meaning?

3. What does Gopnik mean by his claim that statistics are "like the best kind of art history" (paragraph 4)? Why does he introduce this claim before comparing the history of painting (from the fifteenth to the twentieth centuries) to the baseball season (from April to October)?

4. What sports teams serve as the basis of a contrast in paragraph 6? Which team does Gopnik prefer? Why? What conflict in art history does he suggest is parallel or similar to this contrast?

5. Unlike the other paragraphs in this essay, paragraph 7 explores only one of Gopnik's "twin passions." What relationship is there

between art and what he has to say about baseball in this paragraph? (Hint: look closely at the first two sentences of the paragraph.)

6. Have you ever imagined that the outcome of a sporting event could be affected by something you do? Attending the game, perhaps, or wearing a particular item of clothing? Why do you think Gopnik concludes his essay by alluding to this popular fantasy?

Suggestions for Writing

1. Write an essay comparing two apparently dissimilar subjects, interests, or activities. Think carefully about your topic. (We don't make any suggestions here because to do so might stifle your creativity.) Then write an essay that, like "Quattrocento Baseball," makes some significant and unusual observations about the similarities between the two subjects you have chosen.

2. Contrast two sports that at first glance seem very similar; for instance, football and soccer, tennis and squash, baseball and cricket, boxing and wrestling, trots and flats horse racing.

Additional Suggestions for Writing:
Comparison and Contrast

Write a comparison and/or contrast paper based on one of the topics below. Make sure that your thesis statement clarifies the basis of your comparison or contrast, then develop it by providing sufficient and relevant examples and details.

1. People's lifestyles often reveal their personal philosophies. Choose two people of your acquaintance whose ways of life reveal very different attitudes.
2. Compare and/or contrast living in Canada with living in another country. (Be sure to limit this topic to a few specific characteristics before you begin to write.)
3. Compare and/or contrast two sports, teams, or players.
4. Compare and/or contrast men and women as consumers (or voters, or employees, or supervisors, etc.).
5. Compare and/or contrast the appearance, mood, or appeal of a specific place in the summer and in the winter: your home town, a secret hideaway, a neighbourhood park, a favourite hangout.
6. Compare and/or contrast two artists with whose work you are familiar: two painters, poets, film directors, musicians, or actors.
7. Contrast your present career goals with those you dreamed of as a child. How do you account for the differences between the two sets of goals?
8. Choose an issue and contrast the way a typical Reform Party supporter and a typical New Democratic or Bloc supporter would respond to it: free trade, gay rights, equal pay for work of equal value, subsidized day care or elder care.
9. Contrast the way in which you and your parents view a particular issue: premarital sex, postsecondary education, family life, careers for women, raising children.
10. "Love is a gambling table on which women recklessly throw dollars and men carefully place pennies." (Richard Needham)

```
┌─────────────────────────┐
│                         │
│                         │
└─────────────────────────┘
```

Cause and Effect: Explaining "Why"

What? The Definition

Until about 500 years ago, human beings observed the sky, watched the sun come up and the sun go down, and remarked on the comfortable regularity of the sun's journey around our planet. Not until a Polish astronomer named Copernicus doubted the validity of this earth-centred view of the universe did people begin to see that the predictability of the sun had a completely different *cause*: it was we who were going around it! The *effects* of the Copernican theory were momentous. Its publication in 1543 caused much controversy and spurred the study of astronomy and mathematics. Less than a hundred years later, a scientist named Galileo almost lost his life at the hands of conservative religious authorities for supporting the Copernican theory. Ultimately, we earthlings had to cease viewing ourselves as the centre of all existence, and this shift has had profound consequences for religion and science, philosophy and art.

The Copernican theory is an example of the search for causes as well as the attempt to understand effects. Identifying reasons and consequences is one of the ways we try to make sense of the flow of events around us. Asking "Why?" is a fundamental human impulse—just ask the parent of any two-year-old. Finding out "What happened then?" is also part of our natural human curiosity. **Cause and effect**, sometimes called **causal analysis**, is a rhetorical pattern based on these instincts: the writer explains the reasons for something, such as an event or decision, or analyzes its consequences. Sometimes, a writer attempts to do both, which is necessarily a longer, more complex process. Taking one direction, either cause or effect, is usually sufficient in a paper.

Why? The Purpose

Causal analysis answers one of two questions:

1. What are the causes of S?
2. What are the effects or consequences of S?

To write a good causal analysis, you must be honest and objective in your investigation. You must analyze complex ideas carefully in order to sort out the *remote*—more distant, not immediately apparent—causes or effects and the *immediate*—direct, readily apparent—causes or effects. Don't be the prisoner of old prejudices in your causal reasoning. For instance, concluding that the reason for a strike is the workers' greed and laziness, without exploring the motives behind their demands or investigating possible management errors, is irresponsible reasoning: it will lead to an ineffective causal analysis that will convince no one.

Oversimplification is another pitfall in writing cause and effect. To claim, for example, that the increase in juvenile crime is caused by "all the violence on TV" or that women's wages are lower than men's because "men are plotting to keep women down" is an unsubstantiated simplification of complex issues. Such statements contribute nothing to your reader's understanding of causes and effects.

Similarly, you should recognize that an event can be triggered by a complex variety of things. Sometimes, it is necessary to focus on several immediate reasons, while omitting what may be remote causes. For example, if you were asked to identify the causes of a social trend such as the increased consumption of light alcoholic beverages rather than hard liquor, you might have enough space to write only about the concern for fitness and the increasing awareness of the dangers of drunk driving, leaving aside the historical and demographic causes that could not be adequately explained in a short paper. Selecting your focus and scope, then, is very important when you are writing cause and effect.

A common error in causal analysis is assuming that one event that happened to occur before another is the cause of the second event. For example, you walked under a ladder yesterday morning, and this is why you got a speeding ticket in the afternoon. Mistaking coincidence for causation is called the *post hoc* error (from the Latin *post hoc ergo propter hoc*—"after this, therefore because of this"), and it is bad reasoning.

How? The Technique

After looking at some of the problems involved in sorting through cause and effect relationships, you can see that a manageable topic and a clear thesis are essential in any causal analysis. For instance, it would be impossible to explain the causes of all serious eating disorders in a 500-word paper. However, you could adequately explain why a particular person is anorexic. Similarly, you could, after some investigation, describe the effects of anorexia on the patient or on her family. In other words, limit your topic to one you can explore thoroughly. Avoid the unwieldy "Effects of Nuclear Radiation" and choose instead the more manageable "Effects of the Chernobyl Nuclear Reactor Meltdown." The more specific your topic, the more manageable it will be for you and, since you'll be able to support it with specific details, the more interesting it will be for your reader.

Once you have decided on your topic, spend some time shaping your thesis statement. The causes or effects you wish to explain usually become the main points in your thesis statement and outline. In a short paper, each main point can be developed in a paragraph. Your thesis statement may be patterned after one of these models:

> The causes of S are a, b, and c.

Example: The principal causes of failure in college are lack of basic skills, lack of study skills, and lack of motivation.

> There are three effects of S: a, b, and c.

Example: There are three consequences of minor league hockey violence: brutal playing styles, injured children, and angry parents.

To explain both causes and effects is a challenging task in a paper or report. If you choose to analyze both cause and effect in a single paper, be sure that your topic is narrow enough to enable you to develop your points adequately. In this kind of essay, to attempt too much is practically to guarantee confusing, if not overwhelming, your reader.

The final point to keep in mind when writing causal analysis is that your assertions must be fully supported. If you are trying to convince your reader that A causes B or that the inevitable effect of X is Y, you must supply compelling proof. This back-up material may take the form of statistical data, facts gleaned from research, "expert witness" quotations, or well-chosen examples. Don't rely on your audience's indulgence or intelligence; the logic of your identification of causes and effects must be apparent to the reader. Illustrate your causal analysis with sufficient—and interesting—supporting data and examples.

An example of a simple causal analysis follows.

Why Do They Fail?

Introduction (gets attention with a startling statistic)

Statistics show that most people who begin high school finish. Some drop out, of course, but approximately three-quarters earn a diploma. At the post-secondary level, however, fewer than two-thirds of the students complete their program of study. Why do so many college and university students drop out? Knowing the factors that prevent students from completing their post-secondary programs may prove crucial to you regardless of whether you are presently a college student or thinking of becoming one. Most educators agree that the principal causes of failure are lack of basic skills, lack of study skills, and lack of motivation.

Thesis statement

First point (developed with facts and examples)

A firm grasp of basic skills—what are termed the three Rs: reading, writing, and arithmetic—is a must for college or university work. Not only are texts and research material more difficult to understand than they were in high school, but also the quantity of required reading is greater. The ability to express oneself clearly in standard written English is essential; garbled essays, ungrammatical reports, or poorly spelled and punctuated papers will be routinely failed by instructors, regardless of the ideas the writer may think he or she is expressing. Similarly, mathematical skills are essential to a student's success in many post-secondary programs.

Business, science, technology, and some applied arts programs require sound computational skills. Post-secondary students who lack these basic skills often find little remedial help available and little instructor tolerance for poor work; hence, they fall behind and drop out.

Second point (note continuing contrast between high school and college experience)

Occasionally students come to college equipped with the 3Rs but lacking the study skills necessary for success. Time management is critical; keeping up with course work when classes meet only once or twice a week is often a challenge for those accustomed to the high school routine. Students must know how to take notes from texts and lectures because college instructors, unlike high school teachers, rarely provide notes. Basically, good study skills in college or university mean taking responsibility for one's own learning. Going to class, reading and reviewing material, and preparing for assignments and tests are all up to the student. Few instructors will hound or cajole their students into learning as teachers may have done in high school.

Third point (developed by division)

Lack of motivation is also a major cause of failure. Even with good basic skills, a student who doesn't really *want* to be in college, who doesn't possess the necessary drive to do the work, may fail. School must be a priority in the student's life. For instance, if a student works 30 hours a week in a demanding job that she finds more interesting and rewarding than school, it is almost inevitable that her school work will suffer. To be successful, the student must also have a firm commitment to the career for which the college program is preparation. Finally, the successful student is someone with genuine intellectual curiosity. Without the will to learn as well as to succeed, a student is unlikely to complete a post-secondary education.

Conclusion (points out additional benefits)

Basic skills, study skills, and motivation: all are essential to success in college. Students who possess all three will not automatically achieve straight As, but they are on the right road to a degree or diploma. And—an important side benefit—those students will have mastered the traits that will make them as successful in their careers as they have been in school.

Why We Crave Horror Movies

STEPHEN KING

1   I think that we're all mentally ill; those of us outside the asylums only hide it a little better—and maybe not all that much better, after all. We've all known people who talk to themselves, people who sometimes squinch their faces into horrible grimaces when they believe no one is watching, people who have some hysterical fear—of snakes, the dark, the tight place, the long drop ... and, of course, those final worms and grubs that are waiting so patiently underground.

2   When we pay our four or five bucks and seat ourselves at tenth-row center in a theater showing a horror movie, we are daring the nightmare.

3   Why? Some of the reasons are simple and obvious. To show that we can, that we are not afraid, that we can ride this roller coaster. Which is not to say that a really good horror movie may not surprise a scream out of us at some point, the way we may scream when the roller coaster twists through a complete 360 or plows through a lake at the bottom of the drop. And horror movies, like

roller coasters, have always been the special province of the young; by the time one turns 40 or 50, one's appetite for double twists or 360-degree loops may be considerably depleted.

We also go to reestablish our feelings of essential normality; the   4
horror movie is innately conservative, even reactionary°. Freda Jackson as the horrible melting woman in *Die, Monster, Die!* confirms for us that no matter how far we may be removed from the beauty of a Robert Redford or a Diana Ross, we are still light-years from true ugliness.

And we go to have fun.   5

Ah, but this is where the ground starts to slope away, isn't it?   6
Because this is a very peculiar sort of fun, indeed. The fun comes from seeing others menaced—sometimes killed. One critic has suggested that if pro football has become the voyeur's° version of combat, then the horror film has become the modern version of the public lynching.

It is true that the mythic, "fairy-tale" horror film intends to take   7
away the shades of gray.... It urges us to put away our more civilized and adult penchant° for analysis and to become children again, seeing things in pure blacks and whites. It may be that horror movies provide psychic relief on this level because this invitation to lapse into simplicity, irrationality, and even outright madness is extended so rarely. We are told we may allow our emotions a free rein ... or no rein at all.

If we are all insane, then sanity becomes a matter of degree. If   8
your insanity leads you to carve up women, like Jack the Ripper or the Cleveland Torso Murderer, we clap you away in the funny farm (but neither of those two amateur-night surgeons was ever caught, heh-heh-heh); if, on the other hand, your insanity leads you only to talk to yourself when you're under stress or to pick your nose on your morning bus, then you are left alone to go about your business ... though it is doubtful that you will ever be invited to the best parties.

The potential lyncher is in almost all of us (excluding saints,   9
past and present; but then, most saints have been crazy in their own ways), and every now and then, he has to be let loose to scream and roll around in the grass. Our emotions and our fears form their own body, and we recognize that it demands its own exercise to maintain proper muscle tone. Certain of these emotional muscles are accepted—even exalted—in civilized society; they are, of course, the emotions that tend to maintain the status quo of civilization itself. Love, friendship, loyalty, kindness—these are all the emotions that we applaud, emotions that have been immortalized in the couplets of Hallmark cards and in the verses (I don't dare call it poetry) of Leonard Nimoy.

When we exhibit these emotions, society showers us with posi-   10
tive reinforcement; we learn this even before we get out of diapers. When, as children, we hug our rotten little puke of a sister and give

her a kiss, all the aunts and uncles smile and twit and cry, "Isn't he the sweetest little thing?" Such coveted treats as chocolate-covered graham crackers often follow. But if we deliberately slam the rotten little puke of a sister's fingers in the door, sanctions° follow—angry remonstrance° from parents, aunts and uncles; instead of a chocolate-covered graham cracker, a spanking.

11   But anticivilization emotions don't go away, and they demand periodic exercise. We have such "sick" jokes as, "What's the difference between a truckload of bowling balls and a truckload of dead babies?" (You can't unload a truckload of bowling balls with a pitchfork … a joke, by the way, that I heard originally from a ten-year-old.) Such a joke may surprise a laugh or a grin out of us even as we recoil, a possibility that confirms the thesis: If we share a brotherhood of man, then we also share an insanity of man. None of which is intended as a defense of either the sick joke or insanity but merely as an explanation of why the best horror films, like the best fairy tales, manage to be reactionary, anarchistic, and revolutionary all at the same time.

12   The mythic horror movie, like the sick joke, has a dirty job to do. It deliberately appeals to all that is worst in us. It is morbidity° unchained, our most base instincts let free, our nastiest fantasies realized …, and it all happens, fittingly enough, in the dark. For those reasons, good liberals often shy away from horror films. For myself, I like to see the most aggressive of them—*Dawn of the Dead*, for instance—as lifting a trap door in the civilized forebrain and throwing a basket of raw meat to the hungry alligators swimming around in that subterranean river beneath.

13   Why bother? Because it keeps them from getting out, man. It keeps them down there and me up here. It was Lennon and McCartney who said that all you need is love, and I would agree with that.

14   As long as you keep the gators fed.

```
┌──────────────────────────────┐
│                              │
│                              │
└──────────────────────────────┘
```

STEPHEN KING

A master of the horror genre, Stephen King (b. 1947) has written more than two dozen novels and films. Among his enormously popular works are *Carrie, The Shining, Pet Sematary, The Stand,* and *Gerald's Game.* King lives in Bangor, Maine.

Words and Meanings

Paragraph

4	reactionary	ultra-conservative
6	voyeur	someone who gets pleasure (usually sexual) out of watching others

penchant	taste for, liking for	7
sanctions	punishment or penalty	10
remonstrance	scolding	
morbidity	taste for what is horrible and gruesome	12

Structure and Strategy

1. How is the author qualified to explain the causes of our craving for horror films?
2. What INTRODUCTORY strategy does King use? How does it get the reader's attention?
3. Why is paragraph 5 a single sentence?
4. Identify three paragraphs that rely primarily on examples to support their points.
5. What metaphor (see FIGURES OF SPEECH) is the basis of paragraph 9? How does it serve to reinforce King's view that watching horror films is a normal, even healthy, activity?
6. How would you describe the TONE of this piece? (Hint: look closely at paragraphs 8, 10, 11, 13, and 14.)

Content and Purpose

1. What are the "simple and obvious" (paragraph 3) reasons why we like horror movies? What are the less obvious (see paragraphs 4 to 7)?
2. What is "innately conservative, even reactionary" (paragraph 4) about horror movies? Is there a contradiction between this statement and King's contention in paragraph 11 that they are "reactionary, anarchistic, and revolutionary"?
3. What element of the psyche, according to the essay, does almost everyone keep under a tight rein in order to maintain a civilized society?
4. What are the "hungry alligators" referred to in paragraph 12? Explain the meaning and purpose of the complex metaphor (see FIGURES OF SPEECH) King develops in this paragraph.
5. For what kind of AUDIENCE did King write this essay? What was his PURPOSE in writing it?

Suggestions for Writing

1. Write an essay analyzing the causes of our craving for other kinds of movies. Why do people flock to certain film genres (for example, action flicks, tear-jerkers, Disney animated stories, gangster movies, love stories, or cowboy films)? Choose a kind of movie you enjoy and explain the reasons for its popularity.

2. Write an essay in which you argue against King's thesis that horror movies are necessary because they keep our anti-social instincts, the alligators of our psyches, fed. Why not starve them instead, by cutting off people's access to violence and horror as represented in films?

Just Walk On By: A Black Man Ponders His Power to Alter Public Space

BRENT STAPLES

1   My first victim was a woman—white, well dressed, probably in her early twenties. I came upon her late one evening on a deserted street in Hyde Park, a relatively affluent neighborhood in an otherwise mean, impoverished section of Chicago. As I swung onto the avenue behind her, there seemed to be a discreet, uninflammatory distance between us. Not so. She cast back a worried glance. To her, the youngish black man—a broad six feet two inches with a beard and billowing hair, both hands shoved into the pockets of a bulky military jacket—seemed menacingly close. After a few more quick glimpses, she picked up her pace and was soon running in earnest. Within seconds she disappeared into a cross street.

2   That was more than a decade ago. I was 22 years old, a graduate student newly arrived at the University of Chicago. It was in the echo of that terrified woman's footfalls that I first began to know the unwieldy inheritance I'd come into—the ability to alter public space in ugly ways. It was clear that she thought herself the quarry of a mugger, a rapist, or worse. Suffering a bout of insomnia, however, I was stalking sleep, not defenseless wayfarers. As a softy who is scarcely able to take a knife to a raw chicken—let alone hold it to a person's throat—I was surprised, embarrassed, and dismayed all at once. Her flight made me feel like an accomplice in tyranny. It also made it clear that I was indistinguishable from the muggers

who occasionally seeped into the area from the surrounding ghetto. That first encounter, and those that followed, signified that a vast, unnerving gulf lay between nighttime pedestrians—particularly women—and me. And I soon gathered that being perceived as dangerous is a hazard in itself. I only needed to turn a corner into a dicey situation, or crowd some frightened, armed person in a foyer somewhere, or make an errant° move after being pulled over by a policeman. Where fear and weapons meet—and they often do in urban America—there is always the possibility of death.

In that first year, my first away from my hometown, I was to become thoroughly familiar with the language of fear. At dark, shadowy intersections in Chicago, I could cross in front of a car stopped at a traffic light and elicit° the *thunk, thunk, thunk, thunk* of the driver—black, white, male, or female—hammering down the door locks. On less traveled streets after dark, I grew accustomed to but never comfortable with people who crossed to the other side of the street rather than pass me. Then there were the standard unpleasantries with police, doormen, bouncers, cab drivers, and others whose business it is to screen out troublesome individuals *before* there is any nastiness. 3

I moved to New York nearly two years ago and I have remained an avid° night walker. In central Manhattan, the near-constant crowd cover minimizes tense one-on-one street encounters. Elsewhere—visiting friends in SoHo, where sidewalks are narrow and tightly spaced buildings shut out the sky—things can get very taut indeed. 4

Black men have a firm place in New York mugging literature. Norman Podhoretz in his famed (or infamous) 1963 essay, "My Negro Problem—And Ours," recalls growing up in terror of black males; they "were tougher than we were, more ruthless," he writes—and as an adult on the Upper West Side of Manhattan, he continues, he cannot constrain his nervousness when he meets black men on certain streets. Similarly, a decade later, the essayist and novelist Edward Hoagland extols° a New York where once "Negro bitterness bore down mainly on other Negroes." Where some see mere panhandlers, Hoagland sees "a mugger who is clearly screwing up his nerve to do more than just *ask* for money." But Hoagland has "the New Yorker's quick-hunch posture for broken-field maneuvering," and the bad guy swerves away. 5

I often witness that "hunch posture," from women after dark on the warrenlike° streets of Brooklyn where I live. They seem to set their faces on neutral and, with their purse straps strung across their chests bandolier style, they forge ahead as though bracing themselves against being tackled. I understand, of course, that the 6 danger they perceive is not a hallucination. Women are particularly vulnerable to street violence, and young black males are drastically overrepresented among the perpetrators° of that violence. Yet these truths are no solace against the kind of alienation that comes of being ever the suspect, against being set apart, a fearsome entity with whom pedestrians avoid making eye contact.

7   It is not altogether clear to me how I reached the ripe old age of 22 without being conscious of the lethality° nighttime pedestrians attributed to me. Perhaps it was because in Chester, Pennsylvania, the small, angry industrial town where I came of age in the 1960s, I was scarcely noticeable against a backdrop of gang warfare, street knifings, and murders. I grew up one of the good boys, had perhaps a half-dozen fist fights. In retrospect°, my shyness of combat has clear sources.

8   Many things go into the making of a young thug. One of those things is the consummation° of the male romance with the power to intimidate. An infant discovers that random flailings send the baby bottle flying out of the crib and crashing to the floor. Delighted, the joyful babe repeats those motions again and again, seeking to duplicate the feat. Just so, I recall the points at which some of my boyhood friends were finally seduced by the perception of themselves as tough guys. When a mark cowered and surrendered his money without resistance, myth and reality merged—and paid off. It is, after all, only manly to embrace the power to frighten and intimidate. We, as men, are not supposed to give an inch of our lane on the highway; we are to seize the fighter's edge in work and in play and even in love; we are to be valiant in the face of hostile forces.

9   Unfortunately, poor and powerless young men seem to take all this nonsense literally. As a boy, I saw countless tough guys locked away; I have since buried several, too. They were babies, really—a teenage cousin, a brother of 22, a childhood friend in his mid-twenties—all gone down in episodes of bravado played out in the streets. I came to doubt the virtues of intimidation early on. I chose, perhaps even unconsciously, to remain a shadow—timid, but a survivor.

10   The fearsomeness mistakenly attributed to me in public places often has a perilous flavor. The most frightening of these confusions occurred in the late 1970s and early 1980s when I worked as a journalist in Chicago. One day, rushing into the office of a magazine I was writing for with a deadline story in hand, I was mistaken for a burglar. The office manager called security and, with an ad hoc posse°, pursued me through the labyrinthine halls, nearly to my editor's door. I had no way of proving who I was. I could only move briskly toward the company of someone who knew me.

Another time I was on assignment for a local paper and killing   11
time before an interview. I entered a jewelry store on the city's
affluent Near North Side. The proprietor excused herself and
returned with an enormous red Doberman pinscher straining at the
end of a leash. She stood, the dog extended toward me, silent to my
questions, her eyes bulging nearly out of her head. I took a cursory°
look around, nodded, and bade her good night. Relatively speaking, however, I never fared as badly as another black male journalist. He went to nearby Waukegan, Illinois, a couple of summers ago
to work on a story about a murderer who was born there.
Mistaking the reporter for the killer, police hauled him from his car
at gunpoint and but for his press credentials would probably have
tried to book him. Such episodes are not uncommon. Black men
trade tales like this all the time.

In "My Negro Problem—And Ours," Podhoretz writes that the   12
hatred he feels for blacks makes itself known to him through a variety of avenues—one being his discomfort with that "special brand
of paranoid touchiness" to which he says blacks are prone. No
doubt he is speaking here of black men. In time, I learned to smother the rage I felt at so often being taken for a criminal. Not to do so
would surely have led to madness—via that special "paranoid
touchiness" that so annoyed Podhoretz at the time he wrote the
essay.

I began to take precautions to make myself less threatening. I   13
move about with care, particularly late in the evening. I give a wide
berth to nervous people on subway platforms during the wee
hours, particularly when I have exchanged business clothes for
jeans. If I happen to be entering a building behind some people
who appear skittish°, I may walk by, letting them clear the lobby
before I return, so as not to seem to be following them. I have been
calm and extremely congenial° on those rare occasions when I've
been pulled over by the police.

And on late-evening constitutionals° along streets less traveled   14
by, I employ what has proved to be an excellent tension-reducing
measure: I whistle melodies from Beethoven and Vivaldi and the
more popular classical composers. Even steely New Yorkers hunch-
ing toward nighttime destinations seem to relax, and occasionally
they even join in the tune. Virtually everybody seems to sense that
a mugger wouldn't be warbling bright, sunny selections from
Vivaldi's *Four Seasons*. It is my equivalent of the cowbell that hikers
wear when they know they are in bear country.

BRENT STAPLES

Brent Staples (b. 1951) earned a doctorate in psychology, then worked as a journalist for a variety of newspapers before moving to New York. He is an associate editor with *The New York Times* and the author of *Parallel Time* (1991).

Paragraph | **Words and Meanings**

2	errant	unexpected
3	elicit	cause to happen
4	avid	keen, enthusiastic
5	extols	praises highly
6	warrenlike	crowded, narrow, dark—like a rabbit warren
	perpetrators	those who perform or commit a criminal action
7	lethality	deadliness
	retrospect	hindsight, thinking about the past
8	consummation	completion, fulfilment
10	ad hoc posse	group of people quickly assembled to catch a criminal
11	cursory	hasty, superficial
13	skittish	nervous
	congenial	pleasant, friendly
14	constitutionals	walks

Structure and Strategy

1. What is the ALLUSION in the title? Why do you think the author chose this title?
2. What strategy does Staples use in his INTRODUCTION? Identify the details that help the reader picture the scene described. Explain the IRONY in the first sentence.
3. What is the function of the paragraphs that include quotations from writers Norman Podhoretz and Edward Hoagland (paragraphs 5 and 12)? How would the impact of the essay differ if Staples had not included these supporting examples of racist thinking?
4. How are the TOPIC SENTENCES of paragraphs 10 and 11 developed?
5. What is the TONE of this essay?

Content and Purpose

1. This essay reflects on the effects that the author, a black man, has on people in the street, merely by his presence. It also

deals with the effects that this phenomenon has on him. What are they? (See paragraph 2.)

2. Explain what Staples means by his "unwieldy inheritance" and his feeling like "an accomplice in tyranny" (paragraph 2).
3. What does Staples acknowledge in paragraph 6? How does this acknowledgement prepare the reader for the next point he makes about street violence (in paragraphs 7 to 9)?
4. What measures does the author take to minimize his effects on other pedestrians as he walks at night?
5. In paragraph 7, the author observes that his own "shyness of combat has clear sources." What causes does he identify for his dislike of violence?
6. Paragraph 8 deals with the causes of another social tragedy, "the making of a young thug." What are these causes, as Staples sees them? How has this sad reality affected his own life?

Suggestions for Writing

1. It is often suggested that our society is much more violent than it was a few decades ago. Others argue that we are simply more fearful, that the incidence of violent crimes has risen only slightly. Write an essay that explores the causes either for the increase or for the perception of an increase in violence.
2. Write an essay exploring the causes or effects of being an "out-sider," someone who is seen not to "belong." Support your the-sis from personal experience. How did your experience(s) affect you?

Why Young Women Are More Conservative

GLORIA STEINEM

If you had asked me a decade or more   1
ago, I certainly would have said the campus was the first place to look for the feminist or any other revolution. I also would have

assumed that student-age women, like student-age men, were much more likely to be activist and open to change than their parents. After all, campus revolts have a long and well-publicized tradition, from the students of medieval France, whose "heresy" was suggesting that the university be separate from the church, through the anticolonial student riots of British India; from students who led the cultural revolution of the People's Republic of China, to campus demonstrations against the Shah of Iran. Even in this country, with far less tradition of student activism, the populist movement to end the war in Vietnam was symbolized by campus protests and mistrust of anyone over thirty.

2   It has taken me many years of traveling as a feminist speaker and organizer to understand that I was wrong about women; at least, about women acting on their own behalf. In activism, as in so many other things, I had been educated to assume that men's cultural pattern was the natural or the only one. If student years were the peak time of rebellion and openness to change for men, then the same must be true for women. In fact, a decade of listening to every kind of women's group—from brown-bag lunchtime lectures organized by office workers to all-night rap sessions at campus women's centers; from housewives' self-help groups to campus rallies—has convinced me that the reverse is more often true. Women may be the one group that grows more radical with age. Though some students are big exceptions to this rule, women in general don't begin to challenge the politics of our own lives until later.

3   Looking back, I realize that this pattern has been true for my life, too. My college years were full of uncertainties and the personal conservatism that comes from trying to win approval and fit into the proper grown-up and womanly role, whether that means finding a well-to-do man to be supported by or a male radical to support. Nonetheless, I went right on assuming that brave exploring youth and cowardly conservative old age were the norms for everybody, and that I must be just an isolated and guilty accident. Though every generalization based on female culture has many exceptions, and should never be used as a crutch or excuse, I think we might be less hard on ourselves and each other as students, feel better about our potential for change as we grow older—and educate reporters who announce feminism's demise because its red-hot center is not on campus—if we figured out that for most of us as women, the traditional college period is an unrealistic and cautious time. Consider a few of the reasons.

4   As students, women are probably treated with more equality than we ever will be again. For one thing, we're consumers. The school is only too glad to get the tuitions we pay, or that our families

or government grants pay on our behalf. With population rates declining because of women's increased power over childbearing, that money is even more vital to a school's existence. Yet more than most consumers, we're too transient° to have much power as a group. If our families are paying our tuition, we may have even less power.

As young women, whether students or not, we're still in the   5
stage most valued by male-dominant cultures: we have our full potential as workers, wives, sex partners, and childbearers.

That means we haven't yet experienced the life events that are   6
most radicalizing for women: entering the paid-labor force and discovering how women are treated there; marrying and finding out that it is not yet an equal partnership; having children and discovering who is responsible for them and who is not; and aging, still a greater penalty for women than for men.

Furthermore, new ambitions nourished by the rebirth of femi-   7
nism may make young women feel and behave a little like a classical immigrant group. We are determined to prove ourselves, to achieve academic excellence, and to prepare for interesting and successful careers. More noses are kept to more grindstones in an effort to demonstrate newfound abilities, and perhaps to allay suspicions that women still have to have more and better credentials than men. This doesn't leave much time for activism. Indeed, we may not yet know that it is necessary.

In addition, the very progress into previously all-male careers   8
that may be revolutionary for women is seen as conservative and conformist by outside critics. Assuming male radicalism to be the measure of change, they interpret any concern with careers as evidence of "campus conservatism." In fact, "dropping out" may be a departure for men, but "dropping in" is a new thing for women. Progress lies in the direction we have not been.

Like most groups of the newly arrived or awakened, our faith in   9
education and paper degrees also has yet to be shaken. For instance, the percentage of women enrolled in colleges and universities has been increasing at the same time that the percentage of men has been decreasing. Among students entering college in 1978, women *outnumbered* men for the first time. This hope of excelling at the existing game is probably reinforced by the greater cultural pressure on females to be "good girls" and observe somebody else's rules.

Though we may know intellectually that we need to have new   10
games with new rules, we probably haven't quite absorbed such facts as the high unemployment rate among female Ph.D.s; the lower average salary among women college graduates of all races than among counterpart males who graduated from high school or less; the middle-management ceiling against which even those

eagerly hired new business-school graduates seem to bump their heads after five or ten years; and the barrier-breaking women in nontraditional fields who become the first fired when recession hits. Sadly enough, we may have to personally experience some of these reality checks before we accept the idea that lawsuits, activism, and group pressure will have to accompany our individual excellence and crisp new degrees.

11   Then there is the female guilt trip, student edition. If we're not sailing along as planned, it must be our fault. If our mothers didn't "do anything" with their educations, it must have been *their* fault. If we can't study as hard as we think we must (because women still have to be better prepared than men), and have a substantial personal and sexual life at the same time (because women are supposed to care more about relationships than men do), then we feel inadequate, as if each of us were individually at fault for a problem that is actually culture-wide.

12   I've yet to be on a campus where most women weren't worrying about some aspect of combining marriage, children, and a career. I've yet to find one where many men were worrying about the same thing. Yet women will go right on suffering from the double-role problem and terminal guilt until men are encouraged, pressured, or otherwise forced, individually and collectively, to integrate themselves into the "women's work" of raising children and homemaking. Until then, and until there are changed job patterns to allow equal parenthood, children will go right on growing up with the belief that only women can be loving and nurturing, and only men can be intellectual or active outside the home. Each half of the world will go on limiting the full range of its human talent.

13   Finally, there is the intimate political training that hits women in the teens and early twenties: the countless ways we are still brainwashed into assuming that women are dependent on men for our basic identities, both in our work and our personal lives, much more than vice versa. After all, if we're going to enter a marriage system that's still legally designed for a person and a half, submit to an economy in which women still average about fifty-nine cents on the dollar earned by men, and work mainly as support staff and assistants, or *co*-directors and *vice*-presidents at best, then we have to be convinced that we are not whole people on our own.

14   In order to make sure that we will see ourselves as half-people, and thus be addicted to getting our identity from serving others, society tries hard to convert us as young women into "man junkies"; that is, into people who are addicted to regular shots of male approval and presence, both professionally and personally. We need a man standing next to us, actually and figuratively,

whether it's at work, on Saturday night, or throughout life. (If only men realized how little it matters *which* man is standing there, they would understand that this addiction depersonalizes them, too.) Given the danger to a male-dominant system if young women stop internalizing this political message of derived identity, it's no wonder that those who try to kick the addiction—and, worse yet, to help other women do the same—are likely to be regarded as odd or dangerous by everyone from parents to peers.

With all that pressure combined with little experience, it's no wonder that younger women are often less able to support each other. Even young women who espouse° feminist goals as individuals may refrain from identifying themselves as "feminist": it's okay to want equal pay for yourself (just one small reform) but it's not okay to want equal pay for women as a group (an economic revolution). Some retreat into individualized career obsessions as a way of avoiding this dangerous discovery of shared experience with women as a group. Others retreat into the safe middle ground of "I'm not a feminist but...." Still others become politically active, but only on issues that are taken seriously by their male counterparts.

The same lesson about the personal conservatism of younger women is taught by the history of feminism. If I hadn't been conned into believing the masculine stereotype of youth as the "natural" time for freedom and rebellion, a time of "sowing wild oats" that actually is made possible by the assurance of power and security later on, I could have figured out the female pattern of activism by looking at women's movements of the past.

In this country, for instance, the nineteenth-century wave of feminism was started by older women who had been through the radicalizing experience of getting married and becoming the legal chattel° of their husbands (or the equally radicalizing experience of not getting married and being treated as spinsters). Most of them had also worked in the antislavery movement and learned from the political parallels between race and sex. In other countries, that wave was also led by women who were past the point of maximum pressure toward marriageability and conservatism.

Looking at the first decade of this second wave, it's clear that the early feminist activist and consciousness-raising groups of the 1960s were organized by women who had experienced the civil rights movement, or homemakers who had discovered that raising kids and cooking didn't occupy all their talents. While most campuses of the late sixties were still circulating the names of illegal abortionists privately (after all, abortion could damage our marriage value), slightly older women were holding press conferences and speakouts about the reality of abortions (including their own, even though that often meant confessing to an illegal act) and demanding reform or repeal of anti-choice laws. Though rape had been a quiet epidemic on campus for generations, younger women victims were still understandably fearful of speaking up, and campuses encouraged silence in order to retain their reputation for safety with tuition-paying parents. It took many off-campus speakouts, demonstrations against laws of evidence and police procedures, and testimonies in state legislatures before most student groups began to make demands on campus and local cops for greater rape protection. In fact, "date rape"—the common campus phenomenon of a young woman being raped by someone she knows, perhaps even by several students in a fraternity house—is just now being exposed. Marital rape, a more difficult legal issue, was taken up several years ago. As for battered women and the attendant exposé of husbands and lovers as more statistically dangerous than unknown muggers in the street, that issue still seems to be thought of as a largely non-campus concern, yet at many of the colleges and universities where I've spoken, there has been at least one case within current student memory of a young woman beaten or murdered by a jealous lover.

19   This cultural pattern of youthful conservatism makes the growing number of older women going back to school very important. They are life examples and pragmatic° activists who radicalize women young enough to be their daughters. Now that the median female undergraduate age in this country is twenty-seven because so many older women have returned, the campus is becoming a major place for cross-generational connections.

20   None of this should denigrate° the courageous efforts of young women, especially women on campus, and the many changes they've pioneered. On the contrary, they should be seen as even more remarkable for surviving the conservative pressures, recognizing societal problems they haven't yet fully experienced, and organizing successfully in the midst of a transient student population. Every women's history course, rape hot line, or campus newspaper that is finally covering *all* the news; every feminist professor whose job has been created or tenure saved by student pressure, or male administrator whose consciousness has been permanently changed; every counselor who's stopped guiding women one way and men another; every lawsuit that's been fueled by student energies against unequal athletic funds or graduate school requirements: all those accomplishments are even more impressive when seen against the back-drop of the female pattern of activism.

21   Finally, it would help to remember that a feminist revolution rarely resembles a masculine-style one—just as a young woman's most radical act toward her mother (that is, connecting as women in order to help each other get some power) doesn't look much like a young man's most radical act toward his father (that is, breaking

the father-son connection in order to separate identities or take over existing power).

It's those father-son conflicts at a generational, national level   22
that have often provided the conventional definition of revolution; yet they've gone on for centuries without basically changing the role of the female half of the world. They have also failed to reduce the level of violence in society, since both fathers and sons have included some degree of aggressiveness and superiority to women in their definition of masculinity, thus preserving the anthropological model of dominance.

Furthermore, what current leaders and theoreticians define as   23
revolution is usually little more than taking over the army and the radio stations. Women have much more in mind than that. We have to uproot the sexual caste system that is the most pervasive power structure in society, and that means transforming the patriarchal values of those who run the institutions, whether they are politically the "right" or the "left," the fathers or the sons. This cultural part of the change goes very deep, and is often seen as too intimate, and perhaps too threatening, to be considered as either serious or possible. Only conflicts among men are "serious." Only a takeover of existing institutions is "possible."

That's why the definition of "political," on campus as else-   24
where, tends to be limited to who's running for president, who's demonstrating against corporate investments in South Africa, or which is the "moral" side of some conventional revolution, preferably one that is thousands of miles away.

As important as such activities are, they are also the most com-   25
fortable ones when we're young. They provide a sense of virtue without much disruption in the power structure of our daily lives. Even when the most consistent energies on campus are actually concentrated around feminist issues, they may be treated as apolitical and invisible. Asked "What's happening on campus?" a student may reply, "The antinuke movement," even though that resulted in one demonstration of two hours, while student antirape squads have been patrolling the campus every night for two years and women's studies have begun to transform the very textbooks we read.

No wonder reporters and sociologists looking for revolution on   26
campus often miss the depth of feminist change and activity that is really there. Women students themselves may dismiss it as not political and not serious. Certainly, it rarely comes in the masculine sixties style of bombing buildings or burning draft cards. In fact, it goes much deeper than protesting a temporary symptom—say, the draft—and challenges the right of one group to dominate another, which is the disease itself.

27   Young women have a big task of resisting pressures and challenging definitions. Their increasing success is a miracle of foresight and courage that should make us all proud. But they should know that they, too, may grow more radical with age.

28   One day, an army of gray-haired women may quietly take over the earth.

```
┌─────────────────────────┐
│                         │
│                         │
└─────────────────────────┘
```

GLORIA STEINEM

A leading writer and lecturer in the American feminist movement, Gloria Steinem (b. 1934) founded *Ms.* magazine in 1972. Her books include *Marilyn* (1986), a study of Marilyn Monroe, the autobiographical *Revolution from Within* (1992), and *Moving beyond Words* (1994).

Paragraph   ## Words and Meanings

Paragraph		
4	transient	not staying long in any one place
15	espouse	support
17	chattel	property
19	pragmatic	practical, as opposed to idealistic
20	denigrate	diminish, put down

Structure and Strategy

1. What INTRODUCTORY and CONCLUDING strategies does the author use in the essay? Are they effective? Why?
2. Who is the intended AUDIENCE for this essay? How do you know? What is its overall TONE?
3. Which paragraphs explain the reasons that, for most women, the traditional college years are "a cautious time" (paragraph 3)?
4. To what other group does Steinem compare women in paragraph 7? Where in the essay does she reinforce this comparison?
5. Identify three paragraphs that are developed mainly by the use of examples.
6. Which paragraph sums up the four reasons Steinem gives for her belief that women grow more radical with age?

Content and Purpose

1. What assumption of her own does Steinem challenge in the first three paragraphs of this essay? Which sentence best sums up her THESIS?

2. Identify the causes Steinem suggests are responsible for young women's conservatism.
3. What is the source of the cultural norms about the difference between "brave exploring youth and cowardly conservative old age" (paragraph 3)? What is the relationship between these norms and our "conventional definition of revolution" (paragraph 22)?
4. What reasons does Steinem offer to explain why women, when they are college students, are "treated with more equality than [they] ever will be again"? (See paragraphs 4 to 7.)
5. What does Steinem mean by "female guilt trip, student edition" (paragraph 11) and "man junkies" (paragraph 14)?
6. Summarize in your own words the point, supported by her personal experiences, that Steinem makes in paragraph 12.
7. Steinem uses many ABSTRACT terms in this essay; for example, "men's cultural pattern" (paragraph 2), "sexual caste system," and "patriarchal values" (paragraph 23). Does she provide enough CONCRETE examples to make these terms meaningful to her readers?
8. What does Steinem see as the connection between "marriage-ability and conservatism" (paragraph 17)? Is the institution of marriage inherently conservative? Why or why not?
9. Which of the women's issues identified in paragraph 18 are still a concern today, almost twenty years after this essay was published?
10. In the last six paragraphs of the essay, Steinem changes her focus from causal analysis to persuasion. What action does she call for?

Suggestions for Writing

1. Do you agree with Steinem that young women are more conservative than young men, and that women, unlike men, grow more radical as they age? Write an essay that either supports or challenges this thesis. Support your argument with examples and anecdotes drawn from personal experience as well as from external sources.
2. Do you think that a chasm between men and women, a "sexual divide," has opened up on campus? The college years are traditionally the time when many people find life partners. Have issues such as sexual harassment, acquaintance rape, and the feminist re-interpretation of traditional academic disciplines fundamentally changed the way young women and men relate to each other? Based on research and personal experience, write an essay exploring this issue by identifying either causes or effects.

Bound to Bicker°

LAURENCE STEINBERG

1   It's like being bitten to death by ducks. That's how one mother described her constant squabbles with her eleven-year-old daughter. And she's hardly alone in the experience. The arguments almost always involve mundane° matters—taking out the garbage, coming home on time, cleaning up the bedroom. But despite its banality°, this relentless bickering takes its toll on the average parent's mental health. Studies indicate that parents of adolescents—particularly mothers—report lower levels of life satisfaction, less marital happiness, and more general distress than parents of younger children. Is this continual arguing necessary?

2   For the past two years, my students and I have been examining the day-to-day relationships of parents and young teenagers to learn how and why family ties change during the transition from childhood into adolescence. Repeatedly, I am struck by the fact that, despite considerable love between most teens and their parents, they can't help sparring. Even in the closest of families, parents and teenagers squabble and bicker surprisingly often—so often, in fact, that we hear impassioned recountings of these arguments in virtually every discussion we have with parents or teenagers. One of the most frequently heard phrases on our interview tapes is, "We usually get along but...."

3   As psychologist Anne Petersen notes, the subject of parent-adolescent conflict has generated considerable controversy among researchers and clinicians. Until about twenty years ago, our views of such conflict were shaped by psychoanalytic clinicians and theorists, who argued that spite and revenge, passive aggressiveness and rebelliousness toward parents are all normal, even healthy, aspects of adolescence. But studies conducted during the 1970s on samples of average teenagers and their parents (rather than those who spent Wednesday afternoons on analysts' couches) challenged the view that family storm and stress was inevitable or pervasive°. These surveys consistently showed that three-fourths of all teenagers and parents, here and abroad, feel quite close to each other and report getting along very well. Family relations appeared far more pacific° than professionals and the public had believed.

Had clinicians overstated the case for widespread storm and ⁴
stress, or were social scientists simply off the mark? The answer,
just now beginning to emerge, seems to be somewhere between the
two extremes.

The bad news for parents is that conflict, in the form of nag- ⁵
ging, squabbling, and bickering, is more common during adolescence than during any other period of development, except, perhaps, the "terrible twos." But the good news is that arguments
between parents and teenagers rarely undo close emotional bonds
or lead adolescents and their parents to reject one another. And,
although most families with adolescents go through a period of
heightened tension, the phase is usually temporary, typically ending by age fifteen or sixteen.

My own studies point to early adolescence—the years from ten ⁶
to thirteen—as a period of special strain between parents and children. But more intriguing, perhaps, is that these studies reveal that
puberty plays a central role in triggering parent-adolescent conflict.
Specifically, as youngsters develop toward physical maturity, bickering and squabbling with parents increase. If puberty comes early,
so does the arguing and bickering; if it is late, the period of heightened tension is delayed. Although many other aspects of adolescent
behavior reflect the intertwined influences of biological and social
factors, this aspect seems to be directly connected to the biological
event of puberty; something about normal physical maturation sets
off parent-adolescent fighting. It's no surprise that they argue about
overflowing trash cans, trails of dirty laundry, and blaring stereos.
But why should teenagers going through puberty fight with their
parents more often than youngsters of the same age whose physical
development is slower? More to the point: if puberty is inevitable,
does this mean that parent-child conflict is, too?

It often helps to look closely at our evolutionary relatives when ⁷
we are puzzled by aspects of human behavior, especially when the
puzzle includes biological pieces. We are only now beginning to
understand how family relations among monkeys and apes are
transformed in adolescence, but one fact is clear: it is common, at
puberty, for primates living in the wild to leave their "natal group,"
the group into which they were born. Among chimpanzees, who are
our close biological relatives, but whose family structure differs
greatly from ours, emigration is restricted to adolescent females.
Shortly after puberty, the adolescent voluntarily leaves her natal
group and travels on her own—often a rather treacherous journey—
to find another community in which to mate.

In species whose family organization is more analogous° to ours, ⁸
such as gibbons, who live in small, monogamous° family groups,
both adolescent males and females emigrate. And if they don't leave

voluntarily soon after puberty begins, they are thrown out. In both cases, adolescent emigration helps to increase reproductive fitness, since it minimizes inbreeding and increases genetic diversity.

9   Studies of monkeys and apes living in captivity show just what happens when such adolescent emigration is impeded°. For many nonhuman primates, the consequences can be dire°: among many species of monkeys, pubertal development is inhibited° so long as youngsters remain in their natal group. Recent studies of monogamous or polyandrous° monkeys, such as tamarins and marmosets, have shown that the sexual development of young females is inhibited specifically by their mothers' presence. When the mother is removed, so is her inhibitory effect, and the daughter's maturation can begin in a matter of a few days.

10   Taken together, these studies suggest that it is evolutionarily adaptive° of most offspring to leave their family early in adolescence. The pressure on adolescents to leave their parents is most severe among primates such as gibbons, whose evolution occurred within the context of small family groups, because opportunities for mating within the natal group are limited and such mating may threaten the species' gene pool. It should come as no surprise, therefore, to find social and biological mechanisms that encourage the departure of adolescent primates—including, I think, humans— from the family group around puberty.

11   One such mechanism is conflict, which, if intense enough, drives the adolescent away. Squabbling between teenagers and their parents today may be a vestige° of our evolutionary past, when prolonged proximity° between parent and offspring threatened the species' genetic integrity°.

12   According to psychologist Raymond Montemayor of Ohio State University, who studies the relationships of teenagers and their parents, accounts of conflict between adolescents and their elders date back virtually as far as recorded history. But our predecessors enjoyed an important advantage over today's parents: adolescents rarely lived at home much beyond puberty. Prior to industrialization in this country, high-school-aged youngsters often lived in a state of semiautonomy° in which they were allowed to work and earn money but lived under the authority of adults other than their parents. Indeed, as historian Michael Katz of the University of Pennsylvania notes, many adolescents actually were "placed out" at puberty—sent to live away from their parent's household—a practice that strikingly resembles the forced emigration seen among our primate relatives living in the wild.

13   Most historians of adolescence have interpreted the practice of placing out in terms of its implications for youngsters' educational

and vocational development. But did adolescents have to leave home to learn their trade? And is it just coincidental that this practice was synchronized with puberty? Historian Alan Macfarlane notes that placing out may have developed to provide a "mechanism for separating the generations at a time when there might otherwise have been considerable difficulty" in the family.

Dozens of nonindustrialized societies continue to send adoles-   14
cents away at puberty. Separating children from their parents, known as "extrusion," has a great deal in common with the behavior of many nonhuman primates. In societies that practice extrusion, youngsters in late childhood are expected to begin sleeping in households other than their parents'. They may see their parents during the day but are required to spend the night with friends of the family, with relatives, or in a separate residence reserved for preadolescents. Even in traditional societies that do not practice extrusion formally, the rite of passage at puberty nevertheless includes rituals symbolizing the separation of the young person from his or her family. The widespread existence of these rituals suggests that adolescent emigration from the family at puberty may have been common in many human societies at some earlier time.

Conflict between parents and teenagers is not limited to family   15
life in the contemporary United States. Generally, parent-child conflict is thought to exist at about the same rate in virtually all highly developed, industrialized Western societies. The sociological explanation for such intergenerational tension in modern society is that the rapid social change accompanying industrialization creates irreconcilable° and conflict-provoking differences in parents' and children's values and attitudes. But modernization may well have increased the degree and pervasiveness° of conflict between young people and their parents for other reasons.

Industrialization hastened the onset of puberty, due to   16
improvements in health, sanitation, and nutrition. (Youngsters in the United States go through puberty about four years earlier today than their counterparts did a hundred years ago.) Industrialization also has brought extended schooling, which has prolonged youngsters' economic dependence on their parents and delayed their entrance into full-time work roles. The net result has been a dramatic increase over the past century in the amount of time that physically mature youngsters and their parents must live in close contact.

A century ago, the adolescent's departure from home coincided   17
with physical maturation. Today, sexually mature adolescents may spend seven or eight years in the company of their parents. Put a different way, industrialization has impeded° the emigration of

physically mature adolescents from their family of origin—the pre-scription for parent-adolescent conflict.

18   Puberty, of course, is just one of many factors that can exacer-bate° the level of tension in an adolescent's household. Inconsistent parenting, blocked communication channels, and extremes of strict-ness or permissiveness can all make a strained situation worse than it need be. An adolescent's family should seek professional help whenever fighting and arguing become pervasive° or violent or when they disrupt family functioning, no matter what the adoles-cent's stage of physical development.

19   Given our evolutionary history, however, and the increasingly prolonged dependence of adolescents on their parents, some degree of conflict during early adolescence is probably inevitable, even within families that had been close before puberty began. Telling parents that fighting over taking out the garbage is related to the reproductive fitness of the species provides little solace°—and doesn't help get the garbage out of the house, either. But parents need to recognize that quarreling with a teenager over mundane° matters may be a normal—if, thankfully, temporary—part of family life during adolescence. Such squabbling is an atavism° that ensures that adolescents grow up. If teenagers didn't argue with their parents, they might never leave at all.

LAURENCE STEINBERG

Laurence Steinberg (b. 1952) is a professor of child and family studies at Temple University. His publications include *Adolescence* (1985) and, with Ellen Greenberger, *When Teenagers Work: The Psychological and Social Costs of Adolescent Employment* (1986) and *You and Your Adolescent* (1991).

Paragraph   ## Words and Meanings

	bicker	quarrel, argue
1	mundane	ordinary, everyday (see also paragraph 19)
	banality	commonplaceness
3	pervasive	widespread (see also paragraphs 15 and 18)
	pacific	peaceful
8	analogous	comparable
	monogamous	having one mate
9	impeded	hindered, obstructed (see also paragraph 17)
	dire	extremely serious

inhibited	delayed	
polyandrous	relationship involving one female and several males	
evolutionarily adaptive	good for the species as a whole	10
vestige	a remnant, something left over	11
proximity	closeness	
genetic integrity	the health of the gene pool, which would be contaminated by incest (here, the mating of parent and offspring)	
semiautonomy	partial independence	12
irreconcilable	opposed, cannot be made to agree	15
pervasiveness	being widespread, found everywhere (see also paragraph 18)	
impeded	made difficult, prevented	17
exacerbate	increase, aggravate	18
solace	comfort	19
atavism	behaviour that comes from our ancestors	

Structure and Strategy

1. What INTRODUCTORY strategy does Steinberg use? What makes it effective?
2. What two main functions are served by paragraph 5?
3. What ANALOGY does the author develop in paragraphs 7 to 9?
4. What kind of support for the THESIS is presented in paragraph 12?
5. What definition is developed in paragraph 14?
6. How does the CONCLUSION (paragraphs 18 and 19) both summarize the key points of the essay as well as offer practical advice?

Content and Purpose

1. Is Steinberg's title a pun (see FIGURES OF SPEECH)? What meaning(s) do you think he intended?
2. Paragraphs 3 and 4 present three different theories about the sources of adolescent-parent conflict. What are they?
3. According to Steinberg's studies, what biological phenomenon plays a central role in intergenerational conflict?
4. Paragraph 9 focusses on what "unnatural" group? What happens to the young within this group?
5. Why is it "evolutionarily adaptive" (paragraph 10) for adolescents to leave their families at an early age?
6. How do the practices of "extrusion" and rites of passage reduce or even eliminate adolescent-parent conflict in traditional societies?

7. What effects of "industrialization" have increased the potential for adolescent-parent conflict (paragraph 16)?

8. How do you feel about the traditional practice of extrusion (see paragraph 14)? Do you think it could be effectively practised in Canada in the 1990s?

Suggestions for Writing

1. Do you remember bickering with your family during adolescence? Write an essay that explains the causes *or* the effects of this conflict on you and your family.

2. Does your culture practise a "rite of passage," a ceremony or ritual that marks the transition from childhood to adulthood? If so, describe its effects on the person who goes through this initiation. If not, do you think such a ritual would be beneficial to those in your cultural community? Write an essay outlining the need for this sort of ritual and describing a ceremony that would appropriately mark the transition from childhood to adulthood.

Saving the Songs of Innocence

JOHN DIXON

1   When I was a little boy, we called them Blackfish. My father and I would sometimes see them when we strip-cast for coho° at the mouth of the Big Qualicum River. We never got very close to them in that shallow bay, and I don't remember much more than the big dorsal fins coming up and going down in the distance—except that the fishing always seemed to go off then. Dad said that it was because the salmon hugged the bottom, dodging the hunting sonar° of the killer-whale pack. I still don't know if that's true.

2   Last summer, with my own 7-year-old son, it was different. We were spinning for cutthroat° at the mouth of a stream that flows into Pryce Channel, in the Desolation Sound area of British Columbia. It was hot, the deer flies were getting very tough, and we were starting to think more fondly of swimming than catching big trout.

"Puuuff," it sounded far away. But loud enough that we stood 3
still in our little aluminum boat, watching in the direction of the
Brem River.

In less than a minute, the black fin of a killer slowly appeared 4
about a quarter of a mile away. Edge on, it looked for all the world
like a dock piling slowly wavering out the water and then falling
back in, except that pilings don't spout steamy breath. He was
moving along the shore, coming out of Toba Inlet on a course that
would bring him right up to us. His dorsal was so tall that its tip
drooped over in the way that (we say) means it's a big bull.
Excitement! I started our old Evinrude and began idling along the
shore waiting for him to catch up.

The next time he surfaced he was beside us, about 30 feet away 5
on the open water side. I speeded up a bit to match his pace, and we
held our course, staying about 50 feet off the steep shore. With not a
ripple of wind on the water, we could see all of him as he angled
into us a bit, coming up 10 feet closer after his next shore dive.

To say what is seen then is easier than to say what is felt or 6
known. He looked like a huge rubbery thing that had been molded
out of six or seven elephants. And I say "thing" because on one
level he didn't appear, deliberately swimming at such profound
ease, to be alive. Beside the obvious matter of the scale being all
wrong, there was none of the fuss or business we associate with
life, even when it is quietly on the move. But on another level, you
didn't have to know that he ate seals like buttered popcorn in order
to feel the near world humming with his predatory° purpose. And
we were alone with him—primates on a tin half shell.

He went down again, shallow, and angled in another 10 feet. 7
When he came up we saw his eye, and Matthew said, simply and
emphatically: "I'm scared now." "Smart," I said to myself: "You've
just been spotted by one who prefers dining as high up the food
chain as possible." But out loud I did my father stuff: "We're okay.
Let's just go along like this."

The tip of his dorsal slowly slid under again, and I watched it 8
closely for any change of course. "Look!" Matthew yelled: "Look at
the herring!" Under the boat I saw two things at once. We had shal-
lowed up so much that I could see the ground about 20 feet down,
and the boat was over a big school of herring packed against the
shore. And then there was a different "Puuuuff!" as the killer
surged up and dived, turning directly under the boat into the feed.

I saw white and black under us and hit the gas. We squirted 9
away, and turned around to look just as, about 25 yards behind us,
the whale erupted out of our wake. He came out completely, but so
slowly that it was hard to believe, from about the point he was
halfway, that he could possibly go any further. And when he fell

back into the light smoke of our exhaust, it seemed to take as long as the collapse of a dynamited skyscraper.

10   I tend to think of Job whenever I'm whacked over the head with a strong experience of nature. The story of his peek into God's wild portfolio and subsequent attitude-adjustment reminds us of one of the rudiments° of human wisdom: we are out of our depth in this world. In this respect, nothing has changed. What has changed, sadly and urgently, is the gap between our relatively unimproved powers of understanding and the monstrous development of our capacity to despoil. I cannot really know the oceans that Homer called "the whale road," but I can effortlessly reach their deepest regions with a neoprene gumboot that has a half-life of about a million years.

11   Looking that whale in the eye with Matthew has produced at least one point of clarity in me. I don't know how I made my children, but I know that—in a way that has nothing to do with possession—they are mine and I must try to find the strength and wisdom to care for them. Now we know that we have mixed ourselves so completely with the world that not even the mercury and cadmium-laced flesh of the whales has been spared our touch. We have made ourselves so thoroughly immanent° in the world that we have taken it away from nature and hence made it—if only through default—our own.

12   As is the case with God, when the wilderness no longer exists it cannot be invented, no matter how appealing the idea or powerful the human will to realize it. Because an invented God or an invented wilderness lacks the autonomous power that is at the core of its reality. Once innocence is lost, its songs can still be sung but it can never be genuinely restored.

13   This means that the pious path of Job, leaving the running of the world to some separate and autonomous competence such as Spinoza°'s Deus sive Natura ... God or nature, is now forever closed to us. We never understood the significance of that path (the next best thing to not getting kicked out of the Garden of Eden in the first place) until it was too late, and now must search out a future of which the only thing certainly known is that it will require inestimably more from us than patient restraint. We face responsibilities, and obstacles in the way of their being met, of unfathomable° profundity°. The good news—and it didn't have to turn out this way—is that when the world chooses to reveal itself to us, as it does from time to time in Desolation Sound, we continue to fall in love with it as deeply and inevitably as with our children.

JOHN DIXON

A philosophy instructor at Capilano College, John Dixon (b. 1943) has been a guest at the Kennedy School of Government at Harvard, Special Policy Adviser to the Minister of National Defence in Ottawa, Senior Policy Adviser to the Attorney General of Canada, and president of the B.C. Civil Liberties Association. In addition to numerous articles, he has published *Catastrophic Rights* (1990) and is currently at work on a new book, *The Benjamin Franklin Case: The Expression Rights in Canada.*

Words and Meanings

Paragraph

coho	salmon	1
sonar	underwater sound waves whales use to find fish	
spinning for cutthroat	fishing for trout	2
predatory	hunting for prey	6
rudiments	the basics	10
immanent	in-dwelling; we have permeated with chemicals the environment and all life forms	11
Spinoza	seventeenth-century Dutch philosopher who believed that God and Nature were not two different things, but different aspects of one substance	13
unfathomable	so deep we cannot get to the bottom of it	
profundity	idea that is deep, complex, extremely difficult to understand	

Structure and Strategy

1. This essay combines all four RHETORICAL MODES. Identify passages that are primarily narrative, descriptive, expository, and persuasive in nature.
2. Identify five or six descriptive details involving the whale that you find particularly effective.
3. Paragraph 10 contains two ALLUSIONS (Job and Homer). Who were they? Why does Dixon include them to develop his THESIS?
4. How does the CONCLUSION connect with the INTRODUCTION, contribute to the essay's UNITY, and help reinforce the THESIS?

Content and Purpose

1. What is the connection between the brief narrative in paragraph 1 and that which begins in paragraph 2? What is the purpose of the contrast between these two stories?

2. What is Dixon's THESIS?

3. What does the author mean by "primates on a tin half shell" in paragraph 6?

4. Where in the essay does the author move from relating the experience to interpreting it? How does the author interpret the encounter with the killer whale? What does it make him mindful of?

5. Summarize the point of paragraph 10. What is the connection between "God's wild portfolio" and the "neoprene gumboot that has a half-life of about a million years" (paragraph 10)?

6. To what does Dixon compare the loss of the wilderness in paragraph 12? Paraphrase the meaning of the last sentence in this paragraph.

7. What human impulse does Dixon see as positive in its implications for the possible re-establishment of a healthy link between humankind and nature? (See paragraph 13.)

Suggestions for Writing

1. Write an essay recounting an experience you have had in nature (perhaps hiking, camping, fishing, kayaking, skiing, etc.) that had a profound effect on you. Using narration and description to develop your thesis, explain the causal relationship between your experience and its effects.

2. Write an essay exploring the causes or the effects of a particular kind of damage that you, your community, or an industry you are familiar with inflicts on the natural environment.

Clifford Sifton's Medicine Show°

RALPH ALLEN

1   From the start, the story of the two provinces that were carved out of the Northwest Territories [at the turn of the century] has been a story of the unexpected and the unknown. It must remain so for at least another fifty years. For Saskatchewan and Alberta represent a union whose fruit is

"Clifford Sifton's Medicine Show" by Ralph Allen, copyright by Mrs. Gail Chambers. First published in June 1955.

unpredictable almost by definition—the union of a very old land with a very young people. Some of the land, the northern rocks of the Canadian Shield, is as old as any land in the world. The prairies are older than the Nile, older than the hills of Jerusalem, older than Galilee and the valley of the Jordan. And the people are just as spectacularly young. Among voluntary settlers and descendants of settlers, they are second in their newness to their home only to the modern Jews of Israel, and the Jews knew Israel centuries before they returned to it.

It took the old land many millions of years to hew out its rocks   2 and mountains, to bury its twenty-ton lizards and flying dragons, to sift and grind its soil, to hide its lakes of inflammable ooze and its underground hills of coal and metal. It took the young people who came there a maximum of decades and a minimum of weeks to size up the land and guess how best to live with it. In reality they knew very little of what to expect from the climate, or what the soil would stand, or what lay secreted beneath the soil.

It was no accident that they were naive and ill-informed. As the   3 transcontinental railway pushed through the plains in the early 1880s it pushed through empty country. The whole prairie from Winnipeg west had only sixty thousand [European] inhabitants when the decade began. Halfway through the [1880s] the Dominion government had had fewer than twenty thousand takers for the free homesteads it had begun offering more than ten years earlier, and more than half of these had already abandoned their farms and gone back to Ontario or the U.S. The CPR had no traffic for its railway and no buyers for its twenty-five million acres of land along the right of way. By the mid-Nineties the expected wave of settlement still had shown no sign of coming. Clearly, unless something quick and drastic were done the rails would turn to rust and with them the dream of a Canadian nation stretching from coast to coast.

The needed and drastic thing was done, by a quick and drastic   4 man named Clifford Sifton. Sifton was federal Minister of the Interior. His was the chief responsibility for trying to fill a void a third as large as Europe. During the years between 1896 and 1905 Sifton and the CPR, with some help from the Hudson's Bay Company, the Grand Trunk Pacific° and a few private colonization companies, staged the largest, noisiest and most successful medicine show in history. It covered two continents and was conducted in a dozen languages. Its message was simple and direct: whatever ails you, come to western Canada! In his role as chief barker°, Sifton published millions of pamphlets extolling the free land of the Northwest Territories, and offering it gratis° to anyone who would come and get it. In impressive rounded phrases worthy of a multi-lingual W.C. Fields, his literature cajoled the Swedes in Swedish, harangued the Germans in German, beguiled the French in French, coaxed the Hollanders in Dutch, wheedled the Norse in Norwegian.

5   The CPR supported him by sending out equally persuasive pamphlets in Welsh, Gaelic, Danish and Finnish, as well as the more common Western languages. At one time Sifton had twenty-one advertising agencies working for him. He and the CPR brought free-loading American editors to the prairies by the trainload. Successful western farmers from Britain and the U.S. were sent back home, as guests of the Dominion government, to carry the gospel to their old neighbors. Sifton sold huge tracts of Canadian government land at give-away prices to private colonization companies, then paid them a bounty out of the Dominion treasury for every settler they could produce—five dollars for the head of a family, two dollars each for women and children.

6   For every worthy human aspiration°, and for some that weren't so worthy, the new paradise offered the virtual certainty of fulfillment. *Poor?* Where else could you acquire a hundred and sixty acres of land for a ten-dollar registration fee? Where else would a railroad take you halfway across a continent for six dollars? *Opposed by conscience to military service?* What other nation would offer conscientious objectors a guarantee against conscription? *In a hurry?* This from a pamphlet that bore Sifton's name: "The shrewd and sturdy settler who plants a little capital and cultivates it can, with due diligence, in a few years, produce a competency." *Lazy?* J. Obed Smith, one of Sifton's departmental assistants, assured the prospective immigrant: "He can make his crop in less than four months."

7   Sifton and his associate spellbinders answered possible hecklers in advance. *Schools inadequate, sir?* "Educationists," a Sifton circular announced solemnly in 1903, "assert the school system of the Northwest Territories is equal, if not superior, to that of any other country." *Communications unsatisfactory, sir?* "Excellent railway facilities, admirable postal arrangements." *Greater opportunities, my dear sir, in the United States?* As a minister of the crown, Sifton doubtless felt he could not personally denigrate° a friendly nation. The CPR handled the question with a deft effusion° of crocodile tears: "The decadent° condition of many American farms is no doubt due to the prevalence of the tenant system."

8   One CPR circular, aimed directly at attracting immigrants from the U.S.A., borrowed the satisfied-user technique so popular with pill manufacturers. Typical headings above the testimonials read: "Would not Return to Indiana"; "Dakota Farmer Succeeded Without Capital"; "Prefers the Weyburn District to the States"; "Easily Earns Holiday Trips to Ohio."

The cold prairie winters and the hot dry prairie summers were   9
never a serious embarrassment to Sifton, who contented himself
with calling them "splendid." To have said anything less would
have been, according to the relaxed idiom of the times, to have tam-
pered with the truth. Even as late as 1910, by which time a good
deal more evidence about western weather was on the record, not
all of it favorable, a Grand Trunk pamphlet trumpeted: "The time
has probably passed when the impression can exist that western
Canada has a forbidding climate. Such fabrications have been put
forth freely in the past by designing° persons, but the greatest factors in advertising the delightful features of the climate, which
quite submerge the few slight drawbacks, are the people already
settled there, prosperous and happy. The summers are ideal in
every respect with sufficient rainfall properly distributed, and
when winter sets in with its bracing dry atmosphere and clear days,
there is nothing to dread, but much to enjoy in this season of meeting friends and indulging in the sports and pastimes of the season."

The siren song° was heard halfway around the world. Those   10
earthy mystics, the Doukhobors, heard it in Russia and in a single
month seven thousand of them streamed off the gangplanks at
Saint John and boarded the colonist cars for Winnipeg and the central plains of Saskatchewan. Heartsick Ukrainians, without land
and without a country, heard it under the flag of Austria, under the
flag of the Imperial Czar, even under the flag of Brazil. They were
soon to be western Canada's largest racial group, second only to the
Anglo-Saxons. Cockneys heard it in the crowded mews° of
Hackney. Members of the minor gentry heard it on the minor
estates of Surrey and invited their younger sons into the study for a
serious talk about the future. Ontario farm boys heard it as their
time grew near for leaving home. So did ranchers from Texas,
Oklahoma and Montana, cramped by fences.

Once the people started coming, Sifton did his best to retrieve°   11
his promises. At the railway terminals and along the staging routes,
the Dominion government opened ninety immigration halls and
staging camps, where bunks, cookstoves, surveyors' maps, advice
and interpreters were available free of charge. By 1901
Saskatchewan's population was more than ninety thousand and
Alberta's more than seventy thousand and in the next ten years
these figures were quintupled. The dream of a nation had been
redeemed.

The cost of its redemption and its reaffirmation in the half cen-   12
tury since 1905 bore no relation to the estimates on the immigration
folders. The ancient land proved alternately hospitable° and cranky,
kind and savage, benign and spiteful. Thousands of the settlers

were wholly ignorant of agriculture. Even the relatively experienced Europeans knew little about farming large acreages; to them the basic tools were the grub hoe, the scythe, the hand flail and winnow and the wooden plow. Erosion and soil drifting were as foreign to the settlers' thoughts as nuclear energy. Drought, hail and autumn frost were unheard of—at least in the sunny folklore of the Department of the Interior. Grasshoppers, rust° and weeds did not begin to appear north of the border until well after the turn of the century.

13   Thus the pioneers were ripe for ambush. Their mistakes were frequent, and ranged from the tragic to the bizarre. So did the vindictiveness° of nature and the land. Of the first four [European] people to die in Saskatoon, two froze to death in blizzards, one drowned in the Saskatchewan River and the other died of exhaustion after fighting a prairie fire. In Alberta in 1906–7 the Chinook° failed. The owners of the big ranches had no hay for their herds, for they had come to depend on the soft winter wind to uncover the uncut grass. Cattle and horses starved or froze by the tens of thousands. The Bar-U Ranch alone lost twelve thousand head. In 1903, a year of blizzards and bright sunshine, hundreds of horses went snow-blind and lost their lives by tumbling over precipices or blundering into gullies. A physician attached to the famous Barr colony, a mass pilgrimage of English families to Saskatchewan in 1903, complained that he spent most of his time patching up self-inflicted axe wounds.

14   The individual settlers' ideas of how to equip themselves for life on the frontier were often imaginative but odd. Not long ago Ray Coates, who arrived from England in 1903, recalled with amusement that he had come armed with dumbbells, boxing gloves and other muscle-building devices. At least one somewhat earlier arrival is known to have brought a case of Gold Cure, a contemporary remedy for alcoholism. Georgina Binnie-Clark, a spinster lady of quality, arrived in the Qu'Appelle Valley in 1905 with an expensive and ornate bathtub. She discovered that to fill it she would have to haul water three hundred yards, a pail at a time, from a well barely capable of supplying enough drinking water. So she sold the tub to another English lady, who discovered that *she* would have to haul water two miles to fill it. It ended up as a storage bin for seed. Mrs. Robert Wilson, of Bienfait, Sask., recently recalled a disaster that may have been unique: a horse once fell through the roof of her family home, a sod hut which her father had built on a hillside.

15   Their loyal children and their sentimental grandchildren have tried to enforce the tradition that the pioneers endured their troubles, large and small, with unfailing cheerfulness and courage. The theory

is only partly supported by the written history of the period and by a cross-check with almost any of the thousands of men and women who lived through it and are still here to tell about it. Not long ago, I talked to a retired Leduc farmer named Luke Smith, born Lucan Smzt in Poland. Smith arrived in Halifax nearly sixty years ago. His pocket was picked aboard the ship and he docked without a penny. He borrowed two dollars from the fellow immigrant who was later to be his father-in-law and with that and his railway ticket he got to Edmonton. He went to work as a railway section hand at a dollar a day and after four years had saved enough money to make the down payment on a quarter section of land.

It took years to clear the land but he sustained himself by sell- 16 ing willow posts and firewood. By 1946 he had every right to call himself a success. He had raised and seen to the education of five children and he had a good farm with good crops, good cattle and good buildings. A man called in one day and offered him five dollars, plus a per-barrel oil royalty, for his mineral rights. Smith took it like a shot. ("I drilled twenty times for water and got nothing. So who's going to find *oil*? I was so glad about the five dollars I took it to town and bought a bottle of whiskey.") A few months later the Leduc discovery well came in and Smith's next-door neighbor sold his mineral rights for $200,000. If Smith had any regrets on this score, they were not serious enough to remember; his per-barrel oil royalties still run as high as $3,000 a month and Luke and his vigorous, smiling wife give all but $200 of this to their children and grandchildren.

Just before Franklin Arbuckle and I left the cottage to which 17 Luke and Mrs. Smith have retired, I asked a fairly routine question: Were you as happy in the early days as you are now? I half expected a routine answer about the joys and satisfaction of hardship and struggle honourably endured. Luke Smith and his wife have richly earned the right to clothe their memories in sentiment. But Luke was silent for several seconds, his strong, serene face deep in thought. Then he looked up gravely toward the kitchen doorway where Mrs. Smith stood with a dishcloth and the last of the supper dishes. The look they exchanged clearly said: *This question must be answered truly, but is it best that the man answer it, or the woman?* At last it was Mrs. Smith who answered. "He cried lots of times," she said with quiet dignity. "They all did."

In one way or another nearly everyone who was farming in 18 Saskatchewan or Alberta fifty years ago says the same thing. In the last few years the provincial archives office of Saskatchewan has been asking original settlers to put their experiences on paper in order to flesh out the sparse printed records of the time. To the question, "How did you learn farming?", Frank Baines, of Saltcoats, replied succinctly: "By trial and error, with large portions of the latter." R.E. Ludlow recalled: "Nobody had nothing, and we all used it." Mrs. May Davis, who came to Canada from England in 1883, drew a haunting picture of the finality with which so many people committed all their earthly hopes into what for many of them was a literal void. "I can most particularly remember one poor sick-looking woman who was coming to Canada to join her husband, who had left England some months before. She had seven little boys with her, the youngest a baby at her breast. At our last sight of her she was on the wharf at Halifax, seated on a box of her 'effects,' waiting for her husband to come and claim them all. Did he come, I wonder—oh, but surely!—and where did they go and what became of them all? Perhaps by now one of those poor shabby little fellows has his name on the roster of Canada's famous men. Who can say? This is a land of opportunity and it is all a long, long time ago."

RALPH ALLEN

Born in Winnipeg and raised in Oxbow, Saskatchewan, Ralph Allen (1913–66) was one of Canada's best-known journalists. During the course of his career, he worked as writer or editor for many of the major Canadian papers: *The Winnipeg Tribune, The Toronto Globe, Maclean's,* and *The Toronto Star.* He wrote five novels, the best known of which is *Peace River Country* (1958), and a book on Canadian history, *Ordeal by Fire: 1919–1945* (1961).

Words and Meanings

Paragraph

	medicine show	usually a caravan with a barker who would travel from place to place selling "cures" of various kinds
4	Grand Trunk Pacific	financially disastrous rail line built in 1914 and bankrupt in 1919; taken over by the federal government and made part of the Canadian National Railway
	barker	person who urges the crowd to enter a circus, fair, or sideshow; a promoter
	gratis	free
6	aspiration	longing, desire, goal
7	denigrate	say negative things about
	effusion	pouring out, spilling over

decadent	decaying	
designing	self-serving, selfish	9
siren song	the sirens were mythological creatures whose beautiful songs attracted sailors and lured them to their death	10
mews	rooms built out of converted stables	
retrieve	make good	11
hospitable	generous, providing food	12
rust	a disease that devastated wheat fields	
vindictiveness	revenge-seeking character	13
Chinook	warm winter wind	

Structure and Strategy

1. What contrast does the author introduce in paragraph 1? What examples does he use to develop it? Why do you think they are included? How is this contrast extended in paragraph 2?
2. Identify three or four examples of effective DICTION in paragraph 2.
3. What kind of support do paragraphs 3 and 11 use to develop the TOPIC SENTENCE?
4. What image does the author choose to describe Clifford Sifton and the job he did (paragraph 4)? Why do you think he chose this image?
5. Which paragraphs are developed largely by means of quotations? Why?
6. This essay first describes the techniques used by Sifton and his staff to attract European settlers to Saskatchewan and Alberta; then it shifts to describing the consequences of their promotional methods. Where does the transition take place?
7. Identify the TOPIC SENTENCES in paragraphs 6, 10, 12, and 14. How is the topic sentence supported in each of these paragraphs? What development strategies does the author use?
8. What strategies are used in the CONCLUSION of this essay (paragraphs 15 to 18)? Are they effective? Why or why not?

Content and Purpose

1. Who was Clifford Sifton? What was the basic problem he had to solve? Why does the author describe Sifton's solution as a "medicine show"? (See the title and paragraph 4.)
2. What peoples were attracted to the prairies as the result of Sifton's efforts? (See paragraphs 4, 5, and 10.)
3. What does the author think of the promises Sifton made to lure immigrants from Europe? (See paragraphs 5 to 9.)

4. What contrast does the author present between Sifton's promises and the reality the settlers faced (paragraph 12)? Why were the settlers "ripe for ambush" (paragraph 13)? Whose fault was this?

5. What are the causes of failure described in paragraph 13? In paragraph 14?

6. How is the myth of prairie settlement maintained by "loyal children and … sentimental grandchildren" different from the reality (paragraph 15)? Why do you think there is such a contrast between the actual experience endured by the settlers and the "tradition" celebrated by their descendants?

7. The European immigrants were not the only inhabitants of this "ancient land." Indigenous peoples had been there for thousands of years. What were the effects on them of the government's settlement policies?

Suggestions for Writing

1. Did your parents or grandparents come to Canada from another part of the world? How do they remember the experience? Write an essay exploring the effects that their journey had on them and on their descendants. Alternatively, explore the effects that their ethnic group (for example, Ukrainians, Chinese, Italians, West Indians, Portuguese) has had on Canada.

2. Part of Allen's essay focusses on the effects that Canada's climate had on people who were unfamiliar with it and were unprepared to deal with it. Write an essay explaining the impact of a particular climate on culture. For instance, how do very cold, very hot, very dry, or very wet climates influence the culture of the people who live there?

Additional Suggestions for Writing:
Causal Analysis

Choose one of the topics below and write a paper that explores its causes *or* effects. Write a clear thesis statement and plan the development of each main point before you begin to write the paper.

1. sibling rivalry
2. restrictions on smoking in public places
3. the popularity of a current television series
4. the increasing number of working mothers
5. fascination with the lifestyles of the rich and famous
6. the tendency of people to distrust or dislike people different from themselves
7. the pressure on women to be thin
8. the appeal of television evangelists or preachers
9. peer pressure among adolescents
10. the popularity of foreign-made cars
11. the popularity of French-immersion schooling in Canada
12. the trend to postpone childbearing until a couple is in their 30s or even 40s
13. a specific phobia that affects someone you know
14. the attraction of religious cults
15. marriage breakdown
16. alcoholism
17. the popularity of Gordon Korman, or Judy Blume, or any other widely read writer of fiction for adolescents
18. the demand among employers for ever-increasing levels of literacy
19. guilt
20. "Happy families are all alike; every unhappy family is unhappy in its own way." (Tolstoy)

7

Definition: Explaining "What"

What? The Definition

Communication between writer and reader cannot take place unless there is a shared understanding of the meaning of the writer's words. Knowing when and how to define terms clearly is one of the most useful skills a writer can learn. Through definition, a writer creates meaning.

In the biblical myth, which has endured for millennia (a millennium is a period of a thousand years), the Creator presents the animals to Adam in order that he name them:

> And out of the ground the Lord God formed every beast of the field, and every fowl of the air; and brought them to Adam to see what he would call them: and whatsoever Adam called every creature, that was the name thereof.
>
> (Genesis 2:19)

Adam isn't asked to count or catalogue or describe or judge the beasts of creation. They are arrayed before him so that he might *name* them, *define* them, an act which in itself is a kind of creation. This capacity to define things through words and to communicate thought by means of those words makes us unique as humans.

There are two basic ways to define terms: the short way and the long way. The short way is sometimes called **formal definition**. The writer explains in one sentence a word that may be unknown to the reader. An example of formal definition is the explanation of the word "millennium" in the paragraph above. You should include a definition whenever you introduce an unfamiliar word, or whenever you assign a particular meaning to a general term. If you do not define ambiguous words or phrases, you leave the reader wondering which of several possible meanings you intended. You should also provide definitions when using technical terms, since these are likely to be unfamiliar to at least some readers. For instance, a reader who is not familiar with the term "formal definition" might assume it means "elaborate" or "fancy," when in fact it means a one-sentence definition written in a particular form.

The second way to define a term is through **extended definition**, a form of expository writing in which the word, idea, thing, or phenomenon being defined is the subject of the entire essay or paper. Extended definition is required when the nature of the thing to be defined is complex, and explaining *what it is* in detail is the writer's goal.

Why? The Purpose

In your studies, you have probably already discovered that fully exploring a complex subject requires a detailed explanation of it. Definition papers answer the question, "What does S mean?" For example, the word "myth" used above to describe the creation story does not, in any way, mean "untrue," though that is often the way the word is used. A myth is better defined as a traditional or legendary story that attempts to explain a basic truth. Entire books have been written to define what myth is and how it works in our culture. Obviously, myth is a topic that lends itself to extended definition.

Extended definition is especially useful for three purposes: explaining the abstract, the technical, or the changed meanings of a word or concept. If you were asked in a history class, for example, to define an abstract idea such as "freedom" or "misogyny" or "justice," an extended definition would enable you to establish the meaning of the concept and also to explore your personal commitments and aspirations.

Whatever their professional background, all writers occasionally use technical terms that must be defined for readers who may be unfamiliar with them. For example, a Canadian businessperson with a large potential market in the United States may have to define "free trade" to prospective investors. A social worker would be wise to detail what she means by "substance abuse" in a brochure aimed at teenage drug users. An engineer could not explain concepts such as "gas chromatography" or "atomic absorption" to a non-technical audience without first adequately defining them.

Extended definition can also be used to clarify the way in which a particular term has changed in meaning over the years.

For instance, everyone is aware of the way in which the word "gay," which originally meant only "joyful" or "bright," has expanded to include "homosexual," even in its denotative, or dictionary, meaning. Tracking the evolution of a word's meaning can be an effective and interesting way to define the term for your readers.

Clearly, extended definition is ideal for explaining because it establishes the boundaries of meaning intended by the writer. In fact, the very word "define" comes from the Latin word *definire*, which means "to put a fence around." But definition is not restricted to its expository function. Defining something in a particular way sometimes involves persuading other people to accept and act on the definition. Our businessperson will probably want to take a stand on free trade after defining it; the social worker's definition of substance abuse might well form the basis of the argument against drug use. Extended definition is thus a versatile rhetorical strategy that can accommodate the urge we all have to convince and influence the people with whom we're communicating.

How? The Method

Extended definition does not have a single, clear-cut rhetorical pattern unique to itself. Its development relies instead on one or more of the other patterns explained in this text. In other words, depending on the topic and the audience, an extended definition may use any of a variety of forms, or even a combination of forms. For instance, if you wanted to define the term "myth," one way would be to provide *examples* of different myths. Another way would involve *comparing* the terms "myth" and "legend." Or you might choose to explain some of the *effects* of a particular myth on a specific culture. An extended definition of gas chromatography, on the other hand, might focus on the *process* involved in using a chromatograph. An extended definition of substance abuse could *classify* the various addictive drugs. Sometimes a combination of patterns is the best approach. You need to put yourself in your reader's place to determine what questions he or she would be most likely to ask about your topic. Then you'll be able to choose the most appropriate pattern or patterns with which to organize your paper.

It is often helpful to begin your extended definition with a *formal definition*. To write a formal definition, first put the term you are defining into the general class of things to which it belongs; then identify the qualities that set it apart or distinguish it from the others in that class. Here are some examples of formal definitions:

Term		Class	Distinguishing Features
A turtle	is	a shelled reptile	that lives in water.
A tortoise	is	a shelled reptile	that lives on land.
Misogyny	is	the hatred	of women.
Misanthropy	is	the hatred	of people in general.
The gross domestic product	is	an economic indicator	derived by establishing the total value of a country's goods and services.
A résumé	is	a written summary	of a job applicant's education, work experience, and personal background.

Constructing a formal definition is a logical way to begin any task of definition. It prevents vague formulations such as "a turtle lives in water" (so does a tuna), or "misanthropy is when you don't like people." (By the way, avoid using "is when" or "is where" in a formal definition—it's bound to be loose and imprecise.) Notice that a formal definition is sometimes a ready-made thesis statement, as in the last two examples given above. An extended definition of the gross domestic product (GDP) would divide the GDP into its component parts—goods and services—and show how their value is determined. Similarly, an extended definition of a résumé would explain its three essential components: the applicant's education, work experience, and personal background.

There are two pitfalls to avoid when you are writing definitions. First, do not begin with a word-for-word definition copied straight out of the dictionary, even though you may be tempted to do so when you're staring at a piece of blank paper. Resist the temptation. As an introductory strategy, a dictionary definition is both boring and irrelevant. It's *your* meaning the reader needs to understand, not all the potential meanings of the word given in the dictionary. "*Webster's Third International Dictionary* defines love as 'a predilection or liking for anything'" is hardly a useful, let alone an attention-getting, introduction. Second, don't chase your own tail: avoid using in your definition a form of the term you're defining. A definition such as "adolescence is the state of being an adolescent" not only fails to clarify the meaning for your readers, it also wastes their time.

A good definition establishes clearly, logically, and precisely the boundaries of meaning. It communicates the meaning in an organizational pattern appropriate to the term and to the reader. To define is, in many ways, to create, and to do this well is to show respect for the ideas or things you're explaining as well as courtesy to your audience.

Here is an example of an essay that defines a term by exploring its etymological roots.

A Definition of Education

Introduction

Thesis statement

Words don't spring into being out of nowhere: they grow out of other words. It is often useful and interesting to explore the etymology, or origins, of the words we use. The word "education," for example, has a meaningful history. It is derived from two different but related Latin words: *educare* and *educere*.

First point (developed by definition and quotation)

The Latin verb *educare* is most often translated as "to rear" or "to nourish." Originally, the word was applied to both children and animals, because "rearing" means providing food and basic necessities. The *Oxford English Dictionary* tells us that one of the earliest recorded uses of the word was in the context of animal husbandry. In 1607 a man named Topsell wrote that "horses are not to be despised, if they [are] well bred and educated." The word is not used this way today—we teach a dog new tricks; we don't "educate" him. The word retains something of its earlier meaning, however, in that parents and teachers nourish the young with knowledge, which is digested by relatively passive recipients.

Second point (also developed by definition and quotation)

The Latin verb *educere*, on the other hand, has a different, more active meaning. It means "to lead out" or "to draw forth." The English word "educe," a direct descendant of *educere*, means to infer something, or to come up with ideas oneself. In other words, if I use my own faculties, combined with knowledge I've gained, I can actively educe or develop new ideas on my own. The English poet Samuel Taylor Coleridge asserted, "In the education of children, love is first to be instilled, and out of love obedience is to be educed." His use of the word "educed" implies that children can naturally develop obedience out of their own best instincts rather than remain passive receptacles into whom "obedience" is poured (or thrashed). Similarly, a teacher can lead her students or draw them out, but the students must respond actively to develop the behaviour or knowledge themselves. Basically, the *educare* root points to a passive experience in which the learner waits to be filled with facts, while the *educere* root points to a dynamic experience in which the learner interacts creatively with the teacher and the subject matter.

Conclusion (makes use of a short anecdote to make the general point specific)

This distinction was brought home to me recently as I listened to a hotline radio program in which a grade-ten dropout bemoaned his lack of a job: "Unless my education improves," he began, "I won't have a chance." Interestingly, his phrase lacked a "doer." He seemed to understand education only in the sense that derives from *educare*: the experience of being spoon-fed. To this young man, education was something separate from himself, outside his control—something which, like his chances, could only be altered by outside forces. This attitude is clearly self-defeating. It fails to recognize the meaning of education that derives from *educere*: the experience of actively responding to and developing what a teacher has initiated. The relationship between the learner and what is being learned must be an active one. The learner, in other words, must assume responsibility in the process.

Thus, the roots of the word "education" have something to teach us. We can educe useful knowledge from them even today—hundreds of years after the word itself first appeared in our language.

Don't You Think It's Time to Start Thinking?

NORTHROP FRYE

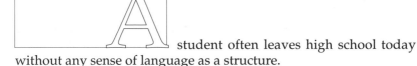 student often leaves high school today without any sense of language as a structure.

He may also have the idea that reading and writing are elementary skills that he mastered in childhood, never having grasped the fact that there are differences in levels of reading and writing as there are in mathematics between short division and integral calculus.

Yet, in spite of his limited verbal skills, he firmly believes that he can think, that he has ideas, and that if he is just given the opportunity to express them he will be all right. Of course, when you look at what he's written you find it doesn't make any sense. When you tell him this he is devastated.

Part of his confusion here stems from the fact that we use the word "think" in so many bad, punning ways. Remember James Thurber's Walter Mitty who was always dreaming great dreams of glory. When his wife asked him what he was doing he would say, "Has it ever occurred to you that I might be thinking?"

But, of course, he wasn't thinking at all. Because we use it for everything our minds do, worrying, remembering, day-dreaming, we imagine that thinking is something that can be achieved without any training. But again it's a matter of practice. How well we

"Don't You Think It's Time to Start Thinking?" by Northrop Frye previously appeared in *The Toronto Star*, January 25, 1986. Reprinted with the permission of the Estate of Northrop Frye.

can think depends on how much of it we have already done. Most students need to be taught, very carefully and patiently, that there is no such thing as an inarticulate° idea waiting to have the right words wrapped around it.

6   They have to learn that ideas do not exist until they have been incorporated into words. Until that point you don't know whether you are pregnant or just have gas on the stomach.

7   The operation of thinking is the practice of articulating ideas until they are in the right words. And we can't think at random either. We can only add one more idea to the body of something we have already thought about. Most of us spend very little time doing this, and that is why there are so few people whom we regard as having any power to articulate at all. When such a person appears in public life, like Mr. Trudeau, we tend to regard him as possessing a gigantic intellect.

8   A society like ours doesn't have very much interest in literacy. It is compulsory to read and write because society must have docile and obedient citizens. We are taught to read so that we can obey the traffic signs and to cipher so that we can make out our income tax, but development of verbal competency is very much left to the individual.

9   And when we look at our day-to-day existence we can see that there are strong currents at work against the development of powers of articulateness. Young adolescents today often betray a curious sense of shame about speaking articulately, of framing a sentence with a period at the end of it.

10   Part of the reason for this is the powerful anti-intellectual drive which is constantly present in our society. Articulate speech marks you out as an individual, and in some settings this can be rather dangerous because people are often suspicious and frightened of articulateness. So if you say as little as possible and use only stereotyped, ready-made phrases you can hide yourself in the mass.

11   Then there are various epidemics sweeping over society which use unintelligibility° as a weapon to preserve the present power structure. By making things as unintelligible as possible, to as many people as possible, you can hold the present power structure together. Understanding and articulateness lead to its destruction. This is the kind of thing that George Orwell was talking about, not just in *Nineteen Eighty-Four*, but in all his work on language. The kernel of everything reactionary° and tyrannical° in society is the impoverishment of the means of verbal communication.

12   The vast majority of things that we hear today are prejudices and clichés, simply verbal formulas that have no thought behind them but are put up as a pretence of thinking. It is not until we realize these things conceal meaning, rather than reveal it, that we can begin to develop our own powers of articulateness.

The teaching of humanities° is, therefore, a militant° job. 13
Teachers are faced not simply with a mass of misconceptions° and
unexamined assumptions. They must engage in a fight to help the
student confront and reject the verbal formulas and stock respons-
es°, to convert passive acceptance into active, constructive power. It
is a fight against illiteracy and for the maturation of the mental
process, for the development of skills which once acquired will
never become obsolete.

NORTHROP FRYE

Northrop Frye (1912–91) was born in Sherbrooke, Que., and raised in
Moncton, N.B. For many years, he taught English at Victoria College,
University of Toronto. His theories of the relationship between myth and
reality have had a wide literary and social influence. Among his books are
The Educated Imagination, Anatomy of Criticism, and *The Great Code.*

Words and Meanings   Paragraph

inarticulate	unexpressed; not put into words	5
unintelligibility	lack of understandable meaning	11
reactionary	ultraconservative	
tyrannical	like a dictator or tyrant	
humanities	the traditional liberal arts subjects, such as	13
	philosophy, history, and literature	
militant	fighting; engaged in battle	
misconception	mistaken belief	
stock responses	standard, predictable expressions	

Structure and Strategy

1. What is the function of paragraphs 1 to 3 and paragraphs 4 to 6?
2. Why is Frye's allusion to Walter Mitty particularly appropriate in
   this essay? (If you aren't familiar with the story, look up "The
   Secret Life of Walter Mitty" in an anthology of James Thurber's
   short stories.)
3. What metaphor (see FIGURES OF SPEECH) does Frye use in paragraph 6 to help reinforce his point? What connection does Frye
   imply between pregnancy and thinking?
4. Identify Frye's formal definition of "thinking."
5. What are the reasons Frye offers to support his opinion that
   thinking isn't often found in our society? How does he develop
   them (paragraphs 8 to 12)?

Content and Purpose

1. What does Frye mean by "language as a structure"? (See paragraph 1.)
2. What does Frye mean by "literacy" and "verbal competency"? (See paragraph 8.)
3. According to Frye, is it possible for an inarticulate person to think? Why?
4. Which groups in our society use "unintelligibility as a weapon"? Why do you think Frye doesn't identify them for us? Why might these groups fear articulateness? (See paragraph 11.)
5. Why are clichés and prejudice enemies of thinking?
6. Explain in your own words what Frye means when he claims that teaching the humanities is "a militant job."

Suggestion for Writing

Write a formal definition of one of the following terms, and develop it by whatever expository techniques you choose into an extended definition: thoughtfulness, imagination, literacy, creativity, respect, pride.

The World View of a Computer Hacker

JONATHAN RITTER

1   The dawn of the electronic age has brought a new breed of individual to life: the computer hacker. A distant cousin of the weekend hobbyist or casual enthusiast, the hacker regards computers and their employment as the single most defining element of his being. He derives both physical and spiritual fulfilment from their use.

2   Viewing *data* as weapons and *programs* as their delivery system, the hacker considers himself a privateer° of the modern era. He likens his computer to a vessel, a battleship for him to cruise the world's computer networks, assailing the weak and subverting the unsuspecting. To his prying fingers, no data base is sacred. He is the underdog, a David against an army of Goliaths, and he fantasizes about bringing big corporations and, indeed, entire governments, to their knees.

Periodically having to detach himself for such things as going   3
to work or gathering food, the computer hacker is decisively in his
element when perched in front of a computer terminal in his basement or attic. Once he has dispensed with his dinner of Alphabits
and cheese toast, secured a plentiful supply of Coke and cleaned
the previous night's tobacco dust from his screen, the hacker will
ready himself for another night's computing session. Consoled by
the soothing hum of his machine's cooling fan, he will bask
momentarily in the warm glow of the monitor before easing forward, after a few minutes of quiet concentration, to quickly, but
gently and with precision, tap out a string of keystrokes. He has tar-
geted his prey.

The computer hacker is not a social animal. He struggles with   4
small talk and has difficulty communicating with technically unin-
formed people, and his introversion confines him to a tightly knit
circle of friends. Arriving unescorted at a party, he will drift about
making perfunctory conversation before gravitating° to the basement (or garage) to happily chat away in technobabble with two or
three like-minded people. At the party's breakup, he will offer genuine thanks to the host, not so much for the Chivas°, but for the
chance to meet a fellow developer of self-propagating°, autonomous
computer programs. A sporadic user of alcohol, the computer hacker breaks his prolonged dry spells with feverish bouts of whisky
drinking with other hackers, who invariably spend the evening con-
triving a plot to destabilize the overseas currency market.

The computer hacker's bizarre fixations and peculiar habits are   5
telling signs of his breed. He will, for example, operate all of his
computers with the covers removed, partly because he relishes the
sight of raw electronics, and partly because he is regularly
installing and removing components. He will speak lustily of the
"techno-aroma" of new equipment and will regularly place his
nose next to the cooling fan to inhale the scents of jet-moulded plastic metal and printed circuit boards. An amorous° relationship
exists between the hacker and his computers. He can often be
found slinking away from a late-night computing session, physically drained and smoking a cigarette.

The hacker will often display perplexing and astonishing   6
behaviour when associating with mainstream society. When planning to move from one dumpy apartment to another, for instance,
the hacker will ask the landlord questions about reliable power and
"clean" telephone lines, and his eyes will expertly scan the
dwelling for an abundance of AC outlets. In a consumer-electronics
shop, the "candy store" for the hacker, he will do such things as
program VCRs and ask to look *inside* television sets. He typically

knows exactly what he wants before he shops, having studied the 600-page *Computer Shopper's Guide* and memorized product evaluations from *Byte Magazine*. Fluent in at least three computer languages, the hacker commonly leaves people bewildered by his speech. He does this unintentionally, absentmindedly forgetting to include English in his conversation.

7   Friends and family who seek advice or help from the hacker frequently regret the decision. Humour is often of a vocational nature to the hacker, who is likely to regard as extremely funny the suggestions to a co-worker that she look "behind the desk" for a missing computer file, or that perhaps a document that didn't get printed is somehow "stuck in the cable."

8   The hacker's preferences, predictably, reflect his personality. He regards Radio Shack as a store for amateurs and any equipment not meeting U.S. military specifications as "Fisher Price playthings." He spends an inordinate° amount of his income on gadgetry, keeps a spare computer around just in case, and is interested in cellular car phones only for the possibility of using them with his laptop computer.

9   To the hacker, a job is only a source of income [with] which he is able to purchase more computing implements. He will usually disguise himself as a white-collar worker and function as a support or development person, burrowing himself away in a back office to work on obscure projects unknown and incomprehensible to most of his co-workers. The anonymity of his circumstances is deliberate, as he loathes the idea of a more public position and does not like people to know of his extracurricular activities. He derides IBM for setting the industry standard—stiffened white shirt, plain tie and dark blazer—and will habitually show up for work wearing the same corduroy jacket, pop-stained tie, untucked shirt and beltless trousers. When the temperature drops, he will simply add layers of mismatched clothing as needed.

10   His company's computer system is almost certainly regarded with disdain°, as it rarely matches the power and flexibility of his home system(s). When his management refuses to authorize the purchase of the computer equipment he has asked for, he contemptuously, but briefly, considers sabotaging° the company's computer network, or at least crippling it enough to justify his requisition.

11   Politically, the hacker is attracted to the Reform Party, solely because of its promise to pour millions into lengthening the information highway. Conversely, he is suspicious of the NDP for its "Luddite° thinking," and instinctively would never vote for a party whose literature was printed on cheap, dot-matrix printers.

Bill Clinton gets praise from the hacker for advertising himself as the first president who can be reached by electronic mail.

The computer hacker can be seen as a manifestation of a soci- 12 ety surrounded and enthralled° by technology. He is awed by its magnitude, inspired by its possibilities and anxious about its future. He can be likened to his ancestors 10,000 years ago, who rubbed two sticks together and changed the course of the world forever.

JONATHAN RITTER

Jonathan Ritter (b. 1965) is a technical writer who was completing his undergraduate degree at the University of Alberta when he wrote this piece. He has worked as a computer salesman, consultant, and service engineer in places as various as Whitehorse, Winnipeg, Calgary, Halifax, and Perth, Australia. When he is not dreaming up new ideas for his four home computers, Mr. Ritter edits a community newspaper, writes software programs, and collects books. His goal is to publish "the definitive work" on computers and society.

Words and Meanings   Paragraph

privateer	pirate	2
gravitating	being drawn toward	4
Chivas	Chivas Regal, a brand of scotch whisky	
self-propagating	producing offspring; that is, offshoots and upgrades	
amorous	loving, passionate	5
inordinate	excessive	8
disdain	contempt, scorn	10
sabotaging	wrecking	
Luddite	antitechnology	11
enthralled	fascinated	12

Structure and Strategy

1. Is there any connection between the INTRODUCTION and the CONCLUSION of the essay?
2. The essay defines a computer hacker by detailing characteristics, behaviours, and personal preferences. Identify the paragraphs that deal with these aspects of the topic.

3. Why does the author include brand names such as "Alphabits" (paragraph 3), "Chivas" (paragraph 4), and "Radio Shack" (paragraph 8)?
4. Why do you think Ritter uses the gender-specific pronouns "he," "him," and "his" in an essay defining a hacker—a person who could presumably be either male or female? What effect does the choice of pronouns have on the reader?
5. What is the TONE of this essay?

Content and Purpose

1. What kind of life does the computer hacker lead? What specific details give us insights into his lifestyle and personality? What does he look like?
2. How do the hacker's friends, family, and acquaintances react to him? Why?
3. What kind of job does the hacker have? How does he view his employer?
4. What is "Luddite thinking" (paragraph 11)?
5. Do you think Ritter himself is a hacker? Why?

Suggestions for Writing

1. By detailing the significant characteristics of a member of a social or vocational subgroup (for example, skatepunks, vee-jays, talk-show hosts, mall rats, vegans, ski bums), define a particular group of people. Keep your tone light.
2. Write an essay defining "the computer age" as it has developed in the past decade or so.

"I'm Not Racist But..."

NEIL BISSOONDATH

1 Someone recently said that racism is as Canadian as maple syrup. I have no argument with that. History provides us with ample proof. But, for proper perspective, let us remember that it is also as American as apple pie, as French as croissants, as Jamaican as ackee, as Indian as aloo, as Chinese as

chow mein, as…. Well, there's an entire menu to be written. This is not by way of excusing it. Murder and rape, too, are international, multicultural, as innate° to the darker side of the human experience. But we must be careful that the inevitable rage evoked does not blind us to the larger context.

The word "racism" is a discomforting one: It is so vulnerable to manipulation. We can, if we so wish, apply it to any incident involving people of different colour. And therein lies the danger. During the heat of altercation°, we seize, as terms of abuse, on whatever is most obvious about the person. It is, often, a question of unfortunate convenience. A woman, because of her sex, easily becomes a female dog or an intimate part of her anatomy. A large person might be dubbed "a stupid ox," a small person "a little" whatever. And so a black might become "a nigger," a white "a honky," an Asian "a paki," a Chinese "a chink," an Italian "a wop," a French-Canadian "a frog." 2

There is nothing pleasant about these terms; they assault every decent sensibility°. Even so, I once met someone who, in a stunning surge of naiveté°, used them as simple descriptives and not as terms of racial abuse. She was horrified to learn the truth. While this may have been an extreme case, the point is that the use of such patently° abusive words may not always indicate racial or cultural distaste. They may indicate ignorance or stupidity or insensitivity, but pure racial hatred—such as the Nazis held for Jews, or the Ku Klux Klan for blacks—is a thankfully rare commodity. 3

Ignorance, not the willful kind but that which comes from lack of experience, is often indicated by that wonderful phrase, "I'm not racist but…." I think of the mover, a friendly man, who said, "I'm not racist, but the Chinese are the worst drivers on the road." He was convinced this was so because the shape of their eyes, as far as he could surmise°, denied them peripheral° vision. 4

Or the oil company executive, an equally warm and friendly man, who, looking for an apartment in Toronto, rejected buildings with East Indian tenants not because of their race—he was telling me this, after all—but because he was given to understand that cockroaches were symbols of good luck in their culture and that, when they moved into a new home, friends came by with gift-wrapped cockroaches. 5

Neither of these men thought of himself as racist, and I believe they were not, deep down. (The oil company executive made it clear he would not hesitate to have me as a neighbour; my East Indian descent was of no consequence to him, my horror of cockroaches was.) Yet their comments, so innocently delivered, would open them to the accusation, justifiably so if this were all one knew 6 about them. But it is a charge which would undoubtedly be wounding to them. It is difficult to recognize one's own misconceptions°.

7   True racism is based, more often than not, on willful° ignorance, and an acceptance of—and comfort with—stereotype°. We like to think, in this country, that our multicultural mosaic will help nudge us into a greater openness. But multiculturalism as we know it indulges in stereotype, depends on it for a dash of colour and the flash of dance. It fails to address the most basic questions people have about each other. Do those men doing the Dragon Dance really all belong to secret criminal societies? Do those women dressed in saris really coddle cockroaches for luck? Do those people in dreadlocks all smoke marijuana and live on welfare? Such questions do not seem to be the concern of the government's multicultural programs, superficial and exhibitionistic as they have become.

8   So the struggle against stereotype, the basis of all racism, becomes a purely personal one. We must beware of the impressions we create. A friend of mine once commented that, from talking to West Indians, she has the impression that their one great cultural contribution to the world is in the oft-repeated boast that "We (unlike everyone else) know how to party."

9   There are dangers, too, in community response. We must be wary of the self-appointed activists who seem to pop up in the media at every given opportunity spouting the rhetoric of retribution°, mining distress for personal, political and professional gain. We must be skeptical about those who depend on conflict for their sense of self, the non-whites who need to feel themselves victims of racism, the whites who need to feel themselves purveyors° of it. And we must be sure that, in addressing the problem, we do not end up creating it. Does the *Miss Black Canada Beauty Contest* still exist? I hope not. Not only do I find beauty contests offensive, but a racially segregated one even more so. What would the public reaction be, I wonder, if every year CTV broadcast the *Miss White Canada Beauty Pageant*? We give community-service awards only to blacks: Would we be comfortable with such awards only for whites? In Quebec, there are The Association of Black Nurses, The Association of Black Artists, The Congress of Black Jurists. Play tit for tat: The Association of White Nurses, White Artists, White Jurists: visions of apartheid. Let us be frank, racism for one is racism for others.

10   Finally, and perhaps most important, let us beware of abusing the word itself.

NEIL BISSOONDATH

Neil Bissoondath (b. 1955) is a Trinidad-born Canadian writer whose works include *A Casual Brutality* (1988), *The Innocence of Age* (1992), and *Selling Illusions: The Cult of Multiculturalism in Canada* (1994).

Words and Meanings

Paragraph

innate	natural, inborn	1
altercation	quarrel, dispute	2
sensibility	feeling	3
naiveté	simple ignorance; lack of sophistication	
patently	obviously, clearly	
surmise	figure out, guess	4
peripheral	side	
misconceptions	mistaken beliefs	6
willful	deliberate, stubborn	7
stereotype	see List of Useful Terms	
rhetoric of retribution	language of revenge, of retaliation	9
purveyors	providers	

Structure and Strategy

1. With what ANALOGY does Bissoondath introduce this essay? Why is it effective?
2. This essay is divided into three parts. Identify the main point of paragraphs 2 to 6, 7 to 8, and 9 to 10.
3. Identify the sentence that most clearly defines what Bissoondath thinks racism is.
4. Do you think the CONCLUSION of this essay is effective? Explain.

Content and Purpose

1. In paragraph 3, Bissoondath draws a distinction between "ignorance or stupidity or insensitivity" and "pure racial hatred." Into which category does he place the kind of racial epithets cited in paragraph 2?
2. What is the difference between the kind of ignorance represented by the examples in paragraphs 4 and 5 and "true racism" as Bissoondath sees it?
3. What does Bissoondath think of Canada's multicultural policies and programs? Do you agree with him?
4. In paragraph 8, Bissoondath maintains that we "must beware of the impressions we create" in the struggle against racism.

Do you agree that ethnic groups are to some extent responsible for their own stereotyping? Is it reasonable to make an ethnic group responsible for counteracting the stereotypical image other groups have of them?

5. What does Bissoondath think of beauty contests, clubs, or organizations that limit participation to a particular ethnic group? Do you think he would be in favour of or opposed to affirmative action programs?

Suggestions for Writing

1. Have you ever experienced the kind of racist stereotyping that Bissoondath describes in this essay? Write a paper explaining the incident, or series of incidents, and its effects on you.

2. Write an essay in which you agree or disagree with Bissoondath's opinion that awards, associations, and competitions that are restricted to people of colour are racist.

3. Read Brent Staples's "Just Walk On By" (Unit Six) and compare his view of racism with Bissoondath's.

Beauty

SUSAN SONTAG

1   For the Greeks, beauty was a virtue: a kind of excellence. Persons then were assumed to be what we now have to call—lamely, enviously—*whole* persons. If it did occur to the Greeks to distinguish between a person's "inside" and "outside," they still expected that inner beauty would be matched by beauty of the other kind. The well-born young Athenians who gathered around Socrates° found it quite paradoxical° that their hero was so intelligent, so brave, so honorable, so seductive—and so ugly. One of Socrates' main pedagogical° acts was to be ugly—and teach those innocent, no doubt splendid-looking disciples of his how full of paradoxes life really was.

2   They may have resisted Socrates' lesson. We do not. Several thousand years later, we are more wary° of the enchantments of beauty. We not only split off—with the greatest facility°—the "inside" (character, intellect) from the "outside" (looks); but we are

actually surprised when someone who is beautiful is also intelligent, talented, good.

It was principally the influence of Christianity that deprived   3
beauty of the central place it had in classical ideals of human excellence. By limiting excellence (*virtus* in Latin) to *moral* virtue only, Christianity set beauty adrift—as an alienated, arbitrary, superficial enchantment. And beauty has continued to lose prestige°. For close to two centuries it has become a convention to attribute beauty to only one of the two sexes: the sex which, however Fair, is always Second. Associating beauty with women has put beauty even further on the defensive, morally.

A beautiful woman, we say in English. But a handsome man.   4
"Handsome" is the masculine equivalent of—and refusal of—a compliment which has accumulated certain demeaning overtones, by being reserved for women only. That one can call a man "beautiful" in French and in Italian suggests that Catholic countries—unlike those countries shaped by the Protestant version of Christianity—still retain some vestiges° of the pagan admiration for beauty. But the difference, if one exists, is of degree only. In every modern country that is Christian or post-Christian, women *are* the beautiful sex—to the detriment° of the notion of beauty as well as of women.

To be called beautiful is thought to name something essential to   5
women's character and concerns. (In contrast to men—whose essence is to be strong, or effective, or competent.) It does not take someone in the throes of advanced feminist awareness to perceive that the way women are taught to be involved with beauty encourages narcissism°, reinforces dependence and immaturity. Everybody (women and men) knows that. For it is "everybody," a whole society, that has identified being feminine with caring about how one *looks*. (In contrast to being masculine—which is identified with caring about what one *is* and *does* and only secondarily, if at all, about how one looks.) Given these stereotypes, it is no wonder that beauty enjoys, at best, a rather mixed reputation.

It is not, of course, the desire to be beautiful that is wrong but   6
the obligation° to be—or to try. What is accepted by most women as a flattering idealization of their sex is a way of making women feel inferior to what they actually are—or normally grow to be. For the ideal of beauty is administered as a form of self-oppression. Women are taught to see their bodies in *parts*, and to evaluate each part separately. Breasts, feet, hips, waistline, neck, eyes, nose, complexion, hair, and so on—each in turn is submitted to an anxious, fretful, often despairing scrutiny°. Even if some pass muster°, some will always be found wanting. Nothing less than perfection will do.

7   In men, good looks is a whole, something taken in at a glance. It does not need to be confirmed by giving measurements of different regions of the body, nobody encourages a man to dissect his appearance, feature by feature. As for perfection, that is considered trivial—almost unmanly. Indeed, in the ideally good-looking man a small imperfection or blemish is considered positively desirable. According to one movie critic (a woman) who is a declared Robert Redford fan, it is having that cluster of skin-colored moles on one cheek that saves Redford from being merely a "pretty face." Think of the depreciation of women—as well as of beauty—that is implied in that judgment.

8   "The privileges of beauty are immense," said Cocteau. To be sure, beauty is a form of power. And deservedly so. What is lamentable is that it is the only form of power that most women are encouraged to seek. This power is always conceived in relation to men; it is not the power to do but the power to attract. It is a power that negates° itself. For this power is not one that can be chosen freely—at least, not by women—or renounced° without social censure°.

9   To preen°, for a woman, can never be just a pleasure. It is also a duty. It is her work. If a woman does real work—and even if she has clambered up to a leading position in politics, law, medicine, business, or whatever—she is always under pressure to confess that she still works at being attractive. But in so far as she is keeping up as one of the Fair Sex, she brings under suspicion her very capacity to be objective, professional, authoritative, thoughtful. Damned if they do—women are. And damned if they don't.

10   One could hardly ask for more important evidence of the dangers of considering persons as split between what is "inside" and what is "outside" than that interminable° half-comic half-tragic tale, the oppression of women. How easy it is to start off by defining women as caretakers of their surfaces, and then to disparage° them (or find them adorable) for being "superficial." It is a crude trap, and it has worked for too long. But to get out of the trap requires that women get some critical distance to see how much beauty itself has been abridged° in order to prop up the mythology of the "feminine." There should be a way of saving beauty *from* women—and *for* them.

SUSAN SONTAG

Susan Sontag (b. 1933) is an American cultural analyst who writes novels, essays, and screenplays. Her works include *Against Interpretation, and*

Other Essays (1966), *On Photography* (1977), *Illness as Metaphor* (1977), and *AIDS and Its Metaphors* (1988).

Words and Meanings

Paragraph

Socrates	Greek philosopher and teacher (469–399 B.C.) who believed the highest meaning of life is attained through self-knowledge	1
paradoxical	a statement or circumstance that seems contradictory, even absurd, at first.	
pedagogical	teaching	
wary	cautious, on guard against	2
facility	ease	
prestige	status, influence	3
vestiges	traces, remains	4
detriment	loss, harm, disadvantage	
narcissism	obsessive self-love	5
obligation	responsibility	6
scrutiny	close examination	
pass muster	be accepted as adequate	
negates	denies, cancels itself	8
renounced	rejected, given up	
censure	disapproval	
preen	groom oneself, make oneself attractive	9
interminable	never-ending	10
disparage	belittle, speak negatively of	
abridged	diminished, reduced	

Structure and Strategy

1. Sontag defines beauty partly through a series of contrasts. Identify two sets of contrasts that are explained in the first seven paragraphs of the essay.
2. What is the THESIS of "Beauty"? Restate it in your own words.
3. Study the examples Sontag uses in paragraphs 7 and 9. Do they provide effective support for her points? Why?
4. Explain the paradoxes with which Sontag introduces and concludes her essay. How do they contribute to the UNITY of the piece?

Content and Purpose

1. How did the ancient Greeks define beauty? How do we define it today?

2. How, according to Sontag, did Christianity change the classical view of beauty?
3. What difference does Sontag identify in the ways in which men and women define themselves? How has this difference affected our culture's perception of physical attractiveness?
4. How does the "obligation" to be beautiful affect the way women see their bodies?
5. What relationship does Sontag identify between a woman's beauty and power? Do you agree with her?
6. According to this essay, physical beauty puts women in a double bind: they are "damned if they do" and "damned if they don't." What does Sontag mean by this? Do you agree?

Suggestions for Writing

1. Define your own idea of beauty. Is it an internal or an external quality?
2. Do you agree or disagree with Sontag that our culture's emphasis on the physical beauty of women is a "crude trap"? Explore the relationship between physical attractiveness and power.

Altruism

LEWIS THOMAS

1   ltruism has always been one of biology's deep mysteries. Why should any animal, off on its own, specified and labeled by all sorts of signals as its individual self, choose to give up its life in aid of someone else? Nature, long viewed as a wild, chaotic battlefield swarmed across by more than ten million different species, comprising unnumbered billions of competing selves locked in endless combat, offers only one sure measure of success: survival. Survival, in the cool economics of biology, means simply the persistence of one's own genes in the generations to follow.

2   At first glance, it seems an unnatural act, a violation of nature, to give away one's life, or even one's possessions, to another. And yet, in the face of improbability, examples of altruism abound. When a worker bee, patrolling the frontiers of the hive, senses the

nearness of a human intruder, the bee's attack is pure, unqualified suicide; the sting is barbed, and in the act of pulling away the insect is fatally injured. Other varieties of social insects, most spectacularly the ants and higher termites, contain castes of soldiers for whom self-sacrifice is an everyday chore.

It is easy to dismiss the problem by saying that "altruism" is   3
the wrong technical term for behavior of this kind. The word is a human word, pieced together to describe an unusual aspect of human behavior, and we should not be using it for the behavior of mindless automata°. A honeybee has no connection to creatures like us, no brain for figuring out the future, no way of predicting the inevitable outcome of that sting.

But the meditation of the 50,000 or so connected minds of a   4
whole hive is not so easy to dismiss. A multitude of bees can tell the time of day, calculate the geometry of the sun's position, argue about the best location for the next swarm. Bees do a lot of close observing of other bees; maybe they know what follows stinging and do it anyway.

Altruism is not restricted to the social insects, in any case. Birds   5
risk their lives, sometimes lose them, in efforts to distract the attention of predators from the nest. Among baboons, zebras, moose, wildebeests, and wild dogs there are always stubbornly fated guardians, prepared to be done in first in order to buy time for the herd to escape.

It is genetically determined behavior, no doubt about it.   6
Animals have genes for altruism, and those genes have been selected in the evolution of many creatures because of the advantage they confer for the continuing survival of the species. It is, looked at in this way, not the emotion-laden problem that we feel when we try to put ourselves in the animal's place; it is just another plain fact of life, perhaps not as hard a fact as some others, something rather nice, in fact, to think about.

J.B.S. Haldane, the eminent British geneticist, summarized the   7
chilly arithmetic of the problem by announcing, "I would give up my life for two brothers or eight cousins." This calculates the requirement for ultimate self-interest: the preservation and survival of an individual's complement of genes. Trivers, Hamilton, and others have constructed mathematical models to account nicely for the altruistic behavior of social insects, quantifying the self-serving profit for the genes of the defending bee in the act of tearing its abdomen apart. The hive is filled with siblings, ready to carry the *persona* of the dying bee through all the hive's succeeding generations. Altruism is based on kinship; by preserving kin, one preserves one's self. In a sense.

8   Haldane's prediction has the sound of a beginning sequence: two brothers, eight (presumably) first cousins, and then another series of much larger numbers of more distant relatives. Where does the influence tail off? At what point does the sharing of the putative° altruist's genes become so diluted as to be meaningless? Would the line on a graph charting altruism plummet to zero soon after those eight cousins, or is it a long, gradual slope? When the combat marine throws himself belly-down on the live grenade in order to preserve the rest of the platoon, is this the same sort of altruism, or is this an act without any technically biological meaning? Surely the marine's genes, most of them, will be blown away forever; the statistical likelihood of having two brothers or eight cousins in that platoon is extremely small. And yet there he is, belly-down as if by instinct, and the same kind of event has been recorded often enough in wartime to make it seem a natural human act, normal enough, even though rare, to warrant the stocking of medals by the armed services.

9   At what point do our genetic ties to each other become so remote that we feel no instinctual urge to help? I can imagine an argument about this, with two sides, but it would be a highly speculative discussion, not by any means pointless but still impossible to settle one way or the other. One side might assert, with total justification, that altruistic behavior among human beings has nothing at all to do with genetics, that there is no such thing as a gene for self-sacrifice, not even a gene for helpfulness, or concern, or even affection. These are attributes that must be learned from society, acquired by cultures, taught by example. The other side could maintain, with equal justification, since the facts are now known, precisely the opposite position: we get along together in human society because we are genetically designed to be social animals, and we are obliged, by instructions from our genes, to be useful to each other. This side would argue further that when we behave badly, killing or maiming or snatching, we are acting on misleading information learned from the wrong kinds of society we put together; if our cultures were not deformed, we would be better company, paying attention to what our genes are telling us.

10   For the purposes of the moment I shall take the side of the sociobiologists because I wish to carry their side of the argument a certain distance afield, beyond the human realm. I have no difficulty in imagining a close enough resemblance among the genomes° of all human beings, of all races and geographic origins, to warrant a biological mandate° for all of us to do whatever we can to keep the rest of us, the species, alive. I maintain, despite the moment's evidence against the claim, that we are born and grow up with a fondness for each other, and we have genes for that. We can be talked

out of it, for the genetic message is like a distant music and some of us are hard-of-hearing. Societies are noisy affairs, drowning out the sound of ourselves and our connection. Hard-of-hearing, we go to war. Stone-deaf, we make thermonuclear missiles. Nonetheless, the music is there, waiting for more listeners.

But the matter does not end with our species. If we are to take seriously the notion that the sharing of similar genes imposes a responsibility on the sharers to sustain each other, and if I am right in guessing that even very distant cousins carry at least traces of this responsibility and will act on it whenever they can, then the whole world becomes something to be concerned about on solidly scientific, reductionist, genetic grounds. For we have cousins more than we can count, and they are all over the place, run by genes so similar to ours that the differences are minor technicalities. All of us, men, women, children, fish, sea grass, sandworms, dolphins, hamsters, and soil bacteria, everything alive on the planet, roll ourselves along through all our generations by replicating DNA° and RNA°, and although the alignments of nucleotides within these molecules are different in different species, the molecules themselves are fundamentally the same substance. We make our proteins in the same old way, and many of the enzymes most needed for cellular life are everywhere identical. 11

This is, in fact, the way it should be. If cousins are defined by common descent, the human family is only one small and very recent addition to a much larger family in a tree extending back at least 3.5 billion years. Our common ancestor was a single cell from which all subsequent cells derived, most likely a cell resembling one of today's bacteria in today's soil. For almost three-fourths of the earth's life, cells of that first kind were the whole biosphere°. It was less than a billion years ago that cells like ours appeared in the first marine invertebrates, and these were somehow pieced together by the joining up and fusion of the earlier primitive cells, retaining the same blood lines. Some of the joiners, bacteria that had learned how to use oxygen, are with us still, part of our flesh, lodged inside the cells of all animals, all plants, moving us from place to place and doing our breathing for us. Now there's a set of cousins! 12

Even if I try to discount the other genetic similarities linking human beings to all other creatures by common descent, the existence of these beings in my cells is enough, in itself, to relate me to the chestnut tree in my backyard and to the squirrel in that tree. 13

There ought to be a mathematics for connections like this before claiming any kinship function, but the numbers are too big. At the same time, even if we wanted to, we cannot think the sense of obligation away. It is there, maybe in our genes for the recognition of cousins, or, if not, it ought to be there in our intellects for having 14 learned about the matter. Altruism, in its biological sense, is required of us. We have an enormous family to look after, or perhaps that assumes too much, making us sound like official gardeners and zookeepers for the planet, responsibilities for which we are probably not yet grown-up enough. We may need new technical terms for concern, respect, affection, substitutes for altruism. But at least we should acknowledge the family ties and, with them, the obligations. If we do it wrong, scattering pollutants, clouding the atmosphere with too much carbon dioxide, extinguishing the thin carapace° of ozone, burning up the forests, dropping the bombs, rampaging at large through nature as though we owned the place, there will be a lot of paying back to do and, at the end, nothing to pay back with.

LEWIS THOMAS

Dr. Lewis Thomas (1913–93) combined the careers of research scientist, physician, teacher, and writer. The recipient of many scientific and academic awards, Lewis Thomas strove in his essays to humanize science and to remind us that medicine is an art. A recurring theme in books such as *The Lives of a Cell* (1974), *The Medusa and the Snail* (1979), and *The Youngest Science* (1983) is the interrelatedness of all life forms.

Words and Meanings

Paragraph		
3	automata	unthinking, machinelike organisms
8	putative	supposed
10	genomes	chromosomal structures
	mandate	contract, requirement
11	DNA	deoxyribonucleic acid; the molecule that carries genetic information
	RNA	ribonucleic acid; the substance that transmits genetic information from the nucleus to the surrounding cellular material
12	biosphere	earth's zone of life—from crust to atmosphere—encompassing all living organisms
14	carapace	outer shell, such as on a crab or tortoise

Structure and Strategy

1. What two ABSTRACT terms does Thomas define in his introductory paragraph? How does he do so?

2. The body of this essay can be divided into sections, as follows: paragraphs 2 to 5, 6 to 8, 9 and 10, and 11 to 13. Identify the main idea Thomas develops in each of these four sections, and list some of the expository techniques he uses in his development.
3. From paragraphs 1 to 8, Thomas writes in the third person. Why does he shift to the first person in paragraph 9 and continue in first person until the end? To understand the different effects of the two POINTS OF VIEW, try rewriting some of the sentences in paragraph 14 in the third person.
4. In paragraph 10, Thomas introduces and develops a similie (see FIGURES OF SPEECH) to explain his faith in the "genetic message." Identify the simile and explain how it helps prepare the reader for the conclusion.
5. What concluding strategy does Thomas use in paragraph 14? How does his conclusion contribute to the UNITY of the essay?

Content and Purpose

1. What is Thomas's thesis? Can you summarize it in a single sentence?
2. In paragraph 1, Thomas introduces the fundamental IRONY on which this essay is based. Explain in your own words the ironic connection between altruism and survival.
3. Identify six or seven specific examples of animals that, according to Thomas, display altruistic behaviour. What ILLUSTRATION does Thomas use to show the altruistic behaviour of human beings?
4. Explain in your own words Thomas's claim that altruism is not an "emotion-laden problem" but that it is based on self-interest (see paragraph 7).
5. In paragraph 9, Thomas identifies two opposing explanations for altruistic behaviour: the cultural and the sociobiological. Summarize these in your own words. Which side does Thomas take and why? (See paragraphs 10 to 13.)

Suggestions for Writing

1. Write an extended definition of the term "parenthood." Explain the reasons why people choose to have children, an act that involves a considerable amount of self-sacrifice.
2. Define another abstract term such as "wisdom," "integrity," "freedom," "evil," or "success." Attempt to define this term as clearly and concretely as Thomas does "altruism."

I'm Having Trouble with My Relationship

LEONARD MICHAELS

1   The word "relationship" appears for the first time in the 1743 edition of *The Dunciad*°. Pope uses it in a way both funny and cruel to identify his enemy Cibber° with the insane. Cibber is said to be related to famous heads, sculpted by his father, representing despondent and raving madness. The heads were affixed to the front of Bedlam°. Pope calls them Cibber's "brothers." Cibber and the heads have the same father; they stand in a blood, brains, "brazen°," family "Relationship." The word effects a contemptuous distance between Pope and Cibber, and makes Cibber one with the sculpted heads. Funny in its concreteness; cruel in the play of implications; luminous in genius. Before Pope, "relationship" may have been part of daily talk, but until he uses it nothing exists in this way, bearing the lineaments° of his mind, the cultural affluence of his self and time.

2   After 1743, "relationship" appears with increasing frequency, with no joke intended, and … it begins to intrude into areas of thought and feeling where it never belonged, gathering a huge constituency° of uncritical users and displacing words that once seemed more appropriate, precise, and pleasing. Among them are "romance," "affair," "lover," "beau," "fellow," "girl," "boyfriend," "girlfriend," "steady date," etc. People now find these words more or less quaint or embarrassingly innocent. They use "relationship" to mean any of them when talking about the romantic-sexual connection between a man and a woman or man, or woman and woman. In this liberal respect, Pope's use of the word is uncannily° reborn.

3   People say, "I'm having trouble with my relationship," as though the trouble were not with Penelope or Max but with an object, like a BMW, a sort of container or psychological condition into which they enter and relate. By displacing the old words for romantic love, "relationship" indicates a new caution where human experience is extremely intense and ephemeral° or a distrust of concrete words in which our happiness might suffer any idea of limit, or

perhaps a distrust of words in general. It could be argued that "relationship" is better than the old words, since it makes abstraction palpable°, generously distributing it among four syllables; a feeling of love in the actions of sex; or philosophy in desire; and, as love is various, so are the syllables of "relationship," not one of them repeating another. Though intended to restrict reference to a single person, the word has the faint effect of suggesting many persons. In its palpableness, syllables bob like Bedlam heads. Strange images of mind.

People also say, "I can relate to that," where no person is   4
intended or essentially involved, just an idea of some kind of experience. The expression is innocuous°, and yet it is reminiscent of psychopathic thinking. In the same modern spirit, people say "mothering" to mean no particular person is essential to the action; that is, "mothering" does not flow from a mother as poetry flows only from a poet, or life from the sun god. "Fathering" has a sexual charge different from "mothering" and cannot be used like this. We talk, then, of "parenting." The political necessity for "mothering" and "parenting," which justifies the words, doesn't make them less grotesque. But this sort of judgment is precious°. The antinomies° of our culture cling to each other like breeders in a slow, violent divorce, and aesthetic considerations are irrelevant. We have no use, in our thinking, for the determining power of essences, or depths of soul, or ideas of value that inhere°, like juice in grapes, in the quiddity° of people. Mom is not by any means an inevitable source of love. She might well be a twisted bitch, and many vile creeps are Dad. The words no longer pack honorific content. Commitments built into blood are honored only by the Mafia. Philip Larkin writes: "They fuck you up, your mum and dad."

What conservatives, feminists, Marxists, and other contempo-   5
rary thinkers have in common is the idea that value has fled the human particular. Larkin might agree. He might even say that, long ago, value went off some place to vomit and it has not returned. If this is true, we have been abandoned to the allure of nonspecific possibility, or the thrill of infinite novelty. A lexical° whorehouse shines in the darkness of the modern mind.... To descend again to my theme: your hot lover has cooled into your "relationship," which in another aspect you have with your grocer or your cat.

This large disposition° in our thinking and speaking arises from   6
impersonal democratic passions, the last refuge of the supreme good. As Simone Weil says, thinking of God, "Only the impersonal is sacred." But it is a little crazy that "relationship," an uppity version of "relation," should be enormously privileged, lumbering across the landscape of English with prefix and two suffixes streaming from a tiny head of substance like ghostly remains of its Latin roots and Germanic ending (*referre*, maybe *latus*, and *ship*).

7   To have survived the guns of our grammarians and displaced more pleasant words in the natural history of English, it must answer to an exceptionally strong need. The other words may seem impossibly quaint, but it isn't only the sophistication of "relationship" that is needed. It is the whole word, including the four-syllable sound, which is a body stumbling downstairs, the last two—"shunship"—the flap of a shoe's loose sole, or loose lips and gossip. In fact, "relationship" flourished in the talky, psychological climate of the modern century as we carried it from the offices of our shrinks and, like a forgotten umbrella, left "romance" behind.

8   Notice well how the syllabic tumble of "relationship" makes a sound like sheer talk, or talking about something, emphasis on "about," not "something." Exactly here, in the eternally mysterious relation of sound and sense, "relationship" confers the dignity of thought upon referential promiscuity°, its objects graced with interestingness, a sound basis in indeterminacy° for interminable° talk.

9   Philosophers might complain that it is a word without much "cash value." Heidegger°, on the other hand, might take it as an expression of "the groundlessness and nullity of inauthentic everydayness." He means the nonstop impetuous trivialization, in "idle talk," of *Dasein*, by which he means anything real, by which he means that thing of which anyone who "is genuinely 'on the scent of' [it] will not speak." Certainly, then, in regard to "relationship," Heidegger might say:

> Being-with-one-another in the "they" is by no means an indifferent side-by-sideness in which everything has been settled, but rather an intent, ambiguous watching of another, a secret and reciprocal listening-in. Under the mask of "for-one-another," an "against-one-another" is in play.

By which he means, "I'm having trouble with my relationship."

10   "The secret king of thought," forerunner of deconstructionism, who spoke of the Nazis as "manufacturing corpses," Heidegger had the deepest grasp of what is authentic and inauthentic in human relations.... But to feel what has been lost in thought, consider this text from a letter by Kafka° to Milena, the woman he loved:

> Today I saw a map of Vienna. For an instant it seemed incomprehensible to me that they had built such a big city when you need only one room.

11   The incomprehensible city is "relationship," or what you have with everyone in the abstract and lonely vastness° of our social reality. The room, all one needs, is romance, love, passionate intimacy,

the unsophisticated irrational thing you have with someone; or what has long been considered a form of madness, if not the universal demonic° of contemporary vision.

The city is also "relationship" in the movie *Last Tango in Paris*, 12 where Marlon Brando texts to his lover, "Everything outside this room is bullshit." He makes the same point as Kafka, but the subtext of the movie is that, in our lust for relationship, we have shoveled all the bullshit into the room. This lust, which is basically for power, or control, or the illusion of possessing something that isn't there—*Dasein*, needless to say, but what the hell—makes us prefer Theory to novels, poems, and people, or flat surfaces in architecture to the various elaborations of material that once engaged our hearts.

Native speakers of Swedish say *förhållande* is close in meaning 13 to "relationship," which suggests the Swedes are in the same boat as the English-speakers, especially since other native speakers say it is difficult to find a close equivalent to "relationship" in other European languages or in Asian languages. "Relationship," then, shouldn't be taken as a mere tendency of English where any noun might lust for sublimity in the abstract extension of itself. It isn't just another polysyllabic fascist on the left or right, but rather something that bespeaks a deeper tendency, in the soul, like what one sees in Andy Warhol's disquieting portraits of Marilyn Monroe and Mao, their faces repeating and vanishing into the static quality of their "look."

"Relationship" has a similarly reductive force, ultimately even 14 an air of death worship. The "aura of death," says Georges Bataille, "is what denotes passion." It also denotes its absence, one might suppose, but this old notion isn't likely to seize our imagination, which is why "relationship" has slipped unnoticed into astounding prominence and ubiquitous° banality°. The word is no less common than death, and it is no less pathetically private; and we use it much as though, after consigning° ourselves to the grave, we had lingered to love the undertaker, having had no such exquisitely personal attention before, nothing so convincing that one is.

LEONARD MICHAELS

Award-winning U.S. writer Leonard Michaels (b. 1933) teaches English at Berkeley. He is the author of two short story collections, *Going Places* and *I Would Have Saved Them If I Could*; a novel, *The Men's Club*; and an autobiographical work, *Shuffle*.

Paragraph

Words and Meanings

1	*The Dunciad*	long, satiric poem by Alexander Pope
	Cibber	playwright Colley Cibber, whom Pope considered rude, vain, and foolish
	Bedlam	popular name for St. Mary of Bethlehem, a hospital in which lunatics were confined
	brazen	made of bronze; shameless (the author intends both meanings here)
	lineaments	distinctive qualities
2	constituency	group
	uncannily	strangely
3	ephemeral	short-lived, impermanent
	palpable	obvious
4	innocuous	harmless
	precious	nit-picking, too fussy
	antinomies	contradictions
	inhere	exist
	quiddity	essence, what makes a thing what it is
5	lexical	having to do with words and their meanings
6	disposition	tendency
8	referential promiscuity	using a word to signify so many different things that it loses all meaning
	indeterminacy	vagueness, having no clear meaning
	interminable	endless
9	Heidegger	twentieth-century German philosopher who thought and wrote much about the problem of "being"
10	Kafka	novelist Franz Kafka (1883–1924), whose central theme was modern man's inability to find meaning or salvation in this life
11	vastness	huge space
	demonic	guiding spirit, inspiration
14	ubiquitous	occurring everywhere
	banality	triteness, having little meaning
	consigning	delivering

Structure and Strategy

1. What INTRODUCTORY strategy does the author employ? What CONCLUDING strategy? Are these linked in any way?
2. Analyze the SYNTAX of the third sentence in paragraph 3, the second sentence in paragraph 8, and the last sentence of the

essay. Contrast the syntax of these sentences with that of the last five sentences of paragraph 4. How would you describe Michaels's STYLE in this essay?

3. Study the DICTION of the essay. Identify sentences where you require your dictionary. Is there an appropriate blend of ABSTRACT terms and CONCRETE support? Cite examples to support your opinion.

4. What AUDIENCE did Michaels have in mind when he wrote this essay? Has he made any effort to make the piece accessible to other readers?

Content and Purpose

1. This complex essay defines the term "relationship," in part by showing how its meaning has changed over time. What is the first recorded use of the word? What did it mean then? What does it mean now? Check the *Oxford English Dictionary* to see how the meaning of the word has evolved over the last 200 years.

2. Consider the words that "relationship" has come to replace (see paragraph 2). Which words are CONCRETE? Which are ABSTRACT?

3. Why does the author object to our abandoning these old-fashioned terms in favour of the trendy, "one-size-fits-all" word "relationship"?

4. What does this trend indicate about people's attitude toward human experience, toward CONCRETE words, and toward our use of words generally? (See paragraph 3.)

5. Paragraph 4 offers examples of other words that are "grotesque" because they "no longer pack honorific content." What does Michaels mean by this? What examples does he provide to support his opinion? Do you agree or disagree with him?

6. Think of two or three instances of the use of the word "relationship" that Michaels would condemn as examples of the "lexical whorehouse … of the modern mind." (For an example, see the last sentence of paragraph 5.)

7. Take a close look at paragraph 7. What aspect of the word "relationship" is Michaels exploring here? How does it help support his dislike of the modern use of the term?

8. In paragraphs 10 and 11 Michaels introduces a complex metaphor contrasting the "city" ("relationship") with "one room" (love). Explain his point in your own words.

9. The meaning of the concluding paragraph of this essay is particularly compressed and therefore difficult to understand. Do you agree or disagree with Michaels's THESIS as it is summarized here?

Suggestion for Writing

Write an essay exploring how a particular word has changed in meaning over time. Words such as "gay," "cool," "black," or even "grammar" reveal interesting changes in denotation and connotation.

Additional Suggestions for Writing: Definition

Write an extended definition of one of the topics below.

addiction

team spirit

superstition

maturity

self-respect

conspicuous consumption

wisdom

terrorism

creativity

censorship

physical fitness

generosity

a typical Canadian

Generation X

feminism

sin

free trade

a conservative

a liberal

the ideal job (boss, employee, parent, roommate, friend, spouse, child)

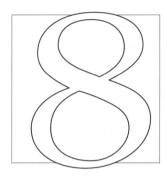

U N I T 8

Argument and Persuasion: Appealing to Reason and Emotion

What? The Definition

We all know what is meant by the word **persuasion**. It's bringing someone over to our side, sometimes with a nod, a wink, usually with a word or two. The meaning of the word **argument** is reasonably clear as well. An argument is a disagreement, an altercation, a verbal brawl of sorts; an argument may occur when someone resists our attempts at persuasion. As Unit Seven on definition pointed out, however, occasionally words have specific meanings different from their generally accepted meanings.

Persuasion is more than encouraging someone to come on side; argument means more than disagreement. In the context of writing, **argument and persuasion** refer to a kind of writing that has a particular purpose—one that differs in degree, if not in kind, from the purpose of expository prose.

The introductions to the first seven units of this text have explained structure patterns commonly found in *exposition*—writing intended primarily to explain. It is true that many explanations contain some element of argument or persuasion: consider Mitford's indictment of embalming in Unit Three, for instance. Nevertheless, the primary purpose of expository writing is to *inform* the reader.

Argument and persuasion have a different primary purpose; they attempt to lead the reader to share the writer's belief and, perhaps, even to act on this belief. Naturally, readers are not likely to be persuaded of anything unless the concept is first clearly explained to them. In this chapter, we will consider argument and persuasion as writing strategies designed to *convince* the reader of an opinion, judgment, or course of action.

There are two ways to convince people: through their minds or through their hearts. *Argument* is the term often applied to the logical approach, convincing a person by way of the mind. *Persuasion* is the term often applied to the emotional approach, convincing a person by way of the heart. Often we can use both routes. We decide which approach to use, logical or emotional—or a combination of the two—depending on the issue we are discussing. For instance, if we want to persuade someone to give money for famine relief, we might appeal to the reader's emotions with descriptions of blighted landscapes, emaciated adults, and starving children. We want our readers to feel the victims' plight and support the cause. However, if we want to argue that a highway needs widening, there is likely to be little emotional punch. In a case like this, we would appeal to the reader's mind by providing logical, well-developed reasons. The issue itself determines which approach is the best one to take.

An important part of convincing the reader is getting the facts straight. An argument is only as strong as the logic behind it. Even when appealing primarily to the reader's feelings, the writer must do so reasonably or risk producing a paper that is sentimental, bullying, or manipulative, and therefore not persuasive. Most of us have been pestered by "persuaders" who attempt to convince us that water fluoridation is a Communist plot, or that all Irish are drunkards, or that people who smoke marijuana inevitably get addicted to heroin. The reasoning that leads to such conclusions is faulty. To be convincing, the reasoning must be sound; if it is not, readers are likely to be confused or insulted rather than convinced.

There are two fundamental ways of reasoning: **induction** and **deduction**. Exploring these logical processes will help you to clarify your own ideas before you try to convince someone else.

Inductive reasoning is the logical process of examining a number of individual cases and coming to a general conclusion. For example, if you order pizza from Guido's Pizzeria once and it's cold when delivered, a one-time-only delay may have occurred. But if you get cold pizzas three times in a row from Guido's, and talk to four friends who have likewise got cold pizza from Guido's, it is fair to make a generalization: Guido's pizzas are usually cold by the time they get to you. You'd better phone another pizzeria. This simple example illustrates the straightforward, let's-look-at-the-facts approach of inductive reasoning. On a more lofty level, we find that induction is also the reasoning of the science laboratory and the law court. For example, if a microbiologist finds bacillus X in the bloodstreams of a significant number of flu victims, she may eventually generalize that bacillus X is the cause of that particular strain of flu.

To use inductive reasoning effectively, you must make sure that your evidence is solid, that it isn't just hearsay or unsupported opinion. You must also ensure that you have sampled enough evidence. You may know three teenage mothers who do not take good care of their babies, but three instances are not enough evidence to dismiss all teenagers as poor mothers.

Deductive reasoning is the flip side of inductive reasoning. Instead of considering specific cases to come up with a general statement, deduction applies a general statement to a specific instance and reasons through to a conclusion. Deduction is the formal logic of the syllogism, a traditional three-part formula:

MAJOR PREMISE:	All humans are mortal.
MINOR PREMISE:	Socrates[1] is human.
CONCLUSION:	Socrates is mortal.

Deductive logic is only as solid as its premises. Deducing specifics from faulty generalizations is dangerous reasoning, as the next example shows:

MAJOR PREMISE:	All Iraqis are terrorists.
MINOR PREMISE:	Yusuf is Iraqi.
CONCLUSION:	Yusuf is a terrorist.

Given the flawed nature of the major premise, the conclusion is erroneous. It is also the product of a bigoted mind.

In short, any writing intended to convince must be grounded in sound logic. Both inductive and deductive reasoning are only as sound as the observations or the premises on which they are based. If your readers are able to detect logical gaps, faulty premises, or

[1]Socrates (469–399 B.C.) was a Greek thinker and teacher who, along with his disciples Plato and Aristotle, is considered the founder of Western philosophy.

unsupportable generalizations in your reasoning, they will not be convinced of anything you say.

Why? The Purpose

Papers designed to convince the reader answer the question, "What are the reasons for—or against—S?" To answer this question, you must first critically assess the belief, proposal, or course of action on which your paper is based. Keep in mind that "critical" means to make a judgment—for or against—not just to "find fault." Once you have tested the logic of your viewpoint, you can use argument and persuasion to accomplish one of two purposes—and sometimes both.

You may simply want your readers to share your opinion, to agree with the argument you present. You may want to bring them over to your side. For instance, you could try to convince readers that Canada's involvement in space exploration is valuable both economically and technologically.

On the other hand, you may intend not only to convince your readers to agree with you but also to convince them to *do* something, to act in some way, on the basis of your opinion. For instance, you might argue that regular exercise promotes health and lengthens life expectancy; hence, the reader should get involved in a regular exercise program. Usually, you need to accomplish the first aim, getting the reader's agreement (especially if the topic is a controversial one), before you attempt the second, moving the reader to act. For instance, a writer might argue for mandatory jail sentences for drunk drivers. The writer might then go on to urge readers to write letters, circulate petitions, and pressure legislators to enact such a law. Proposals such as this one require that you first convince your readers of the validity of your opinion and then motivate them to support your cause.

Learning about the logical processes that underlie argumentation and persuasion has another purpose, one that extends beyond the act of writing. The "hidden agenda" in mastering this rhetorical mode is that learning to reason well enables us to detect other people's attempts to pull persuasive wool over our eyes. If we know the rules of sound logical argument, we can see through the tricks of those who would like to manipulate or lie to us. We frequently meet relatively innocuous examples, such as the promises of television commercials: drink Blue—you'll be part of the crowd; brush with Glitzodent—you'll get your man; buy a diamond—your marriage will last forever. At other times, we encounter profoundly disturbing distortions and lies. Blacks are inferior—they should not be allowed to vote; the Holocaust never happened—the millions who were "murdered" never existed. It is imperative that we recognize the twisted logic of those who would persuade us to evil. It was, after all, Adolf Hitler who forewarned in *Mein Kampf*: "The broad mass of a nation ... will more easily fall victim to a big lie than to a small one." A person aware of the principles of sound reasoning is not easily victimized by lies, big or small.

How? The Technique

Persuasive papers can be developed in a variety of ways. It is possible, as you will see in the readings for this unit, to use a number of different structural patterns to convince your readers. For instance, a *cause-effect* structure might be an ideal way to urge action to end the sulphur emissions that cause acid rain. *Comparison* might offer an opportunity to assess the efficiency of Canada's regulated airline industry as opposed to the deregulated industry in the United States and to argue in favour of one approach. Most of the expository patterns can be adapted to persuasive purposes.

Two patterns are specific to argument and persuasion. One is the classic *their side—my side* strategy, which is particularly useful when you are arguing a controversial position that will provoke serious dispute. This pattern involves presenting the "con" (or "against") points of your opponent first, then refuting them with the "pro" (or "for") side of your argument. For instance, if a writer were to argue that women in the Canadian Armed Forces should participate in combat, she might choose to present the opposing view and then counter each point with well-reasoned arguments of her own. Such a strategy impresses readers with its fairness and tends to neutralize opposition.

The second structural pattern specific to argument and persuasion makes use of the familiar thesis statement. The first step in this procedure is discovering, examining, and stating an *opinion* about an issue. Of course, the logic of your opinion must be scrutinized carefully before the opinion can serve as the subject of a persuasive paper. Here are three examples of clearly stated opinions that could be expanded into thesis statements:

1. General education is an essential part of the college curriculum. (See "'Why Are We Reading This Stuff, Anyway?'" below)
2. Women may be the one group that grows more radical with age. (See Gloria Steinem, "Why Young Women Are More Conservative.")
3. The North American idea of manhood is pitiful. (See Paul Theroux, "Being a Man.")

The crucial test for a satisfactory statement of opinion is that someone could argue the contrary point of view: "General education is not an essential part of the college curriculum"; "Women, like men, usually grow less radical with age"; "The North American idea of manhood is noble."

Once the opinion is clearly stated, the second step is to assemble *reasons* to support it. Here again, logic is essential. Apply the rules of evidence, as they are called in courtrooms. Your reasons should be *accurate, relevant,* and *complete.* Facts, especially statistics, must be precise. For example, a recent letter to *The Globe and Mail* lamented that only 32 percent of the books purchased by the Toronto Public Library were written by women, while 48 percent of the fiction purchased by the Antigonish Public Library was written by women. Given that no totals were provided, that the categories of books are different, and that Toronto and Antigonish are hardly comparable in size and diversity of population, the statistic was misleading and made the writer's entire argument suspect. As Britain's eminently quotable Prime Minister Benjamin Disraeli once said, "There are three kinds of lies: lies, damned lies, and statistics." The writer of a persuasive paper, like the witness in a courtroom, should tell the truth, the whole truth, and nothing but the truth.

Once you have ensured that your reasons are accurate, relevant (clearly related to the stated opinion), and complete (omitting no vital premise), the next step is to arrange these reasons in order. The usual arrangement is climactic order, which means building from least important to most important. In climactic order, you save your most compelling reasons for the end of the paper when the reader may already be inclined to accept your point of view. For example, you might argue that censorship of books is dangerous because it restricts an individual's right to read, it impedes artists' ability to create, and it jeopardizes an entire society's freedom of expression. Arranged in this order, the argument proceeds from the individual level to the threat to the artistic community and on to the larger implications of censorship for society as a whole. The reasons are separate, yet linked, and build upon each other convincingly.

The last step is to link the opinion to the reasons in a grammatically parallel thesis statement (**O** stands for your statement of opinion; **1**, **2**, and **3** represent your reasons):

O because of 1, 2, and 3.

Example: Censorship of books is dangerous because it restricts the individual's right to read, impedes artists' ability to create, and jeopardizes society's freedom of expression.

Example: General education is an essential part of the college curriculum because it enhances one's ability to build a
career and to live a full life.

Clearly, bringing someone over to our side through well-chosen
words is a challenge. Argument and persuasion are probably the
most formidable writing tasks that we undertake, yet they may also
be the most important. When we are engaged in argument and persuasion, we distinguish ourselves from those who can only nod,
grunt, wag a tail, or brandish a club over another's head. It is possible to convince others to agree with us and even prevail upon them
to act, armed with nothing more than our logic, our feelings, our
words, and, ultimately, our integrity. Effective persuasion is an art
that truly deserves to be called civilized.

The essay that follows expands one of the thesis statements
given above into a convincing argument.

"Why Are We Reading This Stuff, Anyway?"

Introduction
(uses an anec-
dote to ask an
important ques-
tion)

As an English teacher in a community college, I encounter large numbers of bright,
highly motivated students who are committed to particular career paths. English
is not their favourite subject. One of these
students—a would-be microbiologist—
challenged me as we worked our way
through a Faulkner piece one gray, wintry
Monday morning. "Why," he demanded,
"are we reading this stuff, anyway?" Not
being especially quick on my verbal feet
so early in the morning, I burbled something about the value of literature and of
empathy, the ability to see the world
through someone else's eyes. I could tell
by his glower that he was unconvinced.

Now I'd like to step back and
answer the larger question inherent in
my student's query. Why do colleges
require anything other than skills training? Why bother with the seemingly
unrelated, "irrelevant" part of the curriculum called "general education"? To
my microbiology student and the many
others who ask this question, I would

Thesis statement

First point (the reason is developed through well-chosen examples)

like to respond: general education is an essential part of the curriculum because it enhances one's ability to build a career and to live a full life.

Skills training alone is enough to get you a job. College or university training will provide you with the entry-level professional skills that most employers require. The important word here, however, is "entry-level." Your degree or diploma does not entitle you to an executive suite; it enables you to find a footing on the very first rung of the ladder. To proceed up that ladder, to build a career, you must continue to learn and to develop numerous other skills. You must be able to read quickly and thoroughly, to analyze the kinds of information logically, to solve problems effectively, and to communicate both in speech and in writing in an articulate and reasonably sophisticated way. In addition, you will be expected to function in a world where people are comfortable with ideas. The latest television miniseries, fashion fad, or hockey brawl will not always be appropriate conversational fare. You may be expected to know who Sigmund Freud, John Maynard Keynes, or Charlotte Brontë was. To be unaware of great cultural epochs or accomplishments, to fail to read significant new publications, to be ignorant of the difference between the Great War and the Black Death will mark you as uneducated and possibly unsuited to high career achievement. The skills and knowledge described here are developed in the "general education" portion of your education, in courses such as history, English, psychology, philosophy, and the natural sciences.

Secondly, one pursues an education to improve the overall quality of life. Working is only one part of living. Most of us hope that it is the means to an end: a comfortable life shared with other people in

*Second point
(again, note the
use of examples
to develop the
reason)*

a way that will bring happiness to ourselves and those around us. We may marry and have children; we will surely make friends; and we will want to contribute to the communities in which we live. The education we acquire will contribute to our family's well-being in a spiritual and cultural sense as well as an economic one. Our education will enable us to make thoughtful choices; it will arm us against manipulation by sham ideas and charlatans. It will even help us to acquire some measure of wisdom and courage and serenity as we face whatever joys and perils life holds for us.

*Conclusion (ties
the essay
together by citing
a quotation from
the writer
mentioned in the
introductory
paragraph)*

Grand promises? Perhaps. However, people with a solid, well-rounded education tend to thrive in the same way that civilizations that place a premium on education continue to flourish. With these thoughts in mind, I return to my young microbiology student and remind him of some lines by William Faulkner, the author whose text we were studying that dreary Monday:

> I believe that man will not merely endure: he will prevail. He is immortal, not because he alone among creatures has an inexhaustible voice, but because he has a soul, a spirit capable of compassion and sacrifice and endurance. The poet's, the writer's, duty is to write about these things. It is his privilege to help man endure by lifting his heart, by reminding him of the courage and honor and hope and pride and compassion and pity and sacrifice which have been the glory of his past. The poet's voice need not merely be the record of man, it can be one of the props, the pillars to help him endure and prevail.[1]

[1]William Faulkner, Nobel Prize acceptance speech, 1949.

The Myth of Canadian Diversity

1   Canadians cling to three myths about their country.

2   The first is that it is young. In fact, Canada is well advanced into middle age. At 127, it has existed as a unified state for longer than either Italy (unified in 1870) or Germany (1871). Less than a third of the 180-odd nations now belonging to the United Nations existed in 1945, when Canada was already a mature 78. We were 51 when Iraq and Austria—two countries many think of as old—came into being.

3   The second myth is that, in everything but geography, Canada is a small country—small in population, small in economic heft. In fact, our population of 27 million is a fair size by international standards, bigger than that of Austria, Hungary, Sweden, Norway, Finland, Romania, Greece, Algeria, Peru and Venezuela, to name only a few. Our economy, by traditional measures, is the seventh-largest in the world.

4   But the most important myth about Canada—the one that distorts our self-image, warps our politics and may one day tear us apart—is the myth of Canadian diversity. Almost any Canadian will tell you that his Canada is a remarkably varied place. "Canada, with its regional, linguistic and cultural diversity, has never been easy to govern," wrote The Globe and Mail when Jean Chrétien became Prime Minister last fall. Provincial politicians routinely parrot° this myth to push for greater regional powers; federal politicians repeat it to let people know what a hard job they have.

5   In fact, Canada is one of the most homogeneous countries in the world. A foreign visitor can travel from Vancouver in the West to Kingston in the centre without finding any significant difference in accent, in dress, in cuisine or even, in a broad sense, in values. A highschool student in Winnipeg talks, looks and acts much like his counterpart in Prince George. Where they do exist, our regional differences are no match for those of most other countries.

"The Myth of Canadian Diversity" from The Globe and Mail, June 13, 1994. Reprinted with permission.

Canada may have a few regional accents in its English-speaking parts—the salty dialect of Newfoundland, the rural tones of the Ottawa Valley—but these are nothing compared with the dozens in the United States or Britain. It may have two official languages, but that is unlikely to impress India, which has 14. 6

To be certain, we have our French-English divide, two "nations" living under one roof. That hardly makes us unique either. Spain has the Catalans and the Basques. Russia has the Tatars, Ukrainians, Belarussians, Chechens, Moldovians, Udmurts, Kazakhs, Avars and Armenians. And, although few would dispute that francophone Quebec is indeed a distinct society, the differences between Quebec and the rest of Canada are diminishing over time. As Lucien Bouchard himself has noted, we share a host of common attitudes—an attachment to the Canadian social system, tolerance of minorities, a respect for government and law. 7

Even our much-discussed ethnic differences are overstated. Although Canada is an immigrant nation and Canadians spring from a variety of backgrounds, a recent study from the C.D. Howe Institute says that the idea of a "Canadian mosaic"—as distinct from the American "melting pot"—is a fallacy. In *The Illusion of Difference*, University of Toronto sociologists Jeffrey Reitz and Raymond Breton show that immigrants to Canada assimilate° as quickly into the mainstream society as immigrants to the United States do. In fact, Canadians are less likely than Americans to favour holding on to cultural differences based on ethnic background. If you don't believe Mr. Reitz and Mr. Breton, visit any big-city highschool, where the speech and behaviour of immigrant students just a few years in Canada is indistinguishable from that of any fifth-generation classmate. 8

This is not to say that Canada is a nation of cookie-cutter people. The differences among our regions, and between our two main language groups, are real. But in recent years we have elevated those differences into a cult. For all our disputes about language and ethnicity and regional rights, our differences shrink beside our similarities, and the things that unite us dwarf those that divide us. 9

Words and Meanings

Paragraph

parrot	repeat mindlessly	4
assimilate	blend	8

Structure and Strategy

1. Is there an INTRODUCTION to this piece? Where does the thesis statement appear? Identify the paragraphs that develop each of the three myths.
2. How does paragraph 2 support its point? Paragraph 3?
3. What contrasts are developed in paragraphs 6 and 7?
4. Which paragraph is developed mainly by the use of quotations?
5. Identify the TRANSITIONS in paragraphs 4, 5, and 7.
6. Is this editorial essentially ARGUMENT or PERSUASION?

Content and Purpose

1. This editorial makes its point by challenging commonly held opinions. What are those opinions and how does the editorial refute them?
2. Why, according to paragraph 4, do politicians encourage the "myth of Canadian diversity"?
3. How does the piece support the notion that "Canada is one of the most homogeneous countries in the world" (paragraph 5)? Do you find this evidence convincing? What would you add to make the point more persuasive?
4. What points does paragraph 7 make about francophone Quebec and "the rest of Canada"? Why does the writer cite Lucien Bouchard as sharing his point of view? Why is this opinion significant to both sides?
5. Explain why the editorial believes the "Canadian mosaic" and the American "melting pot" share more similarities than differences.
6. Describe the target AUDIENCE for a *Globe and Mail* editorial. Would you describe yourself as part of this community? Do you agree or disagree with the point of view expressed in this editorial?

Suggestions for Writing

1. Refute the challenge that this essay makes to traditional wisdom. In other words, write a clear, well-documented, coherent essay arguing that Canada is, in fact, a young, small, and diverse nation.
2. Write an argumentation or persuasion essay based on the proposition: *Canada is becoming more diverse as the media, social change, and increased immigration intensify the differences among its citizens.* If you disagree, write on the converse of the proposition: *Canada is becoming more homogeneous as the media, social change, and increased immigration serve to lessen the differences among its citizens.*

Faking My Way through School

GREGORY A. KLIEWER

h yes, I distinctly remember it. It was the   1
same every year. I'd sit slouching over my desk with my fingers
crossed beneath it, hopelessly attempting to hide my nervousness.
The teacher patrolled the room like a bird of prey … circling, circling, circling … playing out every tense moment until the end of
the day. Behind her back she held a stack of papers some 30 or so
thick. They rustled ominously as she passed. Report cards!

Then the bell would ring, or the principal would make an   2
announcement to the effect that report cards were to be handed out
now, and the teacher would begin her final round of the class. She
always seemed to start at the opposite end of the room from where
I sat, approaching ever so slowly, licking her finger with ravenous
concentration before she would select the appropriate paper and
place it neatly before each student. Eventually, she would reach me
and, without so much as glancing up to see my expression, continue her mechanical procession to the child beside me. Staring at the
paper before me, I'd take a moment to screw up my courage and …

What a relief! Straight B's! Not bad, I'd think to myself, consider-   3
ing I did nothing to earn them. In an instant my view of my teacher
would change. Instead of the horrible monster that was out to get me,
she would transmogrify° into a comrade, a friend, an ally. I'd look up
from my desk at that moment and exchange a conspiratorial glance
with her. Then I'd look around to my friends and nod ever so slightly.
They'd invariably nod back. We'd done it. We'd beaten the system.

Why was I always so nervous about getting my report cards all   4
those years? Because I knew I didn't deserve to pass. I knew that if
just one of my teachers had the integrity to look at what I had
learned over the past year and translate that into a mark, I'd receive
no more than an F. I coasted through my first 12 years of education
on excuses and plagiarism. The way I see it, there can be only three
possible reasons why I managed to make it through: I was so brilliant that I managed to keep my teachers in the dark as to the state
of my education; my teachers were so stupid they never recognized
my rather deviant behaviour; or those who had taken on the

responsibility of educating me had other priorities that prevented them from doing so. I find the first two possibilities highly unlikely.

5   Believe me, I was not alone in my practices. The vast majority of my friends also faked their way through public school and high school, with varying degrees of success.

6   Most, by far, are still caught in what I call "the cycle." They enroll in classes for a year with full intentions of completing them. In the higher grades they now find themselves in, however, excuses are rarely accepted and plagiarism is virtually punishable by death. The tools of their trade being so unexpectedly taken away from them, they find themselves quickly falling behind in their classes and soon drop out. The next year, they start the cycle all over again, hoping to eventually muddle their way through school.

7   Others have found another escape. They drop down through the levels until they're in a stream with a comfortable workload. Heck, if they go down far enough, to the basic stream, they don't have to do any work at all and, in the end, still receive the magic piece of paper that says they completed high school.

8   Still more of my friends have dropped out entirely, seeing a work-free form of income at the end of the welfare line.

9   There are, however, a very few of my friends who are now going through what I am. We have recognized our ineptitude° of the mind, taken responsibility for it, and are spending our time catching up on the past 12 years of our educational lives. It's a hard struggle, but we're making progress.

10   As a result of my experiences in the Ontario educational system, I've sworn that my future children will never endure what I have suffered during my sojourn through the schools of this province. I refuse to subject them to the terror I went through every year of my life on report-card day. I refuse to watch them grow in body while wasting away in mind. They will be confident in themselves and their abilities. I will see to that if it means teaching them myself. Reform of Ontario's educational system must begin now, before another generation is lost to the void of ignorance.

GREGORY A. KLIEWER

When he wrote this article for *The Globe and Mail*, Greg Kliewer (b. 1974) was a high school senior in Orillia, Ontario, where he served on the editorial board of *Shadows of the Prism*. Currently a student in English and philosophy at the University of Toronto, Greg plans to become a teacher.

Words and Meanings

Paragraph

transmogrify	be transformed	3
ineptitude	lack of skill or fitness	9

Structure and Strategy

1. How does the TITLE attract the reader's attention?
2. What INTRODUCTORY strategy does the author use (paragraphs 1 to 3)? Is it effective? Why?
3. Consider the second sentence in paragraph 4. Why is it a sentence fragment? Is this an "error" or is there some reason for it?
4. What is the function of paragraphs 6 and 7? What point do they develop?
5. What CONCLUDING strategy does Kliewer use (paragraph 10)?
6. Is this essay an example of ARGUMENT or PERSUASION?

Content and Purpose

1. Why is the young Kliewer so frightened in the anecdote that opens the essay? What is he afraid of?
2. Summarize the author's THESIS.
3. What are the three possible reasons the author identifies for his ability to "coast through my first 12 years of education on excuses and plagiarism" (paragraph 4)? Which one does he think is a valid reason?
4. What are the four different responses to their school experience that Kliewer's friends choose from?
5. By referring to four or five specific details in the essay, summarize Kliewer's opinion of his teachers.
6. What does the author suggest is the solution to the problem he identifies? Where does he think the responsibility ultimately lies? Do you agree or disagree?

Suggestions for Writing

1. Write an essay based on your own high school experience, arguing that you were *or* were not effectively prepared for post-secondary education or employment. Be sure to identify at least two clear reasons to support your opinion.
2. Is the educational system ultimately responsible for a student's learning? Or is it the person's responsibility to learn? Write a persuasive essay that identifies and supports your opinion.

Rock and Rap Have Never Been Better

LEE BALLINGER

1   Amid the din of complaint created by the whining of nostalgists° and the growling of censors, it's sometimes hard to hear the obvious truth: music in the '90s is more diverse, interesting, and inspiring than at any other time in American history.

2   It all begins with rap. Rap has expanded from the spartan sound of drum machines and voice 15 years ago to become the only art form other than the blues that can incorporate (or be incorporated by) any style of music. For example, at last year's Ojai Arts Festival, director Peter Sellars staged a version of Stravinsky's opera *Histoire du soldat* that not only was inspired by rap (it ended with the audience encircled by smoke and blue and red flashing lights meant to invoke the police) but also was narrated by a female rap group that shared the stage with the Los Angeles Philharmonic. At the other extreme, the rappers in Arrested Development effortlessly blend in elements of blues and even country to create a distinctly southern brand of hip-hop music.

3   Rap has been the primary vehicle for reggae's long-delayed conquest of North America, as the '90s have seen the raplike tongue-twisting toasting of Jamaican "dance-hall" musicians become part of the U.S. mainstream. Rap has sparked experiments in jazz by the likes of Miles Davis; pushed the development of traditional R&B into "new jack swing"; and created the basic instrumental sound that has enabled the likes of Boyz II Men to restore black vocal group harmonies to the limelight. Rap has provided a new voice not only for young black men but also for women (Queen Latifah, MC Lyte), Latinos (Cypress Hill, A Lighter Shade of Brown), and whites (not just the cartoonish Vanilla Ice and Marky Mark, but important artists such as House of Pain and the Beastie Boys).

4   New musical technology has made possible sampling°, which opens up the entire history of recorded music to fresh new uses and makes new generations aware of legends ranging from James Brown to Junior Wells. High tech has also spawned entire new genres of music such as house and industrial.

5   None of this means that the guitar has become extinct. What *has* happened is that we are seeing the full flowering of the seeds sown

in the late '70s by the punk rebels, a harvest now bountiful enough that it has clearly ended the dominance of classic blues-rock. Freed of the conventions of that style, new forms of guitar-based music have rapidly emerged. There's speed metal—which bands like Metallica continue to take to new heights of complex artistry. Various "alternative" guitar-based bands ranging from the funky Red Hot Chili Peppers to the folky R.E.M. are enormously popular even though they're outside the conventions of rock. As for blues-rock itself, it still provides the bedrock for excellent music (Black Crowes, Aerosmith), while Seattle bands like ... Pearl Jam have kept it recognizable even as they refashion it into grunge.

Current pop music has brought women and poets to the fore. 6 While the modern music scene remains a minefield for women, they have made considerable inroads musically (9 of the top 20 singles in late August [1993] were by women, and 6 of the top 20 albums). Women are even numerous in the male-dominated field of hard rock, whether it's in the mainstream (L7, 4 Non-Blondes) or in the underground of the "riot grrrl" movement. Outside the studios women have made real progress in punching holes in the corporate glass ceiling of the music business—rap labels, for instance, have allowed women an unprecedented degree of power, and Madonna owns her own record company.

Poetry is now undergoing a tremendous upsurge in popularity, 7 and Bob Holman, a producer of poetry events in New York City, says it's because "rap is now making poetry cool." This revolution was televised on a July 28 MTV show in which several poets, including punk musician Henry Rollins, read over the backing of a rock band.

Even in this noisy age, music fans are eager for softer sounds, 8 too. *MTV Unplugged*, a weekly show in which musicians of almost every style perform without amplification, has been a smashing success. Country music, still a haven for acoustic pickers and fiddlers, is more popular than ever before.

The U.S. music scene of the '90s is more open to the world 9 around it. Latino artists ranging from El Tri ("the Rolling Stones of Mexico") to Beatles-influenced Dominican singing star Juan Luis Guerra are well known in many parts of the United States. African, Middle Eastern, and even Balkan music have finally become widely available in North America.

As the musicians of the '90s not only listen to each other but 10 also work together, the lines between genres often blur. Speed metal guys in Anthrax record and tour with rappers Public Enemy; *Tonight Show* bandleader Branford Marsalis with Sting; R.E.M. with hardcore rapper KRS-1; reggae star Barrington Levy with Vernon Reid of Living Colour and Puerto Rican acoustic guitar legend Yomo Toro. In 1991, Little Richard made a video with Israel's Ofra Haza and hard rock heartthrob Sebastian Bach of Skid Row.

11   Finally, musicians are forming political alliances with each other and their fans on a scale never even dreamed of in the '60s. With the 1987 maxi-single *Stop the Violence*, two dozen rappers set the stage for the gang truce now moving across the country, and it was rap that popularized the truce as it actually emerged in Watts in the wake of the Los Angeles rebellion. Musicians registered a million new voters last year under the banner of Rock the Vote and Rap the Vote, musicians were the first to raise money for Midwest flood victims, and musicians have carried the discussion of AIDS, homelessness, police brutality, the environment, and abortion into every corner of America.

12   We live in a time when Axl Rose, the bad boy lead singer of Guns N' Roses who once wrote a song about "niggers," now tours with rapper Ice-T. Last year, Rose stood on a stage in Phoenix and blasted the state of Arizona for refusing to honor Martin Luther King's birthday. That alone should make you want to open your ears and stop, look, and listen to the wealth of sounds that are changing the world we live in.

LEE BALLINGER

Lee Ballinger is a combat veteran of Vietnam, a former steelworker, and a leading networker between musicians such as Ruben Blades, John Cougar Mellencamp, Living Colour, and Bruce Springsteen, and community organizations. For the past twelve years, he has been associate editor of the monthly newsletter *Rock & Rap Confidential* (Box 341305, Los Angeles, CA 90034).

Paragraph
Words and Meanings

1   nostalgists   those who look back fondly and longingly on the past

4   sampling   technique used to produce a new musical work out of bits and pieces of previously recorded instrumentals and/or vocals

Structure and Strategy

1. What is Ballinger's THESIS? Where is it most clearly stated?
2. Identify the TOPIC SENTENCES in paragraphs 4, 5, 8, and 9. How are these paragraphs developed; that is, what kind of support does Ballinger choose to support his topics?
3. The first sentence of paragraph 6 identifies two topics. Where is each developed, and how?

4. What CONCLUDING strategy does the author use in paragraph 12?
5. Is this essay primarily ARGUMENT or PERSUASION?

Content and Purpose

1. Identify at least six of the main points Ballinger uses to support his thesis (there are eight). Which do you find most convincing?
2. According to the author, two musical genres have been primarily responsible for promoting women in contemporary music. Which genres? Why do you think women artists would be attracted to them?
3. Paragraph 9 shifts to discuss the influence of world music on the North American "music scene of the '90s." What is the connection between the topic of paragraph 9 and that of paragraph 10? How do both paragraphs 9 and 10 prepare the reader for the political point Ballinger makes in the conclusion?
4. How does the conclusion relate to the thesis of Ballinger's argument, and how does it contribute to the UNITY of the essay?

Suggestions for Writing

1. Do you agree or disagree with Ballinger's argument? Write an essay, using examples from music you're familiar with, that either supports or refutes the thesis that "rock and rap have never been better."
2. Write an essay exploring the way a particular kind of music (for example, reggae, techno, country, jazz, thrash metal, opera, house, salsa, hip hop, folk) reflects the culture of a specific group of people.
3. Write an essay arguing that music, more than any other form of communication, breaks down barriers between people and promotes social harmony.

Being a Man
PAUL THEROUX

here is a pathetic sentence in the chapter   1
"Fetishism" in Dr. Norman Cameron's book *Personality Development and Psychopathology*. It goes, "Fetishists are nearly always men; and

their commonest fetish° is a woman's shoe." I cannot read that sentence without thinking that it is just one more awful thing about being a man—and perhaps it is an important thing to know about us.

2   I have always disliked being a man. The whole idea of manhood in America is pitiful, in my opinion. This version of masculinity is a little like having to wear an ill-fitting coat for one's entire life (by contrast, I imagine femininity to be an oppressive sense of nakedness). Even the expression "Be a man!" strikes me as insulting and abusive. It means: be stupid, be unfeeling, obedient, soldierly and stop thinking. Man means "manly"—how can one think about men without considering the terrible ambition of manliness? And yet it is part of every man's life. It is a hideous and crippling lie; it not only insists on difference and connives° at superiority, it is also by its very nature destructive—emotionally damaging and socially harmful.

3   The youth who is subverted, as most are, into believing in the masculine ideal is effectively separated from women and he spends the rest of his life finding women a riddle and a nuisance. Of course, there is a female version of this male affliction. It begins with mothers encouraging little girls to say (to other adults) "Do you like my new dress?" In a sense, little girls are traditionally urged to please adults with a kind of coquettishness°, while boys are enjoined to behave like monkeys towards each other. The nine-year-old coquette proceeds to become womanish in a subtle power game in which she learns to be sexually indispensable, socially decorative and always alert to a man's sense of inadequacy.

4   Femininity—being lady-like—implies needing a man as witness and seducer; but masculinity celebrates the exclusive company of men. That is why it is so grotesque; and that is also why there is no manliness without inadequacy—because it denies men the natural friendship of women.

5   It is very hard to imagine any concept of manliness that does not belittle women, and it begins very early. At an age when I wanted to meet girls—let's say the treacherous years of thirteen to sixteen—I was told to take up a sport, get more fresh air, join the Boy Scouts, and I was urged not to read so much. It was the 1950s and if you asked too many questions about sex you were sent to camp—boy's camp, of course: the nightmare. Nothing is more unnatural or prison-like than a boy's camp, but if it were not for them we would have no Elks' Lodges°, no pool rooms, no boxing matches, no Marines.

6   And perhaps no sports as we know them. Everyone is aware of how few in number are the athletes who behave like gentlemen. Just as high school basketball teaches you how to be a poor loser,

the manly attitude towards sports seems to be little more than a recipe for creating bad marriages, social misfits, moral degenerates, sadists, latent rapists and just plain louts. I regard high school sports as a drug far worse than marijuana, and it is the reason that the average tennis champion, say, is a pathetic oaf.

Any objective study would find the quest for manliness essentially right-wing, puritanical, cowardly, neurotic and fueled largely by a fear of women. It is also certainly philistine°. There is no bookhater like a Little League coach. But indeed all the creative arts are obnoxious to the manly ideal, because at their best the arts are pursued by uncompetitive and essentially solitary people. It makes it very hard for a creative youngster, for any boy who expresses the desire to be alone seems to be saying that there is something wrong with him.

It ought to be clear by now that I have something of an objection to the way we turns boys into men. It does not surprise me that when the President of the United States has his customary weekend off he dresses like a cowboy—it is both a measure of his insecurity and his willingness to please. In many ways, American culture does little more for a man than prepare him for modeling clothes in the L.L. Bean catalogue°. I take this as a personal insult because for many years I found it impossible to admit to myself that I wanted to be a writer. It was my guilty secret, because being a writer was incompatible with being a man.

There are people who might deny this, but that is because the American writer, typically, has been so at pains to prove his manliness that we have come to see literariness and manliness as mingled qualities. But first there was a fear that writing was not a manly profession—indeed, not a profession at all. (The paradox in American letters is that it has always been easier for a woman to write and for a man to be published.) Growing up, I had thought of sports as wasteful and humiliating, and the idea of manliness was a bore. My wanting to become a writer was not a flight from that oppressive role-playing, but I quickly saw that it was at odds with it. Everything in stereotyped manliness goes against the life of the mind. The Hemingway personality is too tedious to go into here, and in any case his exertions are well-known, but certainly it was not until this aberrant° behavior was examined by feminists in the 1960s that any male writer dared question the pugnacity° in Hemingway's fiction. All the bullfighting and arm wrestling and elephant shooting diminished Hemingway as a writer, but it is consistent with a prevailing attitude in American writing: one cannot be a male writer without first proving that one is a man.

It is normal in America for a man to be dismissive or even somewhat apologetic about being a writer. Various factors make it easier.

There is a heartiness about journalism that makes it acceptable—journalism is the manliest form of American writing and, therefore, the profession the most independent-minded women seek (yes, it is an illusion, but that is my point). Fiction-writing is equated with a kind of dispirited failure and is only manly when it produces wealth—money is masculinity. So is drinking. Being a drunkard is another assertion, if misplaced, of manliness. The American male writer is traditionally proud of his heavy drinking. But we are also a very literal-minded people. A man proves his manhood in America in old-fashioned ways. He kills lions, like Hemingway; or he hunts ducks, like Nathanael West; or he makes pronouncements like, "A man should carry enough knife to defend himself with," as James Jones once said to a *Life* interviewer. Or he says he can drink you under the table. But even tiny drunken William Faulkner loved to mount a horse and go fox hunting, and Jack Kerouac roistered up and down Manhattan in a lumberjack shirt (and spent every night of *The Subterraneans* with his mother in Queens). And we are familiar with the lengths to which Norman Mailer is prepared, in his endearing way, [to go] to prove that he is just as much a monster as the next man.

11   When the novelist John Irving was revealed as a wrestler, people took him to be a very serious writer; and even a bubble reputation like Eric (*Love Story*) Segal's was enhanced by the news that he ran the marathon in a respectable time. How surprised we would be if Joyce Carol Oates were revealed as a sumo wrestler or Joan Didion active in pumping iron. "Lives in New York City with her three children" is the typical woman writer's biographical note, for just as the male writer must prove he has achieved a sort of muscular manhood, the woman writer—or rather her publicists—must prove her motherhood.

12   There would be no point in saying any of this if it were not generally accepted that to be a man is somehow—even now in feminist-influenced America—a privilege. It is on the contrary an unmerciful and punishing burden. Being a man is bad enough; being manly is appalling (in this sense, women's lib has done much more for men than for women). It is the sinister silliness of men's fashions, and a clubby attitude in the arts. It is the subversion of good students. It is the so-called "Dress Code" of the Ritz-Carlton Hotel in Boston, and it is the institutionalized cheating in college sports. It is the most primitive insecurity.

13   And this is also why men often object to feminism but are afraid to explain why: of course women have a justified grievance, but most men believe—and with reason—that their lives are just as bad.

PAUL THEROUX

Paul Theroux is an American-born novelist, travel writer, critic, and poet. After graduating from university, Theroux spent ten years travelling abroad, teaching in Malawi, Uganda, Italy, and Singapore before settling in England. Much of his writing centres on characters whose experiences of a foreign culture have left them disillusioned and critical of the values of their own society. Among his best-known works are *The Mosquito Coast* (1981), *Picture Palace* (1977), *The Great Railway Bazaar* (1975), and *Kingdom by the Sea* (1983).

Words and Meanings   Paragraph

fetish	object to which one is irrationally devoted or attached; here, in the sense of sexual arousal	1
connives	schemes or co-operates secretly	2
coquettishness	flirtatiousness	3
Elks' Lodges	kind of club; fraternal society for men	5
philistine	anti-intellectual	7
L.L. Bean catalogue	American mail-order catalogue for fashionable outdoor wear and sporting and camping equipment	8
aberrant	erratic or abnormal	9
pugnacity	quarrelsome tendency; desire to fight	

Structure and Strategy

1. How successful is the first paragraph in catching the reader's interest?
2. What is the TONE of paragraphs 5 to 8?
3. What is the topic sentence of paragraph 9 and how is it developed in the next two paragraphs?
4. Do paragraphs 12 and 13 form a successful conclusion to this essay? Why or why not?

Content and Purpose

1. What idea or concept does Theroux present in this essay? Is his argument successful or unsuccessful in your opinion?
2. What does Theroux mean when he says he has always "disliked being a man"? What is the distinction between "being a man" and "being manly"?
3. In what ways are both the masculine ideal and the feminine ideal damaging to one's identity and personality? (See paragraphs 3 and 4.)

4. What are the reasons Theroux objects to the way North American society rears male children, the way we "turn boys into men"?

5. Would you describe Theroux as a feminist? Why or why not?

Suggestions for Writing

1. Think of a particular man or some men whom you admire and write an essay defining what it means to be a man.

2. Theroux discusses the difficulty of being a man. Are there difficulties associated with being a woman? Write an essay in which you persuade your readers of the difficulties (or privileges) of being a woman.

A Planet for the Taking

DAVID SUZUKI

1   Canadians live under the remarkable illusion that we are technologically advanced people. Everything around us denies that assumption. We are, in many ways, a Third World country, selling our natural resources in exchange for the high technology of the industrialized world. Try going through your home and looking at the country of origin of your clothes, electrical appliances, books, car. The rare technological product that does have Canada stamped on it is usually from a branch plant of a multinational company centred in another country. But we differ from traditional Third World countries. We have a majority population of Caucasians and a very high level of literacy and affluence. And we have been able to maintain our seemingly advanced social state by virtue of an incredible bounty of natural resources.

2   Within the Canadian mystique there is also a sense of the vastness of this land. The prairies, the Arctic, the oceans, the mountains are ever present in our art and literature. This nation is built on our sense of the seeming endlessness of the expanse of wilderness and the output of nature and we have behaved as if this endlessness were real. Today we speak of renewable resources but our "harvest" procedures are more like a mining operation. We extract raw resources in the crudest of ways, gouging the land to get at its inner

core, spewing our raw wastes into the air, water and soil in massive amounts while taking fish, birds, animals and trees in vast quantities without regard to the future. So we operate under a strange duality of mind: we have both a sense of the importance of the wilderness and space in our culture and an attitude that it is limitless and therefore we needn't worry.

Native cultures of the past may have been no more conservation-minded than we are but they lacked the technology to make the kind of impact that we do today. Canadians and Americans share one of the great natural wonders, the Great Lakes, which contain 20 percent of the world's fresh water, yet today even this massive body of water is terribly polluted and the populations of fish completely mixed-up by human activity. We speak of "managing" our resources but do it in a way that resembles the sledgehammer-on-the-head cure for a headache. On the west coast of Canada, Natives lived for millennia° on the incredible abundance of five species of salmon. Today, the massive runs are gone and many biologists fear that the fish may be in mortal jeopardy because of both our fishing and management policies. Having improved fishing techniques this century to the point of endangering runs yet still knowing very little of the biology of the fish, we have assumed that we could build up the yield by simply dumping more back. But it wasn't known that sockeye salmon fry°, for example, spend a year in a freshwater lake before going to sea. Millions of sockeye fry were dumped directly into the Fraser River where they died soon after. In Oregon, over-fishing and hydroelectric dams had decimated coho° populations in the Columbia River. In one year, over 8 million fry were released of which only seven were ever caught. No one knows what's happening to the rest.

We act as if a fish were a fish, a duck a duck or a tree a tree. If we "harvest" one, we renew it by simply adding one or two back. But what we have learned is that all animals and plants are not equivalent. Each organism reflects the evolutionary° history of its progenitors°; in the case of salmon, each race and subrace of fish has been exquisitely honed by nature to return to a very specific part of the Pacific watershed. Similarly, in the enormous area of prairie pothole country in the centre of the continent, migratory birds do not just space themselves out according to the potholes that are empty. Scientists have discovered that the birds have been selected to return to a very restricted part of that area. And of course, our entire forestry policy is predicated° on the ridiculous idea that a virgin stand° of fir or cedar which has taken millennia to form and clings to a thin layer of topsoil can be replaced after clear-cut logging simply by sticking seedlings into the ground. How can anyone with even the most rudimentary° understanding of biology and evolution ignore the realities of the complex interaction between organisms and the environment and attempt to manipulate wild populations as if they were tomato plants or chickens?

5   I believe that in large part our problems rest on our faith in the power of science and technology. At the beginning of this century, science, when applied by industry and medicine, promised a life immeasurably better and there is no doubt that society, indeed the planet, has been transformed by the impact of new ideas and inventions of science. Within my lifetime, I've seen the beginning of television, oral contraception, organ transplants, space travel, computers, jets, nuclear weapons, satellite communication, and polio vaccine. Each has changed society forever and made the world of my youth recede into the pages of history. But we have not achieved a technological utopia°. The problems facing us today are immense and many are a direct consequence of science and technology. What has gone wrong?

6   I believe that the core of our 20th century dilemma lies in a fundamental limitation of science that most scientists, especially those in the life sciences, fail to recognize. Most of my colleagues take it for granted that our studies will ultimately be applicable to the "big picture," that our research will have beneficial payoffs to society eventually. That is because the thrust of modern science has been predicated on the Newtonian idea that the universe is like an enormous machine whose entire system will be reconstructed on the basis of our understanding of the parts. This is the fundamental reductionist faith in science: the whole is equal to the sum of its parts. It does make a lot of sense—what distinguishes science from other activities that purport° to provide a comprehensive "world view" is its requirement that we focus on a part of nature isolated to as great an extent as possible from the rest of the system of which it is a part. This has provided enormous insights into that fragment of nature, often accompanied by power to manipulate it. But when we attempt to tinker with what lies in the field of our view, the effects ripple far beyond the barrel of the microscope. And so we are constantly surprised at the unexpected consequences of our interference. Scientists only know nature in "bits and pieces" and assume that higher levels of organization are simply the expression of the component parts. This is what impels neurobiologists to study the chemical and electrical behaviour of single neurons in the faith that it will ultimately lead to an understanding of what creativity and imagination are, a faith that I don't for a moment think will ever be fulfilled (although a lot of useful information will accrue°).

Physicists, who originally set this view in motion, have this century, with the arrival of relativity and quantum theory, put to rest the notion that we will ever be able to reconstruct the entire universe from fundamental principles. Chemists know that a complete physical description of atoms of oxygen and hydrogen is of little value in predicting the behaviour of a water molecule. But biologists scream that any sense that there are properties of organization that don't exist at lower levels is "vitalism," a belief that there is some mystical life force in living organisms. And so biochemists and molecular biologists are intent on understanding the workings of organisms by learning all they can about sub-cellular° organization.

Ironically, ecology°, long scorned by molecular biologists as an inexact science, is now corroborating physics. In studying ecosystems, we are learning that a simple breakdown into components and their behaviour does not provide insight into how an entire collection of organisms in a natural setting will work. While many ecologists do continue to "model" ecosystems in computers in the hope that they will eventually derive a predictive tool, their science warns of the hazards of treating it too simply in management programs.

At present, our very terminology suggests that we think we can manage wild plants and animals as though they were domesticated° organisms. We speak of "herds" of seals, of "culling," "harvesting," "stocks." The ultimate expression of our narrow view (and self-interested rationalizations) is seen in how we overlook the enormous environmental impact of our pollution, habitat destruction and extraction and blame seals and whales for the decline in fish populations or wolves for the decrease in moose—and then propose bounties° as a solution!

But Canadians do value the spiritual importance of nature and want to see it survive for future generations. We also believe in the power of science to sustain a high quality of life. And while the current understanding of science's power is, I believe, misplaced, in fact the leading edges of physics and ecology may provide the insights that can get us off the current track. We need a very profound perceptual shift and soon.

___

DAVID SUZUKI

David Suzuki (b. 1936) is a well-known Canadian scientist, educator, journalist, and broadcaster. He has hosted and contributed to television programs such as "Science Magazine" and "The Nature of Things," and writes for a wide range of publications. His most recent works include *Inventing the Future* (1991) and *Time to Change* (1994).

Words and Meanings

3	millennia	thousands of years
	fry	salmon in their second year of life
	coho	species of salmon
4	evolutionary	continuous genetic adaptation of living things to their environment
	progenitors	ancestors; previous generations
	predicated	based
	virgin stand	group of trees that have never been logged
	rudimentary	basic
5	utopia	perfect world
6	purport	intend or seem to
	accrue	result
7	sub-cellular	particle or particles smaller than a single cell
8	ecology	study of the interrelationships between organisms and their environment
9	domesticated	tame; raised in a controlled environment for human use
	bounties	sums of money paid to individuals who have killed "nuisance" animals; for example, wolves

Structure and Strategy

1. Identify five examples Suzuki uses to support his contention that Canada is recklessly abusing its abundant natural resources. Find three or four examples of DICTION that reinforce this contention.
2. What is the topic of paragraph 4? How is the topic supported or developed?

Content and Purpose

1. What are the "illusions" deceiving Canadians that Suzuki identifies in paragraphs 1, 2, and 3?
2. What two reasons does Suzuki identify for Canadians' belief that the "harvesting" of our natural resources is not a cause for serious concern? How does Suzuki attempt to convince us that our notion of "limitless" natural resources is dangerously naïve?
3. Suzuki's essay is both an argument and a warning. Is his primary purpose to convince his readers of the validity of his opinion or to move them to act in some way?
4. Why does Suzuki believe that biologists are lagging behind chemists and physicists in their understanding of the world in which we live?

Suggestion for Writing

Suzuki is a scientist, yet he believes that "in large part, our problems rest on our faith in the power of science and technology." Write a persuasive essay in which you agree or disagree with Suzuki. Use at least three well-developed examples to support your argument.

The Harvest, the Kill

JANE RULE

I live among vegetarians of various persuasions and moral meat eaters; therefore when I have guests for dinner, I pay rather more attention to the nature of food than I would, left to my own imagination.

The vegetarians who don't eat meat because they believe it to be polluted with cancer-causing hormones or because they identify their sensitive digestive tracts with herbivore° ancestors are just cautious folk similar to those who cross the street only at the corner with perhaps a hint of the superstition found in those who don't walk under ladders. They are simply taking special care of their lives without further moral deliberation°.

Those who don't eat meat because they don't approve of killing aren't as easy for me to understand. Yesterday, as I pried live scallops from their beautiful, fragile shells and saw them still pulsing in the bowl, ready to cook for friends for whom food from the sea is acceptable, it felt to me no less absolute an act of killing than chopping off the head of a chicken. But I also know in the vegetable garden that I rip carrots untimely° from their row. The fact that they don't twitch or run around without their heads doesn't make them less alive. Like me, they have grown from seed and have their own natural life span which I have interrupted. It is hard for me to be hierarchical° about the aliveness of living things.

There are two vegetarian arguments that bear some guilty weight for me. The first is the number of acres it takes to feed beef cattle as compared to the number of acres it takes to feed vegetation. If there ever were a large plan to change our basic agriculture in order to feed everyone more equably°, I would support it and give up eating beef, but until then my not eating beef is of no more help than my eating my childhood dinner was to the starving Armenians. The second is mistreatment of animals raised for slaughter. To eat what has not been a free-ranging animal is to condone° the abuse of animals. Again, given the opportunity to support laws for more humane treatment of the creatures we eventually eat, I would do so, but I probably wouldn't go so far as to approve of chickens so happy in life that they were tough for my table.

5   The moral meat eaters are those who believe that we shouldn't eat what we haven't killed ourselves, either gone to the trouble of stalking it down or raising it, so that we have proper respect for the creatures sacrificed for our benefit.

6   I am more at home with that view because my childhood summers were rural. By the time I was seven or eight, I had done my share of fishing and hunting, and I'd been taught also to clean my catch or kill. I never shot anything larger than a pigeon or rabbit. That I was allowed to use a gun at all was the result of a remarkably indulgent° father. He never took me deer hunting, not because I was a girl but because he couldn't bear to shoot them himself. But we ate venison° brought to us by other men in the family.

7   I don't remember much being made of the sacredness of the life we took, but there was a real emphasis on fair play, much of it codified° in law, like shooting game birds only on the wing, like not hunting deer with flashlights at night, like not shooting does°. But my kinfolk frowned on bait fishing as well. They were sportsmen who retained the wilderness ethic of not killing more than they could use. Strictly speaking, we did not need the food. (We could get meat in a town ten miles down the road.) But we did eat it.

8   Over the years, I became citified. I still could and did put live lobsters and crab in boiling water, but meat came from the meat market. Now that I live in the country again, I am much more aware of the slaughter that goes on around me, for I not only eat venison from the local hunt but have known the lamb and kid on the hoof (even in my rhododendrons°, which is good for neither them nor the rhododendrons) which I eat. The killers of the animals are my moral, meat-eating neighbors. I have never killed a large animal, and I hope I never have to, though I'm not particularly tenderhearted about creatures not human. I find it hard to confront the struggle, smell, and mess of slaughter. I simply haven't the stomach for it. But, if I had to do it or go without meat, I would learn how.

9   It's puzzling to me that cannibalism is a fascinating abomination to vegetarian and meat eater alike, a habit claimed by only the most vicious and primitive tribes. We are scandalized by stories of the Donner Party or rumors of cannibalism at the site of a small

plane crash in the wilderness, a boat lost at sea. Yet why would it be so horrifying for survivors to feed on the flesh of those who have died? Have worms and buzzards more right to the carcass?

We apparently do not think of ourselves as part of the food   10 chain, except by cruel and exceptional accident. Our flesh, like the cow in India, is sacred and taboo°, thought of as violated° even when it is consigned° to a mass grave. We bury it to hide a truth that still must be obvious to us, that as we eat so are we eaten. Why the lowly maggot is given the privilege (or sometimes the fish or the vulture) denied other living creatures is a complex puzzle of hygiene, myth and morality in each culture.

Our denial that we are part of nature, our sense of superiority   11 to it, is our basic trouble. Though we are not, as the producers of margarine would make us believe, what we eat, we are related to what we harvest and kill. If being a vegetarian or a moral meat eater is a habit to remind us of that responsibility, neither is to be disrespected. When habit becomes a taboo, it blinds us to the real meaning. We are also related to each other, but our general refusal to eat our own flesh has not stopped us from slaughtering each other in large and totally wasted numbers.

I am flesh, a flesh eater, whether the food is carrot or cow.   12 Harvesting and killing are the same activity, the interrupting of one life cycle for the sake of another. We don't stop at eating either. We kill to keep warm. We kill for shelter.

Back there in my rural childhood, I had not only a fishing rod   13 and rifle, I had a hatchet, too. I cleared brush, cut down small trees, chopped wood. I was present at the felling of a two-thousand-year-old redwood tree, whose impact shook the earth I stood on. It was a death more simply shocking to me than any other I've ever witnessed. The house I lived in then was made of redwood. The house I live in now is cedar.

My ashes may nourish the roots of a living tree, pitifully small   14 compensation for the nearly immeasurable acres I have laid waste for my needs and pleasures, even for my work. For such omnivorous° creatures as we are, a few frugal° habits are not enough. We have to feed and midwife° more than we slaughter, replant more than we harvest, if not with our hands, then with our own talents to see that it is done in our name, that we own to it.

The scallop shells will be finely cleaned by raccoons, then made   15 by a neighbor into wind chimes, which may trouble my sleep and probably should until it is time for my own bones to sing.

```

```

JANE RULE

Jane Rule, a novelist and essayist, was born in 1931 in Plainfield, N.J., and educated at Mills College, California, and University College, London. She moved to Vancouver in 1956 and in 1976 settled on Galiano Island, B.C. Her recent books include *A Hot-Eyed Moderate* (1985) and *After the Fire* (1989).

Paragraph

Words and Meanings

Paragraph		
2	herbivore	creature that eats only plants
	deliberation	thought, consideration
3	untimely	before they are fully grown
	hierarchical	organized in order of rank or importance
4	equably	evenly, fairly
	condone	forgive, excuse
6	indulgent	the opposite of strict
	venison	deer meat
7	codified	written down as rules or laws
	does	female deer
8	rhododendrons	large, flowering bushes common in B.C. gardens
10	taboo	forbidden
	violated	abused, dishonoured
	consigned	delivered, handed over to
14	omnivorous	creatures that eat both animals and plants
	frugal	saving, conserving
	midwife	assist in the birth of animals

Structure and Strategy

1. In paragraph 1, Rule divides her neighbours into two categories: vegetarians and moral meat eaters. What is the function of paragraphs 2 to 4 and 5 to 7? What relation do they have to the opening paragraph?
2. In which paragraph does Rule explicitly state the opinion that forms the basis for her argument? Why do you think she introduces this statement so late in the essay?
3. Explain what makes the concluding sentence of this essay effective and memorable. What powerful images come together to reinforce Rule's point about the interdependency of all forms of life?

Content and Purpose

1. What two classes of vegetarians does Rule identify?

2. What are the "two vegetarian arguments" presented in paragraph 4? Do they appeal to the intellect or to the emotions? Do you find either of these arguments persuasive? Why is Rule not a vegetarian herself?

3. What is a "moral meat eater"? Does Rule herself fit into this category?

4. What childhood experiences contributed to Rule's adult views about the morality of "harvesting and killing"?

5. According to Rule, why is there such a strong taboo on cannibalism? (See paragraphs 9 to 11.)

6. According to Rule, what do humans deny about themselves that leads to an absence of responsibility for the natural world? How does she relate this denial to burial rituals?

7. Paragraphs 12 to 14 illustrate how we exploit nature, consuming far more than we return. What, according to Rule, do we need to acknowledge before we can correct this imbalance?

Suggestions for Writing

1. Write an essay persuading the reader to adopt a vegetarian lifestyle. Appeal to your reader's intellect and emotions in your attempt to convince the reader to give up meat.

2. Do you agree or disagree with the contention that wearing fur or leather clothing is a violation of animal rights? Write an essay in which you convince your reader of the reasonableness of your opinion.

A Meditation on Reading in the '90s

KATIE LYNES

Recently, upon dragging myself out of bed, I tripped over a heap of books that had apparently fallen from and was now growing around my bedside table. As this was the second time in a week that my mid-morning motor faculties (shaky in the best of circumstances) had been tested in this manner, I was driven to engage in a bit of self-analysis. Why, I probed myself, do I have so many books on the go? Whatever happened to the days when one Trixie Belden or Nancy Drew mystery sufficed as bedtime reading? Whatever happened, in other words, to the concept of *one book at a time*?

2   Glancing down at the heterogeneous mass of printed material lying around my bed—with titles ranging from "Feminism and Foucault" to "The Making of the Atomic Bomb"—I was forced to recognize that even the notion of one *interest* at a time was no longer operative in my obviously twisted, late-capitalistic psyche. And with that thought it came to me: perhaps there was a sociological explanation for, to say nothing of rationalization of, my private dementia°; after all, this is the postmodern world, the personal is political, madness is a social construct and the individual—having followed close on the heels of God and the author—is dead. I was compelled, then, in order to exonerate° myself from my own accusations of maladjustment, to generalize from my experience.

3   The self-serving fruit of my generalization is simple: at first glance the culprit appears to be TV. Reading in the '80s was, and in the '90s will continue to be, informed by TV-watching and in particular, by that habit that so infuriates our elders: switching channels. Even in the dark ages of television, when one actually had to get up and walk a few feet to change the channel, the shows themselves were commercial-laden and thus discontinuous. But now, thanks to the remote control, watching TV has become a phantasmagoric° adventure in which, within seconds, "thirtysomething" yuppie gush melds into "Doogie Howser, M.D." inanity, which in turn fuses with those appealing static shots of *objets de consommation* on the Shopping Network. Similarly, reading has become a disjunctive° experience in which the reader "flips" from book to book and from genre to genre. And so, no sooner do I pick up *The Nation* to read the latest wittily phrased invective° against American foreign policy than I find my interest flipping to Kazuo Ishiguro's "The Remains of the Day" and, minutes later, to a borrowed copy of "The Landlord and Tenant's Act."

4   But fun as blaming everything on TV may be, is it really as simple as this? Is the urge to flip when reading actually *caused* by use of the remote control whose current popularity betokens a new privileging of a rapidly shifting (tele)visual? Or are switching channels and flipping from book to book both symptoms of some larger, presumably quite recent, psycho-social phenomenon? The latter explanation seems less simplistic and more likely, especially if one takes into consideration the monumental socio-economic and technological changes that have occurred in the last 200 years.

5   Not the least of these changes has to do with styles and paces of living. For instance, unlike the mostly middle class and female

readers of the early novel, we lack the time to read for extended periods. If we read at all we probably do so on the bus or subway to and from work: when we arrive home at night, exhausted by our nine-to-five, drone-like existence, we are much more likely to watch TV, an activity which, since the advent of the remote control, demands less mental and physical energy than ever.

But it is not just time to read intensively that we lack, it is also the will. And there are both philosophical and psychological reasons for this. In the first place, within today's cultural and intellectual communities there is no longer any consensus° regarding what kind of information one should know: the '60s civil rights movements, the second wave of feminism and the technological revolution have transformed many of the old certainties about God, Man and the State into uncertainties. Knowledge ... has owned up to its illicit affair with Power and, as a result, in almost every field of learning the canon° has died a reluctant but long-overdue death. In its wake has arisen a supermarket of ideas of all kinds, packaged in every manner conceivable. No wonder, then, that soon after settling down to read the latest novel by Margaret Atwood, I begin to think that I should in fact be reading "George Bush, An Intimate Portrait" by Fitzhugh Green.

In the second place, in the psychological arena a condition has emerged which affects both our desire and our ability to read or even watch TV intensively. The condition is metaphorically (mis)named schizophrenia because its sufferers—all of us according to some theoreticians—lack a cohesive subjectivity or sense of self. If we do profess an identity it is a false one which jars with the fragmented reality of our lived experience.

As postmodern schizophrenics, we are incapable of the sustained concentration necessary for focused and relatively uninterrupted reading. But we're not merely incapable of prolonged reading, we're also increasingly uninterested in the genres that require it: since our experience is not logical, linear and progressive we neither expect nor accept such traits in our cultural products. In other words, because we don't possess a centred, coherent and self-sufficient ego° we're not keen on reading about one in, say, the traditional bourgeois novel; nor are we particularly anxious to read—at least continuously—anything that posits° such an ego: i.e., most logocentric° essays, articles or stories.

The unfortunate result of this combination of schizophrenia, information overload, and philosophical doubt is—at least in my case and that of my equally alienated friends—paralysis. It is impossible to know one thing in depth without excluding and potentially marginalizing another, so I choose to know nothing; it is impossible to sift through and evaluate the multitude of "facts," news and images that manages to reach me in spite of my desire not to know, so I accept all as equally (in)significant; finally, given my lack of ego, it is impossible for me even to desire a different state of affairs, so I just don't think about it.

10   Nonetheless, nostalgia for the days of Trixie Belden on the bedside table would be as ridiculous as it would be misplaced. Sure, it was nice to read books from start to finish. It was also comforting to read about charmingly Aryan teenage sleuths who knew right from wrong and who, within the span of 200 pages, were able to use that knowledge to solve complex mysteries. But it was comforting because it had virtually nothing to do with life. Moreover, in its own way it was as paralyzing as the kind of disjointed reading we engage in today, for it left us feeling better about the world beyond the text than we should have. And, at the risk of offending the few remaining upholders of the distinction between high and low culture, I could say the same about much of the "serious" fiction and poetry studied in undergraduate English departments everywhere. What is the effect of a Jane Austen novel if it is not to reassure us that there exists a comfortable place for everyone within a social hierarchy that is as natural as it is benign? Even modernists like Eliot and Waugh, who don't paint a pretty picture of the "real" world, do propose a paralyzingly absurd solution: a return to the days when a man was a man and God was God and each knew his place.

11   Sentimental yearning for the days of one person one discipline° is similarly inappropriate. True, our aging professors and parents displayed the kind of commitment to their particular fields of expertise that few of us can muster. But as the history of literary studies has shown, to know one thing or area in depth is often to know it falsely. In English studies the New Criticism has been discredited precisely because it attempted to analyze literature as an entity in and of itself, separate from and capable of transcending the social and economic context within which it was produced. In the tautological° manner characteristic of this school of criticism, it sought to justify such a project (and conceal its retrograde° political nature) by appealing to the same platonized° "Literature" whose existence its approach presupposed°.

12   As for our lost egos ... well, who really cares anyway? Deep down we all know that the "individual" (the entrepreneur, the self-made man, etc.) is nothing but a patriarchal, ethnocentric construct that keeps us working as cogs in a system not necessarily to our benefit. So good fucking riddance, right? Right. Except what's going to replace it? In a society which constantly bombards us with spuriously° opposed, official versions of the Truth, is it possible to undertake resistant action of any kind—be it in the form of writing, reading or direct political activity—sans ego?

The scenario is pretty depressing but not, I think, entirely hope- 13
less. As egoless individuals or as groups with common interests, we
are capable of acting in a variety of ways. We can, for instance,
allow the dissolution of the ego to infect the work place, where not
to possess a working sense of identity might well constitute a political act in itself. Or less passively, we can combine our habit of dis-
junctive reading with another resistant practice: that of raising our
voices and pens in order to cause a barrage° of our own images,
facts and texts to descend upon the economic and political powers
that be. In these ways we can act to effect change while avoiding
either producing or consuming a "master" plan or narrative which
denies differences and otherness.

So maybe the growing mound of books and magazines beside 14
my bed is a good sign; maybe it signals the end of the hegemony°
of the printed word and, by extension, the demise° of the very idea
of cultural authority (which is far too often complicit with political
and economic authority); like switching channels, maybe it indicates a renewed valorization° of personal experience and desire
over the wisdom of cultural gurus. Perhaps it's even the harbinger°
of a genuine cultural revolution for the '90s. The apex° of such a
revolution, for me, would be the moment when the graffiti artist
realizes that there is only one thing that separates his/her text from
that of, say, Robertson Davies: namely, a set of economically and
politically determined criteria whereby certain (generally white,
middle-class, over-thirty and anally-grammatical) voices are rei-
fied° as "art" while others are silenced or ignored.

In any case, if the printed mess around my bed signifies any of 15
these things, I guess it's worth a few mid-morning tumbles.

KATIE LYNES

Katie Lynes is a freelance writer and a doctoral student in English at the
University of Toronto where she is writing a dissertation on the suburbs and
postmodern fiction. Her influences and interests are wide ranging and include
poststructuralism, French feminism, *Bewitched*, Italian feminism, the canon,
infotainment, suburban neopunk, the Internet, and twelve-step programs.

Words and Meanings

Paragraph

dementia	madness	2
exonerate	declare innocent or free from blame	
phantasmagoric	shifting among reality, fantasy, illusions, and deceptions	3

	disjunctive	unconnected, separating
	invective	violent attack in words; abusive language
6	consensus	agreement among all members of a group
	canon	the traditionally agreed-upon body of work one must know in order to be considered educated in a particular field
8	ego	the part of the personality that governs rational, realistic behaviour; the identifiable "self"
	posits	assumes the existence of
	logo-centric	relying on the reader's understanding of word meanings and logical reasoning
11	discipline	field of study; in this context means "one person, one job"
	tautological	uselessly repetitive; saying something over and over again in different words without adding insight or meaning
	retrograde	moving backward; becoming worse
	platonized	idealized
	presupposed	assumed, took for granted
12	spuriously	falsely, not coming from a right/true/valid source; Lynes is saying that the opposition to "official" versions of the truth is as fake as the version it pretends to oppose
13	barrage	attack; a heavy onslaught
14	hegemony	domination
	demise	death
	valorization	recognition of worth
	harbinger	first or early sign of change
	apex	high point, climax
	reified	certified, labelled

Structure and Strategy

1. Is there any connection between the INTRODUCTION and the CONCLUSION?
2. How does the author develop her point about television channel-surfing in paragraph 3?
3. Analyze the use of TRANSITIONS between paragraphs 5, 6, and 7. How do they connect ideas? How do they ease the reader into the arguments that follow? Study also the major transitional devices in paragraph 10, where the focus of the essay shifts significantly.
4. How do you interpret the repeated use of the (half)parenthesized words in the essay? For example, "(tele)visual" in paragraph 4 and

"(mis)named" in paragraph 7. Can you find any other examples of this trendy punctuation-as-commentary device in the essay?

5. What is the TONE of this essay? The author has, no doubt, an ironic, even self-mocking, attitude toward her subject. But what is suggested by phrases such as "feeling better about the world beyond the text than we should have" (paragraph 10), "aging professors and parents" (paragraph 11), "good fucking riddance" (paragraph 12), and "anally-grammatical" (paragraph 14)?

6. In the final analysis, is Lynes's essay ARGUMENT or PERSUASION or a bit of both? Support your answer with specific references to her essay.

Content and Purpose

1. What is the primary question this essay attempts to answer? What is its THESIS?

2. Who are Trixie Belden and Nancy Drew (paragraph 1)? What do these names tell us about the author and the era she is writing about in this paragraph? What are they seen to be symbols of in paragraph 10?

3. What does the "heterogeneous mass of printed material" in her bedroom lead Lynes to conclude about herself? About the culture of the 1990s?

4. What is the first reason Lynes suggests is responsible for her (and our) inability to finish a single book at a time? Do you agree with her?

5. In paragraph 4, the author begins to develop other, "less simplistic" reasons to account for the "flipping from book to book" phenomenon. What are they? (See paragraphs 5 to 9.)

6. What is the result of this "combination of schizophrenia, information overload, and philosophical doubt" (paragraph 9)? Does the author think she is alone in experiencing this feeling? Do you share it?

7. The focus of paragraphs 10 to 15 shifts from an analysis of the causes of a social phenomenon to a critique of the "postmodern world." What is Lynes's objection to the "'serious' fiction and poetry" taught in college (paragraph 10)? What does Lynes argue about the possibility of specializing in, or even thoroughly learning, any single academic discipline? (See paragraph 11.)

8. What is the one thing, according to Lynes, that separates the work of a graffiti artist from that of a traditional novelist like Robertson Davies (paragraph 14)? Do you agree or disagree with the author on this point?

9. Lynes concludes her essay with a call to action. What "revolution" does she look forward to? What kinds of resistance and

action does she suggest for "egoless individuals" (paragraph 13) in a world that is "nothing but a patriarchal ethnocentric construct" (paragraph 12)? Do you find her argument persuasive?

Suggestions for Writing

1. When is the last time you read a book through from start to finish without significant interruption? What makes you want to finish a story rather than allow yourself to be distracted by other reading material or TV? Write an essay that describes the characteristics and the appeal of such a story.

2. Do you agree or disagree with Lynes's view of our "postmodern" society? Do we live in a world where the traditional economic and political structures, even the traditional college curriculum, are inherently oppressive because they deny "differences and otherness"? Write a convincing argument that explains your views on these complex issues.

Additional Suggestions for Writing: Argument and Persuasion

Choose one of the topics below and write an essay based on it. Think through your position carefully, formulate your opinion, and identify logical reasons for holding that opinion. Construct a clear thesis statement before you begin to write the paper.

1. Equal pay for work of equal value is (or is not) an impractical goal in Canada.
2. Canada Post should (or should not) provide home mail delivery to everyone.
3. The overall quality of Canadian life is improving (or declining).
4. Violence against an established government is (or is not) justified in certain circumstances.
5. Private religious schools should (or should not) receive government subsidies.
6. The federal government should (or should not) make significant changes to the unemployment insurance plan.
7. It is too easy (or too difficult) to get a divorce in Canada.
8. A teacher should (or should not) aim most of the course work at the weakest students in the class.
9. A couple should (or should not) live together before marriage.
10. Student papers should (or should not) be graded for quality of expression as well as for content.
11. The government of Canada should (or should not) decriminalize the use of "soft" drugs.
12. Blondes do (or do not) have more fun.
13. Boys and girls should (or should not) play on the same sports teams.
14. Critically ill patients should (or should not) be permitted to end their lives if and when they choose.
15. The government of Canada is (or is not) helpless to deal effectively with the depletion of fish stocks (or any other environmental hazard).
16. Physical education should (or should not) be compulsory for all able-bodied students throughout the high school years.
17. Fully subsidized day care is (or is not) in the best interests of the whole community.
18. A gay parent should (or should not) be eligible to gain custody of his or her children after a divorce.
19. Dishonesty is sometimes (is never) the best policy.
20. "It is a truth universally acknowledged that a single man in possession of a good fortune must be in want of a wife." (Jane Austen)

Further Reading

Cat Creek

ROBIN SKELTON

wasn't so much wandering that summer 1
as drifting. I had it in mind to explore the interior of British
Columbia and, while doing so, take a few photographs and maybe
write something or other. I told myself it was research, but it was,
in reality, a holiday, and I was enjoying it very much indeed, moving from place to place whenever I felt like it or the weather
changed or a faint stirring of conscience told me that exploration
consisted of more than spending the day driving around back roads
and the evenings sitting in beer parlours. The beer parlours were, in
fact, the most interesting part of my experience. After all, 20 ruined
cabins add little more to the stock of human knowledge than two or
three, while in the beer parlour, there was usually some old-timer
willing to tell improbable and garbled tales and to hint of lost gold
mines, hidden caches and sometimes even undiscovered murders.

It was in one such beer parlour that I met an old-timer who 2
particularly interested me. He was, or had been, a Yorkshireman
and was about as old as the century. He had come over from
England in the lean years of the late '20s, drawn by stories of gold,

and had indeed worked as a placer miner and in the Bullion and other mines before settling down to being a ranch hand. Like many Yorkshiremen—and Irishmen and Scots too, for that matter—he had retained his original accent, though it was somewhat flavoured with Canadian terms and expressions. One such expression caught my attention particularly. We were sitting together in a corner of the beer parlour, watching a large young man, rather loud in the voice and even louder in his shirting, buying drinks for a party of friends and acquaintances and talking of his plans to go back to university in the fall and how great it would be. He played some sort of game, I gathered, and hinted, if comments made at the top of one's voice can ever be called hints, that he had received offers to "go professional." The old-timer looked him over sardonically. "Ah," he said, "he's taking gold from Cat Creek, that one is!"

3   It was an expression new to me. I said, "What do you mean?" "It's a thing they used to say," he told me, "in the old days up Likely way. Taking gold from Cat Creek! Aye!" and he chuckled. "There's a story about Cat Creek?" I hazarded, waving a finger to get more beer, and he said slowly, "You could call it a story, I reckon." I knew by now that there was no use putting the question direct, so I took a pull at my beer and waited, and he took a pull at his. "It was around '31 or maybe '32," he said at last. "This chap had a little place a bit from the lake, a good-sized cabin, and he was well suited with it. He'd been placer mining, had done well with it and then retired, you might say. He wasn't old, though. About 40. Young, really. Maybe that was the trouble." I sat in my chair, and gradually, with many small digressions, he told the story.

4   He explained that the man, who was known generally as Black Joe, though his actual name was James Weatherby, had got his nickname not only because of his black hair but also because of his disposition. He was one of those saturnine creatures who could not bear to give anyone a civil word, and he was inordinately proud of the cabin he had built, of the small garden he had made beside the little creek and of the neatness of everything in his establishment. He had been, like many miners in those days and earlier, a merchant seaman, and the obsessive neatness that seems to become part of the character of many sailors used to living in small cabins, where everything must have its proper place, had become part of his character also. He was a proud man (turkey-proud, the old-timer said) and the more so because his cabin was unlike any other in the country, in its spit and polish and in its garden. The garden was indeed very attractive. Unlike the majority, he had chosen to make a flower garden rather than one for vegetables, and in order to defeat the long winter, he had even constructed a small

glasshouse (a greenhouse, the old-timer called it), which he kept heated with a stove. He'd planted a lot of bulbs on both banks of the little creek that ran through his property. The creek had a name, an Indian name, which meant something like "hurrying water that runs shallow"—it was a very small creek—but naturally, it was generally known as Black Joe Crick, though he called it Weatherby Creek and tried without success to get the name on the maps. Though Black Joe's cabin was set back a good way from the lake and fairly isolated, there were a good many people wandering the area in those days, most of them either prospecting or looking for work, so he sometimes had visitors, whom he invariably made totally unwelcome. He was the kind of man that keeps a dog to chase visitors away, but he didn't have a dog, because dogs dig in gardens and bury bones and generally cause untidiness. He was a very tidy man.

One day in the summer of '31 or '32, another man moved into   5 the country and took up a place on the same little creek, only higher up, and built a cabin there. He was an Irishman, and he was working in Bullion. He had a good job there, but he didn't like living near the mine, so he built this place for his wife and himself. He was called Red Connolly because he had bright ginger hair, and what is more, his wife had ginger hair too, of that vivid kind that you see sometimes in Ireland among the travelling people. As if two lots of ginger hair in the house were not enough, they had a big ginger cat, a huge thing. It must have been almost the only cat in the district. People didn't go in for cats much round there in those days, at least not outside the larger settlements and the ranches. Anyway, this great cat was a wanderer and spent a lot of time roaming the bush and even more in sitting by the creek. It used to take a drink by dipping its paw into the water and then licking it. It had huge green eyes and the sort of tail you'd see on a fox, big, bright and bushy.

Black Joe and Red Connolly didn't get on at all well. For one   6 thing, when Red Connolly was building, all sorts of debris would come floating down and often beach on Black Joe's land where there was a bend in the creek, and for another thing, Red Connolly's wife played the harmonium, and the two cabins weren't so far apart that Black Joe couldn't hear *The Wearing of the Green* and *Finnegan's Wake* coming at him through the trees, which irritated him to the point of frenzy. He'd been in the Black and Tans after World War I and had no love of the Irish. He himself came from Ilkley in the West Riding of Yorkshire (the old-timer pronounced it Ilkla), where there was little singing in the pubs except on Saturday nights and those devoted to music took it out on Handel's *Messiah* once a year round Christmas. All this, however, was as nothing to the irritation caused by the cat. In the early morning and evening, when it felt a natural urge coming on, it would sneak down along the bank of the creek to the softest and most accommodating piece of earth for its purpose, which was Black Joe's garden, and there, after performing its functions with healthy thoroughness, it would scrabble the earth over the deposit with such zeal and energy as to uproot bulbs and smother new shoots. Occasionally, it would thoughtfully urinate over one of the most promising spikes of green. Its attraction to green may perhaps have been due to the Irish in it; who can tell?

7   Black Joe cursed, threw things and generally tried to make life difficult for it, but that ginger cat was the match for any man, and Black Joe found himself spending more time than he liked not only tidying up after the cat but also picking up the things he had thrown which, in truth, often did more damage than the cat had done.

8   This could not go on forever, obviously. One morning, Black Joe rigged up a snare near one of the most promising of his plants and sat in the cabin waiting for the evening visitation. It all occurred just as he had hoped. Just as the dusk was deepening into dark, he heard a great yowl and ran out and found the cat snared by the back leg. He didn't want to make a mess by clubbing the beast, so he got a sack out of the glasshouse and a few stones, tied the cat in the sack, along with the stones, and dumped the thing into the creek, just at the bend where there was a deep bit. Then he went to bed. He had a restless night, it seems. That yowl kept on coming back to him in his dreams, but as it gave him more satisfaction than anything else to recall his victory, he wasn't too disturbed.

9   The next morning, he went down to the creek, reclaimed the bundle and took out the dead cat and buried it in his compost heap. Then he laid the sack out to dry in the sun and put the stones back on the rockery he was making under the cabin window. He was a very neat man indeed.

10   It wasn't long before Red Connolly's wife came down by the creek to enquire after her cat. Black Joe was unusually polite. He said he hadn't seen the cat, and he'd keep an eye open for it. He said it might have got caught in a trap. He wasn't a good liar. The woman looked him over and told him that if that cat didn't turn up, she'd know who to thank for it and that he'd come to regret what he'd done. She was a tall woman, big-boned and with one of those white, freckled faces that go with red hair, and that morning, her face was so white, the freckles stood out like little spots of brown fire. Red Connolly himself did and said nothing. It looked as

if the incident was over, though the tunes the woman chose for her harmonium that day and the following days were more mournful than usual, even a little eerie. They reminded Black Joe of bagpipe music, he said. They wailed a good deal.

It's hard to say what put it into Black Joe's head to straighten the course of the creek that summer. It may have been that the bend in it was still causing debris to land on his property, or it may be just that being a tidy man, he liked the idea of a creek that ran straight rather than crooked. Anyway, he decided to try and take the kink out of it just at the point where he had drowned the cat. He started by cutting into what you might call the inside of the elbow and putting what he took out over onto the other side. It was slow work because of the rocks, but he went at it with energy, and by noon, he had got a good deal done. He took a little time off, then, and would probably have taken longer had not the harmonium started up in the woods behind him, wailing quite indescribably. It was probably some of that Irish music they call traditional, which usually means half tuneless and half tangled. He decided that he would do well to work out his irritation with the pickaxe and shovel and so started to work again, and by the time evening had come and the music suddenly stopped, he was feeling quite cheerful. It was just as the light was beginning to go that he made his discovery. He had decided to take another shovelful out at the bottom of the bank, when he saw a gleam. He bent down and scrabbled for it and found he had a nugget about the size of a small broad bean. He left his shovel and pickaxe where they were, a most uncharacteristic thing for him to do, and went back to the cabin and looked at it under the lamp. It was a funny shape, like most nuggets are, I expect, and an imaginative man might have seen something odd about it. Black Joe wasn't an imaginative man. He'd made his small fortune by mining, and nuggets meant money to him more than they meant romance. If he'd shown it to anybody then, it's likely that someone would have spotted what it was, or at least what it looked like, but naturally, he kept his discovery dark, and the following day, he was very busy attending to all the things necessary to ensuring that he had absolute title to whatever gold he could get out of his creek and the land around it.

Nobody can keep a gold strike quiet, however, and in no time at all, there were prospectors all up and down that creek, except on Black Joe's land and Red Connolly's property above it. Red Connolly said he wasn't interested in working his own claim, he got enough pay for working in Bullion. But he made sure nobody else could move in on him, nevertheless.

Black Joe worked hard for the next few days, but he got very little for it. He got more than anyone else on the creek, however, for he found several very small nuggets—worth practically nothing, admittedly, but promising a good deal, and nobody else found anything. He dug back from the creek into his garden and then took down the glasshouse and dug there. Every day, he found something but never much. It was not like anything he'd come across before. The gold seemed to be scattered at random; there were no big or even medium-sized pockets of it, just occasional tiny nuggets and, once in a while, one as big as a dried pea. He'd got a good sluice box working by now, using the waters of the creek from higher up, diverting it by way of a flume he'd built. Before long, however, he reached the upper end of his land, and it looked to him as if it was Red Connolly's property that had the real stuff in it. The nuggets seemed to be more frequent farther up the creek, certainly. He found it hard to approach Connolly, but at last, he did so. He asked him first if he could stake out a claim or two on his land. Connolly told him no. Then he suggested a partnership, since Connolly wasn't willing to work the property himself. Connolly said no. By this time, Black Joe was in a state that bordered on fury, but he managed to restrain himself long enough to ask if Connolly had any mind to sell out. Connolly said he'd ask his wife and they'd think about it.

14   That night, Black Joe counted up what he had got so far and found that he'd taken out roughly $200 in three weeks' hard work and that he'd spent maybe half of that on equipment and on paying the two Chinese he'd got in to help him after the first few days. A sensible man might have stopped there, but Black Joe was lost to sense by that time. He went to the bank and drew out his money, and he went up to Red Connolly and slapped it all down on the table and said, "Will this buy you out?" Red Connolly looked at him. The wife looked at him. The wife said, in a voice curiously gentle for her, "We might as well, Sean. I've never liked it much here since the cat went." So that was it. Black Joe got the Connolly property. The Connollys moved down nearer Bullion mine, and the very next day, Black Joe and his two Chinese set to work.

15   They found nothing, of course. Not a speck of gold was anywhere to be found, and after a couple of weeks, Black Joe let the Chinese go and went on himself. The rest of it you can guess. Black Joe ran out of money and time and sold first Connolly's cabin and then his own and finally abandoned the whole operation. He hung on to the first nugget he found until the very end. Then he sold it in a beer parlour and went on down to Victoria.

16   At this point, the old-timer paused. I guessed he was expecting a question, and I thought I knew what it was. "So they called the creek after the cat?" I hazarded. "Not exactly," he said slowly, "more like after the nugget. Do you want to see it?" and he put his hand in

his vest pocket and brought out a little washleather bag and spilled a nugget onto his palm. "See!" he said. "That's the cat nugget. That's why they call it Cat Creek. And why they say when anyone blathers a lot, like that chap ower theer, or when folks spend a deal of time on something useless, they're taking gold out of Cat Creek. Here. Take a look." I took it in my hand. I turned it this way and that. It was a nugget all right. There was no doubt about that. But try as I might, I couldn't see that it looked like a cat at all.

ROBIN SKELTON

Born in England in 1925, Robin Skelton emigrated to Canada in 1963. Professor of English at the University of Victoria, Skelton is a poet, editor, biographer, and literary critic who has published more than 80 books. His special interests range from English and Irish literature to the literature of the Pacific Northwest, the visual arts, and the occult. A practising artist, he is also an initiated witch and an authority on spellcraft.

The Softball Was Always Hard

HARRY BRUCE

When I tell young softball players I played the game barehanded, they regard me warily. Am I one of those geezers who's forever jawing about the fact that, in *his* day, you had to walk through six miles of snowdrifts just to get to school? Will I tediously lament the passing of the standing broad jump, and the glorious old days when the only football in the Maritimes was English rugger, when hockey was an outdoor art rather than indoor mayhem and, at decent yacht clubs, men were gentlemen and women were *personae non grata*? No, but I will tell today's softball players that—with their fancy uniforms, batters' helmets, dugouts, manicured diamonds, guys to announce who's at bat over public-address systems and, above all, gloves for every fielder—the game they play is more tarted-up and sissy than the one I knew.

2   Softball bloomed in the Dirty Thirties because it was a game the most impoverished deadbeat could afford to play. For schools, it had the edge that soccer still has over North American football: it required no expensive equipment. It was the people's game in the worst of times. Unlike baseball, which calls for a field the size of a town, softball could flourish in one corner of a city park, on a vacant lot, in any schoolyard. The only gear you needed was a ball, a bat, a catcher's glove and mask, and a first baseman's glove, a floppy affair which I knew as a "trapper." Two amiable teams might even use the same gloves—two gloves for eighteen players.

3   In the Toronto grade school league of the Forties, gloves for all other players were outlawed. This meant that early in the season the hands of a boy shortstop felt as though a 300-lb. vice-principal had given him the strap. Any team that lasted long enough to reach the city finals, however, boasted little infielders with palms like saddle-leather. They learned to catch a line drive with both hands, not by snaring it with a glove big enough to hold a medicine ball. They cushioned the ball by drawing back their cupped hands at the split-second of impact. They fielded sizzling grounders by turning sideways, dropping one knee to the ground, getting their whole bodies in front of the ball, then scooping it up, again with both small, bare hands.

4   A word about balls. The *New Columbia Encyclopedia* says, "Despite the name, the ball used is not soft," which may be the understatement of the tome's 3,052 pages. There were three kinds of softballs, and each was about as soft as anthracite. The best was simply a big baseball, with seams that were pretty well flush with the horsehide cover. Then there was a solid rubber ball with fake seams. After a while, this ball did soften up, but on grounds it no longer hurt enough for competition, it was then retired for use only in practice. Then there was the "outseam" ball. Perhaps it was not a sadist who invented it. Perhaps it was merely someone who sought durability in lean times. But the outseam was a quarter-inch ridge of leather so hard that, when you fielded a rifling, spinning grounder, the ball felt as though its real function was to rip the skin off our palms. The outseam ball was a character-builder.

5   We had no uniforms, but if you reached the city finals team sweaters might magically emerge from some secret cache in the school basement. Certain coaches had the stern theory that even these were bad news, that boys would be so captivated by their own spiffy appearance they'd lose that vital concentration on the game itself, and commit errors. Some boys played in the only shoes they owned, scampers or black oxfords. Others had beaten-up sneakers and, on most teams, some wore short pants and some

long. But these youngsters, gangs or ragamuffins by today's standards of sartorial elegance in softball, played furiously competitive, heads-up ball.

If you played outside the school system, for a team sponsored by a camera shop, dairy, hardware store or greasy spoon, then you did get a sweater. You swaggered in it. You'd earned it. Not every kid was good enough to make a team with sweaters. They were advertisements of ability. Nowadays, of course, any kid with the money can buy an Expos' jacket or a Pirates' cap. They're merely advertisements of disposable income, much like the $25 million worth of gear that the chains of athletic-shoe stores expected to sell in Canada during recession-ridden 1982.

But as a celebrator of softball austerity, I am a pipsqueak beside an eighty-year-old tycoon I know. As a boy in a Nova Scotia coal-mining town, he played cricket and street baseball with home-made bats and balls. To make a ball, boys hoarded string and wrapped it around a rock, or if they were lucky a small rubber ball. "We made very good balls," he said, "and we had just as much fun as kids have today with all their expensive stuff." In line with Canada's hoariest hockey tradition, he added, "We used a piece of frozen manure for a puck. It worked just about as good." It wasn't as durable as rubber, but in those days there was no shortage of horse poop.

I once played with a home-made baseball myself. Indeed, I placed the order for its construction. In the summer of '46, when I turned twelve, my father exiled me from Toronto to spend two months at the Bruce homestead on a Nova Scotian shore. That shore, even now, is as sleepy a spot as you're ever likely to find. Not even most Nova Scotians know where it is. But in 1946, the community was not merely remote, it was an anachronism. It hadn't changed much since Victoria had been queen, and to a kid from what he fancied as a bustling, modern metropolis, its empty beauty was at first desolating. This was the ultimate sticks, the boondocks with a vengeance, and I worked off my loneliness by playing catch with myself. Hour after hour, I hurled a Toronto tennis ball against a bluenose barn, catching it on the rebound.

Then I discovered potential ballplayers.

They lived on the farm next door. They were a big, cheerful family, and my knowing them then started my lifelong love affair with the neighbourhood. As things are unfolding now, I'll end up there for good. Anyway, several of these farm kids—the oldest was a gentle man of fifteen who, with one paralysing hand, pinned me to a hayfield while I endured the sweet, excruciating humiliation of having his giggling, thirteen-year-old sister plant saliva on my face—were old enough to play a form of softball. Amazingly, however, they'd never played it, nor seen it. They'd never even heard the word.

11   I told the fifteen-year-old a softball bat was *this* long, and *this* thick at one end, and *this* thin at the other. He made one in half an hour. It wasn't exactly a Louisville Slugger but it had heft to it, and at the same time it was light enough to enable the smaller kids to take a good cut at the ball. What ball? My tennis ball had split. When I knowledgeably declared that the heart of a real baseball was cork, the fifteen-year-old took me down to the stony shore to negotiate with a character I've preserved in memory as "the Ball-maker." He was a hermit who had just given up commercial fishing on his own. He would never again sail the small schooner he'd built, and she'd begun to rot where she lay, a few feet closer to Chedabucto Bay than the ramshackle hut where he somehow survived the seasons.

12   He was a "beach person," as surely as the salt-stunted spruce were beach trees, and therefore disreputable. If he had known women they had not been church-going women. He was thin, stooped, gnarled, and smelled as though he'd been embalmed in brine, rum, tar, tobacco juice, his own sweat and sinister doings. There was something wrong with one of his eyes and some of his fingers, and though he may only have been as old as I am now (forty-eight), I thought he was ancient enough, and certainly evil enough, to have slit throats for Blackbeard.

13   The Ball-maker conversed with grunts, snarls, illogical silences, and an accent so thick that, to me, it was a foreign language. But we struck a deal. He gave me a dime. If I would walk inland, following a brookside path through a forest of spruce and fir, and on past a sawmill to a general store, and if I would use the dime to buy him a plug of chewing tobacco and, further, if I would then take the tobacco to him ... well, he would meanwhile sculpt a baseball-sized sphere of cork. And he did. He fashioned it from three pieces: a thick, round disc and two polar caps, all jammed together with a single spike. That ball was so flawless it was spooky. I can still see it and feel it in my hand, a brown globe so perfect I wondered if the Ball-maker was a warlock.

14   Back at my friend's farm, we encased the cork in scratchy manila twine till we had something bigger than a hardball but smaller than a softball. For bases, we dropped sweaters among the cowflaps in a pasture, and the lesson began. We would play the kind of teamless ball that's been known in a million schoolyards; as each batter went out, the fielders would all change positions to guarantee that every player got a crack at batting. As the ace from Toronto, I naturally led off. Trouble was, I adored the afternoon's first pitcher. It was she who'd kissed me in the hayfield.

She had hair like a blonde waterfall, eyes like dark chocolate, and 15 skin I ached to touch and smell. Whenever we wrestled, she won. I still dislike that adult sneer, "puppy love." A boy of twelve can love a girl of thirteen with agonizing power. To make matters worse, he hasn't a hope in hell of even understanding the emotion that's racking his skinny being, much less satisfying it. All he knows is that she obsesses him, he yearns for her, he must always appear fine in her eyes.

She had never pitched in her life so it surprised me when she 16 tossed her waterfall in the sunlight and floated the ball gently into the strike zone. Her first pitch. It crept towards me, letter-high. It could have been hanging there in front of me on a string from the sky, and I stepped into it with all the style I'd learned from a hundred Toronto afternoons. Thwack! A line drive so fast no one saw it, and down she went. She crumpled in a heap of blouse, skirt, hair and bare, beloved arms and legs. I had smacked her with the cursed, hairy ball square on her right eye. Her big brother got her sitting up, and we all huddled round her, with me bleating horrified apologies. She never cried. She managed a smile, got to her feet, and shakily went home.

When she turned up for our second game, she had the ugliest 17 black eye I have ever seen on a child. To me, it was a beauty mark. She never blamed me for it. It became a bond, proof of a famous incident we'd shared. She was a tough, forgiving farm girl, and she and her brothers and sisters taught me something I'd not forget about the rough grace of the country folk down home. We played ball for weeks. We played till we pounded the ball to bits, till her eye was once more perfect, and summer was gone.

The car that drove me to the train station passed their farm. 18 Sheets on the clothesline billowed in the usual southwesterly. With her brothers and sisters, she was horsing around with their wolfish mutt. They stopped to watch the car moving along the dirt road, and then they all waved goodbye. I was glad they were too far away to see my face. I still lacked her control.

I have my own cabin on that shore now, and though most of 19 those farmyard ballplayers of thirty-seven summers ago have moved away I still see one of them occasionally. He's a mere forty-six, and I like him now as I liked him then. Sometimes I walk along the gravel beach to a patch of grass, from which a footpath once led to a general store. The Ball-maker's shack is gone, but gray planks and ribs and rusty boat nails still endure the lashing of the salt wind that ceaselessly sweeps the bay. They're all that's left of his schooner. Wrecked by time, like bare-handed softball.

HARRY BRUCE

Harry Bruce, journalist and essayist, was born in Toronto. He has written for the country's leading magazines and newspapers. *Each Moment As It Flies* is a collection of articles and essays. Bruce now makes his home in Halifax.

Her Story, His Story

DENISE CHONG

1   May-ying had never expected that she would have a say in whom she married; no girl or boy did in traditional Chinese society. Marriage was a union between two families and was too important to be left to the whim of the young. Besides, love was not a consideration. In fact, it was seen as a threat to the husband's family, because it would undermine the authority of the mother over her new daughter-in-law. In arranging their children's marriages, parents were most concerned about avoiding any mismatch between the two family backgrounds that might create problems, envy or embarrassment between the families. That was best ensured by a matchmaker, typically an elderly lady from one of the surrounding villages. As well as asking the gods to pronounce on the auspiciousness of a match, she would act as a messenger in negotiations over the dowry (if the girl's family was better off than the boy's), or (if his was the better-off family), the bride-price to be paid.

2   Auntie was not May-ying's real aunt. Born in 1907 into the Leong family, May-ying came from Nam Hoy, one of four counties that comprised the city of Canton and its outskirts, in the province of Kwangtung in south China. As such, she carried a strain of superiority; the people from these four counties were the original native Cantonese, whose dialect and ways were considered more refined than those of peasants further afield. But May-ying's first fall from grace was to be born a girl. No one is glad when a daughter is born; a girl is "someone else's," a mouth to feed until she marries and goes to live in another household. Sons, on the other hand, live at home even after they are married. May-ying's double curse was to be a girl born into a poor family, although not so poor that they drowned or abandoned her at birth.

"Her Story, His Story" from *The Concubine's Children: Portrait of a Family Divided* by Denise Chong. Copyright 1994 by Denise Chong. Reprinted with the permission of Sterling Lord Associates.

She stayed with her family until she was perhaps four; she 3
could remember her mother trying to apply the first bandages to
bind her feet. The practice of binding a young girl's growing bones
had been dying out in China, especially in the south where the
peasant economy needed girls and women to work in the fields.
But some clung to the practice as a way for their daughters to
escape becoming beasts of burden. Diminutive feet, the ultimate
sexual allure, would have elevated May-ying into a social class
where women were artful objects. When hard times struck, as they
surely would, and the family was without rice, her mother might
have hoped to sell her daughter as a child-bride, to have some say
over her future husband. It was not to be. Because of May-ying's
cries of protest, her feet were unbandaged. "Auntie," a stranger,
bought her as a servant.

When May-ying turned seventeen and of marrying age, she 4
was ready to be sold again. Auntie was aware that her girl-servant's
looks would command a high bride-price. No man or woman who
first came upon May-ying could help but stare fixedly at this tiny
figure of a girl, who stood no higher than the average person's chin.
Her delicate features, the bright round eyes and the much admired
heart-shaped mouth, were set in pale skin that had retained its
translucence because Auntie's chores had kept her out of the fields
and out of the baking sun. But for her unbound feet, she had the
body and features much imitated in Chinese porcelain dolls.

May-ying had been squatting over a basin in the courtyard 5
washing Auntie's clothes when she was summoned inside. A stool
was offered, tea poured. May-ying was immediately suspicious; a
mistress does not serve her servant.

"*Ah* Ying, I have found you a *ho muen how*," Auntie declared. 6

A girl expected there to come a day when she would hear these 7
words, announcing a good doorway to another house, that of her
future mother-in-law. The question was where; she wondered if she
would be staying in Auntie's village.

"Where is it, Auntie?" 8

Auntie hesitated. "It is in *Gum San*," she said. 9

"What?!" May-ying could not believe her ears or bite her tongue. 10
"What am I hearing?" Gold Mountain was another continent, a foreign land of white ghosts. Her tone said it was unthinkable that she
would be sent to live in North America. "I don't want to go!"

Auntie had expected the news to come as a shock. She herself 11
had been persuaded only when she saw the bride-price offered. She
took it as a sign that the claims of prosperity in Gold Mountain
were no exaggeration.

"The man is from Heung San," Auntie said, naming the 12
province's county of rice farmers, further south along the Pearl River

estuary. "He has been living in *Gum San* for some years. People living in *Gum San* have wealth and riches; they have to push the gold from their feet to find the road." She met May-ying's eyes. "I am only doing what is best for you. I want you to have *on lock cha fan*."

13   May-ying heard the echo of these words in her head. Her mother had used these same words of farewell. She too had wished her a life of contentment, a life never short of tea or rice. It only reminded May-ying of that tearful parting.

14   In a flash of temper, May-ying kicked the table legs. He's only a peasant, she said. Why couldn't Auntie find a boy from a decent family near Canton? She shoved the table top, splashing the tea. She repeated that she did not want to go, that she did not want to eat rice from a strange land. Auntie was dismayed; she had warned May-ying many times that her quick temper would enslave her to her heart.

15   Auntie had to shout to make herself heard: "You are not going for good." May-ying glared and waited for what had been held back. "He has a *Dai-po* in Heung San," Auntie continued, "and he wants to have a *chip see* in *Gum San*."

16   The effect was more cruel than if May-ying had been told no family would have her. Stunned to hear that she was to join the household of a man already married, that she was to be a concubine, at his whim and in the servitude of his wife, May-ying knew it would be taken as a mark against herself. No decent girl became a concubine, married off in shame without wedding or ceremony. On the other hand, the more concubines a man had, the more prestige and social status he garnered. His parents chose his wife, but he himself recruited his concubines, often from a face he fancied in a brothel.

17   May-ying's ebony eyes flashed a familiar accusing look at Auntie. "Then I might just as well stay in China and be a prostitute," she snapped.

18   At such a stinging rebuke of ungratefulness, such disrespect for the match she had made, Auntie thundered back, "I will not hear any more of this nonsense. When I say go out the door, you will go!"

19   It was early in 1924 by the western calendar when May-ying was married off. Her rebellion was useless; in the Confucian way of thinking, a girl has no authority of her own. She does as she is told. The choice was that or suicide. The village gossip would cast Auntie as the tyrant and May-ying as a girl wronged only if she took her own life, if her body were discovered floating near the stilt-houses over the Pearl River at the village's edge, or hanging from a beam in Auntie's house.

Auntie grew excited about helping May-ying make prepara-   20
tions to leave. She engaged a photographer to record May-ying's
new identity. The photograph had to conform with the age on the
false birth certificate. Perhaps feeling guilty that there would be no
wedding biscuits to distribute to the villagers, no double-happiness
cutouts to hang from the doorways of her house, Auntie hired a tai-
lor to sew two *cheong sams* for May-ying as her going-away present.
May-ying's outburst forgiven if not forgotten, Auntie reveled in
repeating tales of Chinese men going to Gold Mountain and harvesting the money trees and coming home rich men with prestige.
She imagined May-ying, once she came back to China, living in one
of the large houses of the wealthy, where the rooftops are all that is
visible over the wall around the compound. She imagined a harmonious household, where the man's first wife, instead of being jealous, encouraged concubinage. "She will choose you over the other
concubines to serve her," said Auntie. "She will prefer you to occupy the master's bed, you will be the one to produce the sons."

A Chinese knows only one thing for certain: that danger and   21
evil spirits lurk everywhere. According to Chinese belief, jade and
gold are the only talismans, and the more they come handed down,
the more power they have to bestow good luck. May-ying's dangling earrings had been worn by her mother. The pendant, a flawless baize-green jade inlaid in gold, had been retrieved from the coffin of her mother's mother, and was even more precious. She left
Auntie's house as she had left her mother's, with these pieces sewn
inside her clothing.

May-ying's outward journey began by sampan, hailed from   22
among the many plying the Pearl River. After a day downstream,
slowed by the crowd of boat people living on the river, they arrived
in Canton. There, May-ying had her first glimpse of the ancient
trading city, flagstoned lanes choked with shops selling everything
from firecrackers and ready-made herb preparations to sandalwood
and rattan. On the train trip from there to Hong Kong, she peered
out the window as rice fields gave way to a city hinting of people
with greater ambitions. The middleman accompanying her delivered her to an address on Des Voeux Road, and another man there
delivered her to the ship. The officers of the Blue Funnel Steamship
Line found her papers in order, stamped them and accepted her for
passage.

After eighteen days at sea, the ship steamed into the port of   23
Vancouver. Mountains and sea seemed to diminish man's efforts at
fashioning this young cityscape. Among the wide-eyed disembark-
ing passengers was a tiny girl, who, but for her mature hairstyle,
looked too young to have left home. Her birth certificate said she

was born in Ladner, British Columbia. The fertile farmland of the Fraser Valley just outside Vancouver was dotted with Chinese laboring in the fields for white farmers. Presuming she was one of the new generation of Chinese born in Canada, immigration officials accepted her false papers, and the girl who had left her Chinese homeland as Leong May-ying was waved through as the woman Chung Gim-ching returning to her native Canada. "Such a pretty girl alone?" asked the interpreter. No, she was being met, she said, by her husband.

...

24   One Chinese man waiting for the passenger ship to dock at the pier at the foot of Granville Street stood out from the crowd by virtue of his nearly six-foot frame. He had a body that was all limbs, long even in his fingers, which gave his every gesture an elongated emphasis. A fedora graced his head, and he was attired in a custom-tailored three-piece gray suit. His shoes and wire-rimmed glasses were polished and his black hair meticulously combed to expose a high forehead, a physical trait the Chinese considered a sign of intelligence. He owned two suits—one gray, the other brown—and two fedoras. Believing one's appearance mirrored one's inner mind, his appearance today was, as always, immaculate. His manner, like his dress, was sober and serious. At thirty-seven, he was a year younger than the city of Vancouver.

25   A few Chinese were among the waiting crowd of whites, some of their faces familiar to Chan Sam. But he had no desire to squander time in conversation with someone to whom he had no loyalties. He returned to studying that day's *Chinese Times*, to a report of a speech given by a Canadian-born Chinese in Victoria calling for political reform in the homeland. He underlined the characters he did not know; in this way he added two or three new characters each day to his written vocabulary.

26   The dock scene was a marked contrast to what it had been like when Chan Sam himself had first stepped onto this same pier in 1913, eleven years earlier. Today, the Chinese dressed in western dress. Back then, he was one of the few among his compatriots who had spilled off the packed freighter not in mandarin-collared jackets, pajama-like trousers and sandals. Chan Sam had arrived in a western tailored suit. But it had made no difference to his reception; along with the other arriving Chinese, he was herded into a dockside low brick building to spend three months in quarantine behind barred windows and under guard. Despite their protests that they had already stood naked in a line for examination by the white doctor on board ship, the men were fumigated with sulfur, and so were

their belongings. Inside the packed and filthy "pigpen," as the Chinese called it, amid the noise from trains rumbling into the adjacent western terminus of the transcontinental railway, it had been hard for them to keep fast their belief in Gold Mountain's fairy tales, spun from men before them who'd gone to make their fortunes.

They were men from the delta of the Pearl River in Kwangtung 27 province, where seafarers were folk heroes. In the eighteenth century, Canton had been the only Chinese port open to foreigners. Ever since the arrival there of foreign traders offering to exchange opium from India for Chinese silk and tea, distant shores had meant adventure. In 1848, gold was struck in Sacramento, California, and the race was on across the Pacific to Gold Mountain. More Chinese left in 1862, in a second dash for gold up British Columbia's Fraser River to Barkerville. Many, when pushed off the better claims by white prospectors, stayed on to cook and wash clothes, and early Chinatowns sprang up and thrived. Anti-Chinese feelings intensified, and whites up and down North America's west coast began lobbying local governments—state, provincial, municipal—to stem the flow of arriving Chinese and to make it clear to those already there that they were unwelcome. In the 1870s and 1880s, there were limits on the number of incoming Chinese per boat, bans against hiring men with pigtail-length hair and against the use of poles to carry baskets. There were special taxes levied on the Chinese for school and policing, employment, laundry, shoes and even cigars. Worse was to come. Chinese were soon barred from becoming naturalized citizens, from owning land, from working on public works.

Such distaste for the Chinese presence did not deter white con- 28 tractors who were looking for cheap labor to carve out the great transcontinental railways across the United States and Canada. Their governments bought their claim that the Chinese would work for much less and were more reliable than the available white labor, mostly Irish. Though many Chinese, assigned the most dangerous jobs, died building the railway, racist resentment sped along the newly built iron rails. Whites in the east railed against the inevitable eastward settlement of a race they condemned as alien, steeped in moral depravity and degradation.

The Chinese continued to arrive—fathers, uncles, sons and 29 brothers of those who had come before. One was Chan Sam's father. His voyage from China to San Francisco was financed by his clan society in his home county. During his sojourn abroad, he met his own expenses and his wife's at home and still returned home for a visit every third year, three times in all. To further distinguish his name, he more than repaid his debt to his clan society by soliciting overseas donations to help build an ancestral hall.

30   Luck was with him in that he first landed in America before the United States Congress passed the historic Chinese Exclusion Act of 1882. That act gave in to the most fanatical of those lobbying against the Chinese presence and slammed the door shut to new arrivals. Only diplomats, certain scholars and import-export merchants holding temporary visas were to be allowed in. The effect was to condemn Chinese men already in the country to a life abroad without the possibility of their families joining them. The male-female ratio in Chinatowns, already primarily bachelor societies, would change only with the birth of its American-born children. Lest any Chinese try to sneak in by way of Canada, the Americans posted guards at the border.

31   In 1888, Chan Sam's father was back in China cradling him, his firstborn child. That same year, Congress suddenly declared void all Certificates of Return, which had allowed previous sojourners to reenter the United States. Chan Sam's father was grateful that his years abroad had been fat. He had made ten times what he might have had he not gone, enough to buy some thirty *mau tin* (one *mau tin* equals less than one-sixth of an acre of cultivated land), enough to have a second child, a third and a fourth.

32   The only door to the mythical Gold Mountain that the Chinese could still pry open was Canada's. But the Canadian government, aware that some Chinese saw it as a back door to the United States, sought to act in concert with the Americans. In 1885, it tried to put off the average Chinese laborer by imposing a fifty-dollar head tax upon entry. Merchants were exempted for fear they'd go south of the border. In 1904, in the same year that the United States extended its Exclusion Act indefinitely and broadened it to apply to Hawaii and the Philippines, then American possessions, the Canadian government raised the head tax to five hundred dollars.

33   Chinese men were desperate enough to leave China that they found ways to raise such sums. In 1913, when Chan Sam crossed the Pacific, he was one of seven thousand coming to Canada that year, a new high. Such numbers dismayed even the Canadian Chinese Benevolent Association, headquartered in Victoria's Chinatown, Canada's oldest. That year, in an urgent circular to Kwangtung province that was posted in county magistrate offices, the Association painted a picture of the Chinese in Canada as jobless, hungry and cold: "In a nutshell, it is better not to come." The Association's fear was that the Canadian government would overreact to the growing number of arrivals by driving out those already here. Exclusion was the Association's worst nightmare.

34   In Chan Sam's time, the destination of choice was Vancouver's Chinatown. The community had boomed along with the city. But so

too had anti-Chinese sentiment. Within the four to five square blocks of Vancouver's Chinatown, some three to four thousand Chinese, mostly men, lived and worked in virtual isolation from white society. No self-respecting white would be seen anywhere near Chinatown, believing it to be populated with shifty-eyed, pig-tailed Chinamen of the Fu Manchu and Charlie Chan movies showing in North American movie houses. The appetite for painting the Chinese as villains grew when First World War veterans came home to a depressed economy. Newspapers and politicians alike pandered to public hysteria, accusing the Chinese of stealing jobs from Canadian fathers. Chinatowns were denounced as dirty and disease-ridden, as centers of gambling and crime. Vancouver's was depicted in local newspaper editorial cartoons as a congestion of rooming houses, of unmarked doorways to a labyrinth where lascivious Chinamen smoked opium, lay with Chinese prostitutes, fed on rats and enslaved white girls. No one saw the contrasting truth, that there were, among the bachelors, a few upstanding families living there. These included the wives and children of the merchant class who could raise the money to pay for the five-hundred-dollar head tax on each family member, who could install them above their ground-floor businesses, and who could afford to send their children back to China for part of their education. Selling out their business was always an option too, if Canada got unbearably inhospitable, to pay for the family's passage home.

In 1923, the Canadian Chinese Benevolent Association's worst 35 nightmare came true. That year, the Canadian Parliament passed its own exclusionary law, the Chinese Immigration Act. The date it went into effect—July 1—the Chinese marked as "Humiliation Day." In reply to such hostility, many Chinese men went home for good. After ten years abroad, Chan Sam too could have abandoned his plan to sojourn abroad. But to do so would have led to a loss of face, for which he could not look himself in the mirror. Some might have called his pride a character flaw, except that showiness was almost expected of those coming back from Gold Mountain—a sign to others that the dream of riches abroad was still alive.

DENISE CHONG

Denise Chong (b. 1953) was born in Prince George, B.C., trained as an economist, and worked as political adviser to Pierre Elliott Trudeau before she pursued her interest in writing. Her articles have appeared in a number of Canadian magazines and anthologies. Her first book, *The Concubine's Children: Portrait of a Family Divided*, was published in 1994.

Watching the Grass Grow

DON GAYTON

1 At a certain microscopic scale, a leaf begins to lose its biological elegance and starts looking more like a clanking, humming factory. The factory image, in fact, is not far off the mark: a grass leaf is essentially a four-storey, double-sided, solar-driven manufacturing plant, suspended in space. The roof of this factory is made from thick, transparent cuticle cells. Just below the roof, on the fourth floor, is a palisade layer, where photosynthesis takes place. The third floor is the spongy mesophyll layer [which is] where transpiration occurs. The second and first floors form the underside of the leaf, and they are a rough mirror image of the third and fourth. The stomata on the upper and lower roof vent gases and vapors to and from the mesophyll layer to the outside. Xylem and phloem liquid supply lines come in through the utility space between the second and third floors.

2 The interior leaf mesophyll cells are not just the site of water evaporation, they are also the locus for the absorption or "fixation" of carbon dioxide. Plants snatch carbon dioxide from the air around them and transform it into everything from duckweed to hemlock.

3 Here in the mesophyll lies the often desperate exchange that green plants must make: for every bit of carbon dioxide they allow in through their stomata, they lose a dribble of precious water (as vapor) via the same route. The prevention of water loss comes at the expense of carbon gain, and the access to carbon is paid for by lost water. A classic dilemma.

4 I was ignorant of the importance of this plant reality when I first started work in the research greenhouse. One of my first experiments was to attach a delicately-balanced recording boom to an emerging grass leaf. The other end of the boom was attached to a tiny pen which recorded movement on a slowly rotating drum. Upward growth of the leaf allowed the boom to rise, and the pen at the other end would dutifully record that movement on graph paper wrapped around the drum. "Length" is very nearly synonymous with "growth" in grass, making it a good choice for this

experiment. My hypothesis was that leaf growth would start slowly just after sunrise, increase steadily until afternoon, and taper off to a halt at sundown.

When I pulled off the first inked charts I was innocently surprised. These plants grew all night! That violated all my childhood notions about photosynthesis. I redid the experiment with an even lighter boom, thinking that my apparatus was stretching the plants at night, like some medieval torture rack. Then I tried a different grass species, thinking that my first choice had been some sort of anomaly.

All the results were basically the same. Peak growth usually occurred around 11:00 in the morning, followed by a steep decline through the rest of the day and evening, but never a total cessation. Growth began to pick up again at about 2:00 in the morning, with a surge toward the midmorning peak. Puzzling this out, I realized that even with fully watered plants inside a greenhouse, the heat loads from direct summer sunlight could never be dissipated by transpirational cooling. On the average summer day, then, the factory closes its stomata pretty early, but opens them again in late evening. But how could these leaves be growing in pitch dark?

We have a traditional concept of growth as a single, integrated process, a factory with a single product. We try hard to be tolerant of other views of growth, but the expansion of a leaf or the increase of biomass is quite compelling. The plant itself does not share our interest in a single obvious growth process, relying instead on an ensemble of linked partial growth mechanisms.

One of these mechanisms, *carbon fixation*, requires reasonable temperatures, high ambient CO_2 levels, and open stomata to proceed. Fixation is indifferent to light or dark. Another partial process, *nutrient uptake*, requires open stomata, reasonable temperatures, and good soil moisture. It is also indifferent to light. *Photosynthesis*, the capture of light energy, requires light but is indifferent to temperature and water balance. *Sugar production* by the Calvin Cycle needs everything except light. All of these processes need energy, except photosynthesis, which produces it.

So it turns out that plant growth machinery is rarely idle. Except in periods of prolonged drought, cold, and darkness (e.g., Western Canadian winters) there is nearly always something to do.

Carbon fixation, nutrient uptake, photosynthesis, and sugar production are all major precursors to growth, but even growth itself is not a single process. *Cell division* is growth in theory, and can go on independent of sun or water, so long as photosynthate and reasonable temperatures are available. *Cell expansion* is growth in fact, the visible portion we are so keen to measure. It has its own set of specific requirements, namely a supply of recently-divided cells and a positive water balance, but is fairly indifferent to temperature and sunlight. So we arrive now at the basic heresy: plants need sunlight to manufacture the components for growth, but they don't need sunlight to grow.

11   Botanists, ecologists, and agronomists all search diligently for the single key parameter of plant development. Like industrial economists studying a factory, we look for some key integrator that best measures its performance. Volumes have been written, manifestations identified, methodology perfected, formulae promulgated and statistics prepared. But no single measurement of growth seems to hold sway very long. That early morning in the greenhouse taught me that a definition of plant growth is elusive.

12   We have all seen the time-lapse photography of the bean seedling unfolding, each frame showing the secret twists and turns as cotyledon leaves expand outward toward sunlight and destiny. But what we really need to visualize are the blurry instants between the stills.

DON GAYTON

A writer with degrees in agronomy and plant ecology, Don Gayton has been a community developer in Latin America, a hired man on cattle ranches, a steelyard worker, and an agricultural worker on First Nations reserves. He is currently a range manager in Nelson, B.C., and is the author of *The Wheatgrass Mechanism: Science and Imagination in the Western Canadian Landscape* (1990), a prize-winning collection of essays on land management in Canada.

Searching for Stevenson

ROHINTON MISTRY

1   A nd what would you like from Edinburgh?" I asked my friend; I was leaving shortly for the Book Festival there.

2   "Well," he said without stopping to think, as though the answer had been waiting a long time for the question, "a little bust

of Stevenson, if it's no trouble." Like me, my friend is a writer; unlike me, he is also a collector.

"No trouble," I said. "A wee bust of RLS it is, then."   3

The day after arriving in Edinburgh, I prepared to discharge my   4 duties at the Book Festival while the clouds discharged rain. I was scheduled to give a lunchtime reading. The Festival brochure assured its patrons that lunchtime readings were a real bargain: "The best value in town—the price of your ticket includes a filled roll." The comestible was the clincher that would tilt the undecided and send them rushing pell-mell to the reading.

What might it be like, I wondered, to look from stage height   5 upon rows of masticating mouths: would I be treated to privileged glimpses of mayonnaise, bits of lettuce, and shredded chicken? Would the rolls be crusty, thereby igniting a concatenation of crackles and crunches, and multiple mini-avalanches of crumbs? Would the aroma tickle my nostrils and make my stomach rumble? Would the rumbles be picked up by the microphone? Would there be toothpicks? Would I, in short, feel like some watcher of the skies when a new planet swims into his ken, or like stout Cortez, silent, upon a peak in Darien?

The proceedings of the entire Book Festival were being con-   6 ducted under canvas, in Charlotte Square Gardens. There was a jolly carnival atmosphere about the place. It managed to shrug off the rain shower that was now faintly thrumming a military tattoo on the seven or eight large tents. Just inside the entrance to the one where I was to read, a depleted platter sat upon a table of white ash. Looking somewhat abandoned, three forlorn filled rolls rubbed elbows within the platter's vast expanse.

I scanned the audience from the back of the tent and noted with   7 relief that the edible section of the lunchtime reading was mostly consumed. My gastronomic fears had been unfounded—only one person was still chewing. And when it was time to take the stage, the stubby end of that final filled roll, too, had performed its vanishing trick.

The rain continued to practise restrained drumrolls as I read   8 from my novel. Every now and then a wind gust, whipping the drizzle, broke the monotony of the rhythm by injecting a few bars of syncopation. Most of the audience smiled tolerantly and looked skyward. Ah, yes, they seemed to say, the sun was shining this morning, but we're paying for it now. These, I guessed, must be the seasoned veterans of Festivals past. And the few who were irritated by the pitter-patter were obvious novices with unreasonably high expectations such as proper acoustics and a decent sound system.

9   The traffic around the Square did its bit, too, in dashing the hopes of the fastidious. Rising and falling in concordance with the traffic lights, it posed an interesting challenge. But I managed to float with the automobile tide, manoeuvring my voice around obstacles and taking evasive action by incorporating the geargrinding lorries into the punctuation. This, however, made the full stops abnormally long, at times; the sporadic silences imparted a pseudo-Pinteresque quality to the text.

10   Halfway through the reading, I reached a sombre section: the protagonist's best friend had died in hospital, and arrangements were being made for the funeral. At that instant, the sounds of reggae music began creeping into the tent. Well, no, not quite creeping—they stomped in determinedly as though they owned the place, making my audience and me feel that we had no business being there.

11   And my audience—my kind and faithful audience that had gazed heavenward with such understanding—now squirmed in their seats and exchanged disapproving looks. Who had been so stupid as to leave the door open? their faces inquired in silent indignation. Everyone frowned and turned around to look. But the door, of course, was firmly shut.

12   Now this door, which sealed the entrance to the tent, was not a rudimentary tent flap nor a hasty hatch flung harum-scarum into a canvas hiatus. No, it was a proper door, and a fine specimen of its kind, too, polished and hewn of solid, well-grained wood, complete with hinges, door-jamb, lock, gleaming brass knob, and threshold. All the accessories that help to make a Scotsman's home his castle. In fact, it was a most accomplished door which would have done justice to any middle-class dwelling, regardless of ethnic background. It was a multicultural door, a good door, a strong and faithful door; a movable barricade of weight and substance, forming a bulwark against thieves, encyclopaedia pedlars, real-estate agents, and the winter cold; a benevolent barrier to keep in the warmth of the hearth, the dog, two children, cooking smells, and all the memories of a happy family.

13   But, alas, besieged by reggae, this handsome door was revealed in all its helplessness, mournfully out of place. For it was a door without walls. And a door without walls is a doomed door. It is a door without a future. Open or shut, its case is hopeless. It is a door yet to find worthy employment, a door severely in need of relocation.

14   And so, there it stood in all its empty finery, flanked by canvas to left and right, a pitifully over-qualified door. It waited like a spire in search of a church, or a minaret that had misplaced its mosque.

Someone in charge hurried out to try and mute the sounds of 15
reggae. But reggae is nothing if it is not loud, and she returned with
an I-did-my-best look upon her embarrassed face.

The irrepressible rogue music, we learned later, had escaped out 16
of another tent—a very important one, for it even had a title: Beck's
Famous Spiegeltent. The Festival brochure invited visitors to "enjoy
the cafe/bar and cabaret throughout the day in the splendid Beck's
Famous Spiegeltent, brought specially to the Festival from Holland."

For a moment I considered abandoning my reading in favour 17
of leading a sing-along of "Loch Lomond" and "Roamin' in the
Gloamin'" and, of course, the ever-popular "I Love a Lassie, My
Bonnie, Bonnie Lassie." And it would not have been entirely irrelevant, for the protagonist of my novel loves to sing, and these songs
are among his favourites.

Then I thought better of it; my audience, in its present mood, 18
seemed capable of belting out the lyrics with a vengeance, and I had
no wish to be unfair to the reggae crowd or cause an incident. Besides,
I had been invited to read, and not to impersonate Sir Harry Lauder.

So we gamely endured the hour. During the book-signing ses- 19
sion, a number of people congratulated me for managing a fine
reading despite the overwhelming odds. I thought about "The
Charge of the Light Brigade," and was grateful to them for their
kindness.

The official purpose of my trip was behind me. Now I was free 20
to explore the city and search for a wee bust of Stevenson.

"It's closed for lunch," murmured the museum attendant apologeti- 21
cally, when I tried to enter the basement room marked Robert Louis
Stevenson. It was just past two, and he said downstairs could be
viewed after three. So I went upstairs, to the Robert Burns and Sir
Walter Scott sections, which were open. Stevenson, Burns, and Scott
had separate lunch hours.

I was in Lady Stair's House. Built in 1622 by a prominent mer- 22
chant burgess of the city, read my map-guide, it contained portraits,
manuscripts, and relics relating to the three writers. A sign warned
visitors to exercise caution when ascending the stone stairway, for
in Lady Stair's House the steps did not rise equally. It was a seventeenth-century architectural feature, explained the sign, and had
been preserved during restoration of the house. The function of the
dissimilar step was that of a built-in burglar alarm: to make an
intruder stumble, thus warning the occupants.

I went up and down the stairs several times, but could not trip, 23
for the two deviant steps had been painted white. It was like being
told the punch line before the story.

24   Finding the basement room still shut when I had finished upstairs, I walked the Royal Mile and examined a few souvenir shops in the High Street with the bust in mind. Earlier in the day, the guide on the Award Winning Green & Cream Open-Top Double Decker Edinburgh Tour Bus had explained that the Royal Mile, which extended from Edinburgh Castle to Holyrood Palace, was really more than a mile: "It's a shining example of the generosity of royalty, you know," he had said.

25   Almost every shop displayed pewter busts of Burns and Scott, along with miniature editions of their works. Then there were lists of surnames with corresponding clans and tartans, scotch-taped to a prominent wall, enabling visitors from the New World to locate their roots in a jiffy. Bushy-bearded Highland dolls in kilts and sporrans overran the shelves, bearing generic labels like MacGregor and Buchanan and MacLeod. But I did not spot a single Stevenson among them.

26   There were pocket-sized versions of bagpipes, models of haggis, little glass Nessies, videocassettes of Highland Dancing Made Easy in Ten Simple Lessons, plaid scarves, plaid socks, plaid ties, and anything else imaginable in plaid. But of the one who was the object of my friend's veneration, there was never a trace. It seemed quite an unfair state of affairs—squads of Scotts, battalions of Burnses, but not one solitary Stevenson.

27   It's no use going to Switzerland and grumbling about the Alps, my friend always says, the one who requested the bust. But surely a little spot could have been found for RLS, a tiny bit of shelf space, so I could be done with my friend's shopping. Although, given the choice, he (RLS, that is) would probably have preferred this benign neglect to the alternatives on sale.

28   In my place a man of action—someone like my much-mentioned friend, perhaps—would have fired off deliciously pungent letters to the Edinburgh Tourist Board, the Chamber of Commerce, and the Lothian Guild of Souvenir Manufacturers (with carbon copies, in the last instance, to head offices in China and Taiwan). I, instead, kept searching in silence.

29   Next day, I returned to Lady Stair's House, and the Stevenson room was open. Among the usual collections of dark inkpots and warped pens, a straight razor caught my eye. It had belonged to Stevenson's grandfather, who had been nicknamed Beardie, explained the label. Why Beardie? Because he had sworn not to shave ever again until Bonnie Prince Charles was restored to the throne.

30   Then there were Stevenson's things that had been brought back from Samoa: riding boots, stirrups, a crop, a palm-frond fan, a hat,

walking sticks, guns. None of these had an explanatory note as interesting as Beardie's razor. The attendant wandered into the room, and I asked if he knew where I might be able to buy a little souvenir bust of Stevenson.

He held his hands behind his back and swayed a little, like someone appreciating a landscape. "Hmm. I'm sorry, but I'm merely on loan here for two days from the City Art Centre, and not so well-acquainted with this museum." He stroked his ginger moustache. "Might be something in the shop upstairs, though. Let me ask the fellow there." 31

I should have told him I had checked upstairs the day before, but I wanted to see him climb the stone stairway, the one with the uneven burglar-tripping steps. He completed the ascent without mishap, and was back moments later. "They only have a Walter Scott. Have you tried the shops in the High Street?" 32

"Yes, I looked in them yesterday." 33

"You should ask," he advised. "If there is no demand for Stevenson, the shopkeepers might not have him on display. But there could always be something in the back." 34

"Yes, that's a very good idea," I said. 35

He began strolling with me from exhibit to exhibit. "I could let you have that one for five thousand pounds," he joked, when we came to a two-foot bronze of Stevenson standing. We laughed and strolled on. The stern law-enforcement quality of his black uniform seemed increasingly out of place in that quiet little room. 36

On the walls were charts with snippets of biography, and one in particular was of a caretaker reminiscing about the little Stevenson, who would always follow him about the grounds, full of questions, never without his tiny stub of pencil, stopping dead every now and then to scribble "goodness kens what" in his little notebook. 37

I asked my new friend if he could read the bits in dialect with the proper accent. "I don't know what you mean," he answered, testing me, his tone a mix of defence and challenge. 38

"These lines look so rich," I said. "I can hear them in my head but cannot make them sound the way they should." 39

His reluctance melted when he became certain that my request was spurred by genuine interest and not intended to poke fun. There was an old map of the country, and he pointed out the place in the Highlands where he came from. At my prompting, he spoke a few lines in the brogue that was native to his region, and then, to show the difference, followed it with a few words in the border accent (the one with England, that is, he clarified). Before I left he treated me to a beautiful recitation of a Burns poem that began: 40

> Ye flowery banks o'bonnie Doon,
> How can ye blume sae fair?
> How can ye chant, ye little birds,
> And I sae fu' o' care?

His voice, the words, something about Lady Stair's House, all made me nostalgic for places I have never seen, which was a bit silly, though I did not think so then.

41   "Good luck with the Stevenson bust," he called, as I passed through the courtyard and into the street.

42   A piper played at the corner, his hat at his feet. The skirl of bagpipes filled the air like a flock of lazily gliding birds. The sun was shining as I emerged from Lady Stair's House. We'll pay for it by evening, I thought. A quick learner, I had already assimilated the local method of weather forecasting.

43   Yesterday, the shops between here and St. Giles' Cathedral had been examined. Today, I decided to tackle the ones in the opposite direction, towards the Castle.

44   "Would you have a little bust of Robert Louis Stevenson?" I asked at the first place, "something like those, perhaps?" pointing to a glass case where half-a-dozen Walter Scotts pouted in pewter.

45   "A bust of Stevenson?" His tone made me feel like Oliver Twist asking for more. I quickly added that it was for a friend, nothing really to do with me.

46   "Ah, a gift." He brightened. "Would you like to give your friend a Burns instead?"

47   "Do you think he might notice the difference?" I hedged, reluctant to dismiss him outright.

48   He pondered the possibility for a bit. "Aye, that he might. That he might."

49   In the next shop, the woman's suggestion was more to the point, though a trifle impractical. "You must come back next year," she said. "The shops will be full of Stevenson souvenirs then—1994 is his death centenary."

50   The third place had none of the cheap tourist stuff, and was more in the nature of an antique store. If I found a bust here it would be expensive. But I asked my question of the shopkeeper, who could easily have been the model for some of the bushy-bearded Highland dolls I had seen.

51   "Stevenson. Robert Louis Stevenson," he said, spacing the names carefully, as though to make sure we had the right man.

52   I nodded, that's the one.

53   "A fine writer," he continued. "A very fine writer. *Treasure Island. Kidnapped. The Strange Case of Dr. Jekyll and Mr. Hyde.*"

More confirmation of the man's identity. I nodded again. "And didn't he go abroad and live in a faraway foreign land?"

My hopes were rising. "In Samoa," I said "He died there." 54

"Ah, yes, Samoa." His eyes grew distant now, even romantic, 55 before he continued, "I'm sorry, I don't have what you're looking for. But may I ask you something personal? May I ask why you want Stevenson's bust?"

"It's a gift for a friend who adores his writing." 56

"Oh, I see." He seemed disappointed. "Shall I tell you what I 57 thought? I thought, from your skin colour, that you yourself might be Samoan, which might account for your interest in the man." He was amused by his own admission. "And where do you come from?"

"Canada. And before that, India," I volunteered, without wait- 58 ing for the routine follow-up question that was forming on his lips.

"But you can always pretend to be from Samoa," he laughed. 59 "Claim that your family were Stevenson's neighbours on the island. You could write a history of it, become a Stevenson authority." We laughed some more and then I left, too lazy to explain that Samoans and Indians are about as interchangeable as the Scots and the English.

A souvenir store across the road, larger than most, was enticing 60 shoppers inside by offering a taste of shortbread; a man stood in the doorway with a plate. I asked him my question, and got the expected answer. But this time I persevered: "Don't you have any souvenirs of Stevenson? A postcard, perhaps, of the Stevenson museum? Or his childhood home in Edinburgh, or his house in Samoa? Anything?"

A shop attendant who looked like the shortbread man's brother 61 or twin brother (though not identical) overheard me. "This shop is full of Stevenson souvenirs. Overflowing with them," he greeted me, flinging his arms around him to indicate the merchandise. "You're in luck, my friend."

I was willing to listen. 62

"This thimble, for example," he said, extricating it from a tartan 63 sewing kit. "It is the exact copy of the thimble that Stevenson wore while darning his socks after a day of hard writing. It was his way of relaxing."

I couldn't help laughing, but he continued solemnly, picking up 64 a plaid-covered tea cosy. "And this is a perfect likeness of the one with which Stevenson kept his teapot warm."

Now the shortbread fellow, too, got into the spirit of things. "And 65 this mug is the exact model—down to the last detail, mind you—of the one in which Stevenson poured his tea after it had steeped." In a confiding voice he added, "He liked his tea quite strong."

66   "And have you seen this? A superb copy of the sunglasses Stevenson used to wear—the sun was bright in Samoa, far too bright for someone accustomed to the cloud and fog of Scotland."

67   The two passed the gag between them with ease, like a seasoned vaudeville act. They covered all the items within their reach. Shoppers formed a circle to listen. Scarves, ties, wine glasses, teaspoons, dolls, bracelets, pens, ashtrays, cigarette cases, keychains, photo-frames, all were integrated into an instant hagiography and given the Stevenson seal of approval.

68   Finally, the one who had begun the entertainment picked up a plaid-handled toy revolver, cocked it, and raised it above his head. "And this gun, produced in our finest workshop, is the exact replica of the one with which Stevenson, alas, shot himself in the head."

69   "Ah, yes," I interrupted, thinking I had him now. "But Stevenson died of a cerebral haemorrhage. I read it only this morning at the museum."

70   "Of course, that's what it would say in the museum, wouldn't it?" he said patiently. "For is it not the perfect euphemism for blowing out one's brains? Mind you, it's always in the souvenir shops that you get the real story, not in the museums."

71   My search for Stevenson had ended, I decided, and my friend would have agreed with me. Besides, after this bravura performance, everything else was bound to be anticlimactic—good thing I had taken in the Highland Regiments and the Edinburgh Military Tattoo the night before at the Castle.

72   People began drifting out of the shop. The shortbread man held the plate for me: "Won't you try a little piece? It is the exact same recipe that Stevenson used."

73   "Aye, that I will, thank you," I laughed, and went to look for a cup of tea that would complement the shortbread while I pondered the questions of mortality, memory, monuments, and the manufacture and management of fame. I was grateful to my friend for having endowed me with the quest. Without it, my time in Edinburgh would have been the poorer; instead, I felt as exhilarated as though I had returned from a lengthy ocean voyage to Samoa, the seaspray still moist on my cheeks, the tang of salt upon my lips, and clutching with great care against my chest the sweet, freshly baked transubstantiation of RLS.

ROHINTON MISTRY

Born in Bombay, India, in 1952, Rohinton Mistry came to Canada in 1975. He is the author of a collection of short stories, *Tales from Firozsha Baag*

(1987), and a Governor General's Award winning novel, *Such a Long Journey* (1991).

Pornography

MARGARET ATWOOD

When I was in Finland a few years ago for an international writers' conference, I had occasion to say a few paragraphs in public on the subject of pornography. The context was a discussion of political repression, and I was suggesting the possibility of a link between the two. The immediate result was that a male journalist took several large bites out of me. Prudery and pornography are two halves of the same coin, said he, and I was clearly a prude. What could you expect from an Anglo-Canadian? Afterward, a couple of pleasant Scandinavian men asked me what I had been so worked up about. All "pornography" means, they said, is graphic depictions of whores, and what was the harm in that?

Not until then did it strike me that the male journalist and I had two entirely different things in mind. By "pornography," he meant naked bodies and sex. I, on the other hand, had recently been doing the research for my novel *Bodily Harm,* and was still in a state of shock from some of the material I had seen, including the Ontario Board of Film Censors' "outtakes." By "pornography," I meant women getting their nipples snipped off with garden shears, having meat hooks stuck into their vaginas, being disemboweled; little girls being raped; men (yes, there are some men) being smashed to a pulp and forcibly sodomized. The cutting edge of pornography, as far as I could see, was no longer simple old copulation, hanging from the chandelier or otherwise: it was death, messy, explicit and highly sadistic. I explained this to the nice Scandinavian men. "Oh, but that's just the United States," they said. "Everyone knows they're sick." In their country, they said, violent "pornography" of that kind was not permitted on television or in movies; indeed, excessive violence of any kind was not permitted. They had drawn a clear line between erotica, which earlier studies had shown did not incite men to more aggressive and brutal behavior toward women, and violence, which later studies indicated did.

3   Some time after that I was in Saskatchewan, where, because of the scenes in *Bodily Harm*, I found myself on an open-line radio show answering questions about "pornography." Almost no one who phoned in was in favor of it, but again they weren't talking about the same stuff I was, because they hadn't seen it. Some of them were all set to stamp out bathing suits and negligees, and, if possible, any depictions of the female body whatsoever. God, it was implied, did not approve of female bodies, and sex of any kind, including that practised by bumblebees, should be shoved back into the dark, where it belonged. I had more than a suspicion that *Lady Chatterley's Lover*, Margaret Laurence's *The Diviners*, and indeed most books by most serious modern authors would have ended up as confetti if left in the hands of these callers.

4   For me, these two experiences illustrate the two poles of the emotionally heated debate that is now thundering around this issue. They also underline the desirability and even the necessity of defining the terms. "Pornography" is now one of those catchalls, like "Marxism" and "feminism," that have become so broad they can mean almost anything, ranging from certain verses in the Bible, ads for skin lotion and sex tests for children to the contents of Penthouse, Naughty '90s postcards and films with titles containing the word *Nazi* that show vicious scenes of torture and killing. It's easy to say that sensible people can tell the difference. Unfortunately, opinions on what constitutes a sensible person vary.

5   But even sensible people tend to lose their cool when they start talking about this subject. They soon stop talking and start yelling, and the name calling begins. Those in favor of censorship (which may include groups not noticeably in agreement on other issues, such as some feminists and religious fundamentalists) accuse the others of exploiting women through the use of degrading images, contributing to the corruption of children, and adding to the general climate of violence and threat in which both women and children live in this society; or, though they may not give much of a hoot about actual women and children, they invoke moral standards and God's supposed aversion to "filth," "smut" and deviated *preversion*, which may mean ankles.

6   The camp in favor of total "freedom of expression" often comes out howling as loud as the Romans would have if told they could no longer have innocent fun watching the lions eat up Christians. It too may include segments of the population who are

not natural bedfellows: those who proclaim their God-given right to freedom, including the freedom to tote guns, drive when drunk, drool over chicken porn and get off on videotapes of women being raped and beaten, may be waving the same anticensorship banner as responsible liberals who fear the return of Mrs. Grundy, or gay groups for whom sexual emancipation involves the concept of "sexual theatre." *Whatever turns you on* is a handy motto, as is *A man's home is his castle* (and if it includes a dungeon with beautiful maidens strung up in chains and bleeding from every pore, that's his business).

Meanwhile, theoreticians theorize and speculators speculate. Is today's pornography yet another indication of the hatred of the body, the deep mind-body split, which is supposed to pervade Western Christian society? Is it a backlash against the women's movement by men who are threatened by uppity female behavior in real life, so like to fantasize about women done up like outsize parcels, being turned into hamburger, kneeling at their feet in slave-like adoration or sucking off guns? Is it a sign of collective impotence, of a generation of men who can't relate to real women at all but have to make do with bits of celluloid and paper? Is the current flood just a result of smart marketing and aggressive promotion by the money men in what has now become a multibillion-dollar industry? If they were selling movies about men getting their testicles stuck full of knitting needles by women with swastikas on their sleeves, would they do as well, or is this penchant somehow peculiarly male? If so, why? Is pornography a power trip rather than a sex one? Some say that those ropes, chains, muzzles and other restraining devices are an argument for the immense power female sexuality still wields in the male imagination: you don't put these things on dogs unless you're afraid of them. Others, more literary, wonder about the shift from the 19th-century Magic Woman or Femme Fatale image to the lollipop-licker, airhead or turkey-carcass treatment of women in porn today. The proporners don't care much about theory; they merely demand product. The antiporners don't care about it in the final analysis either; there's dirt on the street, and they want it cleaned up, now.

It seems to me that this conversation, with its *You're-a-prude/You're-a-pervert* dialectic, will never get anywhere as long as we continue to think of this material as just "entertainment." Possibly we're deluded by the packaging, the format: magazine, book, movie, theatrical presentation. We're used to thinking of these things as part of the "entertainment industry," and we're used to thinking of ourselves as free adult people who ought to be able to see any kind of "entertainment" we want to. That was what the

First Choice pay-TV debate was all about. After all, it's only entertainment, right? Entertainment means fun, and only a killjoy would
be antifun. What's the harm?

9   This is obviously the central question: *What's the harm?* If there
isn't any real harm to any real people, then the antiporners can
tsk-tsk and/or throw up as much as they like, but they can't right-
fully expect more legal controls or sanctions. However, the no harm
position is far from being proven.

10   (For instance, there's a clear-cut case for banning—as the federal government has proposed—movies, photos and videos that
depict children engaging in sex with adults: real children are used
to make the movies, and hardly anybody thinks this is ethical. The
possibilities for coercion are too great.)

11   To shift the viewpoint, I'd like to suggest three other models for
looking at "pornography"—and here I mean the violent kind.

12   Those who find the idea of regulating pornographic materials
repugnant because they think it's Fascist or Communist or otherwise not in accordance with the principles of an open democratic
society should consider that Canada has made it illegal to dissemi-
nate material that may lead to hatred toward any group because of
race or religion. I suggest that if pornography of the violent kind
depicted these acts being done predominantly to Chinese, to blacks,
to Catholics, it would be off the market immediately, under the present laws. Why is hate literature illegal? Because whoever made the
law thought that such material might incite real people to do real
awful things to other real people. The human brain is to a certain
extent a computer: garbage in, garbage out. We only hear about the
extreme cases (like that of American multimurderer Ted Bundy) in
which pornography has contributed to the death and/or mutilation
of women and/or men. Although pornography is not the only fac-
tor involved in the creation of such deviance, it certainly has upped
the ante by suggesting both a variety of techniques and the social
acceptability of such actions. Nobody knows yet what effect this
stuff is having on the less psychotic.

13   Studies have shown that a large part of the market for all kinds
of porn, soft and hard, is drawn from the 16-to-21-year-old population of young men. Boys used to learn about sex on the street, or (in
Italy, according to Fellini movies) from friendly whores, or, in more
genteel surroundings, from girls, their parents, or, once upon a
time, in school, more or less. Now porn has been added, and sex
education in the schools is rapidly being phased out. The buck has
been passed, and boys are being taught that all women secretly like
to be raped and that real men get high on scooping out women's
digestive tracts.

Boys learn their concept of masculinity from other men: is this what most men want them to be learning? If word gets around that rapists are "normal" and even admirable men, will boys feel that in order to be normal, admirable and masculine they will have to be rapists? Human beings are enormously flexible, and how they turn out depends a lot on how they're educated, by the society in which they're immersed as well as by their teachers. In a society that advertises and glorifies rape or even implicitly condones it, more women get raped. It becomes socially acceptable. And at a time when men and the traditional male role have taken a lot of flak and men are confused and casting around for an acceptable way of being male (and, in some cases, not getting much comfort from women on that score), this must be at times a pleasing thought. 14

It would be naïve to think of violent pornography as just harmless entertainment. It's also an educational tool and a powerful propaganda device. What happens when boy educated on porn meets girl brought up on Harlequin romances? The clash of expectations can be heard around the block. She wants him to get down on his knees with a ring, he wants her to get down on all fours with a ring in her nose. Can this marriage be saved? 15

Pornography has certain things in common with such addictive substances as alcohol and drugs; for some, though by no means for all, it induces chemical changes in the body, which the user finds exciting and pleasurable. It also appears to attract a "hard core" of habitual users and a penumbra of those who use it occasionally but aren't dependent on it in any way. There are also significant numbers of men who aren't much interested in it, not because they're undersexed but because real life is satisfying their needs, which may not require as many appliances as those of users. 16

For the "hard core," pornography may function as alcohol does for the alcoholic: tolerance develops, and a little is no longer enough. This may account for the short viewing time and fast turnover in porn theatres. Mary Brown, chairwoman of the Ontario Board of Film Censors, estimates that for every one mainstream movie requesting entrance to Ontario, there is one porno flick. Not only the quantity consumed but the quality of explicitness must escalate, which may account for the growing violence: once the big deal was breasts, then it was genitals, then copulation, then that was no longer enough and the hard users had to have more. The ultimate kick is death, and after that, as the Marquis de Sade so boringly demonstrated, multiple death. 17

The existence of alcoholism has not led us to ban social drinking. On the other hand, we do have laws about drinking and driving, 18 excessive drunkenness and other abuses of alcohol that may result in injury or death to others.

19   This leads us back to the key question: what's the harm? Nobody knows, but this society should find out fast, before the saturation point is reached. The Scandinavian studies that showed a connection between depictions of sexual violence and increased impulse toward it on the part of male viewers would be a starting point, but many more questions remain to be raised as well as answered. What, for instance, is the crucial difference between men who are users and men who are not? Does using affect a man's relationship with actual women, and, if so, adversely? Is there a clear line between erotica and violent pornography, or are they on an escalating continuum? Is this a "men versus women" issue, with all men secretly siding with the proporners and all women secretly siding against? (I think not; there *are* lots of men who don't think that running their true love through the Cuisinart is the best way they can think of to spend a Saturday night, and they're just as nauseated by films of someone else doing it as women are.) Is pornography merely an expression of the sexual confusion of this age or an active contributor to it?

20   Nobody wants to go back to the age of official repression, when even piano legs were referred to as "limbs" and had to wear pantaloons to be decent. Neither do we want to end up in George Orwell's 1984, in which pornography is turned out by the State to keep the proles in a state of torpor, sex itself is considered dirty and the approved practice is only for reproduction. But Rome under the emperors isn't such a good model either.

21   If all men and women respected each other, if sex were considered joyful and life-enhancing instead of a wallow in germ-filled glop, if everyone were in love all the time, if, in other words, many people's lives were more satisfactory for them than they appear to be now, pornography might just go away on its own. But since this is obviously not happening, we as a society are going to have to make some informed and responsible decisions.

MARGARET ATWOOD

One of Canada's best-known writers, Margaret Atwood was born in Ottawa in 1939. She has published more than twenty books, including novels, short stories, poetry, and criticism. Among her most recent works are *Cat's Eye* (1989), *Wilderness Tips* (1991), and *The Robber Bride* (1993).

Hunger

MAGGIE HELWIG

Consider that it is now normal for North   1
American women to have eating disorders. Consider that anorexia—
deliberate starvation—and bulimia—self-induced vomiting—and
obsessive patterns for weight-controlling exercise are now the ordinary thing for young women, and are spreading at a frightening rate
to older women, to men, to ethnic groups and social classes that
were once "immune." Consider that some surveys suggest that 80
per cent of the women on an average university campus have bor-
derline-to-severe eating disorders; that it is almost impossible to get
treatment unless the problem is life-threatening; that, in fact, if it is
not life-threatening it is not considered a problem at all. I once sat
in a seminar on nutritional aspects of anorexia, and ended up listening to people tell me how to keep my weight down. All this is
happening in one of the richest countries in the world, a society
devoted to consumption. Amazing as it may seem, we have nor-
malized anorexia and bulimia, even turned them into an industry.

We've also trivialized them: made them into nothing more than   2
an exaggerated conformity with basically acceptable standards of
behavior. Everyone wants to be thin and pretty, after all. Some people take it a little too far; you have to get them back on the right
track, but it's all a question of knowing just how far is proper.

The consumer society has gone so far we can even buy into   3
hunger.

But that is not what it's about. You do not stuff yourself with   4
food and force yourself to vomit just because of fashion magazines.
You do not reduce yourself to the condition of a skeleton in order to
be attractive. This is not just a problem of proportion. This is the
nightmare of consumerism acted out in women's bodies.

This is what we are saying as we starve: it is not all right. It is   5
not all right. It is not all right.

There've always been strange or disordered patterns of eating,   6
associated mainly with religious extremism or psychological problems (which some, not myself, would say were the same thing). But
the complex of ideas, fears, angers and actions that make up contemporary anorexia and bulimia seems to be of fairly recent origin.

Anorexia did not exist as a recognized pattern until the 1960s, and bulimia not until later than that—and at first they were deeply shocking. The idea that privileged young women (the first group to be affected) were voluntarily starving themselves, sometimes to death, or regularly sticking their fingers down their throats to make themselves throw up, shook the culture badly. It was a fad, in a sense, the illness of the month, but it was also a scandal, and a source of something like horror.

7   Before this, though, before anorexia had a widely recognized name, one of the first women to succumb to it had made her own scandalous stand, and left a body of writing that still has a lot to say about the real meaning of voluntary hunger.

8   Simone Weil was a brilliant, disturbed, wildly wrong-headed and astonishingly perceptive young French woman who died from the complications of self-starvation in America during World War II, at the age of 34. She never, of course, wrote directly about her refusal to eat—typically for any anorexic, she insisted she ate perfectly adequate amounts. But throughout her philosophical and theological writing (almost all of it fragments and essays collected after her death), she examines and uses the symbolism of hunger, eating and food.

9   Food occupied, in fact, a rather important and valued position in her philosophy—she once referred to food as "the irrefutable proof of the reality of the universe," and at another time said that the foods served at Easter and Christmas, the turkey and *marron glacés*, were "the true meaning of the feast"; although she could also take the more conventional puritan position that desire for food is a "base motive." She spoke often of eating God (acceptable enough in a Christian context) and of being eaten by God (considerably less so). The great tragedy of our lives, she said, is that we cannot really eat God; and also "it may be that vice, depravity and crime are almost always ... attempts to eat beauty."

10   But it is her use of the symbolism of hunger that explains her death. "We have to go down into ourselves to the abode of the desire which is not imaginary. Hunger: we imagine kinds of food, but the hunger itself is real: we have to fasten onto the hunger."

11   Hunger, then, was a search for reality, for the irreducible need that lies beyond all imaginary satisfactions. Weil was deeply perturbed by the "materialism" of her culture; though she probably could not have begun to imagine the number of imaginary and illusory "satisfactions" now available. Simply, she wanted truth. She wanted to reduce herself to the point where she would *know* what needs, and what foods, were real and true.

12   Similarly, though deeply drawn to the Catholic faith, she refused to be baptized and to take Communion (to, in fact, eat

God). "I cannot help wondering whether in these days when so large a proportion of humanity is sunk in materialism, God does not want there to be some men and women who have given themselves to him and to Christ and who yet remain outside the Church." For the sake of honesty, of truth, she maintained her hunger.

Weil, a mystic and a political activist simultaneously until the 13 end of her short life—she was one of the first French intellectuals to join the Communist party and one of the first to leave, fought in the Spanish civil war and worked in auto factories—could not bear to have life be less than a total spiritual and political statement. And her statement of protest, of dissatisfaction, her statement of hunger, finally destroyed her.

The term anorexia nervosa was coined in the 19th century, but 14 it was not until sometime in the 1960s that significant—and constantly increasing—numbers of well-off young women began dying of starvation, and not until the early 1970s that it became public knowledge.

It is the nature of our times that the explanations proffered 15 were psychological and individualistic; yet, even so, it was understood as being, on some level, an act of protest. And of course symbolically, it could hardly be other—it was, simply, a hunger strike. The most common interpretation, at that point, was that it was a sort of adolescent rebellion against parental control, an attempt, particularly, to escape from an overcontrolling mother. It was a fairly acceptable paradigm for the period, although many mothers were justifiably disturbed; sometimes deeply and unnecessarily hurt. The theory still has some currency, and is not entirely devoid of truth.

But can it be an accident that this happened almost precisely to 16 coincide with the growth of the consumer society, a world based on a level of material consumption that, by the end of the 1960s, had become very nearly uncontrollable? Or with the strange, underground guilt that has made "conspicuous consumption" a matter of consuming vast amounts and *hiding it*, of million-dollar minimalism? With the development of what is possibly the most emotionally depleted society in history, where the only "satisfactions" seem to be the imaginary ones, the material buy-offs?

To be skeletally, horribly thin makes one strong statement. It 17 says, I am hungry. What I have been given is not sufficient, not real, not true, not acceptable. I am starving. To reject food, whether by refusing it or by vomiting it back, says simply, I will not consume. I will not participate. This is not real.

Hunger is the central nightmare image of our society. Of all the 18 icons of horror the last few generations have offered us, we have chosen, above all, pictures of hunger—the emaciated prisoners of Auschwitz and Belsen, Ethiopian children with bloated bellies and stick-figure limbs. We carry in our heads these nightmares of the extreme edge of hunger.

19   And while we may not admit to guilt about our level of consumption in general, we admit freely to guilt about eating, easily equate food with "sin." We cannot accept hunger of our own, cannot afford to consider it.

20   It is, traditionally, women who carry our nightmares. It was women who became possessed by the Devil, women who suffered from "hysterical disorders," women who, in all popular culture, are the targets of the "monster." One of the roles women are cast in is that of those who act out the subconscious fears of their society. And it is women above all, in this time, who carry our hunger.

21   It is the starving women who embody the extremity of hunger that terrifies and fascinates us, and who insist that they are not hungry. It is the women sticking their fingers down their throats who act out the equation of food and sin, who deny hunger and yet embody endless, unfulfilled appetite. It is these women who live through every implication of our consumption and our hunger, our guilt and ambiguity and our awful need for something real to fill us.

22   We have too much; and it is poison.

23   It was first—in fact exclusively—feminist writers who began to explore the symbolic language of anorexia and bulimia; Sheila MacLeod (*The Art of Starvation*), Susie Orbach (*Hunger Strike*), and others. However, as their work began to appear, a new presentation of eating disorders was entering the general consciousness, one that would no longer permit them to be understood as protest at *any* level.

24   For, as eating disorders became increasingly widespread, they also became increasingly trivialized, incorporated into a framework already "understood" all too well. Feminist writers had, early on, noted that anorexia had to be linked with the increasing thinness of models and other glamor icons, as part of a larger cultural trend. This is true enough as a starting point, for the symbolic struggle being waged in women's bodies happens on many levels, and is not limited to pathology cases. Unfortunately, this single starting point was seized by "women's magazines" and popularizing accounts in general. Anorexia was now understandable, almost safe really, it was just fashion gone out of control. Why, these women were *accepting* the culture, they just needed a sense of proportion. What a relief.

Now it could be condoned. Now it could, in fact, become the basis for an industry; could be incorporated neatly into consumer society. According to Jane Fonda the solution to bulimia is to remain equally unhealthily thin by buying the 20-minute workout and becoming an obsessive fitness follower (at least for those who can afford it). The diet clinic industry the Nutrisystem package, the aerobics boom. An advertising industry, that plays equally off desire and guilt, for they now reinforce each other. Thousands upon thousands of starving, tormented women, not "sick" enough to be taken seriously, not really troubled at all.

One does not reduce oneself to the condition of a skeleton in order to be fashionable. One does not binge and vomit daily as an acceptable means of weight control. One does not even approach or imagine or dream of these things if one is not in some sort of trouble. If it were as simple as fashion, surely we would not be so ashamed to speak of these things, we would not feel that either way, whether we eat or do not eat, we are doing something wrong.

I was anorexic for eight years. I nearly died. It was certainly no help to me to be told I was taking fashion too far—I knew perfectly well that had nothing to do with it. It did not help much to be told I was trying to escape from my mother, since I lived away from home and was in only occasional contact with my family; it did not help much to be approached on an individualistic, psychological level. In fact, the first person I was able to go to for help was a charismatic Catholic, who at least understood that I was speaking in symbols of spiritual hunger.

I knew that I had something to say, that things were not all right, that I had to make that concretely, physically obvious. I did not hate or look down on my body—I spoke through it and with it.

Women are taught to take guilt, concern, problems, onto themselves personally; and especially onto their bodies. But we are trying to talk about something that is only partly personal. Until we find new ways of saying it and find the courage to talk to the world about the world, we will speak destruction to ourselves.

We must come to know what we are saying—and say it.

MAGGIE HELWIG

Maggie Helwig (b. 1961) is a Canadian poet and editor whose published works include *Apocalypse Jazz* and *Eating Glass*.

Wheels: The Car as a Cultural Driving Force

PIERRE BERTON

1   The astonishing thing about the automobile is that there are people still living who can remember a time when there weren't any. I am not one; but I can remember a place where at one time there were scarcely any. The northern community in which I was raised boasted three livery stables and a blacksmith shop, but in the winter only one motor car was to be seen on the roads. It was the milkman's Model-T Ford and I remember him having to hand-crank it at every stop.

2   In the summer a few more cars took to the gravel streets. As befitted his station, Judge Macaulay had the poshest automobile in town, a black Studebaker with fabric top known then as a "tour car." That was a great word in the 1920s. Few of us owned a car but we all played the popular Parker card game, *Touring*.

3   Of course we lived in a backwater. For in 1926—that was the first year I can remember squatting in Billy Bigg's blacksmith shop watching him hammer horseshoes into shape—the world beyond the Yukon had gone car crazy. We did not know it, but the greatest social transformation in history was under way.

4   We realize now that, more than any other invention, the automobile has changed our lives. It has affected the way we think, the way we act, the way we talk. It has up-ended the class system, sounded the death knell of Main Street, and played hell with the Lord's Day. As a precursor of the sexual revolution, it has been as important as the Pill. It has telescoped time and squeezed geography. It is both our slave and our master. For even as it has liberated us, it has made us its prisoner.

5   There was a time when transportation was the prerogative of the rich. Before the automobile arrived, the carriage, the coach-and-four, the private railway car, and the hansom cab were accepted modes of travel, but only for the well-to-do. We are reminded of that era today when the Governor General rides to Parliament in an open landau.

6   The motor car changed all that. It has been the great leveler in terms of social distance as well as physical grace. The factory worker,

sensing the surge of power under the gas pedal of his truck, feels himself the equal of the businessman in his Dodge convertible. As Marshall McLuhan pointed out, it is the pedestrian who has become a second-class citizen.

The car gave the masses geographical mobility; and that meant 7 social mobility, for the ability to choose is a concomitant of class. With the invention of the automobile, the poor could escape the confines of city tenements and narrow villages. In fact, the development of new mass-production techniques—the legacy of Henry Ford—blurred caste distinctions, creating in North America a vast middle class, most of whom owned cars.

The car brought to a settled world a glorious spontaneity that 8 was not possible in the age of the horse and the railroad. Horses required long rest periods; they could not manage steep inclines without assistance. Railroads ran on schedule to predetermined destinations. But with the coming of the automobile, car owners could leap into their vehicles on impulse and take off in any direction. This ability to control the time and the direction of travel marked for millions the beginning of a new freedom. It is also the reason why most wage earners today get a paid vacation.

With this independence came privacy. Alone in their cars peo- 9 ple can sing, shout, talk to themselves, or quietly plan their day, free from importuning associates or carping relatives. This human desire to be alone is, I believe, the chief reason why the idea of the car pool has never really taken hold in Canada. The highways are crowded with five- and six-passenger automobiles, most carrying only a driver.

As examples of the way the motor car has affected our lives, one 10 need look only at such basics as health care, religion, and education. The ambulance has brought swift medical aid to everyone; the bus has done away with the little red schoolhouse; and rural Canada is littered with boarded-up churches because the car, which made it possible to travel longer distances to worship, also may have made it too attractive to skip worship in favor of a Sunday drive.

Since the early days of the Tin Lizzie we have talked the lan- 11 guage of cars. Just as words and phrases such as *free wheeling, green light, fast lane, going like sixty* and *step on it* indicate the swifter pace of the automobile era, so words like *car hop, motel, passion pit* and *drive-in* suggest a totally different lifestyle.

Urban sprawl, urban rot, and urban renewal all spring out of 12 the motor-car era and hint at the problems created by the suburban explosion, perhaps the single most important demographic change wrought by the automobile. The car made possible the escape of Shelley's "smoky populous cities"; and from the very outset this was seen as its greatest liberating force.

13   As a 1908 advertisement for the Sears motor car put it: "The Sears is the car for the businessman who has tired of home life in a congested neighbourhood and yearns for a cottage in the suburb for his family." Such blandishments were remarkably prescient, even though reality does not quite mesh with the fantasy. The countryside of [the 1990s] is no facsimile of that of the century's first decade. One problem was that the people who escaped from the city insisted on bringing the city with them.

14   It has been determined that, apart from vacations, the trip to work is the longest regular journey most car owners are prepared to make. With the growth of superhighways and faster cars, that trip lengthened in distance but not in time. Business followed the commuters with such amenities as shops, theaters, and department stores. The result was the suburban shopping center.

15   It was the shopping center that helped squeeze out that great Canadian institution, Eaton's catalogue. It sucked the life blood from the main streets of thousands of small towns. It turned the cores of such cities as Edmonton into virtual population deserts after work hours. It changed shopping habits and shopping hours. It encouraged the growth of retail chains, dooming individual merchant enterprise and contributing to the depersonalization and the conformity of the nation.

16   None of this, of course, could have been envisaged in 1900 when the automotive age can be said to have begun. That was the year when the early self-propelled vehicles began to look less like motorized buggies and more like motor cars, with a proper steering wheel instead of a tiller, a hood and a side door, and a speed that could reach a terrifying 40 miles an hour.

17   The universal phrase "get a horse!" suggests the derision in which early automobiles were held. In 1900, the horse was the pivot around which a vast industry revolved, an industry doomed to oblivion within 20 years. There were at least 16 million horses in the United States, perhaps two million in Canada. Harness shops and carriage factories ran full blast. Thousands of wheelwrights and blacksmiths depended on the horse for their livelihood. An entire industry thrived on nails manufactured for horseshoes. Hay was one of the biggest cash crops. Every town had its livery stable, hitching post, and horse trough.

18   Today we think of pollution in terms of automobile exhaust. We forget that in the city of Toronto, in 1890, tons of manure had to be swept off the streets every day. The stench of urine and the clouds of flies rising from the roadway plagued pedestrians and drivers alike. Women crossing the stinking wooden cobbles at Yonge and College streets were forced to raise their skirts and expose their ankles to prevent lumps of dung from sticking to their hems.

Nor is the traffic jam unique to our era. Photographs of   19
Manhattan in the last century show traffic brought to a standstill by
trams, carts, drays, carriages, and buggies.

As was the carriage, the early motor car was a toy for the   20
wealthy, nothing more. After the turn of the century, John Craig
Eaton of the Toronto department store family acquired a Wilton.
Billy Cochrane, the famous Alberta rancher, bought a Locomobile.
R.B. Bennett, then a rising Calgary lawyer, had an Oldsmobile.
Automobile owners were considered eccentric and their cars examples of what many considered "conspicuous waste" (Thorstein
Veblen had just coined the phrase). In 1906, Woodrow Wilson, then
president of Princeton University, termed the motor car "a picture
of arrogant wealth" and announced that "nothing has spread a
socialist feeling more than the use of the automobile." Only a
minority saw the automobile as a boon. Generally, it was reviled.

Like many later 20th-century institutions—movies, radio,   21
television—the motor car was seen initially as a symbol of the
sickness of contemporary society. In his book *The Condition of
England*, published in 1909, C.P.C. Masterman wrote that "wandering machines, travelling at an incredible rate of speed, scramble and smash along all the rural ways. You can see the evidence
of their activity in the dust-laden hedges of the south country
road, a gray, mud colour, with no evidence of green; in the ruined
cottage gardens of the south country villages." The motor car, in
short, was destroying the very countryside it also made available
to the urbanites.

To the Canadian farmer, the car was also an anathema. It scared   22
livestock and killed poultry. "Is it not time something was done to
stop the automobile business?" the Newcastle, Ont., *Independent*
asked in 1904. "They are becoming such a curse to the country that
we cannot stand it...."

If some saw the auto as the wrecker of rural life, others saw it   23
as a means of bringing the joys of the countryside to city dwellers.
But it was one thing to extol those joys and quite another to enjoy
them in the early automobile. The roads were almost impassable—a
tangle of ruts and mudholes that sucked cars down to the axles.
Signposts did not exist. Even towns could not be identified: the villagers knew where *they* lived. Local post offices often bore the sign
Post Office with no other identification. The treadless tires blew
easily and often (they were rarely good for more than 3,000 miles),
while changing one was a nightmare. A rear end projecting from
beneath a hood on a country lane was a typical spectacle in pre-
World War I days. Engines failed so often that one popular song of
the era was "Get Out and Get Under."

24   The early motor car was also a repair shop on wheels. One store sold an automobile repair kit weighing 18 pounds. Driving was an experience akin to mountain climbing. The Damascus Hatchet, a patented device, was advertised, with enormous optimism, as follows: "When the wheel drops out of sight in the mud, get out the Damascus, cut a pole for a lever, right things up, and then on your way again."

25   Touring even required special clothing—linen duster, cap, and goggles for men; and for women, long skirts, sleeves fastened at the wrist with elastic bands, motor coats, and turbans or wide-brimmed hats tied under the chin.

26   Of course women were expected to be mere passengers. It was believed that they could never act with speed in an emergency or muster the strength to push in a clutch or struggle with a gear shift. These myths were shattered in 1909 when Alice Huyler Ramsay drove across the continent in a green Maxwell, without male help.

27   Such ocean-to-ocean trips marked the beginning of the end of the era of the motor car as a toy. Soon it was to become as essential as the telephone. Its change in stature was rapid and complete by the early 1920s, thanks to a succession of ingenious devices that transformed what was essentially a motor-driven buggy into the family car of the mid-century. In 1911, the Dunlop company developed the anti-skid tire; within three years it was outselling its tread-less counterpart. In the same year, the electric self-starter was an option, signaling the ultimate demise of the hand crank. The all-steel body also arrived in 1911, a forerunner to the closed car of the early 1920s, "a power-driven room on wheels—storm proof, lockable ... its windows (closed) against dust or rain." And in 1914, the introduction of the spare wheel eliminated the ghastly business of tire repairing.

28   But the greatest revolution was Henry Ford's introduction, in 1908, of the cheap car—the famous Model-T—followed by the company's development in 1914 of the assembly line. The affordable car had arrived. In 1908, a Model-T runabout cost $825. By 1916, the Ford assembly line was turning out the same vehicle for $345.

29   The assembly line dealt a lethal blow to the old concept of craftsmanship based on long apprenticeship. Young, unskilled men with no previous training could master the simple techniques in a few weeks. To quote a pair of contemporary social observers: "As to machinists, old-time, all-round men, perish the thought. The Ford Motor Company has no use for experience, in the working ranks, anyway. It desires and prefers machine tool operators who have nothing to unlearn, who have no theories of perfect surface speeds for metal finishing, and who will simply do what they are told to do, over and over again, from bell-time to bell-time."

Individuality gave way to conformity with results that none 30 could have foreseen. Since experience was not a precondition, immigrants and other unemployables soon found work on the assembly line—and that changed the demographic make-up of the continent. But the deadly monotony of the line (more easily endured by some than others) also required a much better wage rate and a shorter working day. Ford's $5, eight-hour day brought about the dominance of the middle class.

Again, because work was now seen to be boring and unfulfill- 31 ing, mass production techniques—lampooned in Chaplin's movie, *Modern Times*—brought the Protestant work ethic into disrepute. Since work was no longer satisfying, leisure took on a new importance, aided and abetted by the shorter work week. People began to live for their off-hours.

Mass production was also responsible for the youth cult that 32 has been a feature of North American life in our era. Unskilled 19-year-olds were quicker on the assembly line than their fathers and therefore more valued. As the craftsmen of one generation lost status to the blue-collar workers of the next, respect for age and parental authority began to decline. As the sociologist James J. Fink has pointed out, "maleness" was also to suffer with the slow realization that women could fill any job on the line as easily as a man. Mere strength was no longer a criterion.

As the 1920s dawned, it became clear that the horse had 33 become the toy and the automobile the necessity. Robert and Helen Lynd, the two sociologists who wrote a study on an American community they called Middletown, came up with some interesting revelations about the motor car. Families, they found, were mortgaging their homes to buy one—and most were buying on time payments. The automobile industry had helped launch the revolution in credit that marks this century.

"We'd rather do without clothes than give up the car," a mother 34 of nine told the Lynds. "I'll go without food before I'll give up the car," said another. Pursuing their research, the Lynds asked people in rundown homes: "Do you have a bathtub? Do you own a car?" Of 26 persons questioned who had no bathtubs, 21 owned a car. As one woman is said to have remarked, "You can't go to town in a bathtub."

The car, the Lynds concluded, had revolutionized the concept of 35 leisure. The Sunday stroll, once a feature of the Lord's Day, was abandoned, replaced by the Sunday drive. And the car was the main device holding the family together. One mother declared, "I never feel as close to my family as when we are all together in the car."

The idea of a summer vacation was beginning to take hold 36 because of the automobile. In the 1890s people worked the year round, "never took a holiday," as some boasted. But, by the 1920s, a two-week vacation had become standard among the business class. The blue-collar workers had yet to achieve that status but the rise of unionism in the automobile plants made it simply a matter of time.

37   The car was the perfect symbol for a restless decade, the quintessential artifact of the Roaring Twenties whose hallmarks were speed, sleekness, and glamour. The music was fast and the girls, it was claimed, were faster. So were the cars. The Tin Lizzie had become a joke—a chariot for rubes. The Stutz Bearcat in flaming red and yellow symbolized the era. The Canadian Good Roads Association, founded in 1919 in Montreal to lobby for better highways, was by 1927 also lobbying to cure the "speed mania."

38   No woman, dressed in the cumbersome styles of 1919, could feel comfortable in one of the new, closed automobiles. Overnight, to the horror of their elders, the bright young flappers chopped off their tresses, flung away their stays, hiked their skirts above the knee and piled into the rumble seat. "The auto," one American judge groaned, "has become a house of prostitution on wheels."

39   It had also become a symbol of sudden success. Each new model was awaited with national anticipation. No celebrity had arrived until he or she was pictured beside a custom-built car or at the wheel of a straight 12: Clara Bow, wheeling down Sunset Boulevard in an open Kissel; Gary Cooper dominated by his gigantic red and yellow Duesenberg. The gangsters, too, were motorized and glamorized: Capone with his bullet-proof Cadillac; Dillinger in his Ford (the Number One Public Enemy even wrote a personal testimonial to Henry). The car chase became a cinema staple; "taken for a ride" was the catch phrase of the era.

40   But for most of the continent, the motor car was something more than a glamorous status symbol. It could now be used to drive to work, to go shopping, to visit friends, to drive the kids to school or the dentist, to take the family picnicking. "I do not know of any other invention," Thomas Edison declared, "that has added to the happiness of most people more than the automobile."

41   When the new million-dollar Automotive Building opened at the Canadian National Exhibition in Toronto in the fall of 1929, it set the seal on a car-oriented decade. This was the largest and finest structure anywhere devoted exclusively to the display of automobiles and accessories. Here one would glimpse the tip of the industrial iceberg being created by the invention of the motor car. For behind the shiny new models, with their running boards and big headlamps, stood dozens of other industries, businesses, and services: oil refining, rubber manufacturing, retail sales, used-car lots, gas stations, auto supply stores, car washes, metal and paint and

glass industries, taxi companies; and, in the future, car radios, drive-in theaters, motels, driving schools, car rental firms, and a vast array of roadside fast-food franchises that would turn the entrance to almost every city and town on the map into a true "Gasoline Alley."

Within a matter of weeks, Wall Street crashed and the   42
Depression had arrived. Ironically, its greatest symbol of both hope and despair was a car—in the United States, the decrepit Hudson in which the Joad family in the movie *The Grapes of Wrath* moved from the dust bowl of Oklahoma to the fruit orchards of California; in Canada, the "Bennett buggy" (after Prime Minister R.B. Bennett) of the drought era, a car without an engine, drawn by a horse. For, as the Lynds found when they returned to their Middletown in the midst of the Depression, people refused to give up their cars.

The Joads' western pilgrimage symbolized the gypsy aspects of   43
North American society, a restlessness that goes back to the days of the immigrant ships, the covered wagon, and the Red River cart. The automobile arrived just after the frontier had been tamed. It fulfilled the ancestral urge to move on. And its symbol became the motel, the lineal descendant of the wayside inn.

The "auto tourist camp" of the early 1920s—not much more   44
than a park with washroom facilities, and handy to a garage—became, in 1925, the tourist cabin and the auto court. The tiny, spartan cabins grew more luxurious as the years went by but the lure was always the same: you could park your car at the front door of the motel room. Today, the small-town railway hotel, with its gloomy beer parlor, is all but obsolete; and in the cities, the major hostelries have had to change their entrances to accommodate the car. Who uses the front door of the Hotel Vancouver or Toronto's Royal York nowadays?

The auto court also flourished in the 1930s because people   45
could not afford hotels, any more than they could afford a biannual model change. For 15 years of depression and war, the auto industry was stalled. Cars were sleeker, certainly. "Streamlining" was a word on everyone's lips. The traffic light arrived. People talked of "knee action" and "free wheeling." The roadster, the runabout and the rumble seat became obsolete. But when war came and people could again afford new models, they found there were none. Then, with the introduction of the flamboyant new Studebaker after 1945, the dam burst. The car became more than a workhorse. To quote a Buick ad in the mid-1950s: "It makes you feel like the man you are."

People went car crazy. They cared not a hoot for performance,   46
efficiency, or safety. What they wanted was power, glamour, and status. The car was seen by psychologists as an extension of the

owner's personality. Cadillac drivers were proud, flashy salesmen. DeSoto drivers were conservative, responsible members of the upper middle class. Studebaker owners were neat, sophisticated young intellectuals.

47   "One of the most costly blunders in the history of merchandising," Vance Packard wrote in *The Hidden Persuaders*, "was the Chrysler Corporation's assumption that people buy automobiles on a rational basis." The company decided, in the early 1950s, that the public wanted a car in tune with the times: sturdy, easy to park, no frills—a compact with a shorter wheelbase. That decision almost wrecked Chrysler, but in hindsight we can see that the company was 20 years ahead of its time. The car it thought the public of the 1950s wanted became the status symbol of the late 1970s. The idea of the car as a reverse status symbol—compact, gas-efficient, devoid of tail fins or chrome, and not obviously expensive—derives from a massive about-face of attitudes toward the automobile and what it signifies. The change was spurred, of course, by government decree after the oil shortage, by traffic snarls, by a rising toll of highway deaths, by inner city rot and untrammeled suburban growth, and a consumer attitude that, for the want of a better word, we could call Naderism.

48   As the chairman of General Motors, James Roche, said in 1971, "the American love affair with the car is over." After half a century, the car was again seen as a villain, polluting the air, destroying the countryside, causing death and mutilation, wasting money, time, and gasoline, and fomenting a casual attitude to planned obsolescence.

49   Critics pointed to the car as the least-efficient means of transportation. In 1965, Elinor Guggenheimer, a New York City planning commissioner, pointed out that in 1911 a horse-drawn lorry could travel across Manhattan at an average speed of 11 miles per hour, while a modern taxi then could only achieve six.

50   Streets and parking lots, it was discovered, gobbled up between 35 and 50 per cent of the available space in a large city. Nine miles of freeway could destroy 24 acres of farmland; the average interchange took up 80 acres. Radio stations began to report daily on the pollution index in major cities, with the car as a leading culprit. And car manufacturers ceased boasting about "big car comfort." Foreign compacts became chic. Businessmen and housewives began to boast about how many miles their new car got to the gallon. North America's "Big Three" reeled under these blows and retooled. A new era had begun.

51   The new era has seen a return to the cities. People want to live downtown. Toronto has virtually no apartment space left in the inner city, but there are For Sale signs blossoming in the suburbs.

There is even talk of closing the city centers to all cars except taxis, an experiment that has been tried in some European communities. Does this mean that Marshall McLuhan was right when he predicted that the car is finished? The guru of the 1960s insisted that the home computer would so diversify the work force that commuting would be unnecessary, that the car culture would die.

What he failed to realize, as all critics of the car have failed to realize, is that the automobile's greatest attraction is not as commuter vehicle or as an aid to shopping. The former suburbanites who got rid of their cars when they moved to the inner city still line up on weekends to rent them. For when all is said and done, the major appeal of the motor car, with all its faults and weaknesses, is still what it was at the turn of the century: a liberating force. People want the freedom to move off at will without waiting for the horse to recover or a taxi to arrive; without standing in line for a streetcar or looking up rail or air schedules. In that sense the car remains the genie in the bottle. Release it carelessly and it becomes our master. Guard it vigilantly and it remains what it was always meant to be, a slave ready to serve us at our whim. 52

> [blank box]

PIERRE BERTON

Writer and media personality, Pierre Berton was born in 1920 in Dawson City, Yukon Territory. He is known across Canada for his television appearances (he has been a panelist on "Front Page Challenge" since the show started) as well as for his best-selling books, the most recent of which include *The Mysterious North* (1989), *The Great Depression* (1990), and *Revenge of the Tribes* (1991).

> [blank box]

Further Suggestions for Writing

1. Compare the experiences of Basil Johnston, narrated in "Bush League Business," with those of Carol Geddes, in "Growing Up Native." What similarities did these writers encounter, growing up in the bush in different parts of Canada? What differences?

2. Compare Ann Hodgman's "No Wonder They Call Me a Bitch" and Jessica Mitford's "Behind the Formaldehyde Curtain" as works of satire. Consider each writer's purpose, structure, and tone; then compare their impact on the reader. What similarities can you discover in the techniques these writers use to support their very different subjects?

3. Read Ralph Allen's "Clifford Sifton's Medicine Show," and compare or contrast the experience of immigrants presented in that essay with the one explored in Denise Chong's "Her Story, His Story." Consider the reasons for the different immigrant groups' decision to come to Canada as well as the receptions they received.

4. Contrast Austin Clarke's experience as a Canadian immigrant ("A Stranger in a Strange Land") with that of Eva Hoffman, another person in transition between two cultures ("Lost in Translation").

5. Both Austin Clarke ("A Stranger in a Strange Land") and Brent Staples ("Just Walk On By") deal with the burdens borne by

someone who sees himself and is seen by others as an outsider. Contrast the two writers' responses to the dilemmas they face.

6. Compare Austin Clarke's and Brent Staples's opinions on the causes of violence among young people in their respective communities. Do you agree with them, or do you think there are other significant causes not dealt with by these writers?

7. Read Neil Bissoondath's "I'm Not Racist But..." and compare his view of racism with that presented by Merrily Weisbord in "Being at Home" or Brent Staples in "Just Walk On By."

8. Compare the thesis argued by Wade Davis in "The End of the Wild" with that of John Dixon in "Saving the Songs of Innocence" or that of David Suzuki in "A Planet for the Taking."

9. Read "Altruism" by Lewis Thomas and compare the argument he presents in the conclusion of his essay with Wade Davis's thesis in "The End of the Wild."

10. Compare Jane Rule's thesis in "The Harvest, the Kill" with David Suzuki's in "A Planet for the Taking." What views do these writers share about the relationship between human life and the life of other species on our planet?

11. Compare Susan Sontag's thesis about women's self-image in "Beauty" with that of Maggie Helwig in "Hunger."

12. Compare Gloria Steinem's "Why Young Women Are More Conservative" and Judy Brady's "Why I Want a Wife." What perceptions of women's roles do these writers share? Are there any fundamental principles on which they disagree?

13. Compare the concepts of femininity and masculinity explored by Judy Brady in "Why I Want a Wife" and Paul Theroux in "Being a Man" or John Updike in "Men's Bodies, Men's Selves."

14. Compare the views of manhood and the masculine role as these are explored by John Updike in "Men's Bodies, Men's Selves" and by Paul Theroux in "Being a Man."

15. Compare Paul Theroux's "Being a Man" and Brent Staples's "Just Walk On By" in terms of the restrictions and the sometimes dangerous expectations that young men confront when they are forced to "prove" their manhood.

16. Compare Martin Luther King, Jr.'s explanation of the "dimensions of a complete life" with the "passions" Bertrand Russell identifies as having governed his life in "What I Have Lived For." Do these authors agree or disagree on the values they believe are essential to living a meaningful life?

17. Explore the notion of altruism as it is developed in Lewis Thomas's essay. Then analyze Martin Luther King, Jr.'s view of

altruism in "The Dimensions of a Complete Life." Do King and Thomas agree or differ in their concept of the importance of generosity and self-sacrifice in human life?

18. Read two essays on the subject of sports. (You may choose from Lorne Rubenstein's "Passion Play," Adam Gopnik's "Quattrocento Baseball," and Harry Bruce's "The Softball Was Always Hard.") Although these essays are very different in purpose, structure, style, and effect, they all reveal the authors' deep feeling about their respective sports. Compare the ways two of these essays explore the fascination of "the game."

19. Compare Gregory Kliewer's view of the contemporary school system in "Faking My Way through School" with that of Northrop Frye in "Don't You Think It's Time to Start Thinking?" What similarities or differences do you perceive between these two authors' expectations of and disappointments with education in Canada today?

20. In "Don't You Think It's Time to Start Thinking?" Northrop Frye argues that teaching the humanities is a "militant job." How do you think Professor Frye would respond to Katie Lynes's opinion of a traditional literary education as she presents it in "A Meditation on Reading in the '90s"?

21. How does nostalgia for our childhood experiences affect our adult recollection of them? Compare Harry Bruce's, "The Softball Was Always Hard" with Douglas Coupland's, "Patriotism Redux."

22. Compare or contrast David Fennario's "Black Rock" and David Mamet's "The Rake," both of which are accounts of childhood experiences that significantly affected their authors' views of what it means to be an adult.

23. Consider Laurence Steinberg's thesis in "Bound to Bicker": some fighting within families is inevitable, even healthy. Then consider the family relationships David Mamet portrays in "The Rake." What distinguishes a normal, healthy "bickering" family from one in which the relationships are dysfunctional?

24. In "The Way of All Flesh," Judy Stoffman explains the aging process, something every one of us must undergo. In "Deficits," Michael Ignatieff presents a poignant picture of his elderly mother's struggle with Alzheimer's disease. Contrast the approaches of these two essays to the subject of aging. In your paper, consider differences in structure, style, and tone. Which of the two selections do you personally find more affecting? Why?

25. Larry Orenstein's "Odd Enders" reports stories of bizarre murders, weird deaths, and strange suicides—all factual. Read

Stephen King's essay "Why We Crave Horror Movies" and discuss whether or not King's theory satisfactorily explains our fascination with sensational stories such as those reported in Orenstein's article. Are there other explanations for the public's taste for the macabre?

26. Compare Peter Gzowski's "And the Best Damn Stew-Maker Too" with Paul Quarrington's "Home Ice." Why do these authors find such pleasure in performing what seem, on the surface, to be banal, mundane tasks?

27. Popular culture is often charged with having a negative effect on individuals and society. Compare Lee Ballinger's "Rock and Rap Have Never Been Better" and Stephen King's "Why We Crave Horror Movies," both of which attempt to refute this thesis.

28. Compare the influences of consumerism on men and women as portrayed by Margaret Atwood in "Pornography" and by Maggie Helwig in "Hunger." What assumptions and attitudes do these two essays, on very different subjects, have in common?

29. Compare Thomas Hurka's thesis in "Should Morality Be a Struggle?" with that of Margaret Atwood in "Pornography" or George Galt in "Night Pictures of Peru."

30. Compare two essays written by scientists for the general public: Don Gayton's "Watching the Grass Grow" and Lewis Thomas's "Altruism." What similarities and differences can you discover in the techniques these writers use to make their subjects accessible to the non-scientist?

31. Evaluate Robin Skelton's "Cat Creek" or Rohinton Mistry's "Searching for Stevenson" as an example of narration and description.

32. In "Wheels: The Car as a Cultural Driving Force," Pierre Berton gives us an overview of social history during the last century by focussing on one vehicle: the private automobile. Choose another vehicle or artifact and, by selecting significant moments or advances related to it, present your own history of Canada over the last 50 or 100 years.

33. Contrast Pierre Berton's approach to Canadian history, which focusses on the changes brought about by one technology, with that of Diane Thompson, who focusses on the changes brought about by specific individuals. Which approach makes Canada's past more vivid, more meaningful, to you? Why?

GLOSSARY

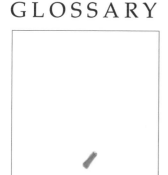

List of Useful Terms

ABSTRACT and **CONCRETE** are terms used to describe two kinds of language. *Abstract* words are for ideas, terms, feelings, qualities, measurements—concepts we understand through our minds. For example, *idea, term, feeling, quality,* and *measurement* are all abstract words. *Concrete* words, on the other hand, are for things we perceive through our senses: we can see, hear, touch, taste, or smell what they stand for. *Knee, song, carburetor, apple,* and *smoke* are all concrete words.

An **ALLUSION** is a reference to something—a person, a concept, a quotation, or a character—from literature, history, mythology, politics, or any other field familiar to your readers. For instance, in an essay on different kinds of employees, we might call one individual "a Rick Moranis type." Immediately, the reader can picture a slight, indecisive, funny character.

The secret of the effective use of allusions is to allude to events, books, people, or quotations that are known to your readers. Suppose one of the references in an essay on employee types is to "a Paul Morel type." Can you picture this type? Are you any better informed? If not, the allusion is a poor one.

Be sure your allusions are clear, single, and unambiguous. A reference to "King" could mean Mackenzie King, King Hussein (or any other male monarch), or Martin Luther King. Or perhaps it refers to the King of Rock. Who knows? Imagine the confusion if the reader has the wrong King in mind.

AMBIGUITY: An ambiguous statement is one that has at least two different and conflicting interpretations. Similarly, an ambiguous action is one that can be understood in various ways. When it's used deliberately and carefully, ambiguity can add richness of meaning to your writing; however, most of the time ambiguity is not planned. It is the result of imprecise use of language. For instance, the statement "He never has enough money" could mean that he is always broke, or that he is never satisfied no matter how much money he has. As a general rule, it is wise to avoid ambiguity in your writing.

An **ANALOGY** is a comparison. Writers explain complicated or unfamiliar concepts by comparing them to simple or familiar ones. For instance, one could draw an analogy between life's experience and a race: the stages of life—infancy, childhood, adolescence, maturity, old age—become the laps of the race, and the problems or crises of life become the hurdles of an obstacle course. If we "fall down," we have let a problem get the better of us; if we "get up again," we are refusing to let a problem beat us. (See the first paragraph of Don Gayton's "Watching the Grass Grow" in Further Reading for an example of an analogy.)

ANALYSIS means looking at the parts of something individually and considering how they contribute to the whole. In essay writing, the common kinds of analysis are process analysis and causal analysis. See the introductions to Unit Three and Unit Six for a more detailed explanation.

An **ANECDOTE** is a little story—an account of an incident—often humorous, that is used to catch the reader's interest. Writers frequently use this technique to introduce an essay. See the first paragraph of Brent Staples's "Just Walk On By" in Unit Six for an example of the effective use of anecdote.

ARGUMENT: See RHETORICAL MODES.

The **AUDIENCE** is the writer's intended reader or readers. Knowledge of their level of understanding, their expectations, is critically important to the writer. Tone, level of vocabulary, the amount of detail included, even the organizational structure, will all be influenced by the needs of the audience.

You know instinctively that when you speak or write to children, you use simple, direct language and, usually, short sentences. You adapt your style to suit your listeners. Before you begin to write, think about your readers' knowledge of your subject, their educational background, and their probable age level. Never talk down to your readers; but don't talk over their heads either, or they will stop reading in frustration.

For example, suppose you were preparing an article on the appeal of sports cars to the public. For a popular women's magazine, you would probably stress style, economy, comfort, and reliability, and you would support your thesis with examples of well-known women who love the sports cars they drive. You would not include much technical automotive jargon. If you were writing about the same topic for a general-audience magazine, however, you would include more specifics about price, ease of maintenance and cost, gas consumption, reliability under various weather and road conditions, with detailed figures comparing several popular makes. And if you were writing for a publication such as *Popular Mechanics* or *Road and Track*, you would stress performance, handling under high speed or unusual road conditions, and the ease or difficulty with which owners could maintain their cars themselves.

The **BODY** of any piece of writing is the part that comes between the introduction and the conclusion. In a PARAGRAPH, the body consists of sentences supporting and developing the TOPIC SENTENCE. In an essay, the body consists of paragraphs supporting and developing the THESIS STATEMENT.

CHRONOLOGICAL ORDER means time order; items or ideas that are introduced chronologically are discussed in order of *time sequence*. Historical accounts are usually presented chronologically. In a chronological sequencing, connectives such as *first, second, third, next, then, after that,* and *finally* are helpful to keep your reader on track. See the Introduction to Unit Three for further details.

A **CLICHÉ** is a trite and familiar expression that was once colourful and original; now it's so familiar it's boring. Clichés often appear in similes or comparisons: for example, your writing will be as "dull as dishwater" and your reader will be "bored stiff" if you are "as stubborn as a mule" and keep on using them. See also STEREOTYPE.

CLIMACTIC ORDER means order of importance. In this ordering pattern, writers arrange their main points so that the most important or strongest point comes last. Thus, the paper builds up to a *climax*.

COHERENCE means a clear connection among the ideas or parts of a piece of writing. In a coherent paper, one paragraph leads logically to the next: ideas are clearly sequenced; the subject is consistent throughout; and the writer has supplied carefully chosen and logical TRANSITIONS such as *also, however, nevertheless, on the other hand, first, second,* and *thus.* If a paper is coherent, it is probably unified as well. (See UNITY.)

COLLOQUIALISM: Colloquial language is the language we speak. Expressions such as *well, okay, a lot,* and *kids* are perfectly acceptable in informal speech but are not appropriate in essays, papers, or reports. Contractions (such as *they're, isn't, it's,* and *let's*) and abbreviations (such as *TV, ads,* and *photos*) that are often used in speech are appropriate in writing only if the writer is consciously trying to achieve a casual, informal effect.

CONCLUSION: The conclusion of any piece of writing determines what will stay with your reader; therefore, it should be both logical and memorable. A good conclusion contributes to the overall UNITY of the piece. This is no place to throw in a new point you just thought of, or a few minor details. Your conclusion should reinforce your THESIS, but it should not simply restate it, or repeat it word for word, which is even more boring. Here are five effective strategies you can choose from when writing a conclusion:

1. *Refer back to your introduction.* This does *not* mean simply repeating the opening lines of your paper; instead, allude to its content and draw the connections for your reader. See the conclusion of "The Social Value of Education" in Unit Two.
2. *Conclude with a relevant, thought-provoking question.* See the conclusion of "Why Are We Reading This Stuff, Anyway?" in Unit Eight.

3. *Ask a rhetorical question*—one that is asked to emphasize a point, not to elicit an answer. See the concluding paragraph of "Bumblers, Martinets, and Pros" in Unit Four.
4. *Issue a challenge.* See the conclusion of "Flunking with Style" in Unit Three.
5. *Highlight the value or significance of your subject.* See the last paragraph of "Why Do They Fail?" in Unit Six.

There are still other techniques you can use to conclude effectively: by providing a suggestion for change, offering a solution, making a prediction, or ending with an ANECDOTE that perfectly illustrates your thesis. Whatever strategy you choose, you should leave your reader with a sense of your paper's unity and completeness.

CONCRETE: See ABSTRACT/CONCRETE.

CONNOTATION and **DENOTATION**: The *denotation* of a word is its literal or dictionary meaning. *Connotation* refers to the emotional overtones the word has in the reader's mind. Some words have only a few connotations, while others have many. For instance, "house" is a word whose denotative meaning is familiar to all and that has few connotations. "Home," on the other hand, is also denotatively familiar, but has a rich connotative meaning that differs from reader to reader.

To take another example, the word "prison" is denotatively a "place of confinement for lawbreakers who have been convicted of serious crimes." But the connotations of the word are much deeper and broader: when we hear or read the word "prison," we think of colours like grey and black; we hear sounds of clanging doors, jangling keys, or wailing sirens; and we associate with the word emotions like anger, fear, despair, or loneliness. A careful writer will not use this word lightly: to refer to your job as a "prison" is a strong statement. It would not be appropriate to use this phrase simply because you don't like the location or the lunch break.

CONTEXT is the verbal background of a word or phrase—the words that come before and after it and fix its meaning. For example, the word "period," which in most contexts means a punctuation mark, means a particular kind of sentence in Eva Hoffman's piece "Lost in Translation."

When a word or phrase is taken *out of context*, it is often difficult to determine what it originally meant. Therefore, when you are quoting from another writer, be sure to include enough of the context so that the meaning is clear to your reader.

DEDUCTION is the logical process of applying a general statement to a specific instance and reasoning through to a conclusion about that instance. See also INDUCTION and the Introduction to Unit Eight.

DESCRIPTION: See RHETORICAL MODES.

DICTION refers to the selection and arrangement of words in a piece of writing. Effective diction depends upon the writer's careful choice of a level of vocabulary suited to both the reader and the subject. A careful writer does not mix formal with colloquial language; standard English with dialect or slang; or informal language with technical jargon or archaisms (outmoded, antique phrases). Good diction is that which is appropriate to the subject, the reader, and the writer's purpose. Writing for a general audience about the closing of the local A&P store, a careful writer would not say, "The retail establishment for the purveyance of merchandise relative to the sustaining of life has cemented its portals," which is pretentious nonsense. "The corner grocery store is closed" conveys the same meaning more appropriately and more concisely.

EMPHASIS: A writer can emphasize or highlight key points in several ways: by repetition; by placement (the essay's first and last sections are the most prominent positions); or by phrasing. Careful phrasing can call attention to a particular point: parallel structure, a very short sentence or paragraph, even a deliberate sentence fragment. These are all emphatic devices. A writer can also add emphasis by developing an idea at greater length, or by calling attention to its significance directly, by inserting expressions such as *most important* or *significantly*. TONE, particularly IRONY or even sarcasm, can be used to add emphasis. Finally, distinctive diction is an emphatic device. (See Ann Hodgman's essay "No Wonder They Call Me a Bitch" in Unit Two for a good example of the use of distinctive diction.)

EVIDENCE in a piece of writing functions the same way it does in a court of law: it proves the point. Evidence can consist of statistical data, examples, references to authorities in the field, surveys, illustrations, quotations, or facts. Charts, graphs, and maps are also forms of evidence and are well suited to particular kinds of reports.

A point cannot be effectively explained, let alone proved, without evidence. For instance, it is not enough to say that computers are displacing many office workers. You need to find specific examples of companies, jobs, and statistics to prove the connection. After all, the number of dogs in Ontario has increased almost as much as the number of computers. Does that prove that dogs breed computers? What makes a paper credible and convincing is the evidence presented and the COHERENCE with which you present it.

EXPOSITION: See RHETORICAL MODES.

FIGURES OF SPEECH are words or phrases that mean something more than the literal meanings of the individual words or phrases. Writers choose to use figurative language when they want the reader to associate one thing with another. Some of the more common figures of speech include similes, metaphors, personifications, and puns.

A *simile* is a comparison in which the author uses "like" or "as." For example, "She is as slow as an arthritic turtle" is a simile. Effective similes are both appropriate and imaginative: trotting out old clichés such as "cool as a cucumber" or "busy as a bee" will only bore, not enlighten, your reader.

A *metaphor* does not use "like" or "as": it claims one thing *is* another. For example, if you write "My supervisor wallowed in his chair," you are implicitly comparing your boss to a pig. "My boss is a pig" is a metaphor, but it is unoriginal and inappropriate. Choose your metaphors with care:

they should enlighten your readers with fresh and original insight, not confuse or tire them with an inappropriate comparison or a cliché.

Personification is a figure of speech in which the writer gives human qualities to an inanimate object or an abstract idea. For instance, if you write "The brakes screeched when he hit them," you are comparing the sound of the car's brakes to a human voice. Strive for original and insightful personifications; otherwise, you will be trapped by clichés such as "The solution to the problem was staring me in the face."

A *pun* is the use of language so that one word or phrase brings to the reader's mind two different meanings. Max Eastman, in *Enjoyment of Laughter*, classifies puns into three sorts: atrocious, witty, and poetic. The person who wrote "How does Dolly Parton stack up against Mae West?" was guilty of an atrocious pun. Margaret Visser's title, "Seeing Red," contains a witty pun. Poetic puns go beyond the merely humorous double meaning and offer the reader a concise, pointed, original comparison of two entities, qualities, or ideas. Dylan Thomas's "Do not go gentle into that good night" is an example of a poetic pun.

GENERAL and **SPECIFIC**: *General* words refer to classes or groups of things. "Animal" is a general word; so is "fruit." *Specific* words limit or narrow down the class of things to something very specific such as "wolf" or "lemon." Good writing is a careful blend of general and specific language. (See also ABSTRACT/CONCRETE.)

GOBBLEDYGOOK is a type of JARGON characterized by wordy, pretentious language. Writing that has chains of vague, abstract words and long, complicated sentences—sound without meaning—is gobbledygook.

ILLUSTRATION: See the Introduction to Unit Two.

INDUCTION is the logical process of looking at a number of specific instances and reasoning through to a general conclusion about them. See also DEDUCTION and the Introduction to Unit Eight.

INTRODUCTION: The introduction to any piece of writing is crucial to its success. A good introduction indicates the THESIS of the piece, establishes the TONE, and secures the reader's attention. The introduction is the "hook" with which you catch your reader's interest and make the reader want to read what you have to say. Here are five different "attention-getters" you can use:

1. *Begin with a story of an interesting incident.* The story or ANECDOTE should be related to your subject. See the first paragraph of "Why Are We Reading This Stuff, Anyway?" in Unit Eight.
2. *Offer a dramatic statistic or striking fact.* See "Why Do They Fail?" in Unit Six.
3. *Begin with a relevant quotation.* Make it interesting but keep it short. See the first paragraph of "Bumblers, Martinets, and Pros" in Unit Four.
4. *Begin by stating a commonly held opinion that you intend to challenge.* See "Flunking with Style" in Unit Three.
5. *Set up a contrast to "hook" your reader.* The opening paragraph of "College or University?" contrasts the postsecondary educational

scene in the United States with that in Canada. See the comparison in Unit Five.

Other strategies you might want to experiment with include posing a question, offering a definition—make sure it's your, not the dictionary's—or even telling a joke. You know how important first impressions are when you meet someone. Treat your introductory paragraph with the same care you would take when you want to make a good first impression on a person. If you bait the hook attractively, your reader will want to read on—and that, after all, is your goal.

IRONY is a statement or situation that means the opposite of what it appears to mean. To call a hopelessly ugly painting a masterpiece is ironic—it's an example of verbal irony, to be exact. Irony of situation occurs when a twist of fate reverses an expected outcome: for example, a man defers all the pleasure in his life to scrimp and save for his retirement but wins a million-dollar lottery at age 65.

Irony is an effective technique because it forces readers to think about the relationship between seemingly different things or ideas. Jessica Mitford's "Behind the Formaldehyde Curtain" is a well-known piece of extended irony. Although she seems, on the surface, to be enthusiastic about the processes of embalming and restoration, Mitford forces her readers to consider whether these practices are not, in fact, barbaric.

JARGON is the specialized language used within a particular trade, discipline, or profession. Among members of that trade or profession, jargon is perfectly appropriate; indeed, such highly technical language is an efficient, time-saving means of communication. Outside the context of the trade or profession, however, jargon is inappropriate, because it inhibits rather than promotes the reader's understanding. Another meaning of jargon, the meaning usually intended when the word is used in this text, is GOBBLEDYGOOK.

METAPHOR: See FIGURES OF SPEECH.

NARRATION: See RHETORICAL MODES.

ORDER refers to the arrangement of information or points in a piece of prose. While you are still in the planning stages, choose the order most appropriate to your subject. There are four main ways to arrange your points:

1. *Chronological order* means in order of time, from first to last.
2. *Climactic order* means in order of importance, leading up to the climax. Usually you would present your strongest or most important point last, your second-strongest point first, and the others in between, where they will attract less attention.
3. *Causal* or *logical order* means that the points are connected in such a way that one point must be explained before the next can be understood. Often used in cause/effect patterns, this order is appropriate when there is a direct and logical connection between one point and the next.
4. *Random order* is a shopping-list kind of arrangement: the points can be presented in any order. Random order is appropriate only when the points are all equal in significance and not logically or causally linked.

PARAGRAPH refers to a unit of composition, usually from five to ten sentences long, all dealing with one topic. In an essay, you present several main ideas, all related to your subject. The main ideas are broken down into points or topics, each of which is developed in a paragraph.

Every paragraph should have a *topic sentence*—a sentence that states clearly what the paragraph is about. It is often the first or second sentence of the paragraph. The rest of the paragraph consists of sentences that develop the topic, perhaps with examples, a description, a definition, a quotation, a comparison—or a combination of these strategies. There should be no sentence in the paragraph that is not clearly related to its topic. A paragraph should lead smoothly into the next (see TRANSITION), and it must also possess internal COHERENCE and UNITY. The essays of Bertrand Russell and Martin Luther King, Jr. (Unit Four) deserve careful analysis: their paragraphs are models of form.

PARALLEL STRUCTURE means similarity of grammatical form. In a sentence, for example, all items in a series would be written in the same grammatical form: single words, phrases, or clauses. Julius Caesar's famous pronouncement, "I came; I saw; I conquered," is a classic example of parallelism.

Parallelism creates symmetry that is pleasing to the reader. Lack of parallelism, on the other hand, can be jarring: "His favourite sports are skiing, skating, and he particularly loves sailing." Such potholes in your prose should be fixed up before you hand in a paper. For example, "What Carol says, she means; and she delivers what she promises, too" would be much more effective if rewritten in parallel form: "What Carol says, she means; what she promises, she delivers."

Because the human mind responds favourably to the repetition of rhythm, parallelism is an effective device for adding EMPHASIS. King's "Dimensions of a Complete Life" (Unit Four) contains many examples of emphatic parallel structure.

PARAPHRASE is putting another writer's ideas into your own words. You must acknowledge the original writer as the source of the idea—if you don't, you are guilty of plagiarism.

You will find paraphrasing very useful when you are writing a research paper. Once you have gathered the information you need from various sources and organized your ideas into an appropriate order, you write the paper, drawing on your sources for supporting ideas, but expressing them in your own words.

A paraphrase would reflect both the meaning and the general TONE of the original. It may be the same length or shorter than the original, but it is not a PRÉCIS.

PERSONIFICATION: See FIGURES OF SPEECH.

PERSUASION: See RHETORICAL MODES and the Introduction to Unit Eight.

POINT OF VIEW, in exposition, means the grammatical angle of the essay. In persuasion and argumentation, point of view can also mean the writer's opinion in the essay.

If the writer identifies himself as "I," we have the first-person point of view; in this case, we expect to find the writer's own opinions and first-hand experiences. All the essays in Unit One, Narration and Description, are written in the first person.

If the writer is not grammatically "present" in the material, we have the third-person point of view. Most of the essays in Units Two to Eight are written primarily in the third person. The writer uses "one," "he," "they," and the result is a more formal essay than one written in the first person.

A careful writer maintains point of view consistently throughout an essay; if a shift occurs, it should be for a good reason, with a particular effect in mind. Careless shifts in point of view throw the reader off track. See paragraph 9 of Lewis Thomas's "Altruism" (in Unit Seven) for an example of a purposeful change in point of view.

A **PRÉCIS** is a condensed summary of an article or essay. It is one-quarter to one-third the length of the original. The examples and illustrations are omitted, and the prose is tightened up as much as possible. All the main ideas are included; most of the development is not.

PROCESS ANALYSIS: See the Introduction to Unit Three.

PUN: See FIGURES OF SPEECH.

PURPOSE means the writer's intent: to inform, to persuade, or to amuse, or a combination of these. See RHETORICAL MODES.

RHETORICAL MODES: The word "rhetoric" simply means the art of using language effectively. There are four classic modes, or kinds, of writing: exposition, narration, description, and argument. The writer's choice of mode is often dependent on his or her PURPOSE.

Exposition is writing intended to inform or explain. If the writer's purpose is to inform, this mode is a likely choice. Expository writing can be personal or impersonal, serious or light-hearted. The various methods of exposition (such as exemplification, definition, comparison, and the rest) are sometimes called rhetorical forms.

Narration tells a story. It is the mode used for fiction. Examples of narrative writing are sometimes found within expository prose: in anecdotes or illustrations, for example. George Galt's "Night Pictures of Peru" and Basil Johnston's "Bush League Business" (Unit One) are good examples of the use of narration to help explain a thesis.

Description is used to make a reader see, hear, taste, smell, or feel something. Good descriptive writing re-creates a sensory experience in the reader's imagination. Descriptive writing is also sometimes found in expository prose. In addition to the essays in Unit One, see the essays by Robin Skelton, Harry Bruce, and Denise Chong in Unit Nine for examples of effective description.

Argument, sometimes called *persuasion*, is writing that sets out not to explain something, but to convince the reader of the validity of the writer's opinion on an issue. Sometimes its purpose goes even further, and the writer attempts to motivate the reader to act in some way. Like exposition, argument conveys information to the reader, but not solely for the purpose of making a subject clear. Argument seeks to reinforce or to change a reader's opinion about an issue.

SATIRE is a form of humour, sometimes light-hearted, sometimes biting, in which the writer deliberately attacks and ridicules something: a person, a political decision, an event, an institution, a philosophy, or a system. The satirist uses exaggeration, ridicule, and IRONY to achieve his or her effect. There is often a social purpose in satire: the writer points to the difference between the ideal—a world based on common sense and moral standards—and the real, which may be silly, vicious, alienating, or immoral, depending on the object of the satirist's attack. The essays by Mitford and Brady (Units Three and Four) in this text are examples of satire.

SIMILE: See FIGURES OF SPEECH.

SPECIFIC: See GENERAL/SPECIFIC.

STEREOTYPE refers to a character, a situation, or an idea that is trite, unoriginal, and conventional. Stereotypes are based on automatic, widely known, and usually incorrect assumptions: all women are poor drivers; all truck drivers are illiterate; all teenagers are boors; all Scots are tight with money. Stereotypical notions about races and nationalities are particularly dangerous: think of the well-known "Newfie" jokes, for example.

A careful writer avoid stereotypes, unless he or she is using them for satiric purposes. Unthinking acceptance of others' assumptions is a sure sign of a lazy mind.

STYLE refers to the distinctive way a person writes. When two writers approach the same subject, even if they share many of the same ideas, the resulting works will be different. That difference is the result of personal style. DICTION, sentence structure, sentence length, TONE, and level of formality all contribute to an individual's style. Compare Harry Bruce's "The Softball Was Always Hard" and Adam Gopnik's "Quattrocento Baseball" as examples of different stylistic treatments of a similar subject.

Good writers adapt their style to their audience; one doesn't write the same way in the business world as one does in the academic world, for example. In this sense, "good style" means one that suits the writer's PURPOSE, subject, and AUDIENCE. An informal and humorous style full of slang expressions would be inappropriate in a paper on teenage suicide. Similarly, a stiff, formal style would hardly be suitable for an article on new toys for the Christmas season.

A **SUMMARY** is a brief statement, in sentence or paragraph form, of the main ideas of an article or essay. See also PRÉCIS and PARAPHRASE.

SYNTAX means the arrangement of words in a sentence. Good syntax means not only grammatical correctness, but also an effective word order and a variety of sentence patterns. Good writers use short sentences and long ones, simple sentences and complex ones, and natural-order sentences and inverted-order ones. The choice depends on the meaning the writer wishes to convey.

A **THESIS** is the main idea or point the writer wants to communicate to the reader in an essay. It is often expressed in a *thesis statement*. (See "How to Write to Be Understood" in the Introduction.) Sometimes the thesis is not stated, but implied. Whether stated or implied, however, the thesis is the central idea that everything in the essay is designed to support and explain.

TONE reflects the writer's attitude to the subject and to the presumed audience. For instance, a writer who is looking back with longing to the past will use a nostalgic tone. An angry writer might use an indignant, outraged tone, or an understated, ironic tone—depending on the subject and purpose of the piece.

Through DICTION, POINT OF VIEW, sentence structure, PARAGRAPH development, and STYLE, a writer modulates the message to suit the knowledge, attitudes, and taste of the people who will read it. Contrast the aggressive, even abrasive tone of Dermody's "Sit Down and Shut Up or Don't Sit by Me" (Unit Four) with the poignant yet somehow positive tone of Staples's "Just Walk On By" (Unit Six). Other examples of superb control of tone are Mitford's scathing "Behind the Formaldehyde Curtain" (Unit Three), Ignatieff's sympathetic "Deficits" (Unit One), and Brady's ironic "Why I Want a Wife" (Unit Four).

A **TOPIC SENTENCE** is a sentence that identifies the topic, or main idea, of a paragraph; it is usually found at or near the beginning of the paragraph.

TRANSITIONS are linking words or phrases. They help connect a writer's sentences and paragraphs so that the whole piece flows smoothly and logically. Here are some of the most common transitions used to show relationships between ideas:

1. *to show a time relation*: first, second, third, next, before, during, after, now, then, finally, last
2. *to add an idea or example*: in addition, also, another, furthermore, similarly, for example, for instance
3. *to show contrast*: although, but, however, instead, nevertheless, on the other hand, in contrast, on the contrary
4. *to show a cause-effect relation*: as a result, consequently, because, since, therefore, thus

   See also COHERENCE.

UNITY: A piece of writing has unity if all its parts work together; each part contributes to the ultimate effect. The unified work has one subject and one tone. Unity is an important quality of a good paragraph: each sentence must be related to and develop the central idea expressed or implied in the TOPIC SENTENCE.

AUTHOR INDEX

Reader Reply Card

We are interested in your reaction to *Canadian Content*, Third Edition, by Nell Waldman and Sarah Norton. You can help us to improve this book in future editions by completing this questionnaire.

1. What was your reason for using this book?

    ☐ university course   ☐ college course   ☐ continuing education course

    ☐ professional   ☐ personal   ☐ other _____
    development   interest   _____

2. If you are a student, please identify your school and the course in which you used this book.

    _____

3. Which chapters or parts of this book did you use? Which did you omit?

    _____

4. What did you like best about this book? What did you like least?

    _____

5. Please identify any topics you think should be added to future editions.

    _____

6. Please add any comments or suggestions.

    _____

7. Please give your reaction to the readings listed by title and author in order of their appearance in the book, rating each essay from 1 (liked least) to 5 (liked best).

Title/Author	Rating	Didn't Read	Title/Author	Rating	Didn't Read
Unit One			*Unit Six*		
Night Pictures of Peru (Galt)	___	___	Why We Crave Horror Movies (King)	___	___
Passion Play (Rubenstein)	___	___	Just Walk On By ... (Staples)	___	___
Black Rock (Fennario)	___	___	Why Young Women ... Conservative (Steinem)	___	___
Growing Up Native (Geddes)	___	___	Bound to Bicker (Steinberg)	___	___
Bush League Business (Johnston)	___	___	Saving the Songs of Innocence (Dixon)	___	___
Deficits (Ignatieff)	___	___	Clifford Sifton's Medicine Show (Allen)	___	___
The Rake (Mamet)	___	___			
Men's Bodies, Men's Selves (Updike)	___	___	*Unit Seven*		
			Don't You Think It's Time ... (Frye)	___	___
Unit Two			World View ... Computer Hacker (Ritter)	___	___
Odd Enders (Orenstein)	___	___	I'm Not Racist But ... (Bissoondath)	___	___
Seeing Red (Visser)	___	___	Beauty (Sontag)	___	___
Being at Home (Weisbord)	___	___	Altruism (Thomas)	___	___
No Wonder They Call Me a Bitch (Hodgman)	___	___	I'm Having Trouble with My Rel'p (Michaels)	___	___
Cdn Women Over Four Centuries (Thompson)	___	___			
The End of the Wild (Davis)	___	___	*Unit Eight*		
Lost in Translation (Hoffman)	___	___	The Myth of Canadian Diversity	___	___
			Faking My Way through School (Kliewer)	___	___
Unit Three			Rock & Rap ... Never Been Better (Ballinger)	___	___
And the Best Damn Stew-Maker ... (Gzowski)	___	___	Being a Man (Theroux)	___	___
Desperation Writing (Elbow)	___	___	A Planet for the Taking (Suzuki)	___	___
Home Ice (Quarrington)	___	___	The Harvest, the Kill (Rule)	___	___
The Way of All Flesh ... (Stoffman)	___	___	Meditation on Reading in the '90s (Lynes)	___	___
Behind the Formaldehyde Curtain (Mitford)	___	___			
			Unit Nine		
Unit Four			Cat Creek (Skelton)	___	___
Speak Low when You Speak FM (Ritter)	___	___	The Softball Was Always Hard (Bruce)	___	___
Sit Down and Shut Up ... (Dermody)	___	___	Her Story, His Story (Chong)	___	___
Toothpaste (Bodanis)	___	___	Watching the Grass Grow (Gayton)	___	___
Why I Want a Wife (Brady)	___	___	Searching for Stevenson (Mistry)	___	___
What I Have Lived For (Russell)	___	___	Pornography (Atwood)	___	___
Dimensions of a Complete Life (King)	___	___	Hunger (Helwig)	___	___
			Wheels: Car ... Cultural Driving Force (Berton)	___	___
Unit Five					
Edmonton vs. Calgary ... (Marken)	___	___			
Should Morality Be a Struggle? (Hurka)	___	___			
Patriotism Redux (Coupland)	___	___			
Stranger in a Strange Land (Clarke)	___	___			
Quattrocento Baseball (Gopnik)	___	___			

(fold here and tape shut)

0116870399-M8Z4X6-BR01

Heather McWhinney
Publisher, College Division
HARCOURT BRACE & COMPANY, CANADA
55 HORNER AVENUE
TORONTO, ONTARIO
M8Z 9Z9